Neoliberalism and the Global Restructuring of Knowledge and Education

Routledge Advances in Sociology

For a full list of titles in this series please visit www.routledge.com

25 **Sociology, Religion and Grace**
   Arpad Szakolczai

26 **Youth Cultures**
   Scenes, Subcultures and Tribes
   Edited by Paul Hodkinson and Wolfgang Deicke

27 **The Obituary as Collective Memory**
   Bridget Fowler

28 **Tocqueville's Virus**
   Utopia and Dystopia in Western Social and Political Thought
   Mark Featherstone

29 **Jewish Eating and Identity Through the Ages**
   David Kraemer

30 **The Institutionalization of Social Welfare**
   A Study of Medicalizing Management
   Mikael Holmqvist

31 **The Role of Religion in Modern Societies**
   Edited by Detlef Pollack and Daniel V. A. Olson

32 **Sex Research and Sex Therapy**
   A Sociological Analysis of Masters and Johnson
   Ross Morrow

33 **A Crisis of Waste?**
   Understanding the Rubbish Society
   Martin O'Brien

34 **Globalization and Transformations of Local Socioeconomic Practices**
   Edited by Ulrike Schuerkens

35 **The Culture of Welfare Markets**
   The International Recasting of Pension and Care Systems
   Ingo Bode

36 **Cohabitation, Family and Society**
   Tiziana Nazio

37 **Latin America and Contemporary Modernity**
   A Sociological Interpretation
   José Maurízio Domingues

38 **Exploring the Networked Worlds of Popular Music**
   Milieu Cultures
   Peter Webb

39 **The Cultural Significance of the Child Star**
   Jane O'Connor

40 **European Integration as an Elite Process**
   The Failure of a Dream?
   Max Haller

41 **Queer Political Performance and Protest**
Benjamin Shepard

42 **Cosmopolitan Spaces**
Europe, Globalization, Theory
Chris Rumford

43 **Contexts of Social Capital**
Social Networks in Communities, Markets and Organizations
Edited by Ray-May Hsung, Nan Lin, and Ronald Breiger

44 **Feminism, Domesticity and Popular Culture**
Edited by Stacy Gillis and Joanne Hollows

45 **Changing Relationships**
Edited by Malcolm Brynin and John Ermisch

46 **Formal and Informal Work**
The Hidden Work Regime in Europe
Edited by Birgit Pfau-Effinger, Lluis Flaquer, & Per H. Jensen

47 **Interpreting Human Rights**
Social Science Perspectives
Edited by Rhiannon Morgan and Bryan S. Turner

48 **Club Cultures**
Boundaries, Identities and Otherness
Silvia Rief

49 **Eastern European Immigrant Families**
Mihaela Robila

50 **People and Societies**
Rom Harré and Designing the Social Sciences
Luk van Langenhove

51 **Legislating Creativity**
The Intersections of Art and Politics
Dustin Kidd

52 **Youth in Contemporary Europe**
Edited by Jeremy Leaman and Martha Wörsching

53 **Globalization and Transformations of Social Inequality**
Edited by Ulrike Schuerkens

54 **Twentieth Century Music and the Question of Modernity**
Eduardo De La Fuente

55 **The American Surfer**
Radical Culture and Capitalism
Kristin Lawler

56 **Religion and Social Problems**
Edited by Titus Hjelm

57 **Play, Creativity, and Social Movements**
If I Can't Dance, It's Not My Revolution
Benjamin Shepard

58 **Undocumented Workers' Transitions**
Legal Status, Migration, and Work in Europe
Sonia McKay, Eugenia Markova and Anna Paraskevopoulou

59 **The Marketing of War in the Age of Neo-Militarism**
Edited by Kostas Gouliamos and Christos Kassimeris

60 **Neoliberalism and the Global Restructuring of Knowledge and Education**
Steven C. Ward

Neoliberalism and the Global Restructuring of Knowledge and Education

Steven C. Ward

NEW YORK LONDON

First published 2012
by Routledge
711 Third Avenue, New York, NY 10017

Simultaneously published in the UK
by Routledge
2 Park Square, Milton Park, Abingdon, Oxon OX14 4RN

Routledge is an imprint of the Taylor & Francis Group, an informa business

© 2012 Taylor & Francis

First issued in paperback 2014

The right of Steven C. Ward to be identified as author of this work has been asserted in accordance with sections 77 and 78 of the Copyright, Designs and Patents Act 1988.

Typeset in Sabon by IBT Global.

All rights reserved. No part of this book may be reprinted or reproduced or utilised in any form or by any electronic, mechanical, or other means, now known or hereafter invented, including photocopying and recording, or in any information storage or retrieval system, without permission in writing from the publishers.

Trademark Notice: Product or corporate names may be trademarks or registered trademarks, and are used only for identification and explanation without intent to infringe.

Library of Congress Cataloging-in-Publication Data
Ward, Steven C.
  Neoliberalism and the global restructuring of knowledge and education / by Steven C. Ward.
    p. cm. — (Routledge advances in sociology ; 60)
  Includes bibliographical references and index.
  1. Education, Higher—Economic aspects. 2. Education—Economic aspects. 3. Neoliberalism—Social aspects. 4. Education and state.
5. Intellectual capital. 6. Knowledge, Sociology of. I. Title.
    LC67.6.W37 2012
    338.4'3378—dc23
    2011031825

ISBN13: 978-0-415-89011-3 (hbk)
ISBN13: 978-0-415-71973-5 (pbk)

For my children,
Kinsey, Kesslyn and Kylie

Contents

	Acknowledgments	xi
	Introduction: The Contemporary Politics of Knowing and Learning	1
1	Changing the Soul: The Contours, Currents and Contradictions of the Neoliberal Revolution	15
2	The Machinations of Managerialism: New Public Management and the Diminishing Power of Knowledge Professionals	46
3	The Neoliberalization of Knowledge: Privatization and the New Epistemic Economy	74
4	The New Marketplace of Ideas: The New Knowledge Makers and Their New Knowledge	101
5	Creating the "Clever Country": Neoliberalism, Knowledge Society Policies and the Restructuring of Higher Education	129
6	"An Island of Socialism in a Free Market Sea": Building the Market-Oriented School	158
7	Aligning Markets and Minds: The Responsibilized Self in the New Entrepreneurial Culture	184
	Notes	213
	References	221
	Index	247

Acknowledgments

First, I would like to acknowledge the research release time and a sabbatical support provided by my university, Western Connecticut State University. Also, I am grateful for the research support for travel provided through two American Association of University Professors—Connecticut State University research grants. Without such institutional support completing a project of this sort would have been impossible. Additionally, I would like to thank those whom I interviewed in both England and New Zealand; those interviews form the basis of some of the materials discussed in Chapters 5 and 6. Also, parts of Chapter 2 are taken from my article in the *Journal of Cultural Economy* in May 2011. I am grateful for permission to use these parts here. Finally, I would like to thank my family Karen, Kinsey, Kesslyn and Kylie for their love and patience throughout work on this rather long project.

Introduction
The Contemporary Politics of Knowing and Learning

The spirit of commerce brings with it the spirit of frugality, of economy, of moderation, of work, of wisdom, of tranquility, of order, and of regularity . . . as long as this spirit prevails, the riches it creates do not have any bad effect. (Montesquieu, 1989 [1748]: 79)

The invention of commerce . . . is the greatest approach toward universal civilization that has yet been made by any means not immediately flowing from moral principles. (Paine, 1942 [1791])

Thus god and nature link'd the general frame and bade that true self-love and social be the same. (Pope, 1824: 50)

Over the last few years we have been in the midst of what at times seems to be a reconsideration and what at other times appears to be a strengthening of one of the most sweeping and dramatic social experiments of the last few centuries. This social experiment, which came to be referred to as neoliberalism in most of the world, or in some instances "advanced liberalism" (Rose, 1999), began in the 1970s and 1980s when a loose affiliation of globally linked policy makers, academics, politicians, corporate leaders and financiers began to forge a broad reaching economic, political and social doctrine and set of policies and practices that would, over the course of the subsequent decades, profoundly alter the way economies and governments operate. Over time this doctrine would also be responsible for reshaping many contemporary social institutions, as well as the techniques and vocabularies individuals use to situate themselves within their societies and understand each other and their world. In doing so, the neoliberal doctrine redefined the relationship between state, society and economy that had existed in many nations at least since the advent of the so-called golden age of capitalism and the welfare state that stretched from the end of the Great Depression into the 1970s.

At neoliberalism's theoretical core was a rearticulation and reconfiguration of the eighteenth and nineteenth century liberalist argument that market exchange captures an essential and basic truth about human nature and the creation and maintence of social order (Dean, 1999: 159; Harvey, 2005). As such, it should become the model for conducting and managing a host of activities that were previously deemed "outside of" or "above" the intrusion of the marketplace. In relying on the activities of markets as a guide for all human affairs and for optimizing social harmony, neoliberals, much like their eighteenth and nineteenth century predecessors, sought to radically transform not only the workings of politics and economics but also the social and moral ties that historically bound individuals to societies, groups and social institutions. Under neoliberalism people were to be reconceptualized less as socially connected citizens of a nation state or morally situated members of a culture and more as self-interested competitors, self-actualized entrepreneurs and rational consumers in a dynamic and ever-changing global marketplace. In this neoliberal reconfiguration of the social, citizenship or social membership did not automatically convey state protected rights and safeguards to all, but rather individual action and responsibility earned one a position and standing in the social order. In this particular updated and modified version of *Homo economicus*, competition and self-interest were again envisioned as universal and fundamental psychological human characteristics before the "local knowledge" and customs of culture, religion and tradition or the protections afforded by the "tribe" or state were added. As such, the social sphere was to be understood as simply an extension of the economic domain and, therefore, reducible to the same basic economic tenants and laws of self-interest that govern the operation of markets. In this framing a new notion of the "self-in-society" was advanced where people's fates were to be determined by their own skills, initiatives, analyses of risk and individual consumptive choices and not by their reliance on the social relationships, obligations or expectations generated by state, society or culture. Indeed, in a strong "tragedy of the commons" (Hardin, 1968) version of this view, social relations, obligations and expectations were depicted as actually holding back both the freedom and advancement of the individual and, as a result, the optimal functioning of society at large.

Since the mechanisms of market exchange were said to best reflect our basic "species being," neoliberals further argued that they should become a normative force for dramatic reforms throughout all parts of government and society. From the neoliberal standpoint the market's competitive dynamism and natural selection process should be used not only to enhance markets through the usual methods of creating new products and services, stoking consumption, generating profits and expanding economies but also to produce the proverbial "greater good" and optimized society at large. This new greater good was seen as being brought about not through cooperation and the governmental leveling mechanisms of the past but through the self-interested activities of actors each working independently and unknowingly to create a spontaneous and balanced social order. These actors were seen as being continuously "disciplined" and "responsiblized" through the steering, motivation and redirection provided by the "messages of the market." This new "greater good" would also be brought into being by fully informed and empowered consumers–citizens and taxpayers whose desires and self-interest would lead them to demand low costs, accountability and transparency from all of those who provided them with products and services, including the state. These empowered consumers would then utilize their "buying power" to essentially "vote" for those products and services that were most in their interests (see Johnston, 2008). In the end, neoliberals envisioned the advent of a utopian capitalism where the market would solve societal problems that were previously thought to be correctable only through state intervention strategies, such as those found in socialism or the welfare state. As such, the expansion of the market into new domains of life would allow the liberal project of individual liberty and freedom begun in the eighteenth and nineteenth centuries to finally be realized after what neoliberals felt were decades of socialist or Keynesian command economic policy and the dependency and moral decay they were responsible for creating.

Promoters deemed neoliberalism not only as a reflection of the "nature of things," or at least the way things should made to be, but also as a pragmatic and inevitable economic and political adaptation to the "market realities" served up by an age marked by the increased global interdependence of economies and people, rapid technological innovation, heightened economic competition and the increased financialization of economies. They maintained the neoliberal policies were the only practical way for economies, states and people to conduct themselves in the highly financialized and consumer driven global economy of contemporary "fast capitalism" (Agger, 1988). For neoliberals, "there is," as Margaret Thatcher (quoted in Felix, 2005: 407) succinctly framed it in the 1980s, simply "no other choice." Indeed, in some settings neoliberal policies became so naturalized that they were frequently offered up as the only viable option available. In these times and places, all political options, policies and opinions were required to be first disciplined by and be in alignment with the "realities of the market" and "the bottom line" before they were considered tenable.

The neoliberalist policies and reform efforts of the last few decades were not just aimed at making national economies more pro-business and firms more economically efficient, however. Many of their efforts were directed at reforming and dramatically reenvisioning, shrinking and transforming the institutions, professions and practices that make up what is commonly referred to as the public sector or public domain. From the vantage point of neoliberalist reformers, the public domain and public institutions, such as in the areas of public housing, health, welfare, transportation or the topic that this book tackles, public knowledge and education, were, in their state supported or public regarding form, "black holes into which money is poured" (Apple, 1998: 81). They were at best incentiveless, unproductive and wasteful systems that were drags on the expansion of markets or at worst destroyers of the moral self-reliance of people. In an ironic twist, the growth of the public domain directed by socialist and Keynesian-leaning governments over the course of the twentieth century to allegedly protect people from the vicissitudes of the market was said to have created an overly public and state-dependent environment that ultimately robbed people of important social benefits. In their effort to expand equality, these Keynesian and socialist systems had killed the profit incentive that was necessary for people to innovate, make things and bring them to market where consumers could then purchase and use them.

Included in these efforts to reform the public domain were attempts to fundamentally rework the conditions under which knowledge was produced and disseminated. Knowledge, from the neoliberalist perspective, had over the course of the twentieth century also become "over-socialized" and much too public. In their present condition, universities, as the historical center of most public knowledge production for the last century and a half, were much too isolated from market forces and the direct productive and workforce needs of corporations and the economy as a whole to serve as needed engines of innovation and economic growth. Universities, with their focus on "basic science," shared, public knowledge and free and open inquiry, had generally followed their own professional and disciplinary determined epistemic concerns. These concerns led them to occasionally and indirectly produce economically viable products or procedures; however, overall their economic impact fell far short of what should be expected of them given the large amount of public funding invested in their operation. Universities, by and large, had failed to "pull their own weight" or maximize their economic impact in the new, often technology driven, global economy. They had failed to understand that the game had now profoundly changed and that the classic "knowledge for knowledge's sake" often identified with the Humboldtian-inspired research university of the late nineteenth and most of the twentieth centuries was no longer possible. Knowledge production, it seemed, needed a major retooling, reorganization and intensification much like other lagging industries or unresponsive state bureaucracies.

In addition to remolding the conditions under which knowledge was produced, neoliberals also took aim at the dissemination of knowledge through public education. Public education, at all levels, was a particularly problematic issue and institution for neoliberalists and the site of some of their most sweeping and controversial global reform efforts. In their view schools and universities around the globe had failed to provide students with the skills and "entrepreneurial values" necessary to compete in an increasingly economically interconnected world. They had also failed to fully recognize and adapt to the new role that knowledge was now required to play in the growth and expansion of regional, national and international economies. For neoliberalists, the failure of education was, like the failures of all public institutions and public realm in general, traceable to socialist and Keynesian economic and social policies that were introduced by governments around the world in the first half of the twentieth century.

These policies essentially "nationalized schooling" by allowing the state in many national contexts to establish an exclusive monopoly over education and professional knowledge workers, such as professors and teachers, to establish and maintain a collective "monopoly of competence" over or to "capture" particular knowledge or education domains (Larson, 1977: xvi). Over time these monopolies created an insular and bloated bureaucratic education system that made both the production and dissemination of knowledge inflexible, inefficient and, ultimately, ineffective. As a result educational institutions at all levels were unable to respond to the changing skill and knowledge needs of corporations.

The state's monopoly on education had also created a system of entitlement that produced complacent, unmotivated teachers and administrators, uninvolved parents and lazy, underachieving students. What was needed in the neoliberalist view was, among other things, the introduction of a "new public management" into these organizations that would be responsible for better managing knowledge and overseeing a major retooling and reorganization of knowledge production and education along the lines of a competitive business enterprise. Bringing economic rationality, consumer choice and the disciplining of the market and its accompanying new managerialistic forms of administration to bear on knowledge production and dissemination would, they contended, finally create a competitive, "entrepreneurial culture" throughout all levels of education. This, in turn, would enable the construction of "post-bureaucratic" (see Heckscher and Donnellon, 1994) or "post-Fordist" (Jessop, 1994) forms of educational organizations and knowledge workers that were flexible, nimble and quick. It would also help "responsiblize" people in educational institutions by constructing self-reliant, fully informed and entrepreneurially-minded students and knowledge workers who didn't need what Margaret Thatcher famously referred to as the "nanny state" to care for them but were capable of using their self-acquired knowledge and skills to adapt to and take advantage of the opportunities the continually evolving global economy served up.

To accomplish these wholesale epistemic and pedagogical reforms neoliberals set out to completely rethink the *raison d' etre* of education and the relationship between public knowledge and education. First they contended that education needed to be reconceputalized as less a public right or direct governmental responsibility, as was the case in other models of state-controlled mass, public education, and more as a private investment in "human capital" made by knowledge consumers in order to better their position and status in the marketplace. Like all commodities in the neoliberal model, education should be obtained, not through welfare-style governmental grants or entitlements but in the marketplace where consumer choice and a "user pays" system would encourage students to "responsiblize" by using their own or borrowed funds to purchase the best product available to them. Education was seen as an investment, like stock ownership, that would pay future dividends. Also, as a result of the cumulative choices made by the student consumer, the education system itself would be further rationalized, optimized and finally turned into a true market.

In this rethinking of education the role of state was to shift from being a purveyor of collective well-being, equality and general social welfare to an information conduit who was responsible for making sure that entrepreneurs and consumers were informed of their options in the marketplace; a manager or auditor who looked to see if established economic goals were being met and accountability mandates were being followed and an agent who would establish a market where none existed before. In this situation market efficiencies and economic fundamentals would determine the types of skills and knowledge that were needed while simultaneously creating the competitive pressures necessary to force educational institutions and teachers and professors to become more flexible and to produce the best product possible for the lowest possible cost.

Neoliberals argued that such a competitive business model would at long last bring Joseph Schumpeter's (1942) infamous process of "creative destruction" that had made market economies so innovative and efficient into the stagnant and wasteful realm of public knowledge production and dissemination. It would enable what a 2004 Organization for Economic Cooperation and Development (OECD) report hailed as the "Schumpeterian Renaissance" (OECD, 2004) to move into another part of the public sector. One of the desired outcomes of this "Schumpterian Renaissance" heralded by neoliberalist reformers was the creation of a "quasi-market" for education and other "public goods" (Gordon and Whitty, 1997). Since the privatization of education would need to move more slowly than in other parts of the public sector, quasi-market incentives could be put in place first to mimic the market and "acclimatize clients" before full privatization would take place—an approach found to some extent in the graduated steps for noncompliance found in the U.S. policy of No Child Left Behind. This quasi-market sought to impose what critics would decry as a "worst of both worlds scenario." Here, a series of competitive market measures and pressures were introduced into education while simultaneously increasing and intensifying state oversight and control.

In this quasi-market situation the education system was deliberately placed in a paradoxical and contradictory position. On the one hand, it was to be left to "competitive market forces" of consumer choice to shape its directions and outcomes. Here, education was "transfigured to act as if embedded in a competitive environment where the laws of economics reign" (Shamir, 2008: 1). On the other hand, however, it faced more rigorous monitoring, auditing and evaluation by the state—a situation that would seem at first glance to limit its freedom to compete in some unfettered educational marketplace, at least as envisioned within the classic liberal economic model. In other words, the education system was seen as being shaped by the forces of competition while also being continuously monitored and evaluated by newly established accountability institutions and mechanisms put in place by governments in the name of efficiency and "accountability to the public" who were now being recast by neoliberalists as "stakeholders" or more commonly as "the taxpayers."

This rather confusing and seemingly contradictory loose–tight arrangement of decentralized centralization is only understandable if we shift our attention away from neoliberalism as a set of strictly economic practices to neoliberalism as a broader form of what Foucault (1991) referred to as "governmentality." In this new neoliberal form of governmentality that emerged over the past few decades the role of the state was dramatically transformed. It became neither a classic *laissez-faire* or capitalist state that stays out of the market economy nor a traditional welfare or socialist state concerned with the social distribution of wealth, maintaining high levels of employment or social planning initiatives. Instead, it became more of a "managerial state" (Clarke and Newman, 1997), "evaluative state" (Neave, 1988) or "small, strong state," (Gamble, 1988) whose purpose is to monitor and assess how well economic and social goals are being met and to control how public monies are being spent. In other words, the neoliberal state that emerged over the last few decades was much less likely to directly intervene in social welfare issues by providing direct services, as had occurred in the traditional welfare state. Instead the neoliberal state privatized or "out sourced" many of its former social welfare functions to private companies competing in newly created markets or quasi-markets to provide services or, in other cases, to already existing state agencies who were reconfigured to operate as if they existed under market conditions. The neoliberal state's role in these circumstances is to continuously monitor and report on these social welfare companies' and agencies' levels of productivity and effectiveness in order to know how to allocate or if to withdraw funding. In essence, the neoliberal state became a state form that sought, as Nikolas Rose (1993) succinctly put it, to "govern at a distance." Under this system of neoliberal governmentality states did "not eschewed intervention; rather they [have] changed its modality" (Gordon and Whitty, 1997: 455). Indeed, it is this characteristic that most separates the liberal from the neoliberal state. Unlike the nineteenth-century *laissez-faire* state or even the early "roll back" neoliberal state (Peck and Tickell, 2002) associated with Margaret Thatcher or Ronald Reagan that wanted to remove the state as much as possible from any direct involvement in economic matters, the neoliberal state used its auditing role to work alongside businesses and firms to create, support and expand markets. The neoliberal state form that emerged in many nations over the last few decades was, thus, not seen as an impediment to economic growth or something that should remain on the sidelines but an integral player in the enhancement of markets and capital accumulation. It was now the job of the state to establish markets or quasi-markets in areas where none had existed before.

In order to implement these neoliberal-inspired political, economic and social changes at the institutional level, reformers around the world began introducing a new form of public management into the operation of most public organizations throughout the 1980s and 1990s. Drawn from public choice theory and the public interest model in economics, this "new public management" sought to run the public sector utilizing the same philosophies, principles and procedures that were found in the private sector. More specifically, this new public management sought both to reorganize the operation of public organizations and to redefine and govern the relationships between administrators and professionals, such as teachers, social workers, professors or physicians and state and government workers who make up the fields that provided direct public services. In the view of neoliberal reformers, public organizations lacked the efficiency, accountability and hierarchical "line management" structure necessary to make fast, definitive and economically prudent decisions. Much like a badly run company, public organizations were too undisciplined either from the prevalence of bureaucratic authority, strong professional or civil service control or traditions of collegial deliberativeness and debate, such as those found in universities, to make quick or efficient decisions. Neoliberals contended that this lack of discipline and rationality had made these organizations outmoded dinosaurs in the age of rapid and unpredictable change and the growing demands for more public accountability. They were drags on economic productivity and a burden to the taxpayers who supported them.

In the context of knowledge producing and disseminating institutions proponents of new public management argued that for educational reforms to succeed it was imperative that a new relationship be forged between those who managed educational institutions and those who delivered the needed educational products. As a result a series of new types of managerial theories and practices borrowed from business firms, such as Total Quality Management (TQM), Human Resource Management or Toyotism, were put in place to redefine, realign and rehierarchicalize the relationship between administrators and knowledge making and disseminating professionals. Under this new managerial regime, teachers and professors in these newly reformed or soon to be reformed schools and universities were to be treated more as employees rather than partners in shared governance or autonomous professionals. As employees they were to follow the dictates as set from "above" by rational, unbiased managerial authority rather than professionally controlling and monitoring their own performance, curriculum and expertise. Teachers and professors were also increasingly required to demonstrate to auditing authorities, often through some form of formal assessment, such as various national research assessment exercises or "high stakes testing" initiatives that they were delivering the curricular or research goods necessary for the organization to reach the "output goals" established by the state's auditing and accountability systems. This, in turn, required continuous and every expanding forms of auditing, assessment and monitoring of these professionals' performances.

As new public management unfolded in public institutions, power and decision-making shifted from the profession's own historically constituted internal and self-administered standards of performance and oversight to "auditors, policymakers and statisticians who need not know anything about the professions in question" (Davies, Browne, Gannon, Honan and Somerville, 2005: 344). As is the case with the importance placed on the high stakes testing of students (and by extension teachers), such as those mandated by the No Child Left Behind policy in the United States or the National Curriculum overseen in the United Kingdom by the Qualifications and Curriculum Authority (QCA), under neoliberalist reforms, knowledge professionals were not to be trusted to follow their own internal professional standards and ethics since these standards fell outside and were not controlled by the state's new accountability mechanisms. They should instead be placed under the continuous purview of the performance and accountability measures of what Power (1997) referred to as the "audit society" (see also Strathern, 2000) to assess the level of their contribution and effectiveness. Otherwise, it was argued, there was no way of knowing if the educational goals established by the state in the name of economic progress were being met or that knowledge consumers and taxpayers were being properly served.

At the broader level of "international policy flows" these neoliberal measures converged in the mid to late 1990s into what are generally referred to as "knowledge society" or "knowledge economy" policies. Advocated by international agencies and groups such as the World Bank, the United Nations Education, Scientific and Cultural Organization (UNESCO), the European Union (EU) and most influentially the OECD, as well as individual governments and non-governmental organizations around the world, this "cognitive capitalism" sought to transform knowledge into an engine of economic development and nations and regions into reflexive, knowledge creating, disseminating and utilizing societies (see World Bank, 2002; OECD, 1996; 2004; UNESCO, 2005). Neoliberalists saw knowledge, particularly the type produced in scientific and technological fields, as holding the possibility of creating what former Australian Prime Minster Bob Hawke described as "the clever country"—a place where increased innovation, production and economic well-being were the central markers of societal development. Under modern economic conditions, knowledge could no longer just be produced following the whims of knowledge-making professionals but needed to be managed, steered and more directly "transferred into technology" and incorporated into national "innovation systems." This management and steering would occur not through the direct or indirect actions of the state for its own political purposes, as had happened under the science policies of socialist and Keynesian states in the wake of the Second World War, but via the needs of the market and the economy in general. Under this arrangement everyone was said to benefit—workers received a higher standard of living, consumers received new products, entrepreneurs, investors and venture capitalists received the profit for providing them and knowledge-making institutions received the funding they needed to continue on or grow without relying on the diminishing pool of public tax support which was now being redirected or returned to taxpayers and corporations to spur further, "demand-driven" innovation and growth. In short, the goals of neoliberalism were to create an entirely new society and new social form where markets and minds would increasingly be aligned.

BOOK OUTLINE

This book is an account of the influence of neoliberal ideas and practices on the way knowledge has been conceptualized, produced and disseminated over the last few decades. I am interested here in grounding knowledge production and education in the context of the contemporary political economy by drawing on various examples of education reform efforts, knowledge society policies, intellectual property law changes, university reform efforts, the discourse and practices of new public management and international trade policies. However, as much as this work is a story about the transformation of knowledge and education, it is also one of the ongoing realignment of the relationship between individuals, state, and market, as well as the growing centrality of markets in everyday life. Knowledge and education are undoubtedly undergoing profound changes but so too are the very social formations that have made particular types of knowledge and particular understandings and practices of education possible.

The reason for grounding the social, political and economic changes discussed here under the term "neoliberalism" rather than a more standard economic framing, such as the "logic of late or advanced capitalism" or organizationally with such terms as "post-Fordist production," or in the more sociologically phraseology such as "the information society," "network society," or "late modernity," is that I want to place special emphasis throughout this work on the political nature of the maneuverings and organizing efforts and principles behind many of the important social changes of the last few decades. The concept of neoliberalism, I believe, has the advantage, despite the *faux ami* and the resulting use of the term for Americans who often confuse liberalism and conservatism, of uniting a series of diverse political, economic and social changes of the last few decades under one dynamic and evocative label. As such it helps us to recognize neoliberalism as not just an economic or political philosophy or "ideological doctrine" but as a broad and multifaceted social movement with widespread implications for all aspects of politics, society and culture. It also helps us recognize these outcomes as the result of human intentionality created through political and social action rather than being abstractions of something called "the economy" or "globalization."

I argue throughout this work that in order to understand global changes occurring in knowledge production and distribution, it is imperative to be both "context sensitive" in order to grasp not only the individual educational reforms and knowledge policies, laws and practices of particular nations but also to be aware of the broader, transnational social, economic and political circumstances in which these policies and practices are embedded. This means it is important, as Gary Rhoades (2005: 11) has framed it, to consider the "comparative importance of the particular." Too often analyses of knowledge and education focus on national or regional aspects of change at the expense of the interdependency or "multi-scalar competitive strategies" at work in various contexts (see Roberston and Keeling, 2008). For example, some of the more famous global educational reform efforts of the last few decades—such as New Zealand's Tomorrow's Schools, England and Wales' Education Reform Act of 1988 and the establishment of a National Curriculum, the U.S.'s No Child Left Behind and the various attempts to restructure higher education in the U.S., Australia, England, Germany and the European Union—cannot be understood without locating them within the larger neoliberal directed global economic, political and social trends of the last few decades. Likewise, it is impossible to understand specific knowledge policies, legislative acts or legal decisions of the last few decades, such as the Bayh-Dole Act in the late 1970s or the more recent wrangle over Google's digitization of books, without considering the broader political and economic ideas and practices in which they are located. Indeed, I believe that much of the discussion surrounding specific knowledge issues such as education reform or changes in intellectual property laws or knowledge and science policies, in the United States and elsewhere, has failed to fully take account of the specific social movements, economic trends and transnational political players that have inspired and directed these reforms.

Accounts of these laws or policies often appear as national or cross-sectional snapshots of one particular policy in one particular circumstance rather than part of more concerted and historically constituted global reform efforts. While each nation's education reforms and knowledge society policies clearly have had their own local features that shape the specificities of their outcomes, these various reform efforts can't be adequately understood in isolation from other reforms in other contexts. The globalization of economies generated by neoliberal policies have also in many ways resulted in the globalization of ideas and practices or "policy flows," some of which are readily adopted by eager governments and others which are sometimes forced on nations and areas by the new "realities" created by the conditions that neoliberal policies have created.

Also, I think it is impossible to fully grasp the reconceptualization of knowledge or educational reform without taking all levels of education into account. For example, in the United States, No Child Left Behind was used as leverage during the G. W. Bush administration in 2006 to establish the Spellings Commission, which sought, but ultimately failed, to make wholesale national level reforms to American higher education. In this respect the conditions under which knowledge is disseminated is always intertwined with the circumstances under which it is produced. Separating education into layers or hierarchies of production and dissemination functions makes sense analytically, since it simplifies analysis; however, in the end it may serve to obscure the interconnectedness and common fate of all knowledge making and distributing institutions and organizations.

Furthermore, I also contend that it is impossible to understand what is happening to educational institutions apart from what has happened to knowledge itself in so-called late modern or postmodern knowledge societies. Pedagogy and the politics of knowledge are, consequently, never far apart. Knowledge is, as Foucault perhaps above all others reminded us, not an innocent bystander to the social change happening around it but a key player and sometimes victim of its manifestation and application. As he framed it,

> we live in a social universe in which the formation, circulation, and utilization of knowledge presents a fundamental problem. If the accumulation of capital has been essential feature of our society, the accumulation of knowledge has not been any less so. Now the exercise, production, and accumulation of this knowledge cannot be dissociated from mechanisms of power; complex relations exist which must be analyzed. (Foucault, 1991 [1978]: 165)

Indeed, it is the fusion and intensification of the relationship between knowledge and capital that so thoroughly marks our own time. These changing conditions under which knowledge and truth are produced don't just change the quantity of knowledge produced but also its "quality" or what Lyotard called "the criterion of truth." In doing so, it also alters the methods and modes in which knowledge will be delivered to others. The commodification, rationalization and privatization of knowledge found in such current practices as the patenting of genetic materials, the general privatization of cultural artifacts, the technology transfer activities of universities, the digitization (or Googlization) of information and the privatization of public domain knowledge, all have far-reaching implication for not only what knowledge is, who controls it and how it is created but also the manner in which knowledge is passed on to others.

Finally, knowledge privatization, education reforms and knowledge society policies are viewed here as some of the key ways in which the neoliberalist ideal of responsiblization are being pursued and enacted. Since within the neoliberalist model it is people and not governments and societies that are ultimately responsible for their own actions and fate, it is the role of knowledge and education to provide the epistemic and moral foundation on which informed agents can make decisions regarding their skills and consumption in the marketplace. In the end, the construction of this responsiblized agent is an outcome and has served to support and reproduce the neoliberalist vision of society and politics. This is, I argue, why both the privatization and commodification of knowledge and education reform have proved so crucial in the expansion, acceptance and partial naturalization of the neoliberal project over the last few decades in countries such as Australia, the United Kingdom, the United States and New Zealand. It is also why so much political energy continues to be directed at changing the way knowledge-making and -disseminating institutions operate. What is a stake here is not just modernizing and "improving" universities or schools but determining how society will be organized and by who.

The chapters that follow fall into four general parts. The first of these, which includes Chapters 1 and 2, examines the contours and manifestations of neoliberalism at the macro level of political economy and the more meso level of national social institutions. Chapter 1, "Changing the Soul," provides a contextual foundation for the book by examining the origins and manifestations of neoliberalism, including the relationship between classic eighteenth- and nineteenth-century liberalism and mid to late twentieth century neoliberalism, as well as the current status of neoliberal ideas and forms of governance. Chapter 2, "The Machinations of the Managerialism," examines how neoliberal ideas were used to reorganize public institutions and the public realm in general beginning in the 1980s and 1990s through the application of public interest theory and its practical offshoot, new public management. Specifically, I describe how the application of neoliberal principles in public organizations was used as leverage to diminish the traditional power and autonomy of knowledge professionals, such as teachers, professors and university researchers.

The second part of the book, which includes Chapters 3 and 4, explores the historical construction of a public domain for knowledge and the way neoliberal ideas, policies and practices have sought to privatize this domain by altering the conditions under which knowledge is produced. Chapter 3, "The Neoliberalization of Knowledge," explores how a fragile public domain for knowledge was carved out in the late nineteenth and early twentieth centuries and how neoliberal influenced polices and shifts in intellectual property law have eroded this domain in the name of privatization, marketization and consumer choice. In Chapter 4, "The New Marketplace of Ideas," I examine the influence that the neoliberalization of knowledge has had on what Jean Francois Lyotard (1984) referred to as "the truth criterion" or "quality" of knowledge. Here I explore how neoliberal policies have altered the conditions under which knowledge gets made, the people who make it and even the very composition of knowledge itself.

The next part, Chapters 5 and 6, surveys the influence of neoliberal knowledge society policies on universities and primary and secondary schools in various national contexts. Chapter 5, "Creating the Clever Country" traces the growing importance of knowledge in national economic and social policy. Specifically, I trace how knowledge policies have evolved from the more general science policies of the post–World War II era to the advent of knowledge society and economy policies, such as those advocated by the European Union, the World Bank and the OECD. I also examine how these policies have been mobilized to reorder tertiary education in different nations, such as in Australia, the United States, England and the European Union's transnational "Lisbon Strategy." Chapter 6, "'An Island of Socialism in a Free Market Sea,'" traces the influence of neoliberal policies on primary and secondary education by examining reform efforts over the last three decades in the United States, New Zealand and England and Wales.

The final part of the book, Chapter 7, shows how these assorted epistemic and pedagogical changes are connected to a larger neoliberal political effort to forge a new type of subjectivity, morality and social order. Specifically, Chapter 7, "Aligning Markets and Minds," examines some of the important dimensions of the moral projects associated with neoliberalism and how these projects have led to the consumerization of choice, the individualization of risk and the entrepreneurialization of work. I conclude the book with a discussion of the limits of liberalism.

1 Changing the Soul
The Contours, Currents and Contradictions of the Neoliberal Revolution

Democracy is the road to socialism. (Karl Marx)

The socialists believe in two things which are absolutely different and perhaps even contradictory: freedom and organization. (Halévy, 1966)

Fundamentally, there are only two ways of co-ordinating the economic activities of millions. One is central direction involving the use of coercion—the technique of the army or the modern totalitarian state. The other is the voluntary co-operation of individuals—the technique of the marketplace. (Friedman, 1962: 13)

As the physical world is ruled by the laws of movement so is the moral universe ruled by laws of interest. (Helvetius, *De l' esprit*)

Practical men, who believe themselves to be quite exempt from intellectual influences, are usually the slaves of some defunct economist. (Keynes, 1964 [1936]: 383)

It is not an exaggeration to say that once the more active part of the intellectuals have been converted to a set of beliefs, the process by which these become generally accepted is almost automatic and irresistible. (Hayek, 1949)

When the capital development of a country becomes the by-product of the activities of a casino, the job is likely to be ill-done. (Keynes, 1964 [1936]: 142)

In the late 1970s and early 1980s a series of bold new social, political and economic experiments were introduced in societies throughout the world. These experiments, which as a collective project came to be labeled by most of the world as neoliberalism, sought to resurrect and extend some of the insights and practices of eighteenth- and nineteenth-century liberalism and apply them to host of late twentieth- and early twenty-first-century problems. Much like the socialist and Keynesian revolutions that remolded many societies in the first half of the twentieth century, this late twentieth-century "neoliberal revolution" sought to fundamentally reconfigure the relationship between society, economy and the state. More importantly, perhaps, it also sought to redefine the relationship between the individual and society—to forge a return to what proponents argued was a more responsible, resilient and independent mode of personhood and self-care. As Margaret Thatcher described the central moral goal of this new liberal project, "economics are the method [but] the object is to change the soul."

Changing something as consequential as the soul involved the introduction of a dramatic new, neoliberal project to "govern the soul" (Rose, 1990). This neoliberal project spawned a series of broad-reaching reconstructive projects that worked simultaneously at the levels of politics, economics and culture. Most important and easily recognizable among these projects were the creation and expansion of a new, more intensified and less regulated "Atlantic" or Anglo-American style of capitalism; the dismantling or "rolling back" of the welfare state and its reconstitution in a new neoliberal state form; new styles of corporate and public management and administration; a casualization and flexiblization of work, firms and organizations; a much more market- and consumer-centered society and the creation of a new entrepreneurial, self-reliant, risk aware and consumer-minded subject.

Like most social movements, neoliberalists spun their own complex and self-serving origin story to both denigrate the status quo and legitimate the need for their particular new political, economic and cultural projects. According to this story as the twentieth century had unfolded, the Keynesian and socialist policies that had prevailed in many Western societies since the Global Depression of the 1930s had, by the 1970s, severely bogged down economic growth, diluted shareholder value, stymied competition and created bloated and crisis prone governments and governmental institutions. Economically, these policies had created a capitalism that was at a "tipping point" as it sought to negotiate the increased taxation brought about by the demands of social movements and the expanding welfare functions of the state within the context of the increasingly global competitive market pressures to provide profits to share and bond holders.

At a more cultural or moral level, this neoliberal origin story contended that socialist and Keynesian policies had lead people to become much too collectivistic and, as a result, much too dependent on "society" and the welfare state, both much maligned terms in neoliberal circles, and their entitlements and social programs to guide their lives and solve their problems. Instead of the state or "society," people needed to look to themselves and their own individual initiatives, or in Thatcher's ironical phrasing their own "personal society," in order to make their way in the world. To do this, people needed to deliberately adopt "the ethos and structure of the enterprise form" (Gordon, 1991: 41). They needed to rediscover the self-affirming and self-deterministic philosophy and independent moral virtues embedded in the long-standing tradition of Anglo-American liberalism—a set of political ideals and practices that neoliberals felt had been washed over, or at the very least, overwhelmed by the socialistic or collectivist leaning philosophies that had prevailed for at least fifty years. For neoliberals, the disciplining and sorting of the market economy was just the tonic individuals needed to rediscover their inner moral virtues of independence and self-reliance. It was also the elixir institutions, governments and societies needed to energize their sluggish, unproductive and over-regulated economic systems and reform their severely over-extended and dependency generating social welfare systems.

As was the case with variants of classic eighteenth- and nineteenth-century liberalism, the late twentieth-century neoliberal conceptualization of the autonomous and free subject was accompanied by the idea of an unfettered or less -regulated "free market" for the exchange of goods and services. Following closely Locke (1980), the ownership of property was envisioned in both classical and neoliberalism as providing the underlying basis of freedom. Property was, as Ludwig von Mises (1983: 21) framed it, "the single word" of the program of liberalism. For neoliberal theorists, such as von Mises, Friedrich Hayek and Milton Friedman, political freedom and free markets require the existence of property-owning individuals and these individuals can only flourish and practice their freedom in a relatively "unfettered" and self-regulating market-style economy. Indeed, neoliberalists wanted to push all this property-based freedom even further than what was advocated in classical liberalism into areas where it only had limited existence before, such as the dramatic expansion of global free trade, the running and reorganization of the public sector, such as hospitals and schools, and the privatization of many social services and public programs, such as public housing, prisons and mental health services (see Sen, 2009; Bourdieu, 2003). For neoliberals, markets, with their internal equilibrium, heightened competition and optimizing effects provided the most rational and efficient pathway available for conducting human affairs. This included not just economic activities but also governance, public and social services and education. In their more utopian moments, neoliberals, particularly beginning in the 1990s, even viewed economic individualism and the markets it spawned as a panacea for correcting a host of difficult and long-standing social issues and problems, such as inadequate housing, urban deterioration, poor education, poverty, the low status of women, underdevelopment, global inequality and pollution—problems the socialist state with its collectivist focus and command economy was supposed to have solved long ago (see, for example, United Nations Development Program, 2004; Sachs, 2005; Yunus, 2009).[1] In neoliberalism's capitalist utopia, these problems could finally be solved if the stifling effects of governments were forever removed and market incentives and the profit motive were unleashed. In the neoliberal framing, "human beings make a mess of it when they try to control their destinies" (Jameson, 1991: 273), as in planned socialist societies. Consequently, markets, with their invisible ordering of things generated by what Hayek (1979: 153) phrased "the

18 *Neoliberalism and Restructuring of Knowledge and Education*

spontaneous process of the interaction of the individuals" should become both a source of social order and a mechanism for ameliorating long-standing and intractable social problems.

In this first chapter I want to examine the origins and the central characteristics of neoliberalism, as well as some of the contours it has taken over the last few decades. It is my contention that in order to grasp the contemporary global transformations taking place in knowledge creation and transmission, it is important to situate them within the broader political and economic theories and practices that have shaped and that are currently shaping states and economies. These political and economic doctrines provide the backdrop from which, and in many cases the legitimation for, the specific epistemic and pedagogical outcomes and practices of the last few decades, such as the introduction of new public management in education, the move toward an auditing and assessment oriented managerial state, changes in intellectual property law, the privatization of knowledge, education reform and global knowledge society and creative economy policies—all issues to be examined in more detail in the new few chapters.

I begin this chapter by briefly situating neoliberal theory and policy in the context of twentieth-century debates over the direction of politics and the economy. Here I look at some of the different forms neoliberalism has taken over the last few centuries, from the classic liberalism of the eighteenth and nineteenth centuries to the so-called "roll back" neoliberalism associated most closely with Ronald Reagan and Margaret Thatcher and the shrinking of the state in the late 1970s and 1980s to the "third way" brand or "roll out" phase of neoliberalism first introduced by Bill Clinton, Tony Blair, the New Democrats and New Labour in the 1990s and 2000s (see Peck and Tickell, 2002). Afterward, I outline what I consider to be ten defining features and characteristics of contemporary neoliberal theory and policy. Finally, I conclude with an examination of the rise of the neoliberal "managerial state" and its role in establishing and expanding markets and auditing and overseeing expenditures in order to control and limit the impact of the public sphere on the private market. I also consider the sometimes conflicting strains within liberalism and how today's political landscape reflects the strange and ironic amalgamation and contradictions of liberal, neoliberal, Keynesian and socialist theories and practices.

NEOLIBERALISM IN THE CONTEXT OF TWENTIETH-CENTURY POLITICAL ECONOMY

As a reaction to the Global Depression of the 1930s, many governments in the West embraced a moderate Keynesian economic policy that sought to put in place "improvements in the techniques of modern capitalism by the agency of collective action" (Keynes, 1926: 13).[2] Keynesianism was, in essence, a "third way" of its own time that sought to forge a middle path between a wholesale socialistic involvement in managing and steering the economy that had emerged in the USSR and a classic liberalist hands off policy that had prevailed in some Western societies during the late nineteenth and early twentieth centuries. In the Keynesian approach, markets were seen as volatile, monopolistic and prone to the radical business cycles of overproduction and retrenchment. These swings would not "clear on their own," as described by the father of general equilibrium theory Leon Walras (1984) in the nineteenth century, but needed active state intervention to right the market's course. Markets, consequently, needed regulation and the guiding hand of the state to operate more efficiently and less erratically. The state form introduced by these policies was not just concerned with purely economic management, however. It also mobilized progressive ideas of social reform to promote the general social welfare and the protection of workers from the swings of the market in order to preserve the state's own legitimacy and that of the economic system. In the Keynesian system it was imperative "to work out a social organization which shall be as efficient as possible without offending our notions of a satisfactory way of life" (Keynes, 1926: 14).

During this Keynesian "high period," the central doctrines of classic liberalism, such as those found in John Locke, Adam Smith, J. S. Mills, Jean-Baptiste Sey, Leon Walras, Herbert Spencer and David Ricardo, often seemed as either ideological justifications for capitalist exploitation by those on the left or as outmoded and impractical doctrines that had outlived their usefulness in the new age of corporate and managerial style capitalism. Instead, the "Keynesian Compromise," as it came to be referred, and its "semi-socialism" as Keynes referred to it (Keynes, 1926: 12), would allow for the functioning of a more moderate, regulated form of capitalism that, under careful government "demand side" management, would be much less susceptible to the radical boom and bust swings of business cycles (Shonfield, 1965). This compromise would also help ameliorate the social upheavals and vast equalities in wealth and income that these swings had caused and would serve as a foundation for what would come to be referred to simply as the welfare state. It would also allow the state to place restrictions on the some of the unwieldy speculative activities of the market; provide backup financial and social support in situations when the market failed or was working ineffectively; help temper and redistribute large discrepancies in wealth through progressive forms of taxation; ease unemployment, social unrest and deprivation through a variety of social welfare and work programs and promote a style of slow and steady economic growth for corporations and their shareholders.

Particularly affected by actions undertaken in the Keynesian compromise were financial institutions such as banks and investment firms. Under Keynesian-influenced controls, these organizations were separated and tightly regulated with regard to backup cash reserves. Their actions were also curbed by both specific state regulators and the regulatory activities of the Federal Reserve or Central Banks. Under the Glass-Steagall Act of 1933 in the U.S., for example, the financial activities of banks and investments firms were separated in order to ensure that banks would stay out of the more speculative and riskier investment side of finance. This would make them less prone to failure during future economic downturns.

Toward the end of World War II, Keynesian economic policy became further ensconced in the monetary policy developed as part of the 1944 Bretton Woods Agreement. Under this agreement that established the World Bank and what became known later as the International Monetary Fund (IMF), gold would be used to create and maintain a fixed exchange rate for each national currency. Under the Keynesian influenced Bretton Woods model, economies would be steered by governments working in concert with corporations to assure steady growth and minimal market disruptions. As described in Article IV of the Articles of Agreement, each member states agreed "to direct its economic and financial policies toward the objective of fostering orderly economic growth with reasonable price stability, with due regard to its circumstances; seek to promote stability by fostering orderly underlying economic and financial conditions and a monetary system that does not tend to produce erratic disruptions" (International Monetary Fund, n.d.). To accomplish these monetary goals, post–Bretton Woods era governments would focus on "capital controls, full employment policies, progressive taxation and expanded social welfare expenditures" (Felix, 2005: 391). Such practices would become the hallmark of the "embedded liberalism" (Harvey, 2005) that came to define the post–World War II welfare state and the "command-and-control economies" found in many Western nations. Capitalism would live on but with slower growth, less profit and more state regulation.

Despite the apparent failures of classic liberal doctrines of unrestricted markets and its version of the *laissez-faire* state, as well as the ascendancy of Keynesian and socialist economic policies in their wake, liberalist theory did not disappear from the intellectual scene during the period of Keynesian dominance from the 1930s through the early 1970s. It was clearly evident in particular policy areas such as the development of U.S. housing policy in the 1940s and 1950s (see Baxandall and Ewen, 2001) and was a key set of ideas mobilized in the McCarthy Hearings of the 1950s. In academic circles, the Austrian-born Friedrich Hayek, a London School of Economics and later a University of Chicago economist and a student of Austrian economist Ludwig von Mises, began in the 1940s to revive and promote a new, revised brand of liberalism by adapting it to some of the lessons created by Soviet-style communism, Nazism and the Global Depression and the Keynesian response to it. Shortly after the Bretton Woods economic conference, in 1947, Hayek convened his own mountainside gathering of economists in a hotel in Switzerland. The group formed there became known as the Mount Pelerin Society (MPS) and would subsequently become key theoreticians and promoters of neoliberal ideas and policies for the later half of the twentieth century (see Hayek, 1984).[3] In addition to Hayek, the Society included both the father of neoliberal thought, Ludwig von Mises, and those who would become its future leaders, including University of Chicago economists, Milton Friedman, and a bit later Gary Becker. At the organization meeting, the MPS decried "the decline of belief in private property and the competitive market" (in Hartwell, 1995: 11). The members dedicated themselves to providing a politically viable liberal alternative to the dominance of Keynesianism and socialism in academia and politics.

Three years prior to the meeting, in 1944, Hayek had published what would become his most influential work and the central theoretical document to guide this resurgent liberalism, *The Road to Serfdom*. Initially the work received only scant academic attention, mostly in the United Kingdom; however, with its publication in the U.S. by the University of Chicago Press and the subsequent printing of shortened version in *Reader's Digest* in 1945, the book began to gain a much wider audience (see Fox, 2009: 90–91). In the work, Hayek, borrowing heavily from von Mises, sought to reconstruct the liberal creed by arguing that all managed economies, whether Keynesian, socialist or nationalist in form, were both the enemies of individual freedom and doomed to economic failure. In this new form of liberalism the enemies of freedom were not the mercantilists, aristocrats and monarchs as they had been for early liberals, such as Adam Smith, but the socialist and totalitarian regimes of the 1930s and 1940s who foolishly believed they could manage their way to happiness and prosperity.

For Hayek managed economies had two interrelated problems: one primarily political in origin and the other one more economic in nature. Politically speaking, managed economies, in every form, create an ever-creeping authoritarian control over people's lives. In this sense, as Hayek (1944: 25–26) remarked, "the Road to Freedom was in fact the High Road to Servitude." In the quest to control production and manage consumption, the state's bureaucratic economic experts had to set limits on profits, production levels, career pathways and pay, among other things, and over time they had to do this across all areas of the economy. They were also required to become "all knowing" and able to "out-guess" demand and the movement of the economy. Accomplishing this elaborate economic management required an increasingly bloated bureaucracy of economic managers and experts and an overtaxed state composed of burgeoning numbers of technocrats and civil servants whose concentrated planning power undermined democracy, individual freedom and the free market. Economically speaking, and flowing directly from the first problem, managed economies were also untenable because they were unable to effectively determine the price of any commodity. Following a earlier paper by von Mises's (1935) that established what became known as the "socialist calculation debate" (Hodgson, 1999: 33) in economics, Hayek argued that socialist efforts to tightly manage production and consumption disrupted the flow of the market and its unique, dispersed and uncoordinated method of determining the value of things. When this occurred the economic actor did not know how to behave toward a commodity, whether to buy, sell, or hoard it, since it was literally without value. In this arrangement, economic activity and price, therefore, must be artificially and continuously created and sustained by even more state intervention and management, this time on the consumption side. The end result of all this escalating economic managing and adjusting was that innovation, motivation and freedom died. In the end, people existed in a totally planed economy and an increasing authoritarian political order where the state was required to manage all activities in order to keep prices and wages stable, production going and the economy functioning. Instead of this totalitarian economic and political system, Hayek (1944: 157) argued that we need "freedom to order our own conduct in the sphere where material circumstances force a choice upon us, and responsibility for the arrangement of our life according to our own conscience." The exercise of this freedom to choose, what to consume and what ideas to support, in turn, would create a functioning economy and society that met the needs of individuals and wider social harmony and balance. There could be no comprise in such a situation either since the mixture of capitalism and socialism was "unthinkable" (von Mises, 1949: 259). A mixture of the two systems, as in Keynesianism, would create a system "worse than if either system has been consistently relied upon" (Hayek, 1944: 31).

The former Keynesian, Milton Friedman, took Hayek's ideas even further and became neoliberalism's chief spokesperson from the 1960s through the 1980s. Friedman, like Hayek, believed it was imperative to combat "the sickness of an overgoverned society" (Friedman and Friedman, 1980: 152). His influential 1962 book *Capitalism and Freedom* (Friedman, 1962) extended some of Hayek's ideas about the connection between the freedom of choice and free markets. In contrasting the freedom of market societies from the authoritarianism required in planned economies, Friedman (1962: 18) wrote:

> In a free market society, it is enough to have the funds. The suppliers of paper are as willing to sell it to the *Daily Worker* as to the *Wall Street Journal*. In socialist society, it would not be enough to have the funds. The hypothetical supporter of capitalism would have to persuade a government factory making paper to sell to him, the government printing press to print his pamphlets, a government post office to distribute them among the people, a government agency to rent him a hall in which to talk, and so on.

Socialist societies with their centralized planning and command economies were, hence, by the necessity of their design, always authoritarian. They would never allow contrarian ideas that somehow threatened the pronouncements of their experts or their carefully planned society to surface.

Market societies, on the other hand, would potentially always generate a free market for ideas, no matter how controversial or "irrational." All ideas needed to exist were to reach a level where they could economically sustain themselves in some manner or find someone who was willing to expend their own capital to support those ideas. Those ideas, positions or products that could not generate such a market had no economic, and consequently no social, value to begin with.

A key argument put forward by Hayek and in European circles by the Freiburg School of Economics or *Ordoliberalen* (i.e., order liberalism), so named because of the school's emphasis on the importance of chosen rather than a forced order, involved the role of the state in the economy.[4] In classic *laissez-faire* liberal theory the state's central role was to only oversee tasks that could not be accomplished by the market, such as the running of lighthouses, protections from other states and establishing the broad legal circumstances for markets to operate. It was, however, not to have any direct role in managing or directing the economy. Hayek and the *Ordoliberalen*, such as Walter Eucken, Wilhelm Ropke, Alexander Rustow and Franz Bohm, however, took a different, more activist view of the state/economy relationship. They maintained that the horrors of National Socialism were made possible by the series of anti-liberal policies that preceded it. In this understanding, National Socialism was, as Michael Polanyi (in Turner, 2003: 66), described it, "not a reaction against socialism, but an outcome of it." Policies, such as protectionism, welfare policies and market interventionism, created the circumstances for the massive growth and increased power of the state (Burchell, 1993: 270). When this economic situation combined with nationalist, nativist and racist sentiments, Nazi ideology was born. With this in mind this branch of neoliberalism essentially dropped much of the classic liberalist thinking about the natural equilibrium of the economy that had been present in the past. They recognized that markets could, under certain circumstances, fall into disequilibrium. As a consequence, markets required a market friendly state to support them and enforce competition—a "free economy and a strong state" as Rustow (in Turner 2003: 84) framed it. In other words, markets need to "be actively constructed by government" (Burchell, 1993: 271)."[5] As Hayek (1944: 17) remarked, "probably nothing had done so much harm to the liberal cause as the wooden insistence of some liberals on certain rough rules of thumb, above all the principle of laissez faire." In this sense, markets, while always politically and economically justifiable and morally superior to government controlled planned economies, were not necessarily natural and perpetual in the way they were envisioned by classic liberal theorists but were more artificial arrangements that needed to be properly nourished and cared for by the state. This *sociale marketwirtschaft* promoted a more constructivist view of the state where markets should not be left alone, as in classic liberalism, or the state used to create various protective buffers between workers and the business cycles of markets, such as in the welfare state. Instead, state policies should be directed toward creating a *Vitalpolitik* that should work to directly aid and encourage the optimal functioning of markets and stimulate the entrepreneurial behavior of citizens. Markets should always be as free as possible but such freedom required the assistance and diligence of a market friendly state, such as found in the so-called "Rhineland form of capitalism" that emerged after World War II and of which many Freiberg school members took part.

While liberal thought remained a minority view in most societies from the 1930s through the early 1970s a series of events and political maneuvers and the formation of a broad neoliberal social movement during the early 1970s began to radically change the course of Keynesian and socialist economic policy in many Western societies and eventually globally. As Milton Friedman (1962: ix) once remarked, "only a crisis—actual or perceived—produces real change. When that crisis occurs, the actions that are taken depend on the ideas that are lying around." By the 1970s neoliberal ideas could be found "lying around" in a number of places waiting to be mobilized.

First among the events of the early 1970s were the abandonment of the gold standard in 1971 and the use of the U.S. dollar as the global backup currency. Two years later, in 1973, came the OPEC Oil Embargo and the Oil Crisis. Indeed, 1973 became, as Prasad (2006: 1) has poetically described it, the year "the dream of reason ended."[6] These two events sent shock waves through the orderly managed economies of the post-Bretton Woods accord and led to the creation of what economists and pundits came to call "stagflation"—a stagnate growth rate coupled with high levels of inflation. For those both in the classic liberal and neoliberalist camps these problems signaled not just the ebb and flow of the market economy but the wholesale bankruptcy of Keynesian- and socialist-style planned economies. Many had attributed the success of capitalism in the post-Depression era to demand management policies and the ability of the state to effectively regulate the market, unemployment and currency exchange (see Shonfield, 1965). These policies now seemed to be collapsing in on themselves as the state seemed no longer able to effectively manage the economy as prices spiraled out of control and long-term unemployment rose. Neoliberalism saw itself as being in a position to offer both an analysis of the "malaise," as American president Jimmy Carter framed it in the late 1970s, and a new political and economic program for ending it and putting the economy back on solid footing through the application of liberal economic and political principles. Now the Keynesian compromise that had yielded some forty years of steady economic growth and near full employment seemed no longer viable or even desirable. In this situation the ideas of the "prophet in the wilderness," as the historian Eric Hobsbawm call Hayek (in Prasad, 2006: 2), seemed poised to return to the mainstream. The "golden age of capitalism" (Felix, 2005: 394) with its "big government and regulated market" seemed now to be ending.

In addition to the specific economic woes wrought by the collapse of the gold standard and the oil crisis on state-managed economies, neoliberals argued that the welfare state that had steadily grown in many countries had become bogged down in the debilitating demands placed on it by unions and popular social movements, or in the denigrative vernacular found in public interest theory" they had been "captured" by "special interests." As evidence critics, such as Milton and Rose Friedman (1980: 96) pointed to the budget of the U.S. Department of Heath, Education and Welfare whose expenditures had grown from $2 billion in 1953 to more than $160 billion in 1978. From the neoliberal perspective, special interest groups placed continuously evolving and escalating economic and political demands on the state that eventually weighed it down in unattainable social obligations and individuals and corporations down in tax burdens to support these obligations. In the Keynesian and socialist arrangement, in order for the state to maintain its legitimacy and for politicians to get reelected they had to adhere to these growing popular demands. In doing so, however, the state increasingly drained wealth from its true source, the private sector, and transferred wealth from producers to the idle and unproductive as it sought to appease various groups petitioning the state for economic relief. In the end such state action killed both innovation and profit making. As a result, everyone, including workers and the poor suffered, not just the socialist bogeymen, the "greedy capitalist" or the "soulless corporation."

The seeming inability of Keynesian policies to deal effectively with the crisis of stagflation and the increasing burdens of the welfare state were also accompanied in the 1970s and 1980s by the introduction of a series of "problematics," "moral panics" and "crisis narratives" into political discourse and public policy that were designed to call into question the prevailing forms of governance and the state's involvement in the management of the economy. Neoliberals offered up these problematics, panics and narratives as both a way to showcase the failures of Keynesian and socialist policies and as a vehicle for offering up their approach as a panacea to the economic and political ills that the inadequacies of these economic policies had apparently created. As with most political programs, the neoliberal problematics were often accompanied by particular icons or imagery that helped to create a broad, far-reaching and influential political semiotics that supported neoliberal arguments and their calls for a fundamental overhaul of society and governance.

First and foremost among these problematics and narratives was an attack on the bureaucratic nature of the state. Here the state was projected as not only a bad economic manager but as a Weberian-style "iron cage" that stymied market innovation and thwarted individual freedom through its "dead hand," while simultaneously providing "bad service." The view is readily seen in the Public Choice Theory associated with James Buchanan and Gordon Tullock (1962) and in the Chicago School of Human Capital Theory developed by Gary Becker (1964). In the context of the civil services, "entrenched bureaucrats" became the particular icon of evil as they were often depicted as indifferent "paper pushers" who were so comfortable and smug in their positions and future guaranteed state pensions that they cared little about those whom they served. Another important problematic introduced in neoliberalist theory focused on the immorality, indolence and corruption inherent in public welfare programs. These programs were said to encourage laziness, abuse and dependence. This focus was accompanied by the imagery and narrative of the "welfare mother," "Cadillac-driving welfare recipient" or "dead beat slacker" who siphoned off the hard earned tax money of the middle class to support their idle and dependent lifestyles. In education this slacker image sometimes showed up in the iconography of the "self serving and monopolistic teacher" who "took summers off" and cared little about their students while simply collecting a taxpayer funded paycheck (see Gleeson and Shain, 1999: 463). These neoliberal policies, problematics, narratives and icons not only proved successful in altering the political players and landscape in many countries, they also were able to shift the general political discourse away from Keynesian-inspired discussions of full employment, the need for a strong and vital public sector, the importance of social welfare programs, progressive taxation, wealth redistribution and the importance of the regulatory role of the state. Neoliberals instead evoked the new vocabulary of free market solutions, choice, privatization and accountability.

While the deployment of these particular "icons of evil," such as the welfare mom, the grumpy and self-serving union member and the smug state bureaucrat, helped delegitimize the welfare state, neoliberals were also successful at redefining progressive Keynesian supporting politicians as somehow outdated, elitist, and, in the case of the U.S., as big government "beltway insiders" who lived off and loved to spend the taxes of "hard working Americans." In doing so they placed neoliberals as the actual anti-establishment "progressives" seeking to bring about positive social change through rolling back the taxing and intrusive regulatory activities of the state. As part of this rhetorical and political transformation, workers came to be redefined as taxpayers, the wealthy were transformed into entrepreneurs, "growth agents" and "wealth generators," citizens were recoded as consumers, private enterprise became simply "the economy," and social movements or groups became, depending on if they were friend or foe, either negatively coded as "interest groups" or positively depicted as "stakeholders."

Ideas, of course, cannot move without actants or networks nor can a sustained critique of the status quo be a tool to actually govern. In this sense, the expansion of neoliberalism as a fully developed and institutionalized social movement during the 1970s and 1980s owes itself to much more than economic theory, powerful icons of evil, crisis narratives or some supposedly inevitable changes manifesting themselves within the world economy. It also reflected a deliberate and sustained political and professional effort to reassert and institutionalize liberal and neoliberal ideas and practices in countries around the globe. This "army of fighters for freedom" as Hayek (in Crockett, 1995: 104) called them, would, over the course of a few decades, be responsible for moving liberalism from the periphery of political popularity back to the center.[7]

During the 1960s and 1970s many corporate leaders and financial leaders began to call for an organized social movement to shake Keynesianism and return to a less regulated marketplace. In the U.S., following the advice of Hayek and the fundraising activities of people like William Simon, who served as Secretary of Treasury in the Nixon administration, a concerted effort emerged to establish and finance a "counter intelligentsia" that would attack Keynesian policies and provide an alternative politics and policies (see Simon, 1978). In 1970 soon to be U.S. Supreme Court member Lewis Powell (1971) wrote and circulated an influential memo directed at the U.S. Chamber of Commerce entitled "Attack on American Free Enterprise System." In the Powell Memorandum, as it came to be referred, Powell proclaimed schools and universities to be socialist enclaves that directly threatened the existence of the American free enterprise system.[8] He argued that only through "careful and long-range planning and implementation" (Powell, 1970: 5) would it be possible to establish the organization and financing necessary to put forward an oppositional intellectual movement to counter the left's hegemonic intellectual control. In the U.S. conservative think tanks, such as the Heritage Foundation, the Manhattan Institute, the American Enterprise Institute (AEI) and the Cato Institute would take on this intellectual and ideological role by creating, disseminating, institutionalizing and legitimating neoliberal ideas and transforming them from the generalities of economic theory into specific policy recommendations that could be channeled to politicians (see Stefancic and Delgado, 1996).[9] The AEI, for example, used direct corporate funding to grow from a small staff of only two residence scholars in 1969 to ninety adjunct scholars by 1985 (Peet, 2007: 89). When Ronald Regan came to power in 1980, more than half of his appointments during his first presidential term came from conservative or neoliberal leaning think tanks (Peet, 2007: 90). Also, of his seventy-six economic policy advisors during his 1980 campaign for president, twenty-two were members of the Mount Pelerin Society (Muller, 2002: 382). Indeed, neoliberal influence had become so widespread that by the early 2000s most politically based think tanks could be identified as neoliberal leaning (Rich, 2004).

In the U.K. a similar neoliberal political activism is also evident beginning with the founding of the Institute of Economic Affairs (IEA) in the mid-1950s to introduce liberal, free market ideas into public policy. Their activities resulted in the so-called "Black Papers" of the 1960s which called for a variety of free market–style reforms including ones to education. In 1974 Keith Joseph and Margaret Thatcher formed the Centre for Policy Studies to promote more direct neoliberal policies in government (see

Spring, 1998: 125). The Centre's first publication was *Why Britain Needs a Social Market Economy* which argued for the need for a West German–style form of neoliberalism in the U.K. The Centre also published other central documents of neoliberal policy including Joseph's own *Monetarism Is Not Enough*. Soon after becoming conservative party leader Margaret Thatcher allegedly threw a copy of Hayek's (1960) book *The Constitution of Liberty* on the table and declared "this is what we believe" (Peet, 2007: 77). After becoming prime minister she appointed Joseph, who has previously been considered a candidate for Prime Minster, as her second Secretary of Education and Science (Peet, 2007: 77). In this role he helped establish much of the groundwork for neoliberal education reform and what would later become the 1988 Education Reform Act and the establishment of the England and Wales' "National Curriculum." Also, many of Thatcher's early economic ministries were filled with people with ties to the IEA (Denham and Garnett, 1998: 109).

In the neoliberal view it was now time that the liberal social contract that linked individuals to society, particularly as found in Locke (1980 [1690]) and, later, Property Rights Theory's linkage of private property and social obligation, to be reinstated. Neoliberals maintained that although the political left may not have succeeded in a full socializing of production or a revolutionary overthrowing of capitalism, its managed style economy had created, in the words of the conservative critic Irving Kristol (in Heilbrunn, 2008: 6) "a system so stringently regulated in detail as to fulfill many of the traditional anti-capitalist aspirations of the left." It was not just the economy that was to undergo a restructuring in the neoliberal revolution, however. The nexus of individual, society and politics was also to undergo a liberalization or "structural adjustment," of its own kind. Society itself was to be "desocialized" and "reindividualized." Much like with the advent of the market economy a few centuries earlier, as described by Karl Polanyi (1957 [1944]), people were to be "pried" from the collective protection, in this case one provided by the state rather than the "tribe," and (re)introduced to a situation that was atomistic, self-interested and individualistic. Here society was no longer to be though of as a superorganic collective represented, overseen and directed by the expert directed state but a collection of free individuals bound together by mutual responsibilities, contractual obligations and community expectations.

In the late 1970s and 1980s neoliberalism began to make the turn from the more "abstract intellectualism" of neoliberal theorists such as Hayek and Friedman to various "state authored restricting projects" led by politicians such as Thatcher, Hawke and Reagan (see Peck and Tickell, 2002: 388). These efforts were supported and given legitimation by organizations such as the Cato Institute, the Heritage Foundation or the Centre for Policy Studies neoliberal politicians and promoted internationally by groups such as the World Bank, Organization for Economic Cooperation and Development and the International Monetary Fund through what would later become known as the "Washington Consensus." By the mid 1980s, neoliberalism had crystallized into a broad, well-organized and increasingly zealous and transnational social movement. By this time it had been successful in establishing majority governments in the U.S., the United Kingdom, Australia and New Zealand and in making important inroads in a number of other countries around the world. It had also been successful at attacking what was considered to be the more socialistic orthodoxy and discourse that had entrenched itself in international organizations, such as the United Nations, various political institutions, non-governmental organizations, universities and the "mainstream media." As the neoliberal movement grew and obtain more power in governments around the world with the siren cries of lower taxes, smaller government, accountability and greater prosperity for all, their ascent set the stage for a series of major economic and political reforms undertaken throughout the 1980s, 1990s and 2000s.

The neoliberal reforms and policies that evolved over the last few decades generally took two forms, a "roll back" form and a "roll out" variety (Peck and Tichell, 2002). The early form of "roll back" neoliberalism associated most closely with economic liberalization and a "withering away of the state" reigned most prominently on the world stage from the late 1970s through the early 1990s and continues on more recently as an important current within neoliberalism, particular as found in various U.S. state governments, the Tea Party Movement and the Big Society policies of the Cameron coalition government in the U.K. Its roots are traceable more directly to eighteenth and nineteenth century liberal thought. However, by the early 1990s problems resulting from the wholesale abandonment of Keynesian economic policy, the increased financialization of markets and radically devolved state responsibility began to become evident to many in the 1987 economic downturn. However, what also seemed clear to many politicians and policy makers were the vast expansions in markets and shareholder value that these "roll back" policies had spawned during the 1980s, as well as the economic and political benefits to state operations of a devolved economic policy and a paired back welfare state. Under these circumstances a new, more nuanced form of the neoliberalism with its roots more directly in the position of *Ordoliberalens* emerged that sought to make a somewhat different calibration in the relations of market and state. This form of neoliberalism sought to establish a "social market" and a "social government." In this newer form of neoliberalism "social government" must, as Rose (1999: 141) described it, "be restructured in the name of an economic logic, and economic government must create and sustain the central elements of economic well-being such as the enterprise form and competition." Going by such names as "the new Democrats," "New Labour" and "third way" (Blair, 1996; Giddens, 1998) and personified in such politicians as Tony Blair and Bill Clinton, these policies sought to forge a path between the more *laissez-faire* approach associated with "roll back" neoliberalism (Peck and Tickell, 2002) and what was now considered by many to be the utter failures of Keynesianism and socialism and their "old style" government intervention strategies. This "social government" or "softer" form of social liberalism, sought to make the state a much more active player in economic development. Here the point was not to destroy the state but "wrest control of it from a 'new class' composed of professors, educators, environmentalists, city planners, sociologist and other trying to steer the economy" (Heilbrunn, 2008: 6)—in other words the bureaucratic, expert elite that Keynesian policy had both created and used as its guideposts. This "roll out" neoliberalism sought to adopt the principles put forward by the *Ordoliberals* by taking what they considered to be the best elements of the operation of markets, such as efficiency, accountability, and choice, and supplement and support them with what they considered to be the best elements of state interventionism, such as regulatory or auditing mechanisms and a concern for social democracy and the general welfare of the citizens. In doing so, it adopted what some termed a more "social development" rhetoric in its policies that sought to support the social aspects of economic growth, such as education and health care (Bergeron, 2008: 352) rather than simply privatizing or eliminating them altogether. However, it remained, like "roll back" neoliberalism, as Peter Mandelson (in Cassidy, 2010: 58) a New Labour politician in the U.K. framed it, "intensely relaxed about people getting filthy rich." In this "roll out" way of thinking, the competitive, disciplining and rationalizing effects of the market were to be admired and utilized to initiate wholesale reforms of the economy and government, as well as to discipline and direct individual behavior. In this situation, the state, however, should not stand on the sideline "or get out of the way" and watch these activities but, in keeping with the doctrines of *Ordoliberans*, should be an active agent in aiding economies to manage and enhance their competitiveness, expand global markets and to create flexible, knowledgeable, marketable and entrepreneurially minded workers. It should also create situations where "stakeholders," as Tony Blair famously referred to them and a term which would soon become one of the key phrases of the political scene, could work to better themselves, the economy and, ultimately, the nation state.

By the time this latter phase of neoliberalism reached maturity in the 1990s and early 2000s, the neoliberal movement had succeeded at ushering in some of the most dramatic and sweeping social experiments to be initiated in the West, and eventually globally, over the last one hundred years—one who's political, economic and social consequences are still being sorted out and debated over now some three decades or more since their introduction. What united these otherwise seemingly incommensurable groups of social conservatives, New Democrats and neoliberalists was a strong conviction in the correcting and disciplining features of competitive markets, the innovation and growth spawned by entrepreneurship and the liberating power of individual or consumer choice. For neoliberals, whether culturally on the right, middle or left or conservative or progressive, the basis of action is not to be found in the traditional sites of society or its political representative, the state, but in individuals and households exhibiting free choices and living up to and upholding their social contract of mutual responsibility. In this vision each individual and household is ultimately responsible for his or her own well-being and society's overall functioning (see Blair, 1996). Consequently, these societal stakeholders must be highly informed consumers of goods and services who continuously analyze situations and make choices that best serve their self-interest as they see them. This "rational choice" style of consumerism serves as fundamental selection principle on which societies, governments and economies should be organized. The goal in all of this choosing is to create what von Mises (1983) referred to as "consumer sovereignty" and a situation where social order is generated through the harmonizing of self-interest in the market (see, Peet, 2007: 73). In such situations governments can only provide the framing, incentives and protection for individuals to manifest this self-interest, choice and responsibility and for market to emerge and be safeguarded. The new society that will emerge from this liberal inspired notion of governance will be one firmly built on "mutual obligation" rather than "state responsibility" or "rights" (see Macintyre, 1999: 125).

SOME CENTRAL FEATURES OF NEOLIBERALISM

The variations of twentieth-century political economy and theory discussed in the last section reveal that neoliberalism is far from a monolithic political ideology or a uniform set of universal practices. The specific local implementation of those ideologies and practices vary considerably with the national political environment in which they were enacted. Based on factors such as the historical nature and types of political parties, the manifestations of cultural progressivism or conservatism, the power and resistant level of social movements, the level of bureaucratic and civil services entrenchment and resistance, existing class and ethnic divisions, the degree of state centralization or federalism, neoliberalism in the U.S., for example, took on a different look than neoliberalism in New Zealand or Chile. Also, it seems important to note that while neoliberalism, particularly the "roll back" variety, shared many of its central features with classic liberalism, it, nevertheless, is a distinct contemporary movement, that in certain circumstances may actually come into conflict with its predecessor. While undoubtedly inspired by liberal ideas, neoliberalism was significantly modified by the political and economic circumstances of the late twentieth century, as well as the perceived problems and lessons learned from the application of classic liberalism in the late nineteenth and early twentieth centuries.

32   Neoliberalism and Restructuring of Knowledge and Education

Despite these historical and doctrinarian variations, however, neoliberalism does contain a number of key elements or generic features that constitute its core principles and practices that transcend the particulars of locality. In this section I want to lay out what I believe to be a few of neoliberalism's most predominant characteristics. Although I will present these distinctly and in a somewhat "ideal typical form," they should, nevertheless, be thought of as interconnected characteristics that intersect and mutually support one other. In some cases, these characteristics are a result of the adoption or modification of basic liberal principles. In other cases, they are the result of neoliberal ideas and policies being applied in particular settings. And in still other cases, they are more general outcomes, intended or not, of other neoliberal policies in operation. The ten particular characteristics of neoliberalism that I want to focus on here are: (1) the advocacy of a particular theory of agency that sees self-interest and avarice as primary elements of human psychology and forces that are both reflected in and can only be adequately tapped, enhanced and contained by generating market-like environments and "contract-like" relationships between individuals, (2) a belief in the inherent and superior rationality, efficiency and optimizing effects of markets not just on economic organizations but all social institutions and activities, (3) an emphasis on loosening and deregulating market activities by the state and the redirection of state activities away from social welfare and regulatory functions and toward capital accumulation, market generation, policy and program auditing and profit-making or -enhancing policies and activities, (4) the use of economics or "the economy" as the final arbitrator or "tribunal of reason" in all institutional and governmental decision making through an economization of social policy, (5) an intensification of the velocity, range and scope of economic exchange, particularly as witnessed by what some have termed the "hyper-financialization" of the economy over the last thirty years and the "denationalization of money," (6) an intense focus on the enhancement of shareholder value or increases in the power of the "rentier class" through, in part, a reorientation of corporate savings and investing philosophies and the refocusing of managers on immediate stock price and shareholder value, (7) an emphasis on deregulating and expanding "free trade" and encouraging the global circulation of commodities including the free movement, marketization and "off shoring" of labor, (8) reforming the public realm and public institutions using market and privatization measures where possible and quasi-market mechanisms that mimic the workings of markets in other cases, (9) an opposition to labor unions, professional associations and other "syndicate like" groups or collectivities that are seen as artificially altering the equilibrium and efficiency of the economy, blocking market reforms, inflating wages, inhibiting freedom of contract and choice and undermining the workings of economic rationality, and, finally, (10) the advocacy of a stakeholder (or shareholder) society where self-interested people are linked to the economic system and society-as-a-whole through private consumption, self-interest, risk analysis and direct investments in the well-being of the general economy, as well as the individual ownership of particular stocks, bonds and mutual funds necessary for their own privately accumulated income and retirement.

With regard to the first characteristic, both liberalism and neoliberalism utilize a particular utilitarian or "game theory" of agency that envision society as a collection of free and independent agents or egos who are best linked to one another through voluntary agreements and mutual interests. Here as John Dewey (1935: 39) described it, "social arrangements were not treated as positive forces but as external limitations." Rather than envisioning individuals in a more sociological or collectivist sense as embedded within and molded by particular pre-existing social forms such as cultures, traditions, religions, groups or societies, liberals and neoliberals see them as "rational utility maximers" whose self-interest leads them to form "voluntary associations" and contractual relationships with one another (see, for example, Becker, 1976). In simple terms this perspective argues that "interest governs the world" (Gunn, 1969: 559). The central form of action in this individualized system is self-interest or what Max Weber (1968) referred to as "instrumental rationality." Here, as von Mises's (1932: 402) framed it, "egoism" is to be understood as "the basic law of society." In this cost/benefit mode of reasoning people in all situations act on the basis of how they perceive they will gain in some manner from a particular course of action rather than due to traditions or values. Such activities occur most obviously in the economy and its instrumentally rational environment; however, it is also a general principle applicable in all other domains of life.[10] Indeed, it is this activity that constitutes the core of Smith's infamous "invisible hand." Echoing themes in Mandeville's (1957) earlier work *The Fable of the Bees*, Smith argued that the individual "by pursuing is own interest . . . promotes [the public good] more effectually than when he really intends to promote it" (Smith, 1904). As an outcome, "the private interests and passions of men naturally led them to divide and distribute the stock of every society, among all the different employments carried on in it" (Smith 1904: 594–595). In the end all this self-interest and the commerce it creates constitutes an effective "order and good government" (Smith, 1904: 385).

Embedded within this idea of the natural state of free individuals is an explicit condemnation of what Milton Friedman (1962: 161) referred to as the "collectivist sentiment." This critique holds the collective, and related concepts such as "state," "society" and the "public," in deep suspicion. Indeed, at one extreme it can even be said, as Margaret Thatcher famously did in a 1987 interview, that for neoliberals society does not really exist, at least in the *sui generis* sociological or collectivist sense.[11] From this view the collective is either a harbinger of an older time of "group think" and authoritarian control that stifled individual freedom, creativity, motivation and innovation or a socialistic concoction used to support their particular collectivist and authoritarian political agenda (see Outhwaite, 2006).

The lessons drawn by neoliberals from this particular reading of human psychology and history is that contemporary politics needs a radical decollectivization and (re)individualization of all collectives such as unions, syndicates, guilds, professional associations, bureaucratic organizations and anything "social" or cooperative that disrupts or inhibits the free association of individuals and their unbounded and spontaneous activities. Any system that must "substitute compulsory for voluntary action" is defined as a threat to human freedom (Friedman, 1962: 195; see also Friedman and Friedman, 1980: 247). Neoliberalism, consequently, contains, as Bourdieu (1998: 2) pointed out, "a programme of the methodical destruction of collectivities—an attempt to call into question any and all collective structures that could serve as an obstacle to the logical of the pure market."

A belief in the inherent rationality and the rationalizing effects of the economy are another central characteristic that neoliberalism shares with its liberal counterpart, although the neoliberals arguably extend this idea much further than even their historical antecedents were willing to.[12] As we saw in the last section, they also significantly modified the classic liberal doctrine of laissez-faire that was used to guide this economic philosophy in many countries throughout the nineteenth century. Classic liberalism was concerned with the conceptual establishment of the market or the economy as an independent realm that was and should be outside of politics and culture. They were also; however, keenly aware of the limitations and proper jurisdiction of markets (see Sen, 2009). For classic liberals there were some important and necessary social and public functions that because of their unprofitability the market was simply unable to provide.

From the classic liberal view markets are both natural and normative. They are natural because markets are reflections of a type of inherent equilibrium evident in both the natural world and human nature. They are normative forces since this naturalness suggested that the best way to allow economies to work was to leave them alone—as in the doctrine of *laissez-faire*.[13] If left alone these markets would, through supply and demand equilibrium, provide what was needed for individual well-being and the public well-being. As Keynes would later describe it, the principle of *laissez-faire* "had arrived to harmonize individualism and socialism ... the political philosopher could retire in favor of the business man—for the latter could attain the philosopher's *summum bonum* by just pursing his own private profit" (Keynes, 1926: 3). In the apt and often-quoted description provided by Adam Smith in *The Wealth of Nations* (1904 [1776]: 14), "it is not on the generosity of the butcher, brewer or baker that we depend for our dinner, but on their self-interest." In France Jean-Bapiste Say (1964) extended Smith's argument by introducing his "law of markets." Markets were in his conceptualization entities that would naturally align and balance themselves if left undisturbed by outside, political forces. Disequilibrium, such as is found in conditions of oversupply, mass unemployment, recession or economic depression were, consequently, caused by meddling in the economy and could only be corrected by removing or cording off such influences. Such an "efficient market theory," as it came to be called in the twentieth century, with its internal balancing of markets was not only a feature of domestic markets but was also possible at the global level. In David Ricardo's (1973) *Principles of Political Economy and Taxation* the liberal economic principles established by Smith and Say are extended to global trade between nations and economies. Here, "gains from trade" are thought of as a means of balancing and distributing goods and wealth globally even in situations where one nation has an obvious "comparative advantage" over another. This also has larger moral effect where commerce "wear[s] off those prejudices which maintain distinctions and animosity between nations. It softens and polishes the manners of men" (Robertson, 1972 [1769]: 67).

Fixed in this classic liberalist way of thinking is a particular way of reading economic history—indeed, it is perhaps only through this particular way of thinking that we can even envision independent entities called economies, markets and economic history set apart from culture, politics or history in general. In this conceptualization liberalist economic history begins to create what Karl Polanyi (1944) called, "the disembedded market." In this conceptualization the market has a genesis and finitude of its own kind that is not reducible to or determined by religion, society, history or any element of culture. Likewise, this "economy *sui generis*," unlike the realms of culture, history or religion, behaves according to its own positive laws and responds to its own natural rhythms much like the human body or the universe (see Boltanski and Chiapello, 2005: 12).[14]

Since outside involvement in the economy disrupts market equilibrium both liberalism and neoliberalism are also well-known opponents of state power and state regulation, or at least where and when they are applied. In such a framing, "the great threat to freedom is concentration of power" (Friedman, 1962: 2) in the hands of the state. Here, "the market economy is understood as distinct from, and ultimately impenetrable by, procedures of government" (Slater and Tonkiss, 2001: 119). Indeed, the state operates on privately produced wealth and not vice versa. As such, state regulation, like other forms of market disruptions such as those caused by cartels or unions, alters the equilibrium present in the market and disrupts its self-correcting features. When a state responds to political pressure to alter the economy through price supports, wage freezes or price controls, it creates conditions that extend and exacerbate the very problem it is trying to correct. Except for the very libertarian fringe of neoliberalists, this does not mean, however, that the state has no larger social responsibility to its citizens, through limited social welfare type supports (see Sen, 2009). As outlined earlier, in contrast to classic liberalism and its doctrine of *laissez-faire*, one key current of neoliberalism views the state as an institution that can be harnessed to generate or expand, rather than simply to secure the conditions for, markets (see Lemke, 2001). It can and should also be used to promote and spread entrepreneurial values throughout society. In this reading, the state is envisioned as a "managerial state" (Clarke and Newman, 1997) or auditing state that oversees and measures prudent economic expansion and one who is a partner in expanding markets and extracting profit. However, such state initiatives are always "fraught with danger" (Friedman, 1962: 2) and should, consequently be minimized. State supports when used should not be so large or intrusive as to drain the economic vitality from markets or destroy the freedom or initiatives of individuals. For instance, in the neoliberal reading put forward by Friedman and others, welfare and employment programs may have a limited place in society; however, they should not disrupt the labor needs of industry or create such onerous tax burdens as to stifle business profits, as neoliberals argue they increasing did in the 1960s and 1970s. It is, consequently, the state's responsibility to create more private wealth, expand markets and profit in order to do a proper and effective job of public governing.

One of the end results of the emphases on the inherent rationality, the positive laws of markets and the opposition to state regulation, and another key characteristic of neoliberalism, is the argument that economics should serve as a tribunal of last resort in all institutional and political decision-making, or as Foucault (in Lemke, 2001: 198) referred to it, *"une sorte de tribunal economique permanent."* This "bottom line" economic determinism or "economization" (see Caliskan and Callon, 2009) has both an obvious economic and a perhaps somewhat less than obvious moral function. Morally speaking markets serve as rationalizing and purifying agents that are capable of solving such widely varying social problems and issues as greenhouse gas emissions (see Esty and Winston, 2009), low income home ownership, global income inequality, and even urban snow removal. For instance, in the so-called carbon market or emissions trading advocated by certain governmental and environmental groups, pollution is to be controlled through establishing a market for its valuation and circulation. Such an approach allows the long-standing problem of air pollution to be solved by bringing the market and its built-in efficiencies to bear through the incentives provided by a government-created market and the possibilities for profit where none existed before. In this "neoliberalization of social problems" the traditional Keynesian relationship of state and economy are reversed; the economy now serves as the principle by which the state and society-at-large must view and gauge its actions rather than the market being measured by its impact on the state or civil society. State or governmental activities that may disrupt the workings of the economy, such as those designed for wealth redistribution including progressive taxes or hikes in capital gains or estate taxes, are actively discouraged because they will cause undue burden on private wealth producers and disrupt the functioning of markets which, as the reasoning goes, will in the end actually create more societal harm than good. As a result the true decision making is shifted from the more contentious and open arenas of Congressional or

Parliamentary battles over fiscal policy to the more hidden monetary policy of Central Banks and the Federal Reserve (see Krippner, 2007: 486).

As this neoliberal reasoning has unfolded and spread over the last few decades, economics and budgets have become the court of last resort for decision-making in all households, organizations and governments. The economic, bottom line argument, with its backing in the supposedly firm principles and laws of the positive science of economics and the pragmatic realities of accounting practices, become effectively "calculating agents," as Michel Callon (1998) has called them, that that can be deployed and mobilized in particular instances to trump all other political or social arguments or considerations. What this ignores, as early critics of neoliberalism such as Foucault and Bourdieu have pointed out, is that budgetary decisions are first and foremost political and moral decisions made from a sea of political options and possibilities. These options and possibilities are, in turn, all shaped by prevailing political and power configurations; although the deployment of economics and law allow for certain considerations to be "bracketed." Decisions are, consequently, never simply economic matters any more than they are simply religious or political ones; they are instead always deeply entwined within culture, history and politics.

Secondly, this form of economic determinism confuses what is arguably an ideological construction: in this case that of the neutrality of the positive science of economics (and the conflation of this in the mathematicalness of accounting), with an exact description of "things as they are." The power of relying on economics as a *tribunal permanent*, consequently, is that it seems to offer the possibility (critics would say illusion) of forever depoliticizing and disciplining decision-making. By mobilizing the economic argument and transforming it into the scientific and mystifying forms of formulas, graphs and expert economic pronouncements the finalizing power of economic decision-making is affirmed (see Mackenzie et al., 2007). With this in place, organizations, institutions and even the state itself are able to present themselves as making proper, prudent and "painful but necessary" budgetary decisions that are rational, wise, "bottom line" oriented and in line with needs of the economy. This process effectively limits or silences the political demands being placed on the state by particular groups, such as those receiving public services, by seemingly creating a situation where certain public services and other state remedies are rendered economically, and hence politically, untenable, "in the red" and out of bounds.

Neoliberal policies have also been responsible for a dramatic intensification of the velocity, range and scope of economic exchange. This even applies to some degree to the overall intensification and rationalization of work and labor under neoliberal regimes. From a neoliberal perspective markets are at their most effective when they are able to quickly respond to changing needs and conditions. Essentially, they must be allowed to "do as they please" and to move and change as quickly as they wish without obstacles or undue regulation that may slow a market's responsiveness. The

Schumpeterian notion of "creative destruction" is often employed in this instance to support the economic and moral outcomes of this intensification. Likewise, economic growth has become the single most important goal of all national economies (see Miller and Rose, 1993: 89). Values can be set, profit derived and growth achieved only when individuals are able to rapidly take advantage of changing conditions, much like in the case of the fast paced movement of the stock market, such as found in the technique of "flash trading." Freeing up markets by removing barriers to trade and state regulations allow products to flow more quickly and efficiently. This process was perhaps most noticeable during the 1990s and 2000s with the financial activities of banks, investment firms and the so-called derivates market. During this time neoliberalist policies promoted a radical financialization of the economy that oversaw "a growing dominance of capital market financial systems over bank-based financial systems" (Epstein, 2005: 3). This financialization, with its emphasis on financial markets, insurance and real estate or FIRE, also brought about a shifting of profit making from traditional avenues, such as the production of goods and trade, to financial channels and instruments. For neoliberals, banks and their financing activities had been unduly regulated since many of them collapsed during the Great Depression. To correct for this in the U.S. context, the 1933 Glass-Steagall Act that had separated the activities of banks and investment banks and investment banks and investment firms was repealed in 1999. In addition to this move post–Bretton Woods economic policies that had sought to maintain stable exchange rates and employment by limiting capital movement were often ignored (Felix, 2005: 394). Advocates of the repeal of Glass-Steagall maintained that the over-regulation of financial activities and financial markets had prohibited this particular sector of the economy from expanding and profiting as much as it could. Such over-regulation slowed economic activity, particularly in post-industrial economies, by limiting the velocity of money and by stymieing the development of a fully actualized market for new financial products, such as derivatives, "mortgage backed securities," "subprime loans," Exchange Traded Funds (ETFs) and other "packaged" investments. What was needed, in Hayek's (1978) terms, was a "denationalization of money." This would essentially create a "free trade in money," which would, in turn, intensify market competition and limit the power of nation states by making them subservient to international monetary markets and creditors. Monetary policy could then be used to ensure that the debts incurred by nation states were always dependent upon their currency rates and treasury markets, such as the conditions in Greece and Portugal in 2010. Under these policies, the state and public sector in general too were now at the mercy of markets, although it was ironically the state and the public who set the legal parameters of economic policy in the first place.[15]

From the neoliberalist perspective in order to fully realize the potential of the classical liberal Ricardoean principle of "comparative advantage" in global free trade, finance and money themselves had to be freed from state regulation and burdens imposed by fixed currency rates and be allowed to flow as readily as goods and services in the increasing globalizing markets. Indeed, a truly global commodities market was impossible without first "unchaining" financial markets. The outcome of this financialization was the removal of restriction on the flow of capital, the abandonment of the Bretton Woods model of fixed and stable currencies, the dramatic expansion of financial markets and the increased power of what Marx (1967: 522) referred to in his own day as the "new aristocracy of finance." In fact, Dumenil and Levy (2001: 578) define neoliberalism expressly as "the ideological expression of the return to hegemony of the financial fraction of the ruling class."

With finance again unshackled, financial markets during the 1990s and 2000s increasingly became crucial mechanisms "driving the allocation of capital between firms, between industries and regions and between whole nations" (Clark and Wojcik, 2007: 3). In the U.S. the financial industry soon came to represent "35 to 40% of all profits by all US corporations." (Volcker, 2010: 12). Over time this move toward an economy based largely on finance would have profound effects on nations and economies, as well as individual companies and firms. With the global movement of capital, particularly when enhanced by the rapid velocity of money created by information technologies, firms were increasing held accountable for fast, immediate profits and ongoing prospects for strong growth. The dream here was that free markets when coupled with technology and "sophisticated financial engineering" would "support both market efficiency and stability" (Volcker, 2010: 12). This situation created what the economist Bennett Harrison (1994) referred to as "impatient capital"—the unmitigated desire for quick profit.[16] This change at the firm level, in turn, created, or at least complimented, a larger push for the major "structural adjustment" of national economies in order to accommodate profitability demands, such as the pressure placed on so-called developing nations by groups such as the IMF and the World Bank and attempts to reform the functioning of government found in New Public Management around the world. Indeed, as Dumenil and Levy (2001: 579) point out financialization was not the result of the "needs" of globalization as pronounced by neoliberal reformers but one of its central drivers.

At the organizational or firm level these international financial changes created an emphasis not only on immediate profits but also on an ongoing industrial restructuring and flexible specialization (Clark and Wojcik, 2007: 3). Industry needed to be continuously streamlined by the ebb and flow of finance. As this happened, "Anglo-American managerial capitalism was overtaken by financial capitalism" (Clark and Wojcik, 2007: 184). Under the new form of financialization corporate managers now had to be concerned not just with the usual managerial tasks of production, labor costs and shareholder value but also bolstering stock prices and bond ratings to attract the attention of rapidly flowing and maniacal financial capital. This change gave much greater power to mutual fund managers, and a series of "independent investment" groups such as private equity firms, venture capitalists and private hedge funds who oversaw, directed and profited from much of these financial flows. It also helped elevate and expand the power of traditional banks, investment firms and the rentier class—the class of individuals whose primary source of income is derived primarily from dividends and interest. In this situation, unlike in classic capitalism, what matters most is not so much the amassing of wealth, although that obviously is still in evidence, but the "the constant transformation of capital, plant and various purchases into output, of output into money, and of money into new investments" (Boltanski and Chiapello, 2005: 5). In this situation the processes of capital accumulation, consequently, never ceases. Those involved in its direction, movement and management are in one sense as entangled and in some sense at its unceasing demand as much as workers; although the consequences of their actions and the benefits derived are obviously quite different.

Another key characteristic of neoliberalism, and one directly traceable to an expansion of the idea of "comparative advantage" introduced by David Ricardo in the nineteenth century, is its advocacy of the virtues of "free trade." Indeed, neoliberalism has been described by Ulrich Beck (2000: 122) as "the high politics of globalization." For neoliberals free trade represents one of the prime opportunities to expand markets into areas where they had not existed before. It also provides an opportunity for workers around the globe to "to trade up" and expand their well-being (Griswold, 2009: 27); thereby generating a burgeoning global middle class of consumers. For neoliberals profit can be extended and GNP expanded only if markets are continuously finding new opportunities and forever growing. In this model there is no room for a "steady state" or no growth economy. Creating forever expanding markets requires the lowering and eventually elimination of tariffs and other structural barriers to the flow of goods and people through the multilateral trade negotiations such as those of the World Trade Organization (WTO), the adoption of OECD policies and the "structural adjustments" measures demanded by groups such as the World Bank and the IMF.

In addition to the ability of forever expanding markets to grow trade, neoliberals also see them as capable of solving long-standing issues of global poverty, North/South wealth divisions or "underdevelopment." Here these problems are viewed as the result of the lack of global free trade rather than being caused by it (see, for example, Griswold, 2009). In the neoliberal argument, countries that practice free markets prosper, while those with state restrictions, socialist governments, high protectionist tariffs and controlled and regulated economies do not. Consequently, trade agreements and cooperatives such as the North American Free Trade Agreement (NAFTA), the Central America Free Trade Agreement (CAFTA) or the

European Union itself, as well as the trade agreements negotiated through the WTO, are ultimately beneficial to all parties. Likewise, as in the Washington Consensus, countries should be "actively encouraged" to open up their markets, reform their public sectors and follow neoliberal guidelines in order to receive loan assistance, such as in the cases of IMF or World Bank support. In fact states can be measured and judged on the basis of their friendliness to these liberal economic policies.

The free movement of money and goods should also be accompanied by the free movement of labor. Labor should, consequently, be flexible and casual enough to move where the jobs are moving. The worker must, in Hayek's (1948: 22) words, "be ready to adjust himself to changes... which to him will often appear unintelligible and irrational." In situations where workers cannot be found in one locality, either the plant should be able to easily move without undue restrictions or new workers should be able to be allowed to migrant, without undue immigration restrictions, perhaps temporarily, to fill the labor void. This applies not only to manual forms of labor but to all types of jobs, including professionals, such as software engineers, graphic artists and educators, such as in the case of the Bridgeport, Connecticut, school district that began importing math and science teachers from India to teach in the city's schools.[17] It turns out that labor is a commodity that too needs to be much more open to the price setting and allocating effects of markets. To make this happen, however, its syndicated protection in unions and professions needs to be curtailed since it prohibits labor markets from establishing equilibrium and workers from reaching their full potential.

Another key characteristic of neoliberalism, particularly in its "third way" or "roll out" version, is the promotion of something widely referred to as the stakeholder or, in some instances, the shareholder society. This strain of neoliberalism views society as a site where autonomous and independent actors each own a stake in a nation's economic activities and, as a consequence, society-at-large. At the policy level this vision promotes the idea that every member of society has a contractual part to play in the overall viability of the economy. At the rhetorical level of institutional and governmental policy this often takes the form of groups being referred to as "stakeholders" who are to "be brought to the table" for important decisions. In this model people gain their stake hold, not through exercising their basic democratic rights or collective responsibilities but, as in stock ownership, through using their effort, income and wealth to "buy into," "own" and "vote their shares" in the general economy and particular companies. Workers, managers and owners are viewed, therefore, not as conflicting social classes vying over power and resources but as individuals who are each responsible in their own way for contributing their part to the creation of the greater good—which in this case is defined as a growing economy free from labor conflicts or other disruptions of private profit making and market expansion[18] Regardless of the unequal distribution of profit between owners and workers, if the economy declines it is the responsibility of both parties to correct it through what is often referred to in the often used but rarely practiced stakeholder rhetoric as "shared sacrifice."

THE NEOLIBERAL STATE AND CONTEMPORARY POLITICS

Today the state form that is left in the wake of the application of neoliberal policies over the last few decades contains elements of both the "roll back" and "roll out" versions of liberalism. As discussed earlier, in classic or "roll back" forms of liberalism the state is portrayed as the enemy of freedom. As such it needs to be kept at a minimum size and continuously watched to make sure it doesn't grow too big or too powerful. The state's basic function in this version of "the government that governs the best governs the least" is to enforce laws that protect property rights and to provide safety and protection, particularly from other states. In contrast, in socialism or even in more moderate forms of Keynesianism the state is presented as the champion of freedom that provides public goods in order to ensure justice and equality. In this sense the state is synonymous with "the people" who need a strong centralized government and robust public domain to protect individuals and promote collective well-being. The neoliberal state that emerged over the last few decades, while politically distinct, borrows particular elements from both of these state forms even, ironically, the very socialist and Keynesian forms that it sought to distinguish itself from and overthrow.

From classic liberalism, neoliberalism borrows the general suspicion of the state and the idea that private enterprise can always do things better and more efficiently than the state. For both liberals and neoliberals the state is not, nor could it ever be, a special, interest free realm that is itself outside of self-interest and power mongering. Likewise, following the views outlined in public interest theory, political leaders are not interest-free public servants motivated by love for their fellow citizens or professionally minded public servants but are driven, like all humans, by greed, avarice and self-preservation (see Downs, 1957; Buchanan and Tullock, 1962; Niskanen, 1971). This being the case the state and politicians need to be monitored and their power continuously checked and dispersed. In contrast the Keynesian or socialist versions sees the state, at least if held by the right political group and monitored by appropriate experts, as the apparatus which creates conditions of equity and fairness. In this sense, the state and political leaders are not driven by self-interest but by ideas of serving the public and creating the greater good and, in some cases, adhering to their creed as government professionals.

Neoliberalism, particularly the "roll out" or third way variety, ironically combines the liberalist focus on individualism and market freedom with the socialist and Keynesian desire to manufacture and steer social change—only this time the social change is envisioned not as expanding and protecting the public domain but as enhancing markets. In this "marketisation of the state" the central task of government is "to construct and universalize competition to achieve efficiency and invent market systems" (Olssen, 2006: 219). Or, as a World Bank (1997: 25) report framed it, society needs "an effective state—not a minimal one." In the socialist system the state was equivalent to society; in the neoliberal system the market is the same as society. In this sense the contemporary neoliberal state model more closely follows the direction laid out by Ordoliberalism, Rhineland capitalism and Hayek than classical liberalism. In this instance, however, the state is not the central overseer of the economy, with its own enterprises and work programs, as in socialist and Keynesian systems, but an institution that works to make sure the markets have the resources and support they need to function optimally and to minimize the tax revenues needed. In this arrangement the state is specifically redesigned to serve as a type of "grand accountant" or manager of the market centered society by auditing and overseeing state services, many of which should be outsourced or privatized as much as possible. In this "Schumpeterian Workfare State," as Jessop (1994) has referred to it, the state takes on a much more activist role than in the *laissez-faire* form as it is used to fuel the development of markets, hone and flexiblize the workforce and further creative destruction and market discipline. Indeed, in one sense what made neoliberalism so appealing to New Democrats and "third way" or New Labour politicians was that it seemed to offer a means of achieving some of the desired outcomes of socialist style planning through other avenues, in this case those of the market.

There is a highly paradoxical notion of oversight at play in the neoliberal managerial state, however, resulting from tensions with the two different forms of neoliberalism. On the one hand, the market is to be further deregulated and allowed to function with minimum oversight. However, agencies that use tax dollars, such as schools, hospitals and universities, are audited and regulated more intensely and frequently than every before since they are, in the neoliberal conceptualization, dependent on private wealth and property for their existence. In the more socialist model wealth is conceptualized as a social accomplishment. It is made possible by the collective efforts and political decisions of society's members and laws and public policies that create the conditions for wealth to be realized. Even the "roll back" form of neoliberalism that railed so loudly against the size and excesses of the welfare state in the late 1970s and 1980s was actually responsible more for a shifting of resources and emphases within the state rather than shrinking it, at least when we examine overall state expenditures during this period. In this case the state's energy and focus moved from ameliorating inequality through various welfare programs and progressive taxation or from serving as a buffer between the well-being of workers and instability of markets to serving as an auditor and marketer.

With this the state became in essence a means of governing without really governing (Olssen and Peters, 2005: 319).[19]

In summary, seeing neoliberalism, as some critics are prone to do, as simply an ideology that markets should always prevail over the activities of the state misses many of the more recent transformation occurring within neoliberal politics and governance and the operations of markets in general over the last few decades (see Rose, 1999: 137–138). With the development of "knowledge societies" and "stakeholder societies" as part of the "roll out" neoliberal thought in the 1990s complex new contours were introduced into neoliberal governance that are clearly not reducible to a simple, *laissez-faire* understanding of the market and the state. The economic downturn of 2008 did little to change this situation. Indeed, the shape that neoliberalism has taken and is now undergoing in the 2010s must be seen as the result of a complex interchange between the state, economic institutions and various social groups present in societies, such as workers, political groups and professions. Its current form, consequently, is best seen as a pragmatic economic and political adaptation to circumstances rather than a straightforward application of a political philosophy.

Although the idealized rhetoric or "enthymeme" of neoliberalism makes it appear to be a unified doctrine and that its ascension to prominence was ordained or inevitable, it would, as I have tried to outline here, take the coordinated efforts of large number of think tanks, donors, political parties, university economics departments and governmental and non-governmental organizations to make it into such an ordinary, natural and, proponents would claim, inevitable, feature of the contemporary political and economic landscape. This being the case, we should envision neoliberalism as a broad, multifaceted and transnational social movement rather than as a singular and unified political and economic doctrine, discourse or "regime of truth." Indeed, even within classical liberalism there was, at least since the nineteenth century, a pronounced tension between "the utilitarians" and "the economists" (Dewey, 1935: 19)—between a political emphasis on "personal freedom" and the economic emphasis on "freedom of contract" (see Hodgson, 1999: 83). What is evident in today's political scene where knowledge and education operate is a complex state-market nexus that blends elements of this classic liberal tension evident in "roll back" and "roll out" neoliberalism. Indeed, in many national contexts the last few decades have witnessed an oscillation between "roll back" and "roll out" forms of neoliberalism as economic conditions change. In so-called "good economic times," "roll out" neoliberalism with its activist, market friendly programs becomes more pronounced. As the market becomes over-extended and the economy declines, "roll back" neoliberalism with its austerity measures and fear of tax increases on "wealth generators" often appears back on the scene in some contexts. This contemporary oscillation also in some contexts blends elements and vestiges of Keynesianism and socialism, not to mention elements of cultural conservatism and cultural progressivism, which continually morph and are reconfigured as conditions change. Neoliberalism is, consequently, something that should be seen as always in motion and always in transformation. Its contours and trajectory are not static or linear but are being continuously shaped and reworked by both an ongoing tension within its own internal camps (e.g., personal freedom vs. freedom of contract) between those who wish to emphasize some of its tenants above others and those on the outside who constantly oppose, challenge and seek to modify its ideas and policies. Indeed, if we stop and consider it, the complex, hybridized and "pragmatic" political and social landscape that we inhabit today is the result of this tension at play.

2 The Machinations of Managerialism
New Public Management and the Diminishing Power of Knowledge Professionals

> Men dilate on the high necessity of a businesslike organization and control of the university, its equipment, personnel and routine. (Veblen, 1918: 85)

> The economy transforms the world, but it transforms it into a world of the economy. (Debord, 1995: 28)

> A quarter of a century of calling the government bad has resulted in bad government. (Soros, 2010: 16)

In the last chapter I was concerned with how neoliberalism developed over the last few decades and how it has played itself out at the broad level of international political economy. In this chapter I want to examine neoliberalism at a more institutional level by focusing on how its ideas and practices have reshaped various public organizations, such as hospitals, schools, universities, and government agencies. I am particularly interested here in how neoliberalism was applied to and transformed public organizations and professions through the application of a particular form of managerialism generally referred to as "new public management" (NPM). Specifically I am interested in NPM's direct connection with the central tenants of neoliberalism discussed in the last chapter and how these tenants managed to make the move from corporate settings into the administrative offices of the public sector over the last few decades. I am also interested here in how NPM has, subsequently, transformed the conditions under which knowledge organizations operate and knowledge workers work.

While it is certainly true that most public service organizations have been "managed" for some time now, they generally have been administered bureaucratically rather than managed managerialistically. In other words, it has only been within the last few decades that public organizations around the world have transitioned from a rule-governed, bureaucratic and administrative model borrowed in part from military organizations to an "output driven" corporate style of managerialism taken from the business world and neoliberal models of organizational governance.

In this chapter I first outline some of the central features of managerialism as both a specific set of organizational practices and as a broad, societal level doxa of modernity. Afterward, I turn to the introduction of NPM in the 1980s and 1990s and how this approach sought to bring the managerialism of the business world into the management of the public sector. Next, I examine some of the implications of NPM for public sector professions and professionals. Afterward, I explore how these changes have affected the way knowledge organizations operate. I conclude with a discussion of how neoliberalism and NPM has sought to transform public professionals from "unproductive" to "productive labor."

MANAGERIALISM AND MODERNITY

The idea that workers need managing seems self-evident. Without the guiding hand of management those working in organizations would be undisciplined, uncooperative and unproductive. Hence, management arose, as the story often goes, "to make people's desires manifest through organized effort" (Wren, 1994: 10). It is, therefore, an essential part of the modernist dream of maximizing the potentials inherent in workers and the organizations in which they are part. With such a vital role to play in the modern world managers were destined "to become the new heroes of the economy" (Boltanski and Chiapello, 2005: 59) and management was likely to, as Peter Drucker (1954: 1) put it in the 1950s, "remain a basic and dominant institution perhaps as long as Western Civilization itself survives."

However, such naturalistic and teleological understandings of the growth of management as both a social class and organizational strata, as well as managerialism as a set of specific practices and a broad societal-level ideology ignores the intricate historical and political antecedents that created such a seemingly natural ordering of managerial authority. It leads is to forget that in most times and places people managed to manage their affairs without the involvement of management. Culturally speaking, this fact did not mean that people were necessarily more disorganized, unproductive, or uncooperative when compared to modernites but that they used other, sometimes less formal and often more phenomenal and socially embedded ways of conducting and coordinating their activities. In an organizational sense, however, management did indeed make people more productive and organized since, to some degree, it is actually its rhetoric and practices that are partially responsible for defining and delimiting what it means to be "rational," "productive," "efficient" and "modern." It did this by enacting and extending elements of what Weber famously referred to as the rationalization process to the levels of institutions and everyday life. In doing so, management helped create a moral and rhetorical ordering that defines and ranks people, activities and things in term of their rationality, efficiency, performity and productivity, while simultaneously legitimating the need for a group of specially trained people to oversee all that defining and ranking.

The insertion of management as a necessary and integral part of the ordering of human affairs and the working of organizations, both large and small, originates in the mid to late nineteenth century with the separation of capital ownership from management and the resulting shift from individual to corporate ownership of companies. This economic shift led to the insertion of a third group between workers and owners for whom, as Marx (1996) describes them, "the work of supervision becomes their established and exclusive function." This new group and strata were "an administrator of other people's capital" and, hence, constituted "a special form of wage-laborer" (Marx, 1996) that would be responsible for the daily workings of the company and the maximization of profit for the new corporate shareholder owners. In broader historical terms the rise of management signaled a switch away from more federative and communal types of social organization toward the centralized bureaucratic organizations that would come to be a central signifier of modernity and to dominate much of modern life (see Weber, 1947; Berle and Means, 1991 [1933]; Chandler, 1977). Over time this switch created a university-trained professional class of individuals whose job it was to discipline the workforce, hone the organization's functioning and continually rationalize economic production in order to increase profit for the now largely absentee shareholder owners. They would accomplish these modernizing feats through the introduction of a continuously evolving series of new managerial theories; techniques of industrial organization and a Tayloristic directed or inspired scientific arrangement and administration of tasks. As this transformation became solidified in the twentieth century, it created what Bousquet (2008: 77) called a "management theory of value"—the widely held belief that it is management and not workers who are ultimately responsible for the rapid production and economic expansion experienced by industrial economies over the last century and a half.

While management as an organizational stratum has been around for some time, managerialism as a particular "regime of truth" (Morley and Rassool, 2000: 170) is a somewhat newer phenomenon. Managerialism can be seen both as a specific set of ideas and practices that, under the direction of managers, arrange a group's activities in particular efficiency- and production-minded ways and as a broader societal-level doxa that legitimates and expands the need for this particular type of control in practically all settings. Managerialism is, then, much more than simply the application of various management practices in organizations. It is, rather, a belief that all organizations or institutions, regardless of their purpose or functioning, can only work properly and efficiently if power, control and decision-making are centralized in some manner in the hands of professionally trained and "objective" managers. Furthermore, this position contends that this organizational form is not only desirable for efficiency purposes but also part of an inevitable historical progression toward better, more effective social structures. Without these uniquely trained, politically neutral professional managers, whose only interest is to make sure the organization works efficiently, institutions risk anarchy, unproductivity and, in a competitive business environment, extinction. Even in situations where an organization purports to be "post bureaucratic" (see Heckscher and Donnellon, 1994) with different, allegedly less hierarchical mechanisms of decision- making, managerialism still entails the notion that productivity and institutional guidance are ultimately the sole forte of managerial authority. In such organizations teamwork and consensus building may be prized, since they signify the absence or at least abatement of organizationally and production disrupting conflicts; however, it is, in the end, the job of management to quell, forge, arrange and interpret those views and convert them into action in keeping with the institution's mission and the wishes of those who ultimately own or control it. Proponents of managerialism maintain that although specific managerial philosophies may vary across time, the fact that people and organizations everywhere need special, dispassionate managers in order to properly and efficiently operate is an uncontestable truism of modern organizational life.

The key feature of managerialism as a regime of truth, consequently, is a belief in the universal application of management principles in whatever form. Without the motivational, disciplinary and organizational techniques utilized by impartial and rationality conscious managers members of all types of organizations, from the Girl Scouts to the Methodist Church to IBM, would veer off course from their institutional missions and become inefficient and unproductive. Such a view has not remained relegated to the working of organizations, however. As Martin Parker (2002: 2) has pointed out over the course of the last century, managerialism became "both a civilizing process and a new civil religion." "If we have a difficulty, with our jobs, our lives, or government or our world, then the answer is often supposed to be better management" (Parker 2002: 2). It is the panacea that is offered up to remold and discipline all types of individual and organizational behaviors in order to make them more efficient, goal oriented and, ultimately, "better." Indeed, as Parker (2002) points out, the practices associated with managerialism often even extend to the level of the individual who must set up something akin to a "strategic plan for living" that helps him or her properly manage their time, households and daily affairs in order to be fully "self-actualized" and "on task."

THE BIRTH OF NEW PUBLIC MANAGEMENT AND THE POST-BUREAUCRATIC ORGANIZATION

Key to the larger restructuring of the economy, society and politics initiated by neoliberals was an attempt to bring the "bottom line" economic rationality and centralized decision-making of corporate organization and functioning into the working of the public sector, such as schools, universities, hospitals and state agencies. Just as the "Reengineering of the Corporation" (Hammer and Champy, 1993) was an economic necessity for businesses so too was the reformulation of governmental institutions. In this case, managerialism, as introduced through the form of NPM, became the primary means through which neoliberalist ideas and practices spread at the level of public institutions. In fact NPM can be seen as the central mechanism through which neoliberalism reconfigured not only the larger political economy of nation states but also the ordinary, day-to-day institutions where people receive services and work. As part of this process, NPM sought to dismantle the classic bureaucratic organization and public administration model and its delegated type of authority structure that had operated in these public service organizations in previous decades. It replaced them with either a business-style managerialism or, in some instances, a "post-bureaucratic" style of management that operates on an entirely different set of devolved relationships, particularly as they relate to decision-making and the role of professionals who work in these public organizations. It also replaced the "rule-driven" behavior of public bureaucratic organizations with the "output-driven" performance of competitive enterprises. As we shall see in more detail in the next section, NPM sought to fold or redirect the professionals who work in public organizations under the wing of managerial authority by creating mechanisms that required a shifting of accountability from the internal ethical and disciplinary protocols of the public professions themselves to either public sector managers or outside auditors who were said to represent the interests of various institutional "stakeholders," taxpayers or the public in general.

The ideas and practices that eventually coalesced into NPM emerged during the 1950s and 1960s with the rise and dissemination of "new institutional economics" and its offshoot, Public Choice Theory (see Downs, 1957; Buchanan and Tullock, 1962; Niskanen, 1971). Public Choice Theory's main proponents were James Buchanan and Gordon Tulloch who established the Center for Study of Public Choice at Virginia Tech University and the journal *Public Choice* in 1966 to promote the study of political institutions using economic principles and methods (see Medema, 2009: 129–159). Embedded in Public Choice Theory's emphasis on bringing the liberal subject and rational choice from economic theory into to the study of political action was an attempt to put these ideas into practice by making public institutions less rule governed, bureaucratic and cloistered and more open, entrepreneurial and consumer oriented. In Public Choice Theory's conceptualization the political process was "a game" where "players with quite disparate objectives interact so as to generate a set of outcomes that may not be internally consistent or efficient by any standards" (Buchanan, 1984: 20). In this game politicians and public bureaucrats are seen as being as self-interested as any other rational actor (see Buchanan, 1972: 12).

As Milton Friedman (1962: 2) described this connection of interests and power, "even though the men who wield this power initially be of good will and even though they be not corrupted by the power they exercise, the power will both attract and form men of a different camp." This being the case public choice theorists argued that public policy should be built around the proper application and containment of this interestness rather than assuming that politicians and bureaucrats operate on more communitarian principles. In this "politics without romance" (Buchanan, 1984: 20), politics should not depend, as Hayek had previously put it, "on our finding good men for running it, or on all men becoming better than they now are" (Hayek, 1948: 12). In order to implement this view of politics and politicians public choice theorists advocated a move away from a "militaristic-bureaucratic idea" of administration to one built on the doctrines of "contestability, user choice, transparency and close concentration on incentive structures" (Hood, 1991: 5). Here politics and policy would not be run by chivalrous "knights" acting virtuously in the name of the people but by self-interested "knaves" whose desires were checked by market-type mechanisms (see Le Grand, 2003). Such an arrangement, in turn, called for the creation of a much more hands-on or entrepreneurial form of management for public organizations borrowed from corporate governance and with its roots in market competition rather than some idealized public service benevolence (see Palumbo, 2001; Clarke and Newman, 1993).

The theories behind NPM began to come to practical fruition in the 1980s and 1990s as public choice theorists became embedded in a number of important positions in universities and government (Medema, 2009) and with the larger rise of neoliberalist-centered politics in the U.S., Australia, New Zealand, the U.K. and, later, other countries throughout the world. Neoliberal politicians were drawn to NPM's calls to control government spending through a fundamental overall of government operations. They argued that in the Keynesian model under which most Western states had operated under since the 1930s public expenditures had grown steadily out of control because of the "ever-increasing demands" placed on the state by "special interest groups" who had "captured" organization to serve "producer interest" (see Dean, 2008: 35). As these public demands increased new bureaucracies had taken root and old ones had dramatically expanded. By the 1970s, public expenditures on education, welfare and infrastructure had become a serious impediment to the expansion of markets, corporate profit, shareholder value and general economic growth. As discussed in the first chapter, this argument built on one of the key problematics and rhetorical strategies introduced by early forms of neoliberalist theory—the idea that welfare-style governments are disabling, unproductive and a drag on the optimal efficiency of the free market and the economic well-being of workers and consumers. As such, private enterprise was presented as always "more effective and efficient than non-profit-making organizations" (Boltanski and Chiapello, 2005: 13). This being the case, all public organizations, regardless of their purpose, needed to fundamentally restructure the way they conducted themselves in order to become more user or consumer oriented, business-like, "incentivized" and efficient. They, should also, ideally and if at all possible, be able to support themselves through a "user pays" system that operates without or with minimal public or taxpayer support. By the late 1980s, NPM has become a "global reform movement" (Kettl, 2000) intent on reorganizing governments and public organizations in places as diverse as Mongolia and Sweden.

Under the direction of neoliberal politicians and ministry and agency heads, NPM introduced a number of wide-reaching changes in the way public organizations around the world operated (see Hood, 1991; Kettl, 2000: 1–2; Osborne and Gaebler, 1992; Kettl and Dilulio, 1995). First and most fundamental among these was a shift to a series of private sector management practices with their emphasis on continuous and ongoing improvements in productivity and efficiency. Since the private sector can, according to the NPM model, always perform tasks cheaper and more efficiently, most pubic sector tasks should be either given over to the private sector directly through privatization measures or indirectly through quasi-privatization tactics such as competitive bidding, incentives or public/private partnerships. In those cases where privatization was not feasible, at least initially, the public organization should be made as productive and efficient as possible by introducing internal market style incentives and procedures that mimic the market. Just as corporate profit is derived, in part, from increases in productivity, NPM maintained that the work of public organizations should be streamlined in order to lower their overall impact on the market and the economy. Here, public organizations were continuously asked "to do more with less" in order to reduce the tax burdens on businesses and individuals. Once freed from their social welfare function, taxes could be lowered and the money saved could be given back to businesses and individuals or in other cases employed by the state in the service of markets where it can be used to spur economic growth and development.

Second, NPM emphasized a type of marketization that used "market-style incentives to root out the pathologies of government bureaucracy" (Kettl, 2000: 1; see Osborne and Gaebler, 1992). This incentivization took a number of different forms depending on the political context of the state implementing it. In some cases it involved creating competition between top-level managers in public institutions for the diminishing tax revenues that were available. This also entailed high salaries for high-ranking agency officials, such as the "superheads" created in the early 2000s to lead underperforming schools in England. In some cases incentivization meant privatizing government-owned property, mineral rights and public enterprises. In broader terms it also involved creating a competitive and entrepreneurial environment throughout the public organizations themselves. Here most regular employees, unlike agency heads, were not necessarily paid higher salaries in order to create competition. In fact, data show that public employees saw a rather profound drop in their overall earnings since the introduction of NPM practices in the 1980s (see Kettl, 2000: 56). In lieu of higher salaries, NPM used either competition to remain employed or surveillance and assessment techniques that monitored performance as mechanisms to spur competitive activity among workers. Once in place, these market or quasi-market incentives (or disincentives) were used to fundamentally rework the traditional modes of bureaucratic operation and decision-making.

Third, NPM introduced a customer service orientation into public organizations and their interactions with the public. Here, the idea was to provide "consumer choice," "client services" and "customer satisfaction" by making all types of public organizations "friendly, convenient, and seamless" (Kettl, 2000: 41). The introduction of this consumer model was often promoted as a response to the call for greater public accountability—that public institutions and the workers and professionals within those institutions should be more accountable to the taxpayers who support them. For example, in the U.S. during the Clinton administration in the 1990s a "Putting Customers First Movement" was launched under the direction of then Vice-President Al Gore and his "National Partnership for Reinventing Government." Based in part on the advice for creating a "customer-driven government" laid out in Osborne and Gaelber's (1992) book *Reinventing Government: How the Entrepreneurial Spirit Is Transforming the Public Sector,* the Partnership's sought to fundamentally remake the delivery of U.S. governmental services (see National Performance Review, 1995). This was to be accomplished by requiring, among other things, that government agencies meet the customer services standards present in the business world as measured through the use of consumer satisfaction surveys. As part of these efforts government employees were given awards such as "the Hammer Award," named for a $400 hammer that was once purchased by the Pentagon, and the "No Gobbledygook Award" which was given to employees as part of Al Gore's "plain language initiative." Related efforts were also found in Government Performance and Results Act (GPRA) of 1993 which sought to judge all federal agency spending based on "outcome assessments." In 2002 this was further strengthened with the introduction of the Program Assessment and Rating Tool created by the Office of Management and Budget to enable measurements of efficiency. Similar measures were also found in England with the recommendation on higher education of the Jarret Committee in the mid 1980s and, a bit later, with the more general "citizen charters" established under the Major government. They were also evident in Germany with the *Kommunale Gemeinschaftsstell zur Verwaltungvereinfachung* (Community Office for the Simplification of Administration), as well as the "whole of client" approach found in various other European governments.

As part of these changes in "customer relations," NPM nudged public organizations to become more "p.r. savvy" or marketing oriented by utilizing the same marketing, pubic relations and advertising techniques as found in corporations. These techniques involved both the use of typical public relations strategies for "handling," "channeling" and placating customers and more sophisticated "branding," marketing and advertising campaigns that sough to always put the organization in "good light" and continually tout its virtues. These strategies were designed to force public agencies to maintain happy customers and to create new markets for their products by expanding their "customer base." They were also designed as labor savings devices since public relations efforts could be used in lieu of increasing or maintaining the overall number of workers in the organization. In this case, successful pubic relations efforts allowed an organization to downsize by deflecting attention away from the "content" of organizations, such as the number and quality of the professionals working there, the use of temporary or contingent workers, budget reductions or worker/management relations, toward a carefully constructed and managerially controlled organizational simulacrum. However, these techniques are not just phony representations without substance but also worked as real techniques to reorient and restructure the organizations themselves (see Symes, 1996). As a consequence of these moves, hospitals began to advertise particular units of their hospitals and think of themselves as being "the best" or possessing "excellence" in a particular area. Also, public universities began touting certain "programs of excellence," engaging in niche marketing to appeal to certain customers fitting particular demographic profiles and producing glossy promotional materials and sophisticated websites filled with air brushed photos of happy students, proud parents and distinguished faculty. This marketization was often fueled by a variety by official and unofficial ranking systems that sought to grade public organizations, such as universities and hospitals, according to consumer satisfaction levels and other so-called "performance measures," such as the *U.S. News and World Report*'s annual ranking of colleges and universities, the UK's League Tables or the newer Academic Ranking of World Universities.

A fourth major change introduced by NPM into public organizations was an emphasis on organizational devolution in the form of administrative decentralization, devolved budgets and the outsourcing of auxiliary functions. In the context of the U.S., decentralization or devolution often meant a shifting of both funding and responsibility from the federal government to individual states. In other national contexts it meant shifting decision making and accountancy to the local or agency level. This shifting often entailed a type of paradoxical "autonomy for accountability" tradeoff that granted greater managerial power to local agencies to make decisions, while, in return, demanding that those agencies implement and adhere to more elaborated accountability and auditing mechanisms instituted by the state. In this "loose–tight" arrangement the state becomes the manager that moved the cost of direct supervision and implementation to the local level while still maintaining control over the functioning of the agency through auditing and oversight (see Clarke and Newman, 1997).

Within public organizations this devolutionary strategy often took the form of a replacement of traditional centralized budgeting with a departmentalized "user pays" system (Arshad-Ayaz, 2007: 86), or "responsibility center management" (Zemsky et al., 2005: 18). In this system of "cost centers and revenue production units," individual areas or departments within an organization were required to become self-sustaining by paying for their own basic operating costs and managing their own domain based on institutionally defined goals or "strategic plans." Instead of the "generalization of costs" aimed at achieving a common organizational purpose, units were expected to become competitive and look after their own particular interests. This "management through objectives" strategy helped managers identify units that were the most productive and had the "lowest overhead." This information could then be used as leverage within the organization by either eliminating or threatening to eliminate departments with low productivity levels or as a mechanism to spur competition between departments for larger budgetary allotments or lines, or as was more often the case, lower budget cuts and fewer layoffs.

Another devolutionary strategy was found in NPM's emphasis on the outsourcing of what it came to frame and label as "secondary," or supporting functions of agencies, such as food and janitorial services, grounds maintenance and increasingly secretarial support. It was also evident in the more general organizational "unbundling" and the "casualization of labor" found at all institutional levels. Supporting functions, and increasing even some parts of the central functions of government agencies, are now often outsourced to the private sector. This enables these agencies to "unbundle" and privatize some of their functions and, as a result, to no longer spend money on the direct management of what were deemed as secondary functions. This created a "bare bones" operation where only the central tasks of the organization were conducted by an often-diminishing pool of full-time agency professionals or employees. In addition, outsourcing helped support a casualization and peripherization of labor that treated a growing number of jobs within the organization as temporary, "on standby" or "as needed."

This transfer of what was essentially a "just-in-time" inventory control strategy in the private sector to a labor management tactic in the public sector–enabled public agencies to operate utilizing the same cost cutting labor principles as found in many newer, globalized industries. Just as this labor strategy allowed for market uncertainty to be passed on to corporate workers (Boltanski and Chiapello, 2005: 218), this flexibility of public service workers allowed for cost-cutting efficiencies to be implemented throughout public services and the tax savings redirected. However, in this "just-in-time" strategy the responsibility of "product storage" was shouldered not by a supplier but by the part-time worker or professional who was to somehow "wait in the wings" or engage in "serial temping" until their labor was needed.

Another central feature of this casualization of labor was the functional differentiation, "agencification" and hierarchicalization of public service labor—a technique also borrowed from the corporate world and post-Fordist production techniques. In this process not only was the organization itself "unbundled" but also the tasks and knowledge base of the existing organizational functioning was "disaggregated" or broken into specific divisions, hierarchies and task segments. Once divided, work within these task segments was often "agencified" into discrete managerial units (see Du Gay, 2006: 151). Here workers could be better managed by being held responsible for specific, agency-determined outcomes. Once agencification was accomplished, the tasks could also then be hierarchicalized with certain parts being performed by the "cheaper labor" that resided on the margins or maybe even outside of the traditional boundary of the profession. For example, "physicians' assistants," medical technicians or nurses, now perform much of the traditional work of physicians. This work segmentation limits the number of high salaried physicians who are needed by hospitals and replaces them with less trained and cheaper "medical workers." This has had the effect of disempowering the profession since administrators deal with more "employees" and fewer professionals who because of their professional focus, allegiances and commitment were considered less manageable. Likewise in academia in the U.S., graduate students or adjunct faculty who are paid a fraction of that of full-time, tenured faculty now do much of the teaching of undergraduates. This enables a public university to spend much less on full-time, tenure-track professor lines while still expanding enrollments and managerial positions.

The work disaggregation process obviously dramatically divided and shrunk both the knowledge base and the overall number of professionals within a profession. As the knowledge becomes diffused, the control of professional expertise also became significantly lessened. The traditional expertise of the profession now becomes something spread between different levels and types of workers, some of whom are in the profession and some who are on the outside. This "profession busting" or change from professional to quasi-professional or casualized work slowly altered the overall power of the profession as lower paid professionals came to make up large segments of the field. As a result, the profession's claim over the exclusive control over their domain of expertise and specialized knowledge was undermined.

All of the changes introduced by the NPM are, however, only part of what has emerged as a very complex picture for the management of contemporary pubic service organizations. Two trends now seem evident in the management of public organizations—both with similar effects for public services professionals. In some instances, the introduction of NPM has meant a more hierarchical and market-based form of decision-making that resembled those found in traditional corporate settings. Thus, hospitals, social work agencies, schools, universities and other public agencies more and more came to resemble and function like corporations, replete with corporate lingoes and "branding," slick advertising campaigns, spin-minded public spokespersons, long-range strategic plans, outsourcing, casualized labor, hierarchical decision-making and worker/employee type of "human resource management." In these settings, NPM has significantly corporatized and hierarchicalized the workings of public organizations and challenged and altered the traditions of professional autonomy that were part of them.

In other situations, however, the introduction of NPM has meant the appearance of a new type of diffused or devolved management style where the managed actually become the managers, as is seen in the "autonomy for accountability" strategy. Here, public professionals essentially became, to use Foucault's (1991 [1978]) phrase, "the self-governing governed"—a situation where the self is disciplined to govern itself. In this "management by objectives" approach, not only were workers in public organizations increasingly under pressure to "be more accountable" in keeping with the practices advocated by NPM and its focus on productivity and the bottom line, but they are also required to continuously manage and report on themselves through managerially overseeing auditing or monitoring systems sometimes adapted from and piggy-backed onto the professional peer review processes already in place. In order to support the new entrepreneurial spirit and practices that neoliberalism deemed so crucial to the remaking of institutional governance, management in these situations was to become less about directly "overseeing" or "managing" and more about helping the worker "self-actualize" or "responsibilize" by reporting on and managing themselves. Just as the state sought to "devolve" its traditional social welfare tasks by pushing implementation and management costs over to local agencies, within public institutions centralized managers or administrators now wished to push many of the tasks of direct management over to the workers and professionals whom they oversaw. In this new scheme, professionals often retained some elements of traditional professional autonomy, particularly those aspects that were seen as fostering competition, self-reporting and organizational innovation. However, they also became even more managed and overseen through ongoing assessment and auditing processes.

The anonymous accountability systems introduced by NPM into the management of professional life sometimes work by adapting or reworking the profession's long-held internal practices of self- and peer review into the newly devised external accountability systems. In these instances, rather than self- and peer-review being used by professionals as internal gatekeeping device into or through their profession, they were used as a method to rank order and reward individuals, departments, units or agencies. In this use of self- and peer evaluation, professionals begin to essentially monitor, report on and discipline themselves. Through their self- and peer evaluation reports it was they who ultimately decided how much money, prestige and new positions would be allotted to particular organizations or units. In this instance, managers simply carried out and enacted the already institutionally embedded funding and performance formulas as specified in the organization's "strategic plan." These strategic plans, which came in vogue in the 1990s, served as "reference points" to redirect institutional activity and employee recognition toward managerial imperatives (see Symes, 1996: 136). They also became coercive by demanding that all institutional activity must pass through the mission and strategic planning documents. Such processes changed the culture of professions by shifting power from the profession with an organization to the auditing system that became the new arbitrator of power. Power was thus slowly and sometimes invisibly drained away from the profession to the auditors and those who managed and enacted the auditing system. Under these anonymous auditing systems, the internal professional peer review processes themselves may remain unchanged, although they are often added to and intensified, their implication and control was drastically altered.[1]

In addition to this expansion of management from the manager to the managed, the practice of management itself was radically transformed under neoliberalism and NPM. Management itself was now expected to become much more post-Fordist by also being flexible, nimble, devolved and disbursed. Ironically, this disbursement saved on the cost of management by "downsizing" management itself, particularly at the middle levels, since the job of managing and disciplining the workforce was now increasingly self-induced and self-directed (see Cloke and Goldsmith, 2002). In this new devolved managerial style, managers were, in some instances, "treated as a variable cost rather than part of the fixed base" (Heckscher, 1995: 4). As a result, they, ironically, fell victim to very same impersonal and autonomous auditing systems they helped introduce.

NEOLIBERALISM, NEW PUBLIC MANAGEMENT AND THE PROFESSIONS

Until the introduction of NPM into public organizations in the 1980s and 1990s, public service professions were able to largely remain outside of the influences of direct management control and corporate-type managerialistic practices. Historically, certain professional groups working in public organizations, such as professors, urban planners, writers, attorneys, physicians, social workers and teachers, were somewhat immune to the intrusion of the oversight of managers and the managerial ethos into their work lives. These groups were given status, autonomy and trust in exchange for "safeguarding our well-being and applying their professional judgment on the basis of a benign moral or cultural code" (Dent and Whitehead, 2002: 1). Their ability to avoid direct managerial oversight and control in a larger historical situation where most work had become increasingly managed and controlled was attributable, at least in part, to the ability of these groups to organize into relatively autonomous and legally protected professions, promote their interest politically through unions and professional organizations and to utilize the power obtain from their legally recognized, and in some cases contractually granted, professional autonomy to insulate themselves from various types of outside influences and managerial oversight. It was also enabled by a system of trust where professionals were seen as promoters and defenders of the public interest. The end result of this professional control was that many professions were able to determine their own criteria for membership, police their own ranks and generally control the knowledge, standards and practices present within their professions (see Krause, 1996). These professions were loosely administered as part of working in a larger, rule-governed bureaucratic organization, but they were not necessarily managed in the managerialistic manner advocated by NPM. In other words, these professional groups may have worked in public bureaucratic organizations, for example, professors in a state-run university or doctors in a city operated hospital, but they were largely allowed to govern their own affairs as long as this governance was in accord with the broader goals and contractual arrangements of the organizations for which they worked. Under this type of "bureaucratic professionalism" (Newman, 1998), professionals were seen as capable of directing their own performance and oversight. Indeed, preserving autonomy was viewed as necessary for creating and maintaining the integrity of professional work fields and the motivation and creativity of professional workers (see Freidson, 1994: 32). Professional power and decision-making was also predicated upon the ability of professionals to follow the standards of their profession rather than the dictates of management. Without the protections from outside control afforded by the professions public professionals would become essentially no different from any other worker in a market-based economy.[2]

Under the bureaucratic organization of the welfare state, the professional's power was based primarily on the delegation of authority to control his or her own affairs. As Newman (1998: 335) describes this bureaucratic professionalism, the "combination of administrative rationality and professional expertise guaranteed the 'neutrality' of the welfare state and protected the exercise of professional judgment in the delivery of social welfare." Within this framework the bureaucratic state organization, with its legal rational framework and official rules of operation, also provided some degree of procedural protection for bureaucratic professionals from undue, outside or non-professional influence and control. Such a civil service structure generated and was supported by relations of high trust and collegiality between professionals and the organizations they worked for (see Olssen and Peters, 2005: 324). Under this high trust arrangement, professionals were trusted to conduct their own activities and socialize and discipline their own members without continuous oversight and control by administrators or the state. In professions, "trust is an almost universal ingredient in social relations" (Schimank, 2005: 370). It is the social mechanism through which professionals engage one another and the publics they serve. In the end these autonomous or semi-autonomous professionals were trusted to create the greater good for the organization or society as a whole by being left alone to pursue their own independent professional and epistemic trends and goals at they saw fit.

Under public interest theory and NPM, the communitarian principles of the public professions and their trustworthiness were viewed as deeply suspect. As a result of this a new managerial arrangement was introduced that altered the traditional role of public service professionals, the mechanisms of trusts and the inner dedication that sustained loyalty and allowed professions to operate relatively autonomously. In this new low trust arrangement, "principle-agent line management chains replace delegated power with hierarchical forms of authoritatively structured relations" (Olssen and Peters, 2005: 324). Under this new regime the professions came to be seen not as magnanimous peer-controlled collectives but as "self-interested groups who indulge in rent-seeking behavior" (Olssen and Peters, 2005: 325). As such, they were to be managed and steered just like any other type of work or self-interested actor under managerialism. Their output, however, still remained less directly overseen relative to other forms of work. Here management is accomplished, as noted earlier, "at a distance" through the establishment of objectives and output goals rather than the mandating of specific regulations to follow (see Schimank, 2005: 366, Gleeson and Shain, 1999). The managerial and oversight techniques themselves, rather than physically present managers or rigid rules of procedure or conduct became the primary means through which professionals were managed and steered under this type of NPM. With these techniques, professionals are to be monitored, assessed and evaluated as part of the ongoing accountability systems and quality control management of the organization. As a result a flat, professionally controlled organizational structure where decision-making was relatively diffuse and democratic (and usually slow) was replaced with a stratified and "more efficient" ordering of line management. Here, true decision-making was made and implemented from above and imposed on professionals, not usually in the form of a manger directly observing and directing, but through faceless, "third person" accountability systems designed to insure efficiency, timeliness and adherence to the organization's output goals.

Politically and organizationally these systems served to create the appearance of "depoliticizing" institutional decision-making by making managerial decisions seem not to be deliberate choices but inevitable and logical outcomes of "economic reality" and what the accountability measures clearly warrant (see Clarke, 2004: 34). Often done as a way to account for limited public funding, these auditing systems served to refocus attention away from the complex and often fractious nature of organizational decision-making to the unquestionabilities of the bottom line. This, of course, forgets, among other things, that the resources that were once available for the operation of the public agency have now been redirected to the very auditing and surveillance systems that were designed to save money (see Davies, 2003: 93).

As a result of the organizational changes introduced by NPM, ongoing interest-based suspicion, monitoring and assessment at a distance replaced the generalized trust in the profession's ability "to do the right thing." Likewise, autonomy was replaced by steering and management from above or even, ironically, from within. In this new arrangement, trust is no longed to be trusted as the central mechanism that promotes adherence to the organization. Those who go unmonitored are viewed warily within the NPM model. Here autonomy is seen as the harbinger of the "unmanaged," and hence the potentially unproductive, undisciplined and unknown, and is, as a consequence, to be held in suspicion and as risky. The "unmanaged" people and areas constitute an indeterminable risk to the organization and even at some level the doctrines of neoliberalism and NPM themselves. After all, unmanaged professionals may be just "goofing off," spending tax money unwisely or pursing their own priorities at the expense of those of the organizations. In such situations they need objective auditing systems and a detached manager to rein them in. All this auditing and oversight, however, reveals one of the central paradoxes of neoliberalism and NPM—"while [it] seeks to operate through autonomous, self-interested subjects, the moral hazard associated with this very same self-interestedness evokes a distrust in the 'self-governing' governed" (Duncan, 2003: 472). In other words, although neoliberalism and Public Choice Theory value, the autonomous, "responsiblized" agent whose self-interestedness would lead her or him to become more entrepreneurial, it also fears that this agent's self-interests would not be in alignment with those of the organization. It, therefore, ironically develops spiraling and ever-expanding auditing systems to keep the supposedly free and autonomous, but ultimately selfish, agent in line and on task.

NPM meant not only the diminishing of traditional professional autonomy, the mechanism of trust and professional power but also the demise of the ability of professionals to think and act collectively, specifically as related to traditional forms of collective representation and bargaining. For instances, under bureaucratic professionalism groups were often able to negotiate the collective rights, responsibilities and the pay structure of the members of the professions as a whole *vis-à-vis* the organization. Here equity was defined in terms of the "going rate" or the "rate for the job" in which compensation was determined by what others were making in comparable areas (see Bailey, 1994). NPM, however, advocated a "decollectivization" that promoted a more individualistic form of labor relations and pay. Under the direction of such managerial programs as human resource management, this approach utilized market-based incentives through direct awards and recognition made to individuals whom they or auditing reports determined had put in the best performance. In the place of collective, group-negotiated contractual rights afforded to all, NPM sought to insert private, individual incentives awarded only to those who were deemed meritorious. Sometimes these incentives appeared in seemingly innocuous and token forms, such as "Employee of the Month," "Awards for Excellence" or "Teacher of the Year"; in other situations, however, they involved more elaborate incentive systems such as "merit based pay increases," "discretionary release time" or other "performance-based" incentives (or punishments). These managerially determined individual incentives were designed to create a competitive environment that, like the entrepreneurial environment of the marketplace, would spur individual motivation and innovation, while also punishing and shaming the "lazy and unmotivated." In this new neoliberal organizational environment, individuals were expected to maximize their own self-interest and forgo the protection of the collective. As with the "collective problematic" discussed in the first chapter, the collective, in this case the profession, was seen as hindering the ability of the individual to maximize his or her abilities and potentials and perhaps income, as well as the organization's ability to make itself more efficient and productive. Here equity was defined exclusively in terms of "what the market will allow" and was based solely on individual performance rather than "the going rate" (see Bailey, 1994). The decollectivization of the profession was seen simply as another necessary step in the responsiblization that neoliberalists believe all members of society should undergo.

Professional collectivism was also made less tenable by the segmentation of professional work and the casualization of labor promoted by neoliberalism and NPM. As professional work became decoupled and broken into segments, certain segments became casualized and reprofessionalized and in some cases deskilled and deprofessionalized. These task segments then sometimes evolved into relatively autonomous forms of work themselves. In instances of reprofessionalization, these segments required their own distinct training programs and formed their own professional organizations. In other instances, where certain segments were deskilled or deprofessionalized, casual, auxiliary workers who had less training and often less job security performed particular tasks. Under these fragmented conditions, it was increasingly difficult for the profession to act collectively since the profession itself was greatly reduced in size, scope and power. The profession also lost its collective bargaining power to some degree because it had also lost its key bargaining chips—an exclusive monopoly over its own unique domain of specialized knowledge and skill and control over its membership. For example, physicians are now just one segment of what has become a behemoth, multilevel medical system consisting of an array of medical personnel with all types of specialized training, skill level, knowledge and pay scales (see Dent, 2006). Likewise, professors are now just a small part of a massified university system that includes a variety of casualized teaching faculty, researchers and a new breed of "quasi-educationalists," such as writing and mathematics laboratory directors, as well as a host of middle-level managers, such as assistant deans, directors of grants and research and technology transfer officers.

Work intensification for professionals became another area, as was the case with the adaptation of peer review, where elements of the pre-existing professional culture were specifically fitted to NPM's agenda of increased efficiency and accountability. Under the bureaucratic conditions described earlier, professional work was regulated by both the broader work rules of the institution and the vocation standards of the profession. In this situation the individual professional generally had a great deal of discretion over the amount of time he or she spent in the profession's secondary or supporting tasks, for example the time professionals spend preparing to be professional, such as reading professional journals, attending conferences, doing professional presentations or even engaging in casual conversations with colleagues. In the face of diminishing state funding, professionals were increasingly asked to teach more students, see more clients or process more patients. When this emphasis was combined with information saturation and the continuous contact enabled by information technologies, professional work under NPM became limitless. In this instance the professional's own ethical commitment to the profession was connected with NPM's auditing mechanisms and technology to help intensify the amount of work done by the professional, particularly as it pertained to things that were countable or auditable. NPM also utilized managerial strategies such as the "high commitment management model" that seeks to create a situation where workers believe their and the organization's best interests are always in alignment and being taken care of by management (see Geare et al., 2006: 1193). Like many corporate jobs this type of high commitment, management encourages workers "to expend high levels of discretionary effort towards the organization" (Geare et al., 2006: 1194). Under conditions of high commitment management, the countable aspects of professional activities are wired into the auditing system of the organization to reward those who produce the most for the organization. In this case, the professional's fate, as well as that of their organizational unit, is no longer determined by meeting their own or the profession's standards but by working hard enough and producing enough "output" to please the auditors and managers who ultimately control the rewards. Under the professionally controlled system, failure to live up the standards of the professions meant marginalization and lowered status within the profession. In the NPM model, professional failure meant punishment for the entire unit or perhaps, if the labor was casualized and decollectivized enough, removal of the individual professional or unit by management for low productivity.

NPM's work intensification was not, however, exclusively an outcome of a "trying to do more with less" type of efficiency or the extra reporting work required by the cooptation of professional review for auditing purposes. It was also an outcome of NPM's emphasis on continuous and ongoing innovation, increased performance and the implementation of the "new and improved" now found throughout all types of public service organizations. This emphasis on novelty, borrowing in part from Total Quality Management founder W. Edwards Deming concept of "continuous quality improvement," sought an ongoing and never-ending emphasis on improvements to the workings of the organization as defined, in large part, by the introduction of new procedures to increase productivity. The role of new public sector managers in this arrangement was to help individuals unleash their "full potential as entrepreneurial innovators" (Grey, 1999: 570). Just as neoliberalists contend that knowledge and technological innovation were at the heart of economic expansion in knowledge societies and the survival of companies in the global economy, NPM considers "continuous programmatic innovation" or the implementation of "best practices" as key to the efficient use of monies in the public sector. At its heart this emphasis on innovation was driven by the demand that the public sector become more and more efficient, accountable and consumer centered. Over time, however, this demand created an "innovation spiral" that used the implementation of the "new" as the key, and sometimes only, signifier that the organization was doing its job. This produces a situation where professionals in the organization were forever caught up in a programmatic escalation of their expectations and performance. In this situation, professionals begin to suffer from a type of "initiative fatigue" as they are asked to perform more and more tasks, not just in order to perform one's job more efficiently for the auditing reports, but also to help the organization continuously "innovate" and "improve quality." Such an emphasis on innovation was also sometimes made possible through a deliberate work intensification strategy of "management by stress." This strategy sought to create an entrepreneurial system of competitiveness throughout an organization that continually and intentionally stresses individuals, often through competition for resources, attention for merit raises, awards or merely to stay employed, in order to increase their performance and hone the most efficient organizational unit possible (see Bousquet, 2008: 104). This process of deliberate and sustained stressing can be seen as part of a broader socio-economic process that Bourdieu (2003: 29) referred to as the "institution of insecurity."

At its heart NPM can be seen as a deliberate strategy "to replace the old regime, dominated by a state-regulated profession, with a new regime, dominated by a market-and state-driven organization" (Schimank, 2005: 366). NPM, whether in the form of increased direct managerial control or the more diffused and post-bureaucratic "management from a distance" approach, has led to the creation of what Gary Rhoades (1998) has referred to as "managed professionals." As Bousquet (2008: 81) describes them, these managed professionals are "increasingly subordinated to the corporate values, ease of command, and bottom line of the management desktop." This has created an important change in the way in which professional identity is constructed and maintained for many public service professionals. In the past, professional identity was constructed via the norms and standards of the profession itself. Indeed, the autonomy of the organization allowed for and encouraged professional identities to be in some sense self-constructed and professionally maintained. The assessment and monitoring associated with NPM has dramatically changed this relatively autonomous situation. Public professionals are now increasingly required to be entrepreneurial in their outlook even if this temperament is at odds with the traditional "professional social ideal" of the professional guild, particular in the public services (see Perkin, 1992: 52). In the end NPM "has involved supplanting the norms of service and dedication with those of competition and customer demand" (Burton, 1997: 226).

FROM SUBSTANTIVE TO TECHNICAL RATIONALITY: NEW PUBLIC MANAGEMENT AND THE TRANSFORMATION OF KNOWLEDGE ORGANIZATIONS

In 1918 the economist Thornstein Veblen (1918: 85) warned in *The Higher Learning in America* of attempts to remold the administration of higher education "after the pattern of a well-conducted business concern." He described this new business order as a situation where "men dilate on the high necessity of a businesslike organization and control of the university, its equipment, personnel and routine" (Veblen, 1918: 85). As has been the case with other public organizations, the introduction of NPM into knowledge organizations, such as public universities and public schools, has greatly intensified the effects that Veblen described almost a century ago by introducing a number of systematic changes in the ways these organizations operate.

Although early twentieth-century businessmen may have wanted to convert the university into a well-managed business, the nascent managerialism that Veblen described was largely kept at bay in most public knowledge-making and -disseminating institutions throughout most of twentieth century by four factors: (1) the growth of the welfare state that promoted and encouraged a relatively neutral and public regarding bureaucratic professionalism in schools and universities, (2) the ability of educational organizations and unions, such as, in the American case, the American Federation of Teachers, the National Education Association, the American Association of University Professors and numerous disciplinary-based professional organizations, to expand and protect professional decision-making and shared governance, (3) a resulting generalizable trust and collaborative norms that allowed professionals in knowledge organizations autonomy to, in varying degrees, control their own work, follow their own epistemic and professional pathways and have an important say in the workings of most knowledge organizations, and (4) a legally protected public domain that envisioned knowledge as a collective product and education as a public good. Under the direction of neoliberalist ideas and NPM, however, each one of these factors that shielded knowledge organizations and makers from the effects of managerialism and the market have been slowly eroded.

As has been the case with other public service organizations, such as public hospitals and state agencies, NPM introduced a number of changes in the way knowledge organizations and professionals within those organizations now operate. The most fundamental of these was a movement of knowledge organizations from operating under a substantive to a technical mode of rationality (Gewirtz and Ball, 2000). As Weber identified it, the ideal type of substantive rationality is a social ordering and form of action that is based on and oriented by a broader set of ideals and ethics and is largely unconcerned with practical outcomes. Here, the central consideration is first and foremost a value-rational or ethical one of "doing the right thing" as prescribed by the prevailing moral code of the group. Under these conditions, people in knowledge organizations have historically spoke of and are motivated by such things as the "love of learning," "teaching as a calling, " " knowledge as enlightenment" or the importance of students' being "well rounded," "enlightened" or "good citizens." While these ideals may be relative and their fulfillment unrealizable, they have historically provided an emblematic basis and orientation for moral action within the group.

Technical rationality, on the other hand, is a type of reasoning that is grounded in and operates on a completely different set of principles. These principles are centered on much more concrete, measurable outcomes, goals and specific objectives. In this instance, action is governed primarily by a consideration of what is countable, pragmatic, measurable, efficient and manageable. Under these types of conditions people in knowledge organizations speak first and foremost about such things as "excellence," "best practices," "assessment outcomes," "test scores," "research productivity," "rankings" and "accountability to stakeholders." Under the new regime of technical rationality, substantive and ethical considerations are viewed as sentimental, inefficient and out-of-date, although they may be useful organizational ideologies to be deployed time to time by managers to inspire workers in knowledge organizations to work harder, create more effective "work cultures" and increase organizational productivity and efficiency.

The prevalence of substantive rationality allowed for the structural conditions necessary for what Basil Bernstein (2000) has referred to as "inner dedication" to arise and be sustained. Inner dedication refers to the type of moral commitment, dedication, ethical responsibility and "calling" to the profession that has often been found in public service fields, such as education, medicine and social work. Since knowledge professions and professionals were allowed to work semi-autonomously with low levels of supervision and oversight, the profession rather than the specific agency was the central authority and moral structure to which members aligned and adhered. As with the "vocational calling" described by Weber (1958) in *Science as a Vocation*, the profession provided the professionals' moral structure, work ethic and identity since it was the profession that decided what constituted "adequate performance," "good work" and a "distinguished career" and not administrators or consumers. In this capacity the profession was insulated and protected from outside influences that might wish to "contaminate" it by absorbing it into its own alternative moral visions and agendas, such as those of the state or the market. Indeed, it is only within the confines of these protected, autonomous and self-administered environs that "genuine ethical responsibility" can arise (Beck and Young, 2005: 188). In the absence of this, other mechanisms, such as oversight, incentives, monitoring or punishment, are needed to put and hold members in their place.

Substantive and technical rationality clearly represent very different ways of ordering people that are made possible by the particular confines, dynamics and morphology of the knowledge organizations themselves. Organizationally, substantive rationality and its accompanying inner dedication is only possible when internal strata are weak, decision-making is relatively diffuse and democratic and the boundaries between inside and outside are comparatively protected or, to put it in the terms set forth by Mary Douglas (1982), when there is a low level of "grid" and high level of "group." In contrast, a technical-style rationality is possible when the strata are strongly delineated, decision-making is more centralized and the boundaries between insiders and outsiders are relatively weak, i.e., in a situation with high grid and low group (see Fuchs, 1992). As NPM moved into knowledge organizations, it significantly altered knowledge organizations' traditional grid/group configurations and boundaries. By implementing more centralized and less collaborative managerial forms, NPM altered the grid system within knowledge organizations. Rather than a relatively flat organizational hierarchy with a diffuse decision-making style, NPM introduced a more layered arrangement, centralized decision-making and a more individualistic ranking of professionals. Also, by promoting consumerism and creating extensive outside accountability and auditing systems, NPM altered the group boundary that allowed knowledge profession an exclusive monopoly and power over their epistemic and pedagogical domains. Knowledge professionals now had to adhere to advice coming from the "outside," such as auditors, alumni, community advisory boards, parents or venture capitalists. In addition, outsourcing and the casualized labor strategies introduced by NPM allowed for the incursion of the knowledge professions by an array of full- and part-time, quasi-professionals who increasingly became part of the knowledge organization as part of its effort to lower costs. This diluted, to some degree, the conventional meaning of professional life and weakening the internal solidarity of the profession's members.

In addition to changes in the organizational culture of knowledge institutions, NPM also sought to centralize the control and operation of these institutions in the hands of a hierarchy of professionally trained "knowledge managers." In Weberian terms, this can be seen as a shift in control of the "insider knowledge" or *Dienstwissen* of knowledge organizations from academics to professional knowledge managers (Weber, 1968). This shift in authority was largely created by a change in the type of people who ran the organization. Past university and school administrators were usually drawn from the ranks of professors and teachers. These were largely what could be referred to as "humanistic intellectuals"—individuals who operated under a system of substantive rationality and who had usually spent years working at various levels of the knowledge organization and who intimately knew its inner workings. These humanistic intellectuals were often trained in classic liberal arts fields, such as history, philosophy and literature, and had found their way into administrative positions, sometimes as simply part of a rotation. Over time with the spread of managerialism and NPM in academia, a "technical intelligentsia" emerged that increasingly replaced these older style "humanistic intellectuals." The newly created technical intelligentsia often had limited or no experience in producing or disseminating knowledge but were instead specifically trained to be managers in specialty degree programs in "higher education management" or "education leadership." In this technical, managerial-style training, new "managers to be" take courses that reflect a managerialistic framing of knowledge and education, such as "Leadership and Change," "Enrollment Management," "Market Price and Margin," and "State Systems and Policy" (see University of Pennsylvania, n.d.). As managerial authority expanded under NPM, the new knowledge managers were more likely to select people with similar training and temperament. This created a continual flow of people from higher education training programs directly into administrative positions, thereby bypassing time spent "in the trenches."

This "MBAization" of educational administration, and public administration in general, created by the rise of professional trained managers in knowledge organizations has, in turn, lead to a flourishing of "leadership discourse" and a new managerial culture throughout all levels of education. As Bousquet (2008: 99) describes it, this new managerial culture seeks to introduce a distinct "system of values and practices" that is very different from "the homelier tone of earlier treatises, over many decades, on the 'art of management.'" Indeed, it is this change from a professional to a business discourse that perhaps most annoys many older faculty members whose careers developed under the "old regime." This new leadership discourse is filled with terms such as "excellence," "quality," "SWOT

The Machinations of Managerialism 69

analyses," "effectiveness," "metrics" and "impact factors" borrowed from the slogans, boardroom posters and such managerial techniques as Total Quality Management, Business Process Reengineering, Management by Objectives and Balanced Scorecard emanating from business schools and found throughout the business world (see Head, 2011: 58).

Since these new centralized managers couldn't be everywhere at all times, they introduced or strengthened auditing and accountability systems to serve as managerial surrogates (see Kleinman and Vallas, 2001). This in turn has called for even more managers to oversee the further rationalization of the university and to monitor all the newly introduced auditing systems (see Hainge, 2004: 42). As with Public Choice Theory's general critique of public administration, NPM considered older forms of knowledge administration to be too concerned with rule following bureaucratic procedure and collaboration. NPM advocates contended that decision-making in this setting was too often based on broad "summary data," such as grades or graduation rates, intuition or ill-defined notions of the virtues of liberal education, rather than empirical data, "data driven decision making" and clearly defined goals and objectives. Making this new technical rationality operate at optimal efficiency required the establishment of the elaborate accountability and auditing mechanisms evident in other public professions. In this instance, they came in the form of "institutional audits," "standardized testing," "teaching quality assessments," "program assessments," "mastery tests" and "research assessments exercises."

Armed with "the facts" and the authority of "data driven decision making," university managers could use formulas and spreadsheets to centralize control and clear away what they considered to be sentiment and opinion when justifying resource allocation, new faculty lines and the startup or discontinuation of research or educational programs. As with the accountability mechanisms in other public professions, the facts were seen as "speaking for themselves" and required no further justification beyond what the indicators indicate. Knowledge managers could also use the reams of data generated externally as evidence of their accountability to various "stakeholders," such as politicians, CEOs, donors, university system's offices and alumni. This created a type of "governance theater" where university senates or faculty meetings became "occasions in which decisions already made [were] announced" (Burtscher, Pasgualon, and Scott, 2006: 250). Under these conditions faculty continued to serve on senates and budget committees; however, the true decisions had already been decided beforehand in the administrative suite by "detached" and "rational" higher education managers.

Accompanying all these managerial changes was a fundamental change in the conceptualization of what knowledge and education are all about. Humanistic intellectuals in educational organizations were largely inspired and governed by a substantive rationality that looked to the larger importance of knowledge and education to society and an often Deweyian notion of the social development and democratic involvement of the individual.

The technical intelligentsia, in contrast, is guided by much more immediate administrative and task-specific concerns. As a consequence, these managers are more "bottom line oriented," "pragmatic," managerialistic and instrumentalist in their thinking. From this managerialistic vantage point, knowledge is a quantifiable and measurable product and can, as a consequence, like any other product, be more effectively packaged, measured and delivered. Knowledge in this instance is conceptualized as being composed of a limitable quantity of skills and information that can be delimited and defined. Once this happens, knowledge can be conveyed to others utilizing standardizable pedagogical techniques and materials and its effectiveness or "uptake" can be quantitatively measured through various standardized tests and assessments. Afterward, these tests and assessment can be "plugged into" the auditing and public accountability systems overseen by the state and various ministries and departments of education in order to allocate funding. As a result of this "externality becomes the principle by which internal life is lived and reproduced" (Cooper, 2000: 128).

FROM UNPRODUCTIVE TO PRODUCTIVE LABOR

NPM maintained that the changes it introduced into the public realm were merely inevitable organizational transformations spurred on and made necessary by global competitiveness, the need for retrenchment in public spending and the growing public distrust of bureaucracies and the professions. These changes made a rebellion against the usual bureaucratic ways of doing things necessary and called for a new, much more "bottom line" and efficient system of managing public institutions. However, as I have tried to show, such a stance does not do justice to the complex politics and policies that spawned NPM or on which it operates today. Indeed, since the introduction of NPM state expenditures have not actually decreased as would have been anticipated given the emphasis on tax savings in neoliberal rhetoric (Cohen and Centeno, 2006). On the other hand, as noted earlier, government employees' salaries have dropped considerably (Kettl, 2000). Given these spending trends, NPM should be seen as much more about the politics of resource reallocation than their purely rational economic curtailment or retrenchment (see Whitty, 2002). NPM is one of the mechanism neoliberals used to force open new market frontiers and break open protected labor. In the case of the public sector, the successful strategies used on union-protected labor in the private sector during the late 1970s and 1980s would not be enough to force change. Public professionals were protected from the forces of marketization by the state bureaucratic apparatus, collective bargaining units and the professions themselves. Each one of these protections required a particular neoliberal strategy of problemitization and redirection. Just as globalization became both the mechanism and rhetorical justification for the transformation and casualization of other forms of labor, NPM became the means through which public organizations were to be converted to private-like and market behaving entities and professional public "unproductive labor" was to be converted to private, entrepreneurial and "productive labor."

In this sense we may characterize NPM's attempts to deprofessionalize and marketize public service professionals as analogous to the social and economic transformation of what Marx referred to as *dritte personen* from "unproductive" to "productive" labor (see Marx, 1967; Harris, 1939; Bell, 1973: 57). Marx defined productive labor as a type of labor that produces profit and aids directly in capital accumulation. In contrast, unproductive labor is that which is largely self-sufficient or, in the modern context, shielded enough from the market that it remains largely outside of the capitalist accumulation process and, consequently, experiences "imperfect subjugation." As the market expands and intensifies its effects, the transformation of work groups from unproductive to productive labor creeps onward and outward. Groups that were largely outside of the market, such as small subsistence farmers and artisans, or those shielded by the church or state, such as priests, social workers, physicians and teachers, are pulled into the full capitalist production process. As Daniel Bell (1973: 57) noted regarding this transformation, "If the worker-capitalist relations were to spread to medical service, amusement and education, the physician, artist and professor would then be wager earners and 'productive'" (see also, Harris, 1939: 287). As this process proceeds globally, no one is left out of or can escape the reaches of the market economy since no protection remains either from geographic isolation, the "tribe," or the state.

The process through which groups are transformed from "unproductive" to "productive" should be seen as occurring economically, politically and organizationally. Economically it involves either constituting new "fictitious commodities" (Polanyi, 1957 [1944]) where the objects or things produced by *dritte personen* are either imbued with exchange value, such as has been happening with knowledge and education, or by a system of removing or dissolving the larger boundaries between commodities and noncommodities, or things of the market and things outside the market, altogether by making all things negotiable commodities that are "for sale" in the market economy. Politically it entails putting into place laws and policies that encourage the expansion of markets and that diminish the ability of groups to resist or retreat from market forces and the changing labor needs of corporations, such as in the cases of the loosening of monopoly restrictions, the shifting downward of tax burdens or welfare reform policies.

At the organizational level these processes manifest themselves in the creation of styles of management that seek to impose a specific ordering and arrangement of work conducive with neoliberalist policies. These organizational orderings and styles of management bring the transformations occurring in the economic and political arenas to the level of institutions where they are used to create a new domain for capital accumulation, a new internal reorganization of the labor process and a further hierarchicalization of managers and workers. In this process, neoliberalism essentially extinguishes the dichotomy of market and non-market. In doing so, market values penetrate the public professions and erode the distinction between the professions and any other forms of work in the market economy both in their values and mode of operation (see Krause, 1996: 281; Weber, 1968). As all groups are pulled into the market economy, the market economy becomes even further normalized and naturalized. When this occurs, as Marcuse (1964) famously argued, the possibility of resistance or alterity is reduced or perhaps even eliminated altogether by rendering all alternatives as "irrational," "unreasonable" or "unthinkable."

Organizationally, NPM also works to mute opposition by giving the impression of "de-politicized" decision-making by making it appear that all decisions are merely reasonable, prudent and inevitable outcomes arrived at by rational management's assessment of reality. Here "managers are the bears of 'real world' wisdom of how to be 'business-like'" (Clarke, 2004: 36). Managerial decisions are made solely in order to make the organization more economically efficient and accountable (see Clarke, 2004: 34; Bourdieu, 2003: 38–52). They present themselves as the only ones capable of dispensing with the internal bickering, partisanship and particularistic knowledge of workers and imparting a universal, "open and transparent rationality" (Clarke, 2004: 36). As Clarke (2004: 37) describes it, "Where managers are pragmatic, politicians are dogmatic. Where managers are rational, politicians are partisan. Where managers are rooted in the 'real world', politicians are either rooted in ideology or rootless, tossed in the winds of public opinion."

Finally, the transformation of knowledge and other public professions under neoliberalism is not unlike that experienced by most occupations within the primary labor market over the last few decades. Within this transformation occupations, such as those in the automobile, airline or steel industries, that once offered stable and permanent work, life-long employment, fringe benefits, union scale and contractual protection have become victims of neoliberalist political and economic policies. As Krause (1996: 283) reminds us, this does not mean that the public professions themselves are necessarily dying out only that their guild-like power to control their own fate is being seriously challenged. NPM in practice is only an extension into the public domain of the new managerial and business policies and practices that many workers have experienced for several decades as a response to the "realities of the market" and the "inevitabilities of globalization." With the extra insularity that working in public bureaucracies created, professionals often saw themselves as somehow outside of the labor process or at least shielded from its more onerous effects. The professions, with their historic monopoly on expertise and political power, have also largely seen themselves apart from and elevated above other occupations and the uncertainties of the labor process in general. It was, after all, that independence that allowed the public professions to operate in a public regarding capacity and to propagate the ideals of "inner dedication" in the first place. As these occupations slowly became reshaped by neoliberalism and its cries of competition, choice and globalization public professions rarely did anything to show their solidarity or to offer assistance. Indeed, in some instances their mutual funds and retirement plans seemed to buy their acquiescence or at least silence. This has created very little sympathy from other occupations about what is now happening to the public realm and public professions. After all, why should they be trusted when all other workers are monitored, evaluated and often fired at will? Why should these professional groups not be transformed into "productive labor" by being exposed to the same policies and processes that have now long affected most other workers in the so-called new economy for decades?

3 The Neoliberalization of Knowledge
Privatization and the New Epistemic Economy

All men strive by nature towards knowledge. (Aristotle, *Metaphysics*)

He who receives an idea from me, receives instruction himself without lessening mine; as he who lights his taper at mine receives light without darkening me. (Thomas Jefferson)

The spirit of American is averse to general ideas; and it does not seek theoretical discoveries. (Alexis de Tocqueville, *Democracy in America*)

Modern industry makes science a productive force distinct from labor and presses it into the service of capital. (Karl Marx)

What is good is given back. (Lewis Hyde, *The Gift*)

Like it or not, the pubic interest will never emerge, even at the cost of a few mathematical errors, from the vision of accountants that the new belief system presents as the supreme form of human accomplishment. (Pierre Bourdieu)

The relationship between knowledge and its various publics has a long and complex history in the West. In certain times and places, such as with Pythagoreanism in Ancient Greece or the Florentine patronage system, knowledge was presented as a sacred object that was creatable by and accessible to only a select few. In other times and places, such as in the writings of the eighteenth-century French *philosophes* or with the founding of public libraries in the U.S., knowledge was advanced, at least in the ideal sense, as a public right open to all with the desire to seek it out. This conflict between a restrictive and often more privatized notion of knowledge and an accessible, more public view can also be found existing within the same society at the same historical moment as various groups vie with one another to either open up or restrict the creation, dissemination or application of knowledge. This historical and ongoing conflict has resulted in series of complex and sometimes contradictory social and legal definitions of what aspects of knowledge should fall within either the private or public domains and what forms should properly constitute and delimit what today are referred to as "intellectual property" or "fair use."

The reasons for restricting access to knowledge vary considerably according to the groups advocating them and the time periods in which they are advocated. In some situations, such as with the banning of books or restricting sex education, some forms of knowledge are seen as simply too dangerous or morally threatening and, therefore, in need of tight regulations, restrictions or controls. In this framing only certain exclusive groups within society, such as experts or religions leaders, are viewed as being beyond corruption and deemed worthy of "being in the know." In other situations, such as with sedition acts or designations of "state secrets," certain types of knowledge may be seen as politically destabilizing forces that, if held in the wrong hands (or minds), jeopardize the legitimacy of the state or the prevailing political order. Restricting the flow of knowledge may also be done to protect the proprietary interest of the knowledge maker or owner, such as in the cases of craft guilds, product patents, trademarks, copyright laws or even the secretive "asset strategies" of hedge funds. In these situations, laws, "letters of patent" or charters are used to manufacture scarcity and create and sustain a restrictive knowledge monopoly (see Krause, 1996). In this framing, knowledge is a commodity that will decrease in value if overexposed and easily available. It will, like all other market commodities, cease to flow and have value if the economic incentives and legal protections that encourage knowledge producers to make more of it are not in place.

Promoting knowledge as an open and accessible public good also has considerable historical and social variability. In some situations, such as with Thomas Jefferson's or John Dewey's distinct projects of democratic education, access to knowledge and information are intractably linked with the ability of citizens to fully participate in a democratic community. Here, freedom and an actively and engaged citizenry are impossible without open, unfettered access to knowledge and information. In other situations, such as with Montessorianism or Paulo Freire's (1970) "radical pedagogy," open access to knowledge is a prerequisite for the personal quest for "moral improvement," enlightenment, *Bildung* or political emancipation. In these instances, self-enlightenment, emancipation and individual creativity are only possible if knowledge is freely available to all who seek it out. In some cases, such as with the open source software movement, Lawrence Lessig's "free culture movement" (see Lessig 2004; 2008) or Lewis Hyde's (1983) "cultural commons project," access to knowledge is part of the constitution of an independent and "recursive public," "commons" or as Lessig (2004: 24) refers to it, "a lawyer-free zone," that stands outside of corporate or governmental direction or manipulation (Kelty, 2008). Without open access to knowledge, so the argument goes, a civil society that resists both the co-optations of the market and the hegemonic aspirations of the state is impossible. Open and accessible knowledge has also been promoted as a necessity for creating fully informed, free and responsible liberal agents who use their acquired or perhaps purchased knowledge to make choices about what to consume and what course of action to follow. In this neoliberal framing the free flow of knowledge is as essential for a functional marketplace as the free flow of capital. Indeed, from this vantage point, innovation and informed consumer choice can't happen without complete and unregulated access to knowledge and "full information;" although in some instances this knowledge may itself need to be purchased in the marketplace, such as with the case of college degrees, self-help books or sales or leadership seminars.

In this and the next chapter, I turn from the more general discussion of neoliberalism to how its ideas and practices have altered the location, production and meaning of knowledge over the last few decades. The general theoretical argument put forward here is somewhat straightforward: changes in political and economic policies and practices affect the organizational and institutional context in which knowledge is produced, the mechanisms through which it is diffused and the social networks in which knowledge makers and disseminators work and interact. These changes, in turn, affect the definition of what knowledge is, the form it takes and even, as I will argue in more detail in the next chapter, the very content and "quality" or makeup of knowledge itself. More specifically, in this chapter I want to examine how a historical tension between knowledge as a public good versus knowledge as a private commodity, or in more legalistic terms a "public-regarding" understanding of knowledge versus a "monopoly privilege" view (Sell and May, 2001: 495), shaped the historical course of knowledge conceptualization and production over the past few centuries. Essentially I argue that his tension between the state and market created a continuum where knowledge (or particular forms of knowledge) was pulled back and forth between the polls of the public and the private as political ideologies and conflicts changed. I explore here how, over the course of the last few decades, neoliberalism has recast the conditions of knowledge production by attempting to privatize vast domains of knowledge and by using market or pseudo-market mechanisms to restructure the organizations, institutions and networks where knowledge has been traditionally produced and disseminated. This change has resulted in the both the movement of knowledge into the market and the market into knowledge, if you will. As this occurred, the public domain has often been reconfigured from a shared, common space into a fallow, lethargic and unproductive space, such as when public domain works are characterized as "abandoned" or that a work has "fallen into" the public domain (see McSherry, 2001: 30). In this presentation the public domain resembles "more a junkyard ... than a popular, shared, 'live' space" (Gains, 1995: 146). In contrast, today the private domain is usually touted as the only area in which the true value and benefits of knowledge are achievable for the "owner" of "intellectual property" and "knowledge consumers."

In the first section of this chapter, I trace the historical construction of the pubic realm and its role in socializing or communalizing knowledge. In the second section I explore how neoliberalist-influenced policies and legal decisions have reprivatized some forms of knowledge over the last few decades through polices and legislation, such as the Bayh-Dole Act, the World Trade Organization's Agreement on Trade Related Aspects of Intellectual Property Rights and, more recently, the ongoing legal debate over Google's digitization of books. In the conclusion, I revisit the historical oscillation between private and public conceptualizations of knowledge.

CONSTITUTING THE PUBLIC DOMAIN: THE PRIVATE/PUBLIC KNOWLEDGE HYBRID

One of modernity's most enduring legacies can be found in its attempt to divide the world into the distinct realms of the private and the public. In doing so, modernity eroded notions of the "common good" found in scholastic philosophy and the *salus populi* or "welfare of the people" that subjected the individual to the needs of the community as found in Roman law (Gunn, 1969: ix). Such a division between the realm of things private and things public began to slowly emerge in late Medieval Europe with a growing emphasis on economic and political individualism; an expanding division of labor that "chopped up" and limited collective experience; the culture value of personal privacy and the growing sanctity and subsequent cocooning of bourgeois family life (see Moore, 1984; Webb, 2007, Durkheim, 1964; Habermas, 1989). As part of this division, modernites created, or at least intensified, the two often-contradictory processes of privatization and collectivization and slowly began constituting what would become the distinct and seemingly mutually exclusive realms of the private and the public (see Elias, 1978). They also launched an ongoing conflict over the types of things that properly belonged in each realm, as well as series of legal and political sorting mechanisms for determining what went where (see Latour, 1993). As this new modern formation solidified over time, certain things were said to belong firmly in the private realm where private ownership would ensure proper stewardship. In other instances, however, other things were seen as clearly belonging in the collective or public realm where in some instances that very same autonomy, this time in the form of avarice, greed and the monopolistic activity of individuals and firms, should be held in check in order to create the greater collective good for society or the public or simply to ensure political balance, stability and plurality.

This friction between what sorts of things should be private and what things should be public generated one of the most familiar political struggles of the last two centuries and hailed the birth of the two great political and economic systems of liberalism and socialism. Both liberalism and socialism contained their own unique and variable constructions of these society/individual arrangements. Within liberalism, theorists as diverse as Locke, Smith, Mill and Ricardo sought to support and protect the private realm of individuals, private property and personal choice. Within socialism or collectivism, on the other hand, theorists as varied as Rousseau, the Utopian Socialists and Marx advocated and defended the realm of society, "the social," the public good, collective rights or the sanctity of the "commons." Early liberalism's advocacy of the private was not in any sense a monolithic stance, however. It contained inherent contradictory tendencies that created two distinct but mutually enforcing forms of liberalism, one primarily economic in nature and the other generally political. The more economically focused variant maintained that all things are better off privatized and outside of state control. Here, the ownership of property served as the basis of all human dignity, political action and civic engagement, such as found in Locke's social contract. In the other, more politically focused variant of liberalism, the fear of state power was retained but was combined with an equal distrust of economic monopolies. In this case, privatization was always preferable to "socialization" or collectivization, but it was important to be aware of and prevent the concentration of both economic wealth and political power. Preventing such monopolies was seen as one of the central activities of the state. For liberals, of both varieties the body politic or the greater social order was both tyrannical and unproductive without the guidance, direction and control of free, autonomous individuals operating in an independent space outside of the structures of the state or its spawn "society." This included free individuals operating relatively unrestrained in the marketplace. In contrast, for those on the collectivist or socialist side of the divide, individual freedom was impossible without the social, political and state mechanisms for making order and economic equality possible. For liberals the coercive power of society/culture/politics/state must be held in check in order to allow individual freedom to flourish. For socialists, unbridled personal freedom and self-interest must be controlled to allow for the fulfillment of the greater public good. Those in the socialist camp would also be divided between those who viewed the collective good as synonymous with the state's interests, e.g., state socialism, and those who viewed the state as needing a democratic counterbalance to limit its power, e.g., democratic socialism.

At certain times and places, a temporary settlement ensued from this division in which some societies, specifically socialist ones, would emphasize the power of and seek to expand the power and range of their version of the social and the *civitas*, and other societies, particularly capitalistic ones, would promote the virtues of and seek to expand the private domain and individualism. A historical continuum also developed in which some societies would move back and forth across this range as political and economic conditions warranted a change in direction (e.g., from a thorough state-centered socialism to a *laissez-faire* liberalism).

All the social and political forms of liberalism and socialism did, in their own way, advocate for the importance of a public domain. They were, however, deeply divided on what this public domain should look like and how to achieve it. In more socialistic societies, freedom was seen as only possible when a robust social space and publicly controlled enterprises were present. Here, the communal ownership of things usually via the state provided the political and economics conditions necessary for individual liberty, freedom and equality. In more liberal or capitalistic societies, the public good is obtainable only through the economic and political actions of free individuals who are or should be beyond state manipulation. For this group, it is actually the private realm that makes the public possible, both in the wealth it provides in taxes and its generation of the greater good—private avarice turns into a public good ala Bernard Mandeville and Adam Smith. Part of this theoretical and practical arrangement separated political economy into the distinct modern realms of "politics" and "economics" and, for those in Western capitalist societies, assigned politics to the realm of the public and economics to the private. In these societies, politics was to be governed by public consensus and debate while economic matters were largely to be determined privately and individually and outside the public and political domains.

The friction between "socializers" and "privatizers," or socialist and liberals if you will, was not only relegated to the contours of the modern political landscape and the death of unified vision of political economy in the West. It was also at the heart of the Enlightenment's contorted, fiercely contested conceptualization of what knowledge was about. In this sense knowledge was one of the issues that became entangled in modern political and legal attempts to sort things into the distinct realms of private or public (see Hagstrom, 1974). In terms of the production of knowledge, the Enlightenment sought to overthrow the more privatized version of knowledge associated most famously with the Florentine patronage system and its "sponsored knowledge." Here an independent public realm was necessary not just morally or politically but also epistemically in order to purify the "context of discovery and revelation." In this instance, the "idols of the marketplace," as Bacon (1960) famously referred to one set of idols that distorted knowledge acquisition in *The New Organon*, was seen as a barrier to the production of objective, true and trustworthy knowledge. The unrealized objective of this enlightenment of knowledge was the establishment of a "Republic of Letters"—"a realm with no police, no boundaries, and no inequalities other than those determined by talent" (Darnton, 2009: 9). This was equally true for the dissemination of knowledge, where from the mid to late nineteen century onward schooling was increasingly seen as something public that should be open to all.

This modern arrangement of knowledge which sought to free knowledge from the clutches of private control and the distortions of patronage required that its production be socialized through open and public display and dissemination. At the epistemic level, knowledge claims needed witnessing and public replication in order to have validity and reliability (see Shapin and Shaffer, 1985). Knowledge claims that were cloistered or private ran the risk of manipulation and contamination by self-interest or self-promotion and were, consequently, not worthy of the label "knowledge." This is one reason why early scientific experiments were modeled after and closely resembled the public proceedings found in courts of law (see Fuchs and Ward, 1994). They needed, indeed required, public display to obtain legitimacy as a knowledge claim. Once publicly made, witnessed and inspected, this knowledge could then ideally flow freely to all those who wished to, or at least those who were in a position to, receive it.

However, the Enlightenment ideal of the public demonstration of knowledge was not without its own social limitations or restrictions. As much as knowledge risked distortion if overly privatized, it also risked contamination if overly publicized and democratized. In this case, another set of Baconian idols—the "idols of the theatre"—also threatened the legitimacy of knowledge production. Here a much more "ruffian" and less democratic view of the public prevailed where the uninitiated who lacked the proper background and methodological mastery to properly understand what was really going on or charlatans who threatened to aggrandize or distort knowledge threatened the legitimacy of scientific truth claims. As such, knowledge production needed supervision by a core of experts who would protect knowledge from both the manipulations of private interests and the distortions of public sophistry and quackery. In other words the unwieldy marketplace of ideas needed a regulatory authority.

In organizational terms, the solution to the Enlightenment's paradoxical juxtaposition of the problematics of the public and private was to be found in the extension of the university guilds into the establishment of the knowledge professions in the eighteenth and nineteenth centuries. While knowledge in this Enlightenment conceptualization ideally belonged in the public domain, since it could and should be used to enlighten and improve all of human kind, its practical creation and dissemination required a controlling body of peers, professionals or "gentlemen scientists" who were capable of seeing that knowledge was properly produced, distributed and interpreted. Such a conceptualization of the role of organizations in the preservation of professional knowledge was key to the establishment of the British Royal Society, the French Academy of Sciences, and somewhat later on, the organization of the individual academic professions and the National Academy of Sciences in the U.S.. As this process became further institutionalized and "modernized" over the course of the nineteenth century, relatively independent professions, rather than private individuals, patrons, states or monarchs, increasingly became the primary vehicle for controlling most knowledge production and dissemination in Europe and the Americas. These "priestly professions" were responsible for ensuring that the production of knowledge remained, at least to some degree, independent of politics and economics.

The fusion of liberal Enlightenment and democratic ideas, while emphasizing the public nature of knowledge and the importance of shared innovation to society, did not, however, mean the complete and unadulterated collectivization of all knowledge. In addition to lauding the virtues of the public knowledge, the more liberalist side to Enlightenment thought also often lionized the author as the principle source for the inspiration and ingenuity found in a work (see Foucault, 1977). In this account, epistemic creativity was seen as being housed inside the human mind where the inimitable personal qualities of experience, dedication and ambition worked to create a uniquely inspired and highly idiosyncratic knowledge. Previous views of knowledge had often ignored the author or viewed him or her as a mere craftsperson or assembler who was no more important to the production of the printed word that the printer, the binder or the book seller (see Woodmansee, 1984: 425).[1] The emerging Enlightenment view, however, simultaneously generated both a creative genius whose ownership of his or her ideas required recognition (and some compensation) and a public domain and a society that urgently needed that authorial knowledge to advance.

The Enlightenment's particular hybrid of the private/pubic conceptualization of knowledge found its legal manifestations in an attempt to balance the public need for knowledge and the private right to compensation for creating that knowledge.[2] The first Western legal protections of copyright began to appear in early forms in Venice as early as the fifteenth century (M. Rose, 1993). In Great Britain, copyright protection appears with the Statute of Anne in 1710. The Statute was promoted as an "Act for the Encouragement of Learning" and sought to end the monopoly over published books effectively established by London Stationer's Company (Darnton, 2009: 9). A few decades later the U.S. constitution also promoted a particular "public regarding" conceptualization of knowledge in Article 1, Section 8. Here, Congress was granted the power to "promote the Progress of Science and useful Arts, by securing for limited Times to Authors and Inventors the exclusive Right to their respective Writings and Discoveries." Indeed, from this more liberal and utilitarian perspective, the only way to overcome the so-called "public goods problem" (Boyle, 1996: 123) and create a public domain for knowledge was through some form of limited privatization.[3]

Neither the establishment of the knowledge professions or the public regarding tendencies of early copyright law were in themselves enough to open up or sustain a significant and perpetual public domain for knowledge, however. A more thorough communalization of knowledge also required broader institutional protection to ensure that it was relatively independent and public and to protect it from always-present privatization efforts and political steering. Such protection also required knowledge making and disseminating institutions that could both house and sustain the knowledge professionals in a relatively independent environment and provide the legal, political and ideological protection necessary to keep outside forces minimized. Knowledge could never be free nor could a vigorous public domain exist if knowledge was forever dependent on patronage and sponsorship; if individual knowledge owners held unchecked monopolistic private power over their copyrights or patents or if political power such as in the newly emerging nation states could easily redirect it to serve its own interest. In addition, although the emerging professions had used their guild-like organization structure to become increasingly powerful, they generally lacked a broader, institutional base from which to act on that power. Without such an institutional base they would be unable to financially and socially ground their activities (see Krause, 1996).

This institutional protection of knowledge and the newly constituted professional "knowledge workers" would be made possible by what Collins (1998: 663) called "the university revolution" in the nineteenth century. Indeed, the system of control of scholarly professions would have been "unattainable without legitimization by the universities" (Geiger, 1986: 21). In *The Conflict of Faculties* Kant described this new modern arrangement of knowledge as one guided by the principles of reason and organized around university produced and monitored knowledge.

> It was not a bad idea, whoever first conceived and proposed a public means for treating the sum of knowledge (and properly the heads who devote themselves to it), in a quasi industrial manner, with a division of labour where, for so many fields as there may be of knowledge, so many public teachers would be allotted, professors being trustees, forming together a kind of common scientific entity, called a university (or high school) and having autonomy (for only scholars can pass judgment on scholars as such); and, thanks to its faculties (various small societies where university teachers are ranged, in keeping with the variety of the main branches of knowledge), the university would be authorised to admit, on the one hand, student-apprentices from the lower schools aspiring to its level, and to grant, on the other hand—after prior examination, and on its own authority—to teachers who are 'free' (not drawn from the members themselves) and called 'Doctors', a universally recognised rank (conferring upon them a degree)—in short, *creating* them. (Kant, 1979[1798])

Knowledge was now relatively free; however, this freedom was to be overseen and safeguarded by the university and guided by the organizing norm and principle of reason.

This meant that rather than seeking out legal protection from the state, such as what happened with medicine and other professions, most scholarly organizations sought out protection within the university and its department systems (Geiger, 1986: 21). Historically, universities and colleges had been relatively small institutions entrusted with the moral training and transformation of a selection of upper-class young men and teaching limited subject areas. However, under the influence of Enlightenment, democratic and bureaucratic ideas and practices, they were slowly and somewhat ironically transformed from small, moral seminaries of the elite into massive repositories, protectors and disseminators of public knowledge and legally recognized credentialing agents. Much like the hybridized public, yet private legal provisions found in the Statute of Anne or the U.S. Constitution, the professionals who worked within the confines of these organizations were able to "own" their ideas through the legal protections afforded by copyright, as well as the anti-plagiarism norms of the professions and the norms of ownership for their lectures. However, they also lived and worked under a limited "gift" or status-based economy, as well as the now legally established concept of "fair use" and the epistemic and communitarian notion of "scientific accumulation." In this context it was expected that as part of their institutional support and protection that the knowledge they generated would be shared with students, colleagues and the public in general. This configuration did not necessarily mean that these knowledge producers were at all times selfless and community minded, as anyone who has worked in academia can surely attest, but that the organizations in which they worked, the instructional structures, such as departments and schools, that supported them and the networks in which they were embedded created conditions that made cooperation and public mindedness a moral virtue and a practical and financial possibility. In other words, self-interest or community mindedness are outcomes of social conditions rather than an inherent human nature. From the somewhat unique organizational configuration of the modern university, an academic culture evolved that exalted the collective nature of knowledge making and the public nature of its dissemination.

By the early twentieth century, universities and colleges had begun to store, monopolize and control a majority of formal knowledge production in many Western societies. Indeed, universities had by this time "absorbed or rendered obsolete such 'amateurs' as the freelance inventor, and even the autonomous intellectual [had become] a threaten species" (Nowotny et al., 2001: 79). This monopolization of knowledge was made possible, in part, by the confluence of Enlightenment ideals, professional control and university structural insularity. These institutional features had by the twentieth century begun to carve out a relatively open and public view of university-generated knowledge and had created what we might call a small, fragile and relatively compact "knowledge commons" in many Western societies. This knowledge commons was support by a new knowledge accord that had been forged over the course of the nineteenth century. In this accord colleges and universities, regardless if they were private or public in origin, were granted a charter by the state to operate relatively autonomously, even if their funding was mostly or entirely state derived. In turn, the professionals working within these organizations were entrusted to work on their knowledge projects and pursue knowledge as they and their professions defined it without undue regulation, manipulation, steering or supervision from outside political and economic forces. This lack of interference included university administrators whose position in the organization made them particularly susceptible to political and economic pressures coming from business people and politicians, who often served on boards of trustees, in some contexts. Although university administrators would increasingly be influenced by business and management tactics in the day-to-day activities of the university, they would leave the direct oversight and control of knowledge work to the academics in their respective departments. Under this arrangement, university knowledge became as McSherry (2001: 55) described it, "usefully useless." Society would indirectly reap the benefits of this knowledge arrangement of professional, university and state through the creation of public domain knowledge, as well as through an increased numbers of educated citizens, basic knowledge, new techniques of social planning and administration and technological innovation. Knowledge makers would, in turn, benefit in a limited financial sense through both the terms of copyright that granted narrow monopoly rights and some compensation but more importantly through the financial support and protection afford by the university through salaries, and beginning in the late nineteenth and early twentieth centuries with the rise of broad-based professional groups such as the American Association of University Professors (AAUP), and the Association of University Teachers in the U.K. (now the University and College Union), formal tenure and recognized academic freedom. In this agreement the care of knowledge was entrusted to the professions and universities who, in keeping with the Enlightenment configuration, would see that its creation was shielded from direct outside political and economic concerns, that its dissemination was widely available and that it served greater societal purposes rather than purely the private interests of individual knowledge producers or the powerful (see Newfield, 2003: 15). The professionals themselves, through an emerging collegial arrangement found in a department structure, would also see to it that the members of the knowledge-producing professions were properly socialized, mentored and monitored (see Geiger, 1986: 36–37). In this arrangement knowledge workers, unlike most workers elsewhere, would constituted a type of "labor aristocracy" (Newfield, 2003: 80) who would not need direct supervision by the state or management guided by overseers but would be "self-managed" by the collegial rules and norms of their own professionalism and the peer review and shared governance structures of departments and universities in general. The knowledge work performed within these institutions was seen as largely independent, creative work that did not need direct oversight or heavy handed "management" in order to be produced. Indeed, that type of overt and direct managerialism was viewed as detrimental to the creative process that made novel and innovative knowledge possible.[4]

The expansion and deprivatization evident in university-produced knowledge directly paralleled the more general late nineteenth- and early twentieth-century expansion of the public domain and the burgeoning of a more general public space in many societies around the world. This expansion was evidenced by such occurrences as the setting up of large public universities and primary and secondary schools, public libraries, public parks, public transportation and public housing, as well as the establishment of socialist or Keynesian-leaning governments in many corners of the world. It is also seen in the expansion of free public education, free public libraries, the increased democratization of schools and universities and the slow desegregation of public education along ethnic, class and gender lines.

Much like the eighteenth-century establishment and defense of the public domain, the late nineteenth- and early twentieth-century deprivatization of knowledge was supported by a strong "public-regarding conception" (Sell and May, 2001: 469; May and Sell, 2006) in intellectual property law. Following the provisions put forward in the U.S. Constitution this conception maintained that although knowledge was produced by individuals and groups who deserved ownership, at least for a period of time, their intellectual property and patents were not to be forever monopolized and held away from the public.[5] Here, as in the Constitution, "access and the curtailment of privilege" became the primary legal concern (Sell and May, 2001: 481). This curtailment had two general social purposes: One was a more collectively centered argument that assured that knowledge was a public good that could promote social progress. The other was a more liberal purpose to make sure that knowledge was not monopolized and could be used to innovate and enable future profit making. Much like eighteenth-century concerns, prevailing legal opinions in the late nineteenth and early twentieth centuries maintained that copyright or intellectual property which was too tightly controlled or monopolized risked thwarting innovation and the greater advancement of society.[6]

The vision of a relatively autonomous, self-organizing university where, as Cicero put it, truth was to be kept separate from "necessary cares" was at the heart of a number of influential idealized accounts of nineteenth- and twentieth-century university life. Cardinal John Henry Newman's of the Catholic University in Dublin (1996 [1852]: 77–78) 1852 book *The Idea of a University* proclaimed the university to be "a pure and clear atmosphere of thought" where the pursuit of knowledge "was its own reward." In a similar vein, Andrew White, the first president of Cornell University in the U.S., described the university as "a place for liberally minded men of learning" where "truth shall be sought for truth's sake" (White in Schweber, 1992: 153). Cornell was envisioned by White as a place "where intellectual culture might restrain mercantilism and militarism" (White in Schweber, 1992: 153).[7] Such a vision of the university was also central for Wilhelm von Humboldt's plans for the establishment of the University of Berlin. Humboldt (in UNESCO, 1993: 616) maintained that "the sole purpose of education must be to shape man himself." In his model it was imperative that education be autonomous. It "lives and continually renews itself on its own, with no constraint or determined goal whatsoever" (Humboldt in Lyotard, 1984: 32). To do this it had to "take place entirely outside the limits ... within which the State must confine its own activities" (Humboldt in UNESCO, 1993: 616).[8] Such a view generated a *Kulturstaat*, or in other terms a "facilitatory state" (Kogan and Hanney, 2000: 30), where the state respected the internal decisions of the university and its unique generation of culture and knowledge while funding and regulating its activities remotely and indirectly (see also Burtsche et al., Pasqualoni and Scott, 2006: 243).[9]

By the early twentieth century a public configuration of knowledge production involving the knowledge making professions, law, the universities and the state had been established. In this configuration, governments would supply a great deal of the funding for university knowledge production in the public universities of many Western countries and the dissemination of knowledge through public education; however, they would generally stay out of directing what that knowledge would be like or the form it would take. By and large knowledge production would be left to the epistemic norms and vicissitudes of the knowledge making and disseminating professions operating within the largely "self-organizing" institutions of universities, with some state or market steering taking place on the margins of knowledge production (see Marginson and Considine, 2000: 1). Law would support these knowledge-making norms through a public–regarding conceptualization of intellectual property that, while recognizing the authorship and ownership of ideas, generally placed public need, in either the liberal or social progressive models, ahead of straightforward private gain. In some more federated national systems governments would even have limited influence on what knowledge was actually disseminated in public elementary and secondary schools, since much of that funding was locally derived and controlled by individual states and towns and overseen by a group of increasingly professionalized and unionized teachers. In this scenario national and state governments helped establish schools, colleges and universities through legislative efforts, such as the Morrill Act of 1862 in the U.S. that helped individual states to establish state universities to support "agriculture and the mechanical arts." However, they generally stayed out of overseeing the content and direction of the knowledge taking place there. In exchange, knowledge-producing institutions would see to it that knowledge was produced as, and remained largely, a public good. They would also retain control over the process of credentialization that the state and other groups saw as increasingly important. The private interests of industry and corporate involvement in university knowledge production would be, with a few exceptions, such as the "institutes of technology," limited to a type of indirect donor or supporting role. They, too, would wait on the sidelines while knowledge was produced by those in the professions and until it entered the public domain where it could be then used for profit within the protocols established by intellectual property law. If industry and corporations wanted to exclusively control and profit from knowledge, they would have to produce it themselves; otherwise, knowledge was, with a few caveats, a public resource open to all.

CONSUMING THE PUBLIC DOMAIN: THE DE-SOCIALIZATION OF KNOWLEDGE

Although the late nineteenth and the early twentieth centuries saw the further transformation of knowledge from a private to a public good, there was never a complete socialization of knowledge in most Western societies. University-produced knowledge generally followed the public-regarding model with its more public or collectivized understanding of knowledge production and dissemination. As universities came to dominate knowledge production and dissemination throughout the course of the early to mid twentieth century, their particular public regarding view of knowledge generally prevailed, at least for certain types of knowledge in particular places. In addition, until the twentieth century, it was "virtually impossible for the links between science and industry to have any rational or planned basis" (Bernal, 1953: 36). During this time, science and industry knowledge transfer links were much too rudimentary and "unthinkable" to produce any significant and continuous technology, "knowledge, outflows" or to establish "innovation systems."

Despite the broadening and socializing of knowledge in the nineteenth and early twentieth centuries the forces of privatization were always close at hand. As early as the 1830s Alexis de Tocqueville (1899: 52) lamented that in the U.S. "a science is taken up as a matter of business, and the only branch of it which is attended to is such as admits of immediate practical application." A century later Thornstein Veblen (1918) railed against the connection of the market and knowledge in his infamous 1918 book *The Higher Learning in America*. In the work, Veblen lamented the growing influence of business interests on academic life in the late nineteenth and early twentieth centuries. By the time of Veblen's book, foundations and businesses were becoming active shapers of some types of scientific work (Kohler, 1991; Newfield 2003: 37). For instance, in 1912 the University of California Berkeley Research Corporation was founded to license patents and support applied research (see Mowery, 2004: 58–63). A bit later in the 1920s at the University of Wisconsin, programs and foundations dedicated to the administration of university-produced patents were founded, such as the Wisconsin Alumni Research Foundation which was formed to oversee the commercialization of Vitamin D (McSherry, 2001: 147;

Holbrook and Dahl, 2004: 92). At MIT close bonds were established with industry during the early 1920s as part of creating what was referred to as the "Technology Plan" (Schweber, 1992: 151). Indeed, MIT was founded in the mid nineteenth century with the expressed purpose to establish a closer link between the economic development of New England and university science and engineering (Etzkowitz, 2002). As part of the MIT's Technology Plan, the "Division of Industrial Cooperation and Research" was developed to make available to business and industry for a fee the university's "scientific and industrial experience and creative aptitude" (Maclaurin in Schweber, 1992: 151). In other cases, such as most famously with corporate laboratories such as General Electric's, founded in 1900, the Dupont Company's, founded in 1902, Eastman Kodak's, founded in 1912, and Bell Telephone (AT&T) founded in 1912, companies forged their own for-profit knowledge by creating their own research centers and laboratories on par with those found in top research universities (see Hounshell, 1992; Geiger, 1986: 95). These labs and research centers could essentially bypass the system of university-centered, public knowledge production and seek viable, commercially centered, private and for-profit research from the start, although they continued to rely on universities for the training of engineers and scientists.

During the early and middle twentieth century the modern knowledge compact with its particular configuration of the public domain, autonomous professional knowledge producers, state support and broad and indistinct social benefits began to come under serious challenge from both industry and the forces of production and the state and the forces of control in the name of public interests. While industry and business had always sought to privatize knowledge like other commodities, the slow dismantling of the liberal university actually began not with direct economic pressure placed on universities for more marketable commodities but with a change in the way nation states conceptualized and situated themselves with regard to knowledge and education. As discussed earlier, in the past when a more politically liberal understanding of governance prevailed, states in many contexts had simply provided the general funding for knowledge production and education to happen, such as in the cases of land grant universities created in the U.S. in the Morrill Act of 1862, university-centered agricultural experiment stations created by the Hatch Act of 1887 and the more general training of teachers in state supported "normal schools" in the U.S. The state nudged and encouraged academic institutions to take on certain areas of knowledge, such as agriculture and education, and to produce and credential certain type of workers, such as teachers and engineers; however, except for a few areas such as the Geological Survey and the Agriculture Department in the U.S. context, they generally stayed out of the day-to day operation and large-scale steering or what would later become known as "knowledge management." However, with the growth of state power even by the early 20th century this was showing signs of change. For example, by

1900 the U.S. government was spending around $11 million annually on various types of scientific activities (Geiger, 1986: 59). Yet, this would be small scare relative to the level of spending that would soon be introduced. By the late 1930s, despite the Great Depression, government spending on science had increased to over $100 million.

By the middle of the twentieth century, as the state dramatically expanded under progressive, Keynesian and socialist governments, it increasing became interested in more directly shaping the direction both knowledge and education should take. This changing relationship between knowledge producing institutions and the state would, as neoliberalism gain prominence in the latter part of the twentieth century, also ultimately be responsible for knowledge's changing relationship with the market in the development of, first, state serving science policies and, later, more market serving knowledge society policies (see Chapter 5).

Perhaps the most important turning point in the redefinition of the involvement of the state in steering knowledge occurred during World War II, particularly in the U.S. case with the Manhattan Project and efforts by the government to build the atomic bomb. Prior to this time frame large-scale government involvement in steering university knowledge had been rather limited, marginal and sporadic, occurring only in a few times, such as during World War I, and in a few subject areas. However, during the War government spending on physics increased over ten fold as part of the Manhattan Project (Galison, Hevly and Lowen, 1992: 46). By the end of the War the federal government in the U.S. financed three-fourths of all research being conducted (McSherry, 2001: 147). As a result of the success of the Manhattan Project in building the atomic bomb in a relatively short period of time a new nexus of knowledge and the state began to take shape.

In 1945 Vanneavar Bush (1945), the Director of the Office of Scientific Research and Development and former Vice President and Dean of Engineering at MIT, exemplified this new attitude when he presented his influential report to the President entitled "Science—the Endless Frontier." The report called for a fundamental shift in the deployment of knowledge and the development of a specific science policy in the U.S. In the place of professional and institutionally defined direction of knowledge, Bush called for the dramatic increase in the role of the state in directing and funding science to better and more directly serve the public interest. Bush envisioned science as the "key to our security as a nation, to our better health, to more jobs, to a higher standard of living, and to our cultural progress" (Bush, 1945: 3). Over time the report became an impetus for establishing the National Institutes of Health (NIH), the National Science Foundation (NSF) and the Office of Naval Research (ONR) in order to better align national and scientific interests. Bush's statements, while calling for a bigger role for university knowledge in moving society forward, were not, however, a call for state controlled knowledge, as had occurred in Nazi Germany and was occurring in the Soviet Union. Bush was quite leery of direct governmental control over science outside of government laboratories; although he welcomed a grant driven, state funded science that allowed science to remain independent (Schweber, 1992: 154). Indeed, the report contained many elements of the public regarding conception of knowledge that had been constructed over the course of the past century. Bush's report emphasized the need for universities to remain centers of basic research that were distinct and indirectly linked to industry. Under these university conditions, scientists were, in Bush's (1945: 17) description, able to "work in an atmosphere which is relatively free from the adverse pressure of convention, prejudice, or commercial necessity." Furthermore, universities were seen as the only institutions that were able to "provide the scientific worker with a strong sense of solidarity and security, as well as a substantial degree of personal intellectual freedom" (Bush, 1945: 17). Scientists should be encouraged to pursue certain lines of inquiry that paralleled social needs through government grants and within the confines of government laboratories but they should not be told exactly or directly what to research.

In the post-World War II context knowledge was becoming recognized as something that needed a "policy" and, hence, more state management for guidance. It was also becoming viewed as something that could be more directly harnessed to enhance industrial production and the general economic well being of society. This more direct form of governmental involvement and steering was justified based on the massive spending that was being directed toward university research and university funding. In this sense the post War University was becoming "the federal grant university," as former University of California President Clark Kerr (1964: 46) referred to it in the 1960s. During this post war time period at MIT, for example, 85% of its research budget came from the U.S. military and the Atomic Energy Commission (AEC) (Kevles, 1992: 315). In 1949 the Defense Department and the AEC accounted for 96% of all federal dollars spent on for research in the physical sciences (Kevles, 1992: 315).

In keeping with the liberalist and Enlightenment narratives, knowledge during the 1940s through the late 1970s was, at least conceptually, recognized as something that should largely stay in the public domain, while also recognizing its growing importance for serving private industry, the military and social planning goals of the state. This change was the most pronounced on the natural and physical sciences. The rather small scale, "tinkering" science of the eighteenth and nineteenth century had been replaced, at least in the natural sciences and some of the social sciences, with the "big science" of the post World War II research university (see Weinberg, 1961; Price, 1963; Kerr, 1964, Galison and Hevly, 1992). Indeed, much of the scientific research of the 1950s and 1960s was fueled directly by U.S. government expenditures as part of the cold war (see Leslie, 1993; Lowen, 1997). During this period federal support of research constituted 60–70% of all university research and development (see Mowery et al.,

2004: 24). However, even during the height of state supported "big science" the University of California put into place its "Regulation No. 4" that, while acknowledging the importance of industry connections, maintained that basic science rather than applied research was to remain the central focus on the university (Shapin, 2008: 212–213).

While university produced knowledge's remained largely independent, the seeds of change that would be reaped later in the century had been planted during the period of the dramatic growth of big state science during World War II and afterward. The university's involvement with the state during the Cold War renewed calls to more directly harness knowledge for industry and corporations. If knowledge was useful for the state's military and political efforts and if state and industry efforts were often in accord, at least in the military-industrial complex, why could knowledge not be made more directly applicable to other businesses and industries? A more elaborate privatization of this type would, however, require a new notion of the state and yet another shift in the relationship between the state, profession and market. The socialist or Keynesian state of the middle of the century, was simply too active of player with too varied and progressive of an agenda to be sidelined by private industrial interests alone. Likewise, the earlier liberalist state, despite its vaunting of the private sector, was much too concerned with political liberalism and preserving individual liberty and the evils of monopolization to completely privatize knowledge in the name of the unfettered market and free enterprise. However, as neoliberal governments came to power in the late 1970s and 1980s, a much closer connection between the state, university knowledge production and business interests was initiated. Indeed, university produced knowledge would come to be recognized as a commodity that would drive economic development and spur private profits. The commodification of knowledge was no longer viewed as an evil to be epistemically and practically avoided for fear of contamination, as in the Enlightenment conceptualization, but would now, in keeping with the tenants of economic liberalism, be promoted as the best avenue for promoting the greater social good.

During the 1970s a series of legal and policy changes began to set the stage for the neoliberalization of knowledge that would happen over the subsequent decades. By the 1970s technology-based businesses had begun popping up in zones around universities such as the University of California, Berkeley, Stanford and MIT. These zones developed to both take advantage of university graduates as a labor pool and as outgrowths of new businesses formed by their graduates. During this time the National Science Foundation also began looking for ways to support their funding by developing what was coming to be called "technology transfer" or knowledge transfer links between universities and businesses (McSherry, 2001: 149). Even as late as the early 1940s only twenty American universities had developed formal patent polices (Shapin, 2008: 212). Indeed, before 1970 fewer than 200 patents were awarded annually to American universities, making up less that .05% of all patents awarded (Geiger, 2004: 216). Additionally until this time the transfer of technology from universities to businesses had been guided by a number of government agencies with their own rules of ownership and transfer protocols. For example, a study conducted under the Lyndon Johnson administration in the 1960s found that no pharmaceutical that the government held a patent on had every been developed commercially (Etzkowitz, 2002: 117). In the American context this situation changed with the passing of the Patent and Trademark Law Amendments Act, also known as the Bayh-Dole Act, which was enacted into law in 1980, the same year the U.S. Supreme Court recognized the patenting of life forms. Proponents hailed the law as "probably the most inspired piece of legislation to be enacted in American over the last half-century" (quoted in House of Representatives, 2008: 7–8). Critics, however, decried its effects on the independence of university research. They saw it as a step toward the privatization of university produced public domain knowledge and end of independent basic science.

Prior to the Act's passage the U.S. government retained title to most federally funded research that resulted in the creation of new knowledge, patents and technology. The government made these products available through "non-exclusive licenses" to anyone who wished to use them. Under this model the licenses were non-exclusive since the public provided the funding for these innovations and they, consequently, should be relayed back to the public in an open and freely available form. Indeed, prior to Bayh-Dole leading American research universities often limited patenting because of the political embarrassment that might result from using public funds for their own benefit (see Mowery et al, 2004: 4). Advocates of Bayh-Dole, maintained, however, that such a broad and overly public conception of university produced knowledge and the lack of "marketplace exclusivity" (House of Representatives, 2008: 13) failed to provide the economic incentives necessary for companies, venture capitalist or individual entrepreneurs to take on risk and develop and market these discoveries. They pointed out that in the 1970s, prior to the Bayh-Dole Act, fewer than 5 percent of the some 28,000 patents held by the U.S. government were licensed for product development in industries (Holbrook and Dahl, 2004: 90). These patents, like most academic products, simply sat around the university despite their potential importance and profitability and were never marketed and made available to people. In this reasoning the normal public regarding idea was essentially flipped on its head—it is actually the lack of privatization that denies the public access to knowledge, not its public availability.

One of the stated objectives of the Bayh-Dole Act was "to promote the commercialization and public availability of inventions made in the United States by United States industry and labor" (U.S. Code Collection, n.d.). This was to be accomplished by allowing universities and companies to own through "excusive licensing" the knowledge and technology that resulted from federally funded research. This meant that universities and individual researchers, through newly established Technology Transfer Offices at universities, could directly benefit from selling or controlling the patents or licenses that were produced through federally funded research. Proponents argued that this would create a competitive system where universities would not only vie with one another for government grants, which still made up the majority of science funding, but would also begin to compete to offer corporations and venture capitalists the opportunity to invest in and support their research in exchange for licensing opportunities. Likewise scientists would become more entrepreneurial and less state dependent as they sought out new, private means for increasing their research funding, status and income. This would, in the long run, lessen the need for state support for universities and lower tax rates.

Proponents claim that since its inception the Bayh-Dole Act has been being responsible for thousands of patents, $30 billion of economic activity each year and has supported of 250,000 jobs in start up and existing companies (University of California Office of Technology Transfer, n.d.). For example, today U.S. universities receive almost four thousand patents a year (Greenberg, 2007: 4). In 2007, for example, New York University led the list of universities in the U.S., earning nearly $800 million "from technology transfer on 227 active licenses" (Masterson, 2009: A16; see also Association of University Technology Managers, 2007). This proliferation of patents also helped forge a new "spin-off economy"—a series of products and firms started by professors and researchers often backed by private equity and venture capital firms seeking manufacturing licenses and new patents (see Greenberg, 2007: 54; also, Shapin, 2008). In 2007 this spin-off economy accounted for 686 new products and 555 new startup companies (Masterson, 2009: A16). More fundamentally, advocates maintain that the Act also helped establish a new relationship between business and the university that was, in the end, economically beneficial for both parties. It also greatly benefited the public who now had products and services that would not have had under the old, public regarding model and its non-exclusive licenses. Critics, however, pointed out that many of these patents were awarded for basic research that used to be shared freely and widely disseminated but was now horded and private (Wirten, 2008: 68). In addition, critics charged that Bayh-Dole had undermined the basic purpose of the modern university—to produce knowledge independent of commercial or political interests. It was also likely, critics charged, that many of the changes attributed to Bayh-Dole would, in actuality, have occurred without the legislation (Mowery, et al., 2004).

By the 2000's the Bayh-Dole Act had so penetrated academia that it had begun to alter the internal standards and procedures of academia, such as the standards for tenure. The Texas A & M University System, for example began to allow "patents and the commercialization of research" to count toward the criteria for tenure (Greenberg, 2007: 56; see also Holbrook and Dahl, 2004: 98–99).[10] As a former Dean of the Graduate School of Arts and Sciences at Emory University, Donald Stein (2004: 8-9), described the situation created by Bayh-Dole, "publish or perish" has been supplanted by "publish, patent or perish." A similar situation emerged in the U.K. where the Research Assessment Exercise (RAE) installed during the Thatcher government and required of departments and universities in order to be allocated government funding now contains patents and research income for knowledge transfer partnerships as part of the assessment materials (see Willmott, 2003). Globally many other nations, such as India, South African, Brazil, Jordan and Malaysia, have developed their own Bayh-Dole type of laws to encourage knowledge transfer (see International Centre for Trade and Sustainable Development, n.d.).

Other neoliberal attempts to privatize knowledge, this time in a more global context, can be found in the formulation of international trade agreements on intellectual property and trade in services directed by the World Trade Organization and found in the General Agreement on Trade in Services (GATS), as well as the Free Trade Act of the Americas (FTAA). During the 1980s and 1990s intellectual property rights emerged as one of the priorities of the many American and European firms, as well as the U.S. government (Ryan, 1998: 1). During the 1980s American businesses, particularly IBM and the pharmaceutical company Pfizer, began a move to institutionalize American standards of property law in countries around the world (Ryan, 1998: 67-68). Pfizer in particular wanted important reforms to the Paris Convention for the Protection of Industrial Property that had first established international property law in 1883 (Ryan, 1998: 68). The 1994 Agreement on Trade-Related Aspects of Intellectual Property Rights (TRIPS), which was negotiated as part of the Uruguay round of the General Agreement on Tariffs and Trade (GATT), sought to create uniform international laws on intellectual property rights modeled after those existing in many Western nations. Negotiators of the agreement received both encouragement and considerable legal support from an entity known as the International Property Committee, which was composed of a group of U.S. corporations whose products fell under the domain of intellectual property (May and Sell, 2006: 154). They were also supported by the U.S. government and the U.S. Trade Representative who saw the strengthening of intellectual property as a key feature of creating a new "competitive advantage" in trade relations, particularly with regard to film and video content, pharmaceuticals, biotechnology and computer programs. As with other trade provisions, the TRIPS agreement allowed the WTO to force members to adhere to protections on intellectual property in order to maintain membership in the Organization (see World Trade Organization, 1994). In the end, TRIPS passed through a type of "bananas and shirts" for "drugs and pop culture" free trade compromise that opened up agricultural and textile imports from many poorer nations who generally opposed the Agreement in exchange for following the TRIPS guidelines (see May and Sell, 2006: 155).

GATS also legally established the idea that education could be treated as a commodity that could be exchanged in a transnational trading system like any other commodity. Just as some countries' comparative advantage might be in bananas or airplanes, some might be in educational products, such as their tertiary education system. Under one reading of this argument even the idea of publicly financed education, like other type of state subsidized industry, might be viewed as a violation of the treaty unless private organizations received similar state subsidies (see Klees, 2008: 335). This argument along with the FTAA also sought to regulate the flow of knowledge production through textbooks and curriculum (see Lipman, 2007: 52). These efforts to commodify and privatize knowledge were also supported by efforts by the World Bank directly and also through its arms the International Finance Corporation (IFC) and EdInvest that sought to make education an opportunity for investors. In 2001 education was declared by the Bank as a "frontier sector" for future investment (Klees, 2008: 335).

The international privatization efforts advanced by neoliberals through the WTO, the World Intellectual Property Organization (WIPO) and other agencies such as the World Bank also set off the privatization of a number of epistemic areas that were once seen as simply "traditional," "tacit" or "culture-based knowledge." For example, native groups in societies around the world have, over the course of the last few decades, begun to assert their "collective copyrights" over their art, stories, folk music and traditional medical practices and remedies (see Brown, 2003). Items once considered as common or public knowledge have been increasingly sealed off through intellectual property law decisions. One such case in Australia, *Bulun Bulun and Milpurrurru v. R & T Textiles Pty Ltd* pitted aboriginal artists against a textile company that put native designs on shirts without acknowledgment and compensation (see Brown, 2003: 43–68). This process is also evident in the formation of the Intergovernmental Committee on Intellectual Property and Genetic Resources, Traditional Knowledge, and Folklore by the WIPO which seeks to protect native ownership rights over their intellectual property (May and Sell, 2006: 194). This type of cultural privatization and propertization was done to protect the rights of native groups who have seen their culture being plundered, not just for its gold or cheap labor as in the past, but for cultural artifacts and knowledge that can be turned into everything from t-shirts, tourist art, sampled in pop music or transformed into patentable drugs or procedures. In an ironic, post-colonial twist, although often it is poorer countries who have historically been the targets of the new intellectual property law changes of the WTO because of their alleged piracy of copywritten and patented materials, in this instance it is largely Western corporations who are guilty of pirating the biological and cultural products of non-Western societies (see May and Sell, 2006: 195). This sealing off of cultural ownership has created a "propertization" of culture where new "fictitious commodities" (Polanyi, 1944) are created out of items, objects and ideas that were once simply "there" and open for sharing (see Hann, 2007). In this case neoliberal privatization efforts have created a unique global situation where only more privatization is considered the proper legal response for problems created by privatization measures in the first place.

Another key moment in the neoliberalization of knowledge came in 1998 with the passage of the Sonny Bono Copyright Term Extension Act (CTEA) in the U.S., also sometimes euphemistically referred to as "The Mickey Mouse Bill" or "The Mickey Mouse Protection Act" (see Sprigman, 2002; Lessig 2001: 1065) due to the involvement of the Walt Disney Company in the law's creation and passage (see U.S Government, 1998). CTEA's origins are traceable to the late 1990s when the Disney Corporation approached members of the U.S. Congress regarding its copyright protection on Mickey Mouse which was due to expire in 2003 (see Wirten, 2008: 121). Disney maintained that if Mickey Mouse entered the public domain the economic viability of the company with its theme parks and cast of characters and products would be put in jeopardy. The passage of CTEA extended existing copyright provisions from fifty to seventy five years after the death of author. For works written for hire this time frame was extended to ninety-five years. The change in the law effectively extended the copyright on Mickey Mouse until 2023.

Opponents of the law maintained that not only did it severely restrict the use of works in the public domain, but it also represented a clever duplicity on the part of The Disney Corporation whose movie content often contained materials mined directly from the pubic domain, such as Rudyard Kipling's *Jungle Book* and Victor Hugo's *The Hunchback of Notre Dame*. What Disney had actually accomplished with the passage of CTEA was a further conversion of public domain materials into private commodities. The company was then successful at using legal measures to extend and strengthen their control over these previously public goods. Other critics maintained that CTEA, somewhat like the earlier *Basic Books v. Kinkos* decision which took away the ability of university instructors to make course packets for their students under the doctrine of "fair use," also placed further restrictions on the doctrine that has been an integral part of the public regarding conceptualization of knowledge for some time (see Wirten, 2008: 133).

A more recent court decision that will undoubtedly have profound and far-reaching implications for knowledge residing in the public domain is the debate surrounding the still unresolved tentative Google settlement of 2008 and its 2009 amended settlement (see Books Rights Registry, 2011). The tentative settlement, which was set aside for the time being in March 2011 stemmed from a class action lawsuit filed by a group of authors and publishers in 2005 over an alleged violation of copyright by Google resulting from its ongoing digitization of books from research libraries around the world (see Darnton, 2011). When finished, Google's new digital library would create the world's largest library that would "dwarf the Library of

Congress and all the national libraries of Europe" (Darnton, 2009: 11). In the tentative results of the settlement announced in the fall of 2008, Google will be able to sell access to these digitized works via a library purchased database. Public domain works would continue to be offered "free of charge," except for exposure to advertising on the website. Authors whose works had not become part of the public domain would be compensated through a newly created entity call the "Books Rights Register." Critics of the agreement maintain, however, that this enables Google to create a new kind of monopoly, "not of railroads or steel but of access to information" (Darnton, 2009: 11). As a result of their digitization, libraries are likely to remove these works from their shelves as they continue on their transformative journey to become large internet cafes. This means that in the future anyone wanting to have access to these works, even those in the public domain, will have to either pay a private company for that privilege or be exposed to Google's for-profit advertising. In this new situation, public libraries will perhaps no longer exist, thereby creating a concentration of books in the hands of a few private companies such as Google and Amazon. Such a situation is already present in the move toward electronic subscriptions for journals rather than a print copy that may be owned by a university library. In this move, knowledge stays in private hands and can only be accessed through a continuous fee system rather than the free availability offered by a public university or library (see Ciancanelli, 2008).

Critics maintain that this electronic concentration of knowledge in essence creates a privatized public domain—a domain that appears accessible and public but because of its commercial restrictions is actually private and profit based. It also, as with the case of the Disney extension, essentially transfers public works into private goods where they are used not for the public good but to generate company profit for shareholders. Much like the argument in support of the Bayh-Dole Act, supporters of Google responded that they are providing a valuable service by making readily available books that had sat around unused. For that service to the public and their customers, they should receive compensation, much like a bookbinder or distributor. In this case the fallow public domain had failed to provide the public with what it wants and perhaps needs. It was, therefore, time for the private sector to take control in the name of the consumer and public dissemination.

In isolation these policy and legal changes of the last few decades may seem as merely pragmatic, local adaptations to particular circumstances. However, when taken together they constitute a fundamental shift in the way knowledge is conceptualized and practiced. As universities gained a virtual monopoly over knowledge production and the credentialization of experts in the twentieth century, its model of public knowledge, autonomous knowledge professionals, indirect market relevance and limited state oversight become a dominant mode of knowledge production in many Western societies. During this time knowledge was predominantly publicly oriented. Although its ideational products could be temporarily protected and its technological products patentable, these were limited in time and scope and within the scientific community could still fall under the communal principle of fair use. The neoliberalization of knowledge evidence in the legal and policy changes of the last few decades have sought to fundamentally change this public regarding conceptualization. As neoliberal governments came to power and enacted new policies, they promoted a resurgence of the private conceptualization of knowledge just as they did in other areas that that felt had been "overly socialized," such as public welfare, public housing, water rights and public space in general. In this instance if the public wanted or needed knowledge they would need to pay for its production through copyrights, patents or consumer products (see Ciancanelli, 2008: 69). As a result of these neoliberal privatization efforts the state and law changed from supporting the long-standing public regarding view of knowledge to advocating for a much more privatized and monopolized conceptualization. As this happened, the ownership of ideas became paramount over their public application. If ideas were to come to the public, it would be through the consumer-based mechanisms of markets rather than through the "free use zones" of public space. As this occurred, intellectual property began "behaving more like real property" (Murray 2003: 739). Laws were expanded to increase the marketization of knowledge, to protect intellectual property rights and to assert a competitive and private conceptualization of science, knowledge and culture.

THE POLITICAL ECONOMY OF KNOWLEDGE

In order to understand the somewhat contorted origins of the public domain and the historical tension between the public and the private realms over the last couple of centuries, it is important to recognize the role early both liberalist and collectivist or socialist ideas and practices played in shaping the form knowledge would take. In simple terms, it is possible to conclude that the forces of early Enlightenment liberalism of the nineteenth century set knowledge free and those of state socialism and neoliberalism of the twentieth century made it serve new masters. Prior to the advent of the neoliberalization of knowledge, three predominant views of university-based knowledge and the private/public division are evident. One variant drew from liberalist ideas about the importance of private property and free markets and contended that all things are better off when privatized, including science and knowledge in general. A second view, found most readily in state-centered socialism, wished to completely or partially socialize the public domain and knowledge by both limiting the extent of the private domain and collapsing the distinction between the interests of the state and those of the public. A third position, with some of its roots in the liberal fear of both the state and the monopolizing tendencies of markets wished to constitute and protect a freestanding public domain independent of both state and market. This public domain was only possible with a vigorous, non-monopolistic private domain.

Much of the university-produced knowledge of the nineteenth and twentieth centuries was born and sustained within the political and social space that the third position made possible. Here, as Robert Nisbet (1971: 34) described it, "the service rendered by the university lay not so much in what it did, but in what it was." Tucked away from direct control by either the state or market and politically insulated to some extent by the relatively independent state, governmental bureaucracies and the professions, the "usefully useless" (McSherry, 2001: 55) knowledge of the university could flourish relatively, although never completely, independently. In this position the foundation of what would become the modern, publicly minded and oriented knowledge domain was born.

This situation was less the result of the actions of some "free floating intelligentsia," as Karl Mannheim (1991) famously described them or of the independent knowledge as projected by the Enlightenment *philosophes*, however, although Enlightenment and democratic understandings of knowledge figured importantly here. It was rather more of a structural outcome of a compromise (or perhaps stalemate) between state, professions and market and the variants of liberalism and socialism.[11] Indeed, the shape of knowledge during this time in many Western national contexts would reflect the somewhat contradictory political contours of fear of the state and monopolization, an embracing of the economic and political sanctity of the individual and the need for public view of knowledge that allowed individuals or citizens to learn for themselves. When these quintessential liberal ideals were coupled with the insularity and the public service orientation of the professions and the relative institutional independence of the university, the fragile and paradoxical configuration of public knowledge came into being.

When knowledge is allowed to "roam free," at least relatively speaking, in structural situations where the professions are relatively strong and can shield knowledge from both the market and the state, its shape and form are quite different from situations when it is confined and steered. If the power of the market is more pronounced, knowledge changes to become more private, commodifiable and marketable. If, on the other hand, the state is more powerful knowledge is modified to serve the needs of political authority. If, as in neoliberalism, the state is reconfigured to serve the market, knowledge is pulled quickly and sharply toward the market. In other situations it may contain a type of private/public hybrid liminality that holds contradictory indications as some knowledge is pulled one way and other forms are pulled another. This relationship is, in turn, closely linked to and reflects larger changing notions of the public and private realms. In this sense it is important to take account of how knowledge is continuously entwined with the expansion or shrinkage of the larger modern public domain. In historical periods when the public domain is growing, for example with the expansion of the state in the form of public housing, transportation, public parks or public education, knowledge too becomes more public, accessible and "communalized." In times when the private domain expands and absorbs elements of the public domain this latter domain retracts and knowledge too becomes increasingly privatized, commercialized and commodified. In these latter settings, knowledge, like all aspects of life, must "pull its on weight," "make a direct contribution to the economy," or be "put to use."

The structural condition where an independent, professionally produced knowledge or the "knowledge for knowledge sake" position can exist is, thus, significantly altered by both the fully socialized, stated based systems and purely privatized systems. An "oversocialized version" of knowledge, particularly in a state-driven form, may lead knowledge to become the exclusive servant of state interests and power, as was the case with the Nazi or Soviet sciences and to some degree with the university-military-industrial alliance in the U.S. after World War II. Although these interests may serve the public domain in some instances, at least if the state and public are in alignment, as they supposedly are in democratic socialist systems, they may also threatened the independence of knowledge and the autonomy of knowledge producers who must bend their focus to fit with the will of the state. Likewise, in situations where knowledge becomes overly privatized, its independence is again threatened, this time by the interest-driven concerns or "Baconian idols" of knowledge entrepreneurs, venture capitalists, "cultural poachers," corporations or even now the market savvy universities themselves who must mold knowledge to fit with the search for balanced budgets and non-profit profitability.

The history of knowledge illustrates that knowledge operates under its own uniquely constituted "epistemic economy" that shapes its directions and outcomes (see Mittelstrass, 2003). While the age of "merchantable knowledge," as Thornstein Veblen (1918: 85) referred to almost a century ago, is not particularly new, neoliberal ideas, policies and practices have been instrumental in both intensifying many of the markets effects and more fundamentally in reconfiguring the market/state continuum that gave modern knowledge much of its form and character and knowledge producers and teachers much of their relative autonomy in the twentieth century. Under neoliberalism the forces of state and market were essentially combined into a new, united nexus that worked in unison to create a much more private, market-centered, version of knowledge. The new form knowledge is now taking, consequently, is less the result of shifting epistemic standards or "inevitable changes," as is sometimes argued, than variations in the larger political economy in which knowledge in the West, and increasingly globally, is embedded.

4 The New Marketplace of Ideas
The New Knowledge Makers and Their New Knowledge

> You are lost if you forget that the fruits of the earth belong equally to us all, and the earth to nobody. (Rousseau, 1992 [1755]: 59)

> Poetry can only be made out of other poems; novels out of other novels. All of this was much clearer before the assimilation of literature to private enterprise. (Frye, 1957: 96–97)

> Knowledge has entered the industrial (and postindustrial) product system. But with equal force, the production system has entered knowledge. (Shipman, 1999: 95)

> The actual corrosive "materialism" of our times does not proceed from science. It springs from the notion, sedulously cultivated by the class in power, that the creative capacities of individuals can be evoked and developed only in struggle for material possessions and material gain. (Dewey, 1935: 89)

In the preceding chapter I was concerned with how knowledge has been shaped by a historic and ongoing political tension between state, market and profession and a resulting struggle over defining and delimiting and expanding or shrinking the private and public spheres. Historically knowledge in general, as well as specific forms of knowledge, have oscillated along the range of a continuum between a completely privatized version where knowledge is owned or privately controlled by individuals or groups and its complete socialization and in some cases, politicalization, by the state. In the middle of this continuum was a type of "balance point" where knowledge was largely controlled by the knowledge-making professions and was generally more publicly oriented. The practical outcomes of this oscillation were an ironic "private but at times public" and "public but at times private" conceptualizations of knowledge that has prevailed in many Western societies. In the first case, in certain times and under particular situations, knowledge was at its core a private good but one with a social value that must be legally managed and protected in order to be properly utilized. From this vantage point, it is privatization that creates the incentives and mechanisms for transforming private knowledge goods into public use. In the latter case knowledge is, first and foremost, a non-rivalrous public good but one that may, in some cases, have some limited form of temporary private ownership that legally recognizes the property rights of the producer. As the last chapter tried to illustrate, over the last few decades neoliberal politicians and policy makers have presided over and helped direct the swinging of the pendulum toward a much more private, monopolistic and proprietary view of knowledge, as evidenced by the series of legislation, international trade policies, knowledge society doctrines and court decisions examined in the last chapter.

In this chapter I want to extend the discussion of the neoliberalization of knowledge begun in the last chapter further by examining the meaning this most recent swing in knowledge creation has for the organizational conditions under which knowledge is produced, those who traditionally make knowledge, particularly professors and researchers in the university setting, and the effects of this transformation on "what is thinkable" (Swidler and Arditi, 1994: 315) or the actual "quality" or composition of knowledge itself. Over the last few decades three general trends have become evident in the neoliberal treatment of knowledge. In the first trend, associated most closely with "roll back" neoliberalism, knowledge production, particularly in public universities, is to be streamlined in the name of efficiency, economic rationality, accountability and taxpayer savings. In the second trend the outcomes of university knowledge production are to be increasingly transformed into private, marketable goods that can finance universities and fuel profit making and economic growth. In the third trend, state-led auditing and assessment mechanisms are to be used to enable consumer choice and to direct knowledge production and education delivery more closely to the needs of the market. These political trends, I will argue in this chapter, have spawned new institutional forms of knowledge production, new forms of entrepreneurially minded knowledge producers, different, more market-relevant types of knowledge and even different, more performative standards of truth, or what Lyotard (1984: 46) called "the truth criterion."

This latter point is, undoubtedly, the most difficult proposition to empirically support or even to acknowledge. While most would readily accept that knowledge varies, at least to some extent, with the historical conditions under which it is made, (see, for example, Collins, 1998) it is quite another matter to argue that the very content, or what I refer here to as the "quality of knowledge," or standards of truth are altered by the "epistemic economy" or organizational conditions under which it is produced. Knowledge, unlike ideology, commonsense or opinion is not supposed to operate in such a crass and deterministic manner. Knowledge, at least in the version put forward in the Enlightenment and cultural narratives that served as legitimation and as a foundation for most modern knowledge production, is supposedly driven by its own internal logic of unfolding, revelation or discovery that is only indirectly influenced by the political and economic context in which it operates. Indeed, as I argued in the last chapter, protecting knowledge from this type of market and state-borne "contamination" was one of the goals behind the general socialization of knowledge that began in the seventeenth and eighteenth centuries.

In order to outline the transformations occurring in the late modern organization of knowing, I being this chapter with a brief discussion of the application of general neoliberal principles to the topics of knowledge and education. Here I want to outline what university knowledge and public forms of education look like from the vantage point of neoliberal theory. In the next section, I examine the transformation and reculturing of knowledge-making institutions. In the next section, I explore the impact that this transformation and reculturing has had on the professors and researchers who have traditionally produced and disseminated knowledge in a university setting. I conclude with a discussion of the meaning these transformations have for the current makeup or composition of knowledge itself.

KNOWLEDGE AS COMMODITY: THE NEOLIBERAL CONCEPTUALIZATION OF KNOWLEDGE AND EDUCATION

In the Enlightenment, cultural or expert-rationalist conceptualizations and legitimations of knowledge and education traditionally found in the university and public education, particular types of knowledge are seen as indispensable regardless of what individual knowledge or education consumers may consume or their marketability. Following the rationalist model, people need truth, enlightenment, growth or political socialization not just what is popular, marketable or "in demand" at the moment. However, at the heart of the neoliberal way of thinking, at least in what we might call its ideal typical or pure theoretical form, nothing, not even the enlightenment's once sacred and public thing called knowledge, has value until it enters the marketplace. Knowledge is to be seen as, in Hayek's framing, a scarce and dispersed resource (Hayek, 1945; 1948; see Hodgson, 1999). In this "capitalization of knowledge" the value of knowledge (and education) are to be determined by their usefulness to individuals and this usefulness is best determined by markets composed of freely trading and consuming people. Adam Smith (in Pribram, 1983: 134) maintained that "no human knowledge or wisdom" could perform "the duty of superintending the industry of private people and of directing it towards the employment most suitable to the interest of society." Echoing Smith and Michael Polanyi's understanding of the diffusion of scientific knowledge, Hayek (1948: 77–78) envisioned the "economic problem of society" as the "problem of the utilization of knowledge which is not given to anyone in its totality." This means that "human reason . . . does not exist in the singular, as given or available to any particular person, as the rationalist approach seems to assume, but must be conceived as an interpersonal process in which anyone's contribution is tested and corrected by others" (Hayek, 1948: 15). In the end "no man is qualified to pass final judgment on the capacities which another possesses or is to be allowed to exercise" (Hayek, 1948: 15). It is only under rationalist truth regimes and socialistic political regimes where a particular knowledge's "price" is subject to the artificial adjustments generated by the state. Rationalists believe in a "correct view of things" independent of knowledge's exchange value. From the liberal view the expert or state control of knowledge or education is essentially a form of monopoly that imposes a particular world view, as described by J. S. Mill (1951). Protecting any commodity in this manner, or even by placing it in the public domain through political or legal measures, destroys its practical value and renders it useless for economic exchange and, consequently, for individuals who need this valuing in order to know what or if to buy, what price to pay and what use it has. In this conceptualization, knowledge is not to be prized as a sacred object or public good that is somehow outside or above the dynamics of private exchange but as an object that can and should be turned into a commodity in the same manner as land, money or labor. Indeed, as found in endogenous growth theory, GATT and OECD and World Bank policies, knowledge is now considered to comprise a unique new fourth "factor of production" that makes it as commodifiable and exchangeable in a marketplace as anything else. In addition, this transition of knowledge and education into commodities and capital is not just simply the appropriation of more things for profit by capitalists, although this is certainly a necessary precondition for the establishment of a free knowledge market, but is, in terms that would have been recognizable to Adam Smith, the only reliable means for creating the conditions for the larger good. Without incentives for producing knowledge and pricing mechanisms for allocating value to those knowledge products, knowledge and education are valueless and, as a result, useless. Under such incentiveless conditions knowledge and education, like people in a protected or embedded environment, becomes self-indulgent, idiosyncratic, unproductive, insular and lazy—perhaps as in certain protected and "useless" knowledge areas within the university. The uncommodifiable is, hence, the valueless, the useless and the unactionable. Only the market can discipline knowledge making and dissemination in a manner that makes it socially useful.

The economic principles used to determine the value of commodities are, consequently, also moral principles for valuing or "pricing" all aspects of culture. In this formulation only those things that can generate a market sufficient to sustain them should exist. The market serves as an "epistemic machine" (Gray, 1989) that values knowledge and education by determining both the types that are useful and their dispersion among individual consumers. At the level of the production of knowledge this means that only knowledge that is "in demand" and can become self-sustaining by creating a market for its epistemic wares should continue to survive. In simple, pure market terms knowledge should be "demand driven"—if there is a demand for the knowledge form or product it will and should be produced. If there is no demand and one cannot be generated through marketing techniques, then it will not nor should it be produced (see Etzkowtiz, 2008). In this understanding, it is, as Richard Matasar (1996: 790) Dean of the New York Law School argued in his controversial piece "A Commercialist Manifesto," not the duty of a university to support "the boutique courses" of faculty members regardless of their alleged importance to society. In more direct terms what this means is that the university is "a business, deal with it" (Matasar, 1996: 783). Such a view is also echoed in the sentiments of many academic deans and provosts across the country who, following the sound economic and managerial principles drawn from neoliberalism and trickled down to universities through New Public Management, will not run a course without what they and the university deem to be an enrollment level sufficient enough to support the faculty member's salary. One extreme version of this view was initiated at Texas A & M in 2010 when the university released a report with the cost/benefits of each professor at their university. This was followed in 2011 with a similar measure in the University of Texas system (see Simon and Banchero, 2010: C1–C2). In these cases a table was created that compared professors' salaries with the money they brought into the university either through grants or student tuition. Under these types of accounting schemes, all courses and departments must have a "business plan" that enables them to draw a large enough paying audience of choosing and consuming students or from private donor support to legitimate their existence. In a truly spontaneous market society no knowledge domain is important enough to overcome the restrictions imposed by the absolute of the bottom line or the economization of consumer choice. Regardless of what a course or area may contribution to "society" its legitimacy must be first vetted by the economic demand created by consumers before its intellectual merits are considered tenable.

Much like the neoliberal critique levied against the Pubic Broadcasting System (PBS) or National Public Radio (NPR) in the U.S. over the last few decades, if there is not a market for a knowledge form or a cultural expression and one can't be generated, it should not exist, regardless of its supposed educational, enlightenment or other "morally useful" role (see McCauley, 2005). In this reading it is not the role of the state to impose or support particular ideas or perspectives. Indeed, even government agencies that support knowledge, such as the National Science Foundation or the National Foundation for the Humanities, are considered in some "roll back" neoliberal circles as "undesirable and should be terminated" (Friedman and Friedman, 1980: 68). A knowledge form's level of influence, or perhaps if we take this argument to its logical extreme we can even say its truthfulness, can only extend as far as its market and consumer demand will carry it. Of course, as with farm subsidies or governmental price supports, a type of pseudo or artificial demand may be generated by governments who wish to use knowledge for particular ideological or administrative purposes but this process is both difficult to sustain and, as is the case with all state managed endeavors, works to undermine the "natural selection" and "creative destruction" found within markets. Such a rationalist approach to knowledge and education is also deeply authoritarian as it seeks to use the legal power of the state to coerce adherence and to elevate some knowledge forms above others.

Knowledge making and distribution is consequently better off if privatized and commodified. In this sense, knowledge is conceived of as being as tangible and important of a product as steel or oil, particularly in the transformation from an industrial to a post-industrial knowledge society. The public knowledge commons that has supported a "free use knowledge" needs, therefore, to be enclosed and privatized in order to be better protected and more productive (see Boyle, 2003; 2009). From this vantage point, just as in the first enclosure movement when peasants were removed from the land in order to unleash the lands potentiality and in order to aid economic development, today knowledge and education must be freed from the stifling and unproductive grip of the public realm and the stranglehold of the public professions and turned over to various knowledge entrepreneurs who can use market incentives to value various forms of knowledge and education and increase their usefulness, much like the argument behind the Bayh-Dole Act. The misty-eyed humanists who lament the horrors of either the enclosure of land or the current enclosure of the "knowledge commons" and the public domain in general overlook what the biologist Garrett Hardin (1968) famously referred to as "the tragedy of the commons"—the propensity of individuals to overuse or neglect common things until they are destroyed since they have no incentive to protect them. In their opposition to the privatization of knowledge and education these critics are as misguided as those who opposed the enclosure of land in earlier centuries. The marketization of knowledge is, consequently, not a throwback to some "cut throat" past but is a progressive, transformative, mechanism for the future. In fact it brings necessary reforms, opportunities, innovations and efficiencies to people and institutions, including schools and universities, who are often backward looking, fear averse and still clinging to the protection of the collective. In the neoliberal model, what is true will prevail, and what prevails is true.

THE REORGANIZATION AND RECULTURING OF KNOWLEDGE-MAKING INSTITUTIONS

As we saw in the last chapter, the fragile public knowledge commons that was established in universities in the late nineteenth and twentieth centuries was a complex accomplishment resulting from a particular interaction and compromise between state, market, universities and the newly established knowledge professions. This accomplishment created a tenuous space for a particular type of public knowledge organization and a specific style of public knowledge to grow and prosper. This was less the idealized manifestation of enlightenment ideals as it was a social and political accomplishment of a particular time and place. This accomplishment allowed for existence of such things as "basic science," "public regarding," "fair use," "university produced," or, in summary, "Mode I" (Gibbons et al., 1994) knowledge. It also allowed for the drawing of distinctions between pure and applied knowledge and knowledge produced for commercial purposes and that produced for the public good. Under Mode I conditions, knowledge was seen as politically disinterested, epistemically and internally focused, professionally controlled, organizationally independent and publicly available. This mode of knowledge production provided both the practical conditions under which most knowledge was produced and the normative and narrative framework that would guide future knowledge production, as well as working to establish the work cultures of universities.

Under conditions of Model I knowledge production "problems are set and solved in a context governed by the, largely academic, interests of a specific community" (Gibbons et al., 1994: 3). Here it was the contours of the profession and its uniquely constituted form of "peer pressure" that determined what projects could be undertaken, what procedures were acceptable and what outcomes would be considered appropriate. Such a style of knowledge production was made possible by strong professional organizations and a political boundary that kept both the market and the state at bay or relegated to the fringe of the organization. This type of knowledge form was marked by "limited marketability" and "limited governmentality" where both the commodification of particular epistemic realms were not thinkable or, at least practical, nor was their incorporation by the state for its own governance agendas.

Under Mode I, knowledge production was often legitimated through what Lyotard (1984) famously referred to as the "grand narrative of emancipation." This narrative envisioned the goal of knowledge production in all domains as the liberation of both the human spirit and society-at-large from tyranny, authority and ignorance. In this context, the university existed primarily to, as Kant (1979 [1798]) viewed it, promote reason and liberate humanity from arbitrary authority. Within this influential Kantian narrative, knowledge, as opposed to superstition, myth or ideology, was capable of producing both socially beneficial knowledge and progressive ideas that would move society forward and improve the condition of humanity. This approach drew a sharp distinction between the relatively freely flowing and independently determined "basic science" or general knowledge of the academy and the conversion of that knowledge into technology or application for governments or industries.

In the terms put forward by Robert Merton (1968) in his famous treatise on science, this type of knowledge formation promoted an academic culture emphasizing universalism, communism, disinterestedness and organized skepticism. The value of communism, which can be viewed in one sense as one particular cultural manifestation of the public regarding view of knowledge, promoted the idea that knowledge was both an outcome of collective effort, since it always relied on the accumulation of the knowledge that went before, and a collective force, since it should be disseminated to all who wished to receive it. Even if some knowledge was "locked up," so to speak, in elite university settings and was closed to large numbers of people, other modes of distribution, such as public libraries and public universities would provide alternative avenues for making knowledge publicly available. Individual authorship and control, while acknowledged and sometimes glorified in the well-worn "inspired genius trope," were in themselves not the ultimate goal of knowledge production in this mode. Rather the goal was to search for basic knowledge and to solve intellectual issues that flowed from the cumulative history, practices and discourse of the knowledge profession itself. As I argued in the last chapter, this did not mean that this was an ideal, conflict-free utopia, but rather that the conflicts and contradictions that did exist were largely internal to the status economy of the university or the profession.

Under Mode I the application of knowledge or its translation into technology was viewed as positive and beneficial in many instances, although the mechanisms for making this happen were usually either ill defined or were assumed to be directed by groups outside of academia, such as governments or industries. Simply put, universities produced and stored knowledge as part of their emancipatory mission to spread reason, it was mostly up to others, however, to apply it or covert it into technology. Under Mode I conditions application and technological innovation was never really the prime consideration for making or spreading knowledge. Here knowledge could simply exist and be advanced for its own sake, such as in the case of "basic science." Furthermore, since academia operated on a status rather than a market economy, glory, reward and fame was more likely to go those who advanced "the frontiers" of basic science rather than to someone who invented something directly useful. Indeed, invention and application were in some more purist academic circles actually looked down upon since they may have involved a promotionalism and individualism that ran counter to the prevailing Baconian communal norms of science. The public nature and free availability of this basic science created the public knowledge stock that anyone could draw upon and convert into application if they so wanted (see Eisenberg and Nelson, 2002).

The neoliberal-directed (re)privatization and marketization of knowledge that has occurred over the last few decades has fostered the emergence of a dramatic new mode and style of knowledge production and a fundamental "reculturing" of parts of the university along with it (see Anyanwu, 2004). Within this "post normal" (Funtowicz and Ravetz, 1993), "post-academic" (Ziman, 2000), "postmodern" (Lyotard, 1984), "triple helix," (Etzkowitz, 2008) or Mode II (Gibbons et al., 1994) knowledge production has been remolded into a new form, particularly in certain fields. First, and most fundamental among these changes, is that the production of knowledge has become much more decentralized than it was under Mode I conditions. With the growth of think tanks, governmental agencies and laboratories, policy institutes, corporate laboratories and consulting firms, universities have become just another locale where knowledge work is carried out. As a result knowledge now has become "socially distributed," "trans-disciplinary" or "application oriented" with "multiple accountabilities" rather than unilocal and accountable to the profession or home university (Beerkens, 2008: 22). In the decentralized mode the new model of knowledge production, both inside and outside of the university, has become the "research institute" or "sustainable excellence clusters" (Grafton, 2010: 32) rather than the traditional academic department. In many ways this new "flexible project work" resembles the post-Fordist models of production found in industry where work is more "team oriented," temporary and flexible. In some instances these institutes or clusters contain "multidisciplinary teams" who work on a very specific problem, project or issue and then offer up "practical advice" or application in the form of policy recommendations and research studies to governments and industry about what plan of action to follow.[1] In the sciences they often involve centers, "business incubators" or laboratories devoted to specific topical research, such as nano- or biotechnology, that are capable of producing products or procedures than can be patented by universities, licensed and transferred to corporations or organized in spin-off companies the university and faculty members develop themselves. In physical appearance these institutes and centers, particularly outside of the sciences, often more resemble corporate office settings with cubicles and conference rooms rather than typical academic offices. While a significant portion of Mode I research took place with the lone scholar pursing his or her work in his or her own study or laboratory, work in this new mode is made by a "production team" that contributes individual bits and pieces to the production of reports, patentable products, licenses and "directly relevant" positions papers.

The growing importance of Mode II forms of knowledge production signals a profound change in the way knowledge flows and the relationship between knowledge "producers" and "consumers." Groups that were once dismissed by those in academia as merely disseminators or users of university-produced knowledge or basic science, such as corporations, think tanks or government agencies, are now in the position to produce and spread their own knowledge. Their knowledge facilities and products are even sometimes more advanced than those found in the increasingly cash strapped and tax starved public university settings. Likewise, thanks to the new flow of information created by the internet those who were once passive consumers of knowledge now become "media co-designers" and are able to "talk back" to those who produce knowledge (see Cope and

Kalantzis, 2008). The disciplines and professions that comprised the core of knowledge production in the Mode I model become much less crucial under this newer mode of production (Gibbons et al., 1994: 5). They are merely one component of an increasingly vast and unwieldy knowledge-generating and -disseminating innovation system—a system that can now be overseen and directed by knowledge managers to increase production. As a result of these changes, university knowledge producers themselves become both "a less privileged group" since they are no longer hold a special place in knowledge production and a "problematic category" (Nowotny et al., 2001: 89) because they are seen as requiring constant regulation, incentivization and oversight by managers. Likewise, universities become less crucial sites for the creation of knowledge, although they are still generally seen as the central sites for the training and credentialization of scientists and other future knowledge producers; although with the growth of for-profit on-line universities and a proposal for a Wal-Mart University this too may be changing.

The decentralization of knowledge found in new Mode II production has spawned an "entrepreneurial science" that is centered neither in the activities of university or even in traditional industries (see Nisbet, 1971; Shapin, 2008). In the early stages this movement was largely an internal reordering within the university where, as Robert Nisbet (1971: 74) described it over four decades ago, the "new bullion" goes to "academic entrepreneurs for companies known as centers, bureaus and institutes." Today, however, the new entrepreneurial science has gone external, and the bullion is no longer just a metaphor for status. Now scientists can appeal much more directly to the "third stream" funding provided by corporations for product licenses and venture capitalists for startup funds for new ideas and companies rather than tinkering around the university lab, pursing traditional governmental grants or working directly in industry (Shapin, 2008). Although government funding still makes up the vast majority of science funding, the last twenty-five years have shown a steady shift away from governmental toward private sources of funding for scientific research, particularly in the biosciences (see Biddle, 2007; Krimsky, 2003; Mirowski and Sent, 2002). In this new system government grants are also redirected more to projects that involve direct applicability, as required, for example in the U.S., in the Government Performance and Results Act (GPRA) of 1993 and the 2002 introduction of the Program Assessment and Rating Tool (PART) by the Office of Management and Budget that uses a funding formula based on outcomes assessment to fund programs (see Cozzens, 2007). In addition venture capitalist and "angel investors" also increasingly become an important new partner or "stakeholder" in the production and distribution of knowledge.

In the new knowledge organization professors are also increasingly judged by either the ability to produce applicable products or to generate grants that hold the likelihood of producing product patents and licenses.

For instance, with the emergence of "strong evaluation systems" (see Cozzens, 2007) such as the Research Assessment Exercise (RAE) in the United Kingdom, the Research Quality Framework (RQF) in Australia (which was replaced in 2010 with The Excellence in Research for Australia Initiative, ERA), and the Performance Based Research Fund (PBRF) in New Zealand, as well as other similar neoliberal-inspired exercises found around the world, part of the research funding of departments and universities directly tied to the publication and grant-receiving performances of their professors. This directly links productivity to funding and, in turn, generates greater competition between departments and universities. However, more recently these performance-based mechanisms have begun to move away from simple "output measures" to ones that more closely examine "impact."

While these assessments have been controversial and results mixed, at best, even proponents have noted the changes they have made in the orientation of university research.[2] Even if we set aside what Merton (1968b) famously dubbed the "Matthew Effect" in science, evidence from New Zealand and the U.K. suggests that these types of performance-based funding scenarios have created a series of "adaptive mechanisms" (see Glaser and Laudel, 2007) at the university level and have altered, in many but not all cases, the type of inquiry that professor and researchers are willing to undertake and publish.[3] For instance Talib (2001: 42) studied changes in the behavior of academics since the 1992 RAE in England found that academics were "increasingly choosing research topics based on RAE panel members' preferences" and that "more academics seem to avoid speculative research and also publish at an earlier state than they would have preferred." As could be expected, he also found that more academics were "giving less time to activities given no recognition by RAE" (Talib, 2001: 43). Similar outcomes have been found in Australia where Glaser and Laudel (2007: 142) found an "adaption to indicators" resulting from its assessment exercise. In this "economy of the same" research "becomes more applied, approximates the mainstream, narrows and its results become less reliable (less rigorously tested)" (Glaser and Laudel, 2007: 146). Interestingly, the study also found that by narrowing the focus of research and intensifying competition between researchers the assessment exercise may have ironically reduced the "docking points" available for research collaboration, hence, further reducing the ability to generate novel integrated research projects (Glaser and Laudel, 2007: 146). Also, the costs of administering the various research assessment exercises, with their army of evaluators and reams of data, seem to outweigh their supposed benefits (see Hicks, 2008).

The alterations of the academic organization and behavior created by these various exercises seem to happen in several ways, some overt and others more subtle. First, since evaluation committees must employ an "economy of logic" in order to complete their review of all the pertinent documents they must reduce the complexity of judgment to easily countable items, much like the effects of standardized testing movement on pedagogy. As a result they are more likely to value certain kinds and presentations of knowledge over others. In this case the research article with its compactness and established and quantified pecking order of journals and citation indexes becomes preferable over other forms of presentation, such as the monograph. This has the effect of disadvantaging fields where the monograph or a small number of quality papers are the normal mode of publication (see Marginson and Considine, 2000: 168). In addition, articles published in high status journals are given substantially higher scores than those published in lower status journals. This obviously greatly increases submission to these journals and magnifies their particular line of research and the perspective of established researchers. In the field of management, for instances, another study in the U.K. found that the RAE had altered the focus of research by creating a myopic focus in much of management and organizational studies (Dunne et al., 2008). So while the volume of submissions increase the spectrum of what constitutes good and worthwhile endeavors seems to narrow.

In Mode I conditions of knowledge production, the narrative of reason and the "emancipation of the human spirit" legitimated the production of most public knowledge. In Mode II, however, knowledge is guided almost exclusively by the "metanarrative of performativity" (Lyotard, 1984). Under Mode I a knowledge form could exist simply because of the epistemic contours and the strength of the profession supporting a knowledge form. Under Mode II, however, knowledge must perform a service for some type of paying client or the state or market (or the market-state nexus) in order to have validity. Knowledge, now, must "be useful to someone whether in industry or government, or society more generally" (Gibbons et al., 1994: 4). As this shifting of modes has occurred the traditional rallying cries of "collegiality," "academic freedom " and the "pursuit of truth" have been replaced with "accountability," "efficiency," and "research output" (see Dollery et al., 2006: 86).

Such a rearrangement of knowledge production also influences the way knowledge is delivered and who delivers it at all levels of education. Since in the new system knowledge only has a performative rather than a transformative value, there is no need for anyone to possess a "knowledge base" or an overarching body of knowledge. Knowledge, then, can simply be applied by a new class of "educational technicians" (formerly known as teachers) who are trained in the techniques of delivery but not the content of knowledge, as is the case with the new model of teacher education reform now being promoted in the U.S.. These knowledge workers essentially "act as technicians or functionaries" (Derby et al., 1990: 136) rather than reflexive professionals. The specific content they will deliver will be produced somewhere "above" the teaching ranks by "curriculum specialists" or "knowledge companies," then purchased and provided as needed to the education practitioners who will then execute the knowledge.[4] Once delivered to these knowledge consumers in their particular knowledge segments, state-mandated and -directed assessment techniques can swoop in and gauge the success of their delivery by the teaching technicians and the degree of "uptake" by particular knowledge consumers. In this setting, education becomes a stratified commodity with stratified suppliers providing varying items of quality for different marketing niches and class segments, much like the division between consumers who shop at Neiman Marcus or Wal-Mart.

Just as the production of knowledge has increasingly become reduced to formula and marketable bits of information, education also becomes condensed and reified into a series of things "that students should know" as found in standardized testing, company-produced curricula, "teaching platforms" and various student assessment exercises generated by the "metrics enterprise" (Brooks, 2011: 12). Here a profound distrust of both the ability of students to properly learn and teachers to teach have created "scripted lessons" that are designed to be "teacher proof" (see Saltman, 2006: 352). As a consequence, a "mutual instrumentality" (Pollard et al., 2000: 290) has emerged where formulistic knowledge has led to formulistic delivery and assessment by teachers, which, in turn, has led to formulistic learning by students.[5] For example, in standardized testing a student produces a score that then can be used to both measure the student's worth to and place in the quasi-market of the school and eventually the larger global economic marketplace. Standardized testing also serves to assess the amount of knowledge that was imparted by a particular school or teacher. With such a system in place, individual students can be ranked and sorted into appropriate slots for further education, remediation or employment. In addition, schools can be ranked and sorted into league tables for the expansion or retraction of funding, and teachers can be sorted for merit raises, retraining or dismissal. Like the commissioned salesperson who lives by the amount of units sold, the entrepreneurial knowledge model produces teachers, students and schools whose only marker of success is the degree to which test scores increase. Likewise the "curriculum packets" or "platforms" sold to increasingly standardized schools by such companies as Scholastic, American Education Corporation or Blackboard provide the structure and content for a prefabricated curriculum to this group of increasingly deprofessionalized, deskilled and marginalized teachers whose jobs have increasingly become about the effective delivery of standardized information through standardized pedagogical techniques.[6] With a new labor model in place that seeks to lower the cost of knowledge production and dissemination, cheaper, less-skilled knowledge workers can be used to deliver the increasingly standardized curricular goods. In this case, standardization allows for the easy substitution, flexibilization and deskilling of knowledge professionals as has historically occurred in other occupations (see Braverman, 1974).

Another outcome of the organizational transformation of knowledge that is underway can also be found in the changing production of scholarly books and academic journals over the past few decades. In the past, university presses and professional journals were a central means through which scholarly ideas were disseminated. Under Mode I conditions university presses were funded by the larger university which moved money from some units to others in order to support what was seen as one of the vital missions of a university—to produce high quality, peer-reviewed knowledge regardless of its popularity or marketability (see Clawson, 1997; Thompson, 2005). This resembled the way in which money in a university might be moved from a popular program to support a less popular one if that knowledge was deemed important and indispensible for a university education. This can be seen as a type of "socialization of responsibility," seen in areas such as socialized medicine, pension funds or social security, where costs are spread across a broad population in order to create a larger social benefit rather than individualizing it in people and departments.

With the introduction of "user pays," "financial accountability" and "responsibility centered management," this "cost sharing" has changed (see Thompson, 2005: 108–109). Under the principles of performativity each unit of the university is required to "pay its own way," including university presses and departments with lower enrollments. In this new scenario works or bodies of knowledge that can't identify a clear audience, "distinguish themselves in the marketplace of ideas," as is the case with publishing, or promise wide dissemination in the lucrative library, online and secondary sales markets risk being rejected outright (see James and McQueen-Thomson, 2002). University presses thus begin to become indistinguishable from private ones, except maybe for where their main offices are located.[7] Indeed, in this new arrangement, private universities often become the preservers of less popular fields and knowledge domains primarily because of their endowments or religious-based missions and their positioning away from the neoliberal state's economizing and practicalizing pressures while, in contrast, state-funded universities are further directed toward the dictates of the state-supported marketplace. The endowments and status prestige of private, "Ivy League" universities, such as those in the U.S. context or the elite publicly funded sandstones and Oxbridges in the Australian or British contexts, allow for the preservation of older academic norms than are increasingly impossible in most publically funded universities.

FROM SCHOLARS TO KNOWLEDGE WORKERS: THE END OF THE AGE OF THE PROFESSOR?

As knowledge-producing and -disseminating organizations have changed so too have the so-called knowledge workers who inhabit them. Indeed, even the concept of a "knowledge worker" as opposed to that of a scholar, professor, academic or researcher signals both a shift in how knowledge makers are positioned and perceived and the proliferation of the places where knowledge can now be produced. Under the historical metanarratives of reason and culture prevalent under Mode I knowledge production, the professor held a particularly powerful and relatively independent position with regard to knowledge production and dissemination. They were the source of knowledge making, and administrators, who were often drawn from these ranks, were in place to ensure that the conditions of knowledge making and dissemination were protected. Under contemporary neoliberal notions of performativity, however, the position and power of the professor has been seriously eroded while that of the administrator has greatly expanded.

Although neoliberals have advocated for knowledge economy and society policies that emphasize the importance of knowledge to economic development, knowledge's marketability can't be fully realized until certain efficiencies are introduced into the knowledge-making system. Simply put, knowledge, like a range of other commodities, has become much too expensive to make and distribute under neoliberal standards of efficiency. Furthermore, knowledge has not fully entered the profit-generating private domain where it could more directly impact the economy and expand wealth. In order for this to happen, knowledge makers too need to be placed under the labor compressing, rationalizing and casualizing effects of market mechanisms. For this to happen, knowledge making and dissemination first need to be brought under a managerial efficiency and accountability regime, such as new public management, that is capable of reducing their costs. This requires a thorough transformation of not only the organizational conditions under which knowledge is made but also a "desocialization" of academic culture and a reconstitution of those who make it through the formation of a new, more individualistic and competitive culture of knowledge making.

As we saw earlier, in the neoliberal schema, knowledge is no longer something that happens only in universities. It is now more "social distributed" and can be made equally well, at least in the performative and quantitative sense, in think tanks, the private laboratories of biotech firms and government labs, as well as a host of newly crafted liminal public/private spaces. This being the case, university professors and teachers are simply just one form of knowledge worker performing one particular type of knowledge work in one particular knowledge-making environment. Indeed, depending on the classification system used, knowledge work is now the largest segment of workers in the newly formed knowledge societies and traditional university professors and researchers are but one segment of those knowledge workers. As a result they are no longer thought of as a Manheimian *freischwebende Intelligenz* who possess the professionally based, expert monopoly over a particular domain of knowledge as found in the Kantian and Humboldtian models of the university (see Baert and Shipman, 2005: 159).

Historically universities have always contained a variety of individuals motivated by various things, including professionalism, progressive change, *bildung*, and yes even power and money. While neoliberalism may not be responsible for creating the latter two motivations, it has been responsible for making them more rewarded and hence more pronounced. This has contributed to the growth of a new, much more entrepreneurial model of academic culture and knowledge producers. As Steve Shapin (2008: 209) describes the advent of this new breed of scientific entrepreneurs, "By about the 1970s, it had become common to think that to be a scientist was to do a job much like any other professional job and that scientists were morally and motivationally pretty much the same as anybody else with their backgrounds and in their station of society." These new entrepreneurially oriented professors or "practitioner professors" who are often more oriented toward the promotion of their own profession rather than contributing to a larger community of inquiry have begun to "crowd out" or overshadow the space previously occupied by traditional professors with their emphasis on teaching and research (Symes, 2000).

This erosion of the status of traditional professors resembles that faced by public officials whose public calling, according to public interest theory, is just another word for their "private interest." This status deflation also parallels and is fueled by the greatest massification of education in history. This massification and the permeation of the boundary of expert and non-expert and basic and applied knowledge allows various groups to produce their own knowledge and "speak back" to the official knowledge emanating from universities (Nowotny et al., 2001). As Usher (2000: 106) describes it, "anything, anywhere is now potentially researchable by a wide variety of knowledge producers no longer accountable solely to the gatekeepers and epistemological policing of disciplinary communities." As this happens the opinions and judgments of professors or experts in general come to be on par with and indistinguishable from those of other knowledge makers or even bloggers or TV pundits—everyone is just selling their knowledge wares. Such an occurrence undermines the university as a "well defined territory" with its "own specialized goals" (Henkel, 2007: 91) and with it the professional power of knowledge producers and the epistemic and social magnitude of their truth claims.

For neoliberal reformers, traditional university professors represent the "old guard" of the new dispersed knowledge labor force. With their bureaucratic encapsulation, life-long employment and protection through tenure, and politically engaged organizational involvement through shared governance, they were able to encase themselves in numerous layers of job protection. This protection afforded them the luxury of being shielded from the demands and efficiencies of market forces. While other occupations have had to respond to the demands of the market, academics have seldom noticed the shifting political economy under their feet. Indeed, under Mode I organization such isolation was deemed necessary and desirable for creating the conditions of creativity and of maintaining the integrity of knowledge—of producing novel, accurate and unbiased knowledge. Despite this protection, they are from the neoliberal vantage point the slow, aging and expensive knowledge dinosaurs in an age of increasingly fast and mobile capital, "fast knowledge" and cheap labor. Indeed, tenure, the protection so important for maintaining the independence and power of knowledge producers under Mode I production, is seen in this new light as analogous to the guaranteed job security or union protection afforded other workers in other areas—as something no longer tenable in the post-Fordist age of efficiency, mobility and flexibility. Professors' standing and pay were made possible by both their virtual monopoly over knowledge production and dissemination and their lack of outside accountability—both of which must now come to an end under neoliberal directives. This combined with "delegitmation and the predominance of the performance criterion are sounding the knell of the age of the Professor" (Lyotard, 1984: 53).

As with the management of other workers a central concern for new knowledge managers is determining what strategies can be used to make knowledge workers work cheaper and be more productive and efficient. One means to cheaper knowledge production, as in other areas, is through the casualization of work and workers. This casualization of knowledge work means in part that knowledge work is now carried out, not just by the diminishing numbers of traditional permanent and full-time academics, but also by a slew of newer forms of flexible and increasing expendable knowledge workers. These new knowledge workers appear in the form of contingent or part-time faculty, research assistants, limited-term appointments, "non-tenure stream" faculty, laboratory technicians, graduate students, "soft money" grant workers, post docs and other "supporting" or secondary knowledge workers. These divisions of knowledge workers "mirror the differential skill/status levels of post-Fordist work" (Ozga, 1998: 44) with its various layers and modes of flexibility. Much like the labor market segmentation and flexibilization evident in other professions, such as medicine or pharmacy, that created a diminishing core of relatively well paid professionals and an increasing periphery of lower paid wage earners, knowledge work has become segmented into its own categories, layers and wage structures. In some places, such as regional state universities in the U.S., this labor market segmentation has become so pronounced that it now threatens the core itself; thereby reversing both the meaning of and relationship between the core and periphery labor market. For instance, in many U.S. universities these new secondary knowledge workers now make up the majority of academics and are responsible for the majority of the knowledge dissemination and a growing segment of the normal, day-to-day research taking place. This new layer is often overseen by core knowledge workers who now increasingly take on the role of line managers rather than colleagues. This makes it both difficult to tell who is actually in the core or periphery and, as we saw in Chapter 2, has transformed the managed into the managers. This confusion spreads to outside the university where the public and students are unable to recognize any differences residing in these groups and their respective levels of expertise. For instance, students rarely know the position of the individual delivering the knowledge they are now "consuming."

The new model of the academic that is emerging in the wake of this transformation of the role of professor is one of a grant driven, "piece worker" or "project manager" who lives and dies under a "limited-term contract" made possible by the presence of "soft money." This new type of contingent knowledge worker must live by individual entrepreneurial cunningness and agility rather than the protections afforded by tenure or bureaucratic encapsulation in the university (see Marvizon, 2008). Much like the replacement of the "old line" workers in the new global economy with flexible and temporary workers, the newly inaugurated knowledge worker must be flexible, clever and agile enough to be able to quickly change his or her research agenda to stay abreast of the latest, grant-funded research fashion or research that holds the greatest promise for technology transfer or is likely to gain the attention of venture capitalists. The value of this type of worker is to be measured by his or her "degree of activity, ability to adapt, flexibility and mobility" (Burtscher et al., 2006: 249). Under this performative model projects that are long term or hold little potential "yield" are to be shied away from because their market costs are simply too high. Such a system, therefore, discourages working on projects with "deviant goals with unorthodox methods" (Whitley, 2007: 16). Consequently, despite the often used adventurous rhetoric of the entrepreneur that proponents use to promote these changes, in the end "playing it safe" comes to the most prudent form of academic behavior under these circumstances. As a former Dean of Graduate School of Arts and Sciences at Emory University describes this situation,

> Both young and more seasoned faculty members know that the reward structure of the university often favors those who bring in cash. . . . leading to competition rather than collegiality, paperwork rather than productivity, and increasing pressure to do what will sell rather than what is intellectually stimulating, innovative, and important to teach and learn. (Stein, 2004: 3)

This incentivization and entrepreneurialization lead knowledge workers to, in essence, "capitalize knowledge" (Collins and Tillman, 1988). Here researchers and professors must continually "find ways for research to generate income as well as more knowledge" (McSherry, 2001: 33). This creates a new type of knowledge work steering or management—one already in evidence to some degree with the increased competition for tenure generated by fewer and fewer tenure track jobs—where research and scholarship must first and foremost be based on "potential yield" rather than determined by the inner vicissitudes of the discipline. Likewise, things that may distract from this work intensification, such as informal discussions with colleagues or long term and exploratory projects, are shelved or pushed off for the increasingly rare full professor years which are themselves brought under increasing pressure with the expansion of "post tenure review." In this setting a new production of behaviors ensues where academics must "begin to think like entrepreneurs" (Marginson, 1994: 19). Here incentives are put into place to entice through monetary rewards, such as shares of patents rights or merit pay, to enhance status competition and to generate fear through feelings of inadequacy, failure or unemployment. The central outcome of this entrepreneurialization of research is that "the more a researcher depends on external sources of funding, the less autonomous he or she is when choosing a problem to study" (Lamont, 2009: 11). For example, Sehnhav's (1986: 29) study of this process in Israel found that externally funded research had a "low degree of autonomy, a high degree of structural formalization, and low influence of the scientific literature on problem-choice." This finding is supported by a long line of classic research on the effects of various sources of funding on different sciences (see Ezrahi, 1971; Blume, 1974; Barnes and Edge, 1982; Useem, 1976).

These changes in the way research is conducted also signal a switch from a more bureaucratic and professional model of accountability and trust to a consumer and managerial model (see Olssen and Peters, 2005: 328). Under bureaucratic professionalism, accountability was "measured in terms of process; formulated in terms of standards, based on expertise of those who work in a particular area" (Olssen and Peters, 2005: 328). However, in the more consumer model, accountability is based more on market systems that reward or punish based on "pre-set market targets" (Olssen and Peters, 2005: 328). These changes are also responsible for fundamental remolding the traditional career structures of the knowledge-making professionals from one defined by "craft or skill, with monopolization of socially valued knowledge" (Kanter, 1989: 510) to an entrepreneurial career model "in which the growth occurs through the creation of new value or new organizational capacity" (Kanter, 1989: 516). With this come a shift from the "university scholar schooled in a discipline, a member of a distinct status group pursing its own interests, to that of the modern project manager—the (usually male) achievement-oriented subject whose actions have an almost imperial quality, namely the forging of alliances and reputation in order to land lucrative and prestigious research projects" (Burstscher et al., 2006: 249). As this happens "a life- and work-style previously associated only with academic superstars has become a generalized expectation and measure of success" (Burtscher et al., 2006: 249).

As with the transformation of other forms of work, neoliberal reformers contend that the creation of the new work environment for academia and academics is but an inevitability placed on universities by the demands of the new economy, limited state budget and the public's demand for transparency and the desire to keep costs and taxes under control. By altering and expanding the knowledge labor force and by creating new forms of knowledge work, neoliberal policies are helping forge a cost efficient and rational knowledge production and dissemination system just as they have done in other industries and areas of the public sector. Much like the old industries of steel and automobiles that were forced to undergo "creative destruction" and reorganization in order to reborn in new, flexible and cheaper forms, knowledge organizations too need retooling and public knowledge workers need to become more flexible and much cheaper.

THE NEOLIBERAL CONDITION OF KNOWLEDGE: THE SHIFTING OF EPISTEMIC STYLES

Not only do knowledge organizations begin to look different and knowledge makers begin to act differently under neoliberal policies, knowledge itself begins to take on new forms. Jean-Francois Lyotard's (1984) *The Postmodern Condition: A Report on Knowledge,* written during the early turn toward neoliberal policies in Europe, was among the first works to outline what all these changes may mean for the way knowledge is practiced and enacted. In his prediction, "knowledge is and will be produced in order to be sold, it is and will be consumed in order to be valorized in a new production: In both cases, the goal is exchange. Knowledge ceases to be an end it itself, it loses its 'use value'" (Lyotard, 1984: 4–5). Yet, how specifically does the neoliberal reorganization of knowledge production and dissemination change the types of knowledge that can exist and the form it takes (see Gumport and Snydman, 2002)? For instances, under neoliberal policies does knowledge become more standardized, performative and rationalized? Do new knowledge hierarchies and power configuration emerge? Do some forms of knowledge or epistemic styles become privileged above others or maybe even die out altogether? And, at a more normative level, if knowledge indeed changes under these circumstances is this merely part of the inevitable "evolution of knowledge" or one directed to suit a political purpose?

The simplest and most straightforward way to begin to answer these complex questions is to first examine what types and styles of knowledge and epistemologies flourish under the structural conditions created by neoliberal policies and which do not. As part of this examination it is also important to note what epistemic standards and practices are compatible with these new conditions and which are not, either because they are too slow, superfluous or perhaps even critical. First of all, it is clear that some traditional forms of university-produced knowledge seem to thrive under neoliberal conditions, although their orientation has been significantly redirected. On the other hand, however, some traditional epistemic areas become malnourished or perhaps even starved. This differential treatment happens in somewhat subtle ways with the types and maintenance of facilities of the different knowledge areas and in much more overt forms with the gaining or loosing of faculty lines, the allocations for department budgets or in some cases the shutting down of departments or phasing out of programs altogether. The humanities seem to be a particularly problematic knowledge form in the new neoliberal knowledge schemata. While the "enabling sciences" (Bullen et al., 2004: 15), or STEM areas of science, technology, engineering and mathematics, can provide the items and techniques needed for technology transfer, although never as easily and straightforwardly as advocates perhaps have wished, and the social sciences, specifically economics, help support governmentality and the social control and management efforts of the state, the humanities are in a nebulous position under the new standards imposed by neoliberal policies. While seen as having some value in producing "critical thinking skills," national historical myths, "cultural capital" and marketable cultural products, such as works of music, fiction or plays, the humanities, particularly what we might call the theoretically based humanities, such as philosophy, the classics or literary criticism, or historical works that fall outside of the state's nationalist and governing agendas, are often viewed with suspicion or outright disdain in neoliberal circles. This reflects both their dubious marketability and also their inability to be easily simplified and made formulaic and transportable in the knowledge market. Such a view of the humanities was particularly evident in the 2003 statements of former British Education Secretary Charles Clarke when he described medieval history as an "ornamental" subject that should not be subsidized by the state (Woodward and Smithers, 2003: 7). Instead, the state should only pay for subjects with, what he described as, "clear usefulness." The purpose of universities was, according to a spokesperson for Clarke, "to enable the British economy and society to deal with the challenges posed by the increasingly rapid process of global change" (quoted in Woodward and Smithers, 2003: 7). Such a stance can also be found in American universities such as Michigan State which dropped its classics program and the Louisiana's Board of Regents decision who in the spring of 2009 voted to eliminate the philosophy major at the state's campuses in order to help make the universities more "effective and efficient" (Zernike, 2010: 17). A similar orientation can also be found throughout numerous knowledge society documents where the role of the humanities is rarely mentioned and in the instances when they are invoked in these reports, such as in writings on the "creative economy" (see Florida, 2002), it is usually to promote their ability to produce good technical writers, entertainment, cultural products for export or as part of a city's redevelopment strategy. In some instance, if the humanities are to continue on, they are expected to become increasing self-supporting much like public radio and television in the U.S. In doing so, the long-held "humanist principle that humanity rises up in dignity and freedom through knowledge is left by the wayside" (Lyotard, 1984: 34).

This same type of neoliberal "natural selection" of knowledge fields can also be observed in critical disciplines and critical sub-disciplines within fields as well as across them. As Newfield (2008: 209) describes it,

> .... disciplines that focus on basic skills, on the past, on difficultand controversial social and cultural domains, meaning fields like sociology, anthropology, history, literature, philosophy, music drama, classics, and linguistics, in short, studies of the whole spectrum of human life.... lost money, caused trouble, and were not seen as part of society's economic engine. When that engine faltered cultural study could be cast as an expensive luxury; resource should, in culture-war doctrine, be diverted to the rock face of technological innovation.

Simply put, in the neoliberal academy the notion has began to prevail in some circles of the administration that "technology makes money and culture loses it" (Newfield, 2008: 210). In this instance, fields that directly contribute to marketability or neoliberal-style governability, thrive at the expense of more theoretical, critical or speculative areas which have a considerably lower "exchange value" or direct convertibility. What would have been unthinkable in the Kantian and Humboldtian notions of the university, a university without critique and culture and void of disciplines such as philosophy or history, is, under neoliberal performativity, not only possible but also maybe desirable. After all "Humboldt is dead," as a former Germany minister for education, science, research and technology framed it (in Krucken, 2003: 325).

In contrast to the experiences of the humanities and some social sciences under the neoliberal knowledge regime, the bio- and technosciences or STEM areas have done particularly well, at least in terms of funding, facilities, new positions and support. During the period of neoliberalism's dominance spending on the biosciences increased dramatically, including the building of hundreds of new science buildings. The physical sciences that have a long history of government support also faired well under neoliberalism. However, some of the neoliberal-inspired reforms have created problems even for these fields. For example, under the Research Assessment Exercise in Britain departments that are expensive to operate, such as Chemistry, are often placed in the position of needing to score highly on the RAE or face shutdown.

While these changes in the orientation of knowledge introduced by neoliberal policies into academia are organizationally, economically and politically driven, the results are, nevertheless, deeply epistemic. They have helped generate a new "post-explanatory" style of knowledge or what Cooper (2002) refers to as "post-intellectuality." This style of knowledge sets aside and in some cases is even irritated by the so-called "big questions" of a more ponderous, critical or slow science or weighty political and social issues that can't be answered easily and quickly through pragmatic standards or by standardized positivistic methods. The foundational or so-called "big" questions that previously animated much of university life seem either as quaint holdovers from the past or as actual irritants to the practically minded and productive entrepreneurial university. Instead, the big questions are to be replaced with smaller, empirically narrower issues they are of a more immediate relevance to policy decision makers or companies. For instance, Slaughter and Leslie's (1997) comparative study of the advent of market-centered policies in four countries found a shift from "basic or curiosity-driven research to commercial or targeted or strategic." (Morey 2003: 79). In their interviews with faculty they found that

> with regard to altruism, professors engaged in academic capitalism were ambivalent. Although they still hoped their research would benefit humankind, they began to speak about research paying its own way ... merit was not longer defined as being acquired primarily through publication; rather it encompassed at least in part success with market and market-like activities. (Slaughter and Leslie, 1997: 21)

Such a reorientation of research and knowledge may lead to a type of "funding effect" that in some instances leads researchers to align conclusions with those that are in the interests of the funder (Bekelman et al., 2003). For example, a study conducted a few years after the introduction of Bayh-Dole (Blumenthal et al., 1986) found that 30 percent of faculty who received industrial support said that "commercial considerations" influenced their choices of projects compared with only 7 percent of those who did not receive such funding. Likewise, the same study found that faculty who received support from industry said that their research had resulted in trade secrets (see also, Kleinman and Vallas, 2001: 457). In addition, in one study, researchers examining the effects of private funding on university research found that about 50 percent of the time corporate sponsors of research reserve the right to withhold or block publications in order to preserve industry secrets that could be threatened by publicity (Thursby and Thursby, 2004). Indeed, under patent law ideas, procedures or techniques that are written about in a public forum such as a scientific journal may fall into the public domain and become unpatentable.[8]

Such changes generate an anti-reflexive, "matter of fact" pragmatism throughout the university and society-at-large. The "dereferentialization" of the university generates a type of "institutional pragmatism" where the university is no longer capable of making transcendental claims regarding its purpose (see Readings, 1996: 166–168). Its purpose is now clear and practical: to aid in the generation of products, economic growth and to provide an effective, flexible workforce. This matter of fact neoliberal "modal personality," if you will, that is not so much the affirmative and instrumentalist game player or abnegating escapist dreamer famously described by Max Weber in the early twentieth century (see Scaff, 1991) but more of a "so what" pragmatist that doesn't quite care for either option left open for the conduct of late modern life. In this situation, as Lyotard (1984: 41) defines it, "most people have lost the nostalgia for the lost narrative." They no longer care to be liberated or even an "informed citizen." They need marketable skills to exchange in the marketplace—nothing more. In the end, pragmatism's critique of philosophical idealism is finally represented in a social form. In this move, a new postmodern style of cynicism is born where anything not directly practical, productive or of consumptive value is deemed unworthy of much attention. Cynicism, or in some instances even a "vicious know-nothingism" (Brooks, 2011: 12), thus becomes "the norm of all action and behavior" (Bourdieu, 1998). This norm fits well with and in fact encourages and supports the standardization and marketization of education that has been introduced or intensified by neoliberal regimes. Here critical reflections that are not directly marketable or items that are not "on the test," so to speak, are neither sought after nor needed.

Such an epistemic reorientation has also created a unique style of "hurried empiricism" (Lyotard, 1984: 52) in which speed and sheer output volume are associated with increased rationality, productivity and truthfulness. This "hastening of science" alters knowledge production's uniquely constituted "timescape" (see Pels, 2003). As Pels (2003: 2) describes this traditional timescape, "compared with other professional pursuits such as journalism, politics or business management, science indulges in a typical delay and deferral of decisions about what the world is like, how to describe and explain it, and what to do about it." The speed at which knowledge is produced, particularly with the use of various information technologies, has increased dramatically over the last few decades. For example, the literature in chemistry increases by over a million articles every two years. Likewise, historians have produced more works since 1980 than in the history of the history profession (Morey, 2003: 73. As this hurried empiricism increases, as Simmel (1990) phrased it over a century ago, quantitative values are eroded and replace qualitative ones. Measurable units of speed and efficiency come to represent the new standards of academic performance.

Another epistemic outcome of the neoliberalization of knowledge has also involved a discrediting of not only traditional forms of knowledge as being contaminated by "interests" but an "interestization" of all knowledge and a questioning of the very idea of objective knowledge itself. As Marx first argued, in market based societies all things including social relations, labor and human psychology come to appear to always be interest driven and, hence, commodifiable. Even if our "better angels" prevail under certain circumstances they are envisioned in liberal and neoliberal theory as merely cultural apparitions that can only temporarily thwart people's adversarial nature or perhaps these angels are themselves merely interests in disguise. Under this arrangement universities and professors are as interest driven and untrustworthy as any other organization or profession. As such they are to be held in suspicion and their power checked. Such suspicion in combination with the performative criteria generates a series of new questions about academia and academic professions that were not prevalent in the past, such as "Do all academics work? Do they work effectively? Is what they do worthwhile? Or might they be using their privileged status to subvert the very same society that is feeding them? Do 'we taxpayers' have to keep supporting them, and if so, under which conditions?" (Baert and Shipman, 2005: 163).

In terms of varieties of knowledge certain braches of the sciences, such as chemistry and physics, have been relatively untouched by the interestization of knowledge, primarily because of their seemingly direct applicability and falsifiability. However, other fields, even some within the sciences, such as branches of biology concerned with population ecology, evolution and the environment sciences, have been opened to an ongoing criticisms and doubt about the credibility of their knowledge claims. Medical knowledge and the social sciences have been particularly affected by this suspicion. Since knowledge claims are seen as moves in a particular interest-driven language game or "power by other means," they have no larger functioning than providing and "covering over" particular interests and political maneuverings. In this sense, knowledge and information become leveled and all knowledge symmetricalized. University knowledge becomes indistinguishable from "talk show discourse" where various operatives state their case, argue and then walk away. Interestization, consequently, eventually generates relativism (see Jameson, 1991). Everyone is seen as existing within a particular political nexus and consumer "lifestyle niche" whose only validity occurs through the fact that it is allegedly freely chosen and practiced. In this context everyone can have their own bit of knowledge which they chose to legitimate their lifestyle niche made by their favorite knowledge producers, much like consumers have their favorite line of clothing or shoes.

With this, "truth" fades into "perspective." As the location of knowledge production spread and the public-regarding and -defending notion of knowledge declined, the idea that the university is a center of unbiased knowledge and the objective pursuit of truth is too on the wane. Indeed, the varied location of knowledge production in both private and public settings and the emergence of "hybrid communities" (Henkel, 2007: 90) that combine basic and applied knowledge confuses the traditional boundary between a type of knowledge that is "interested" and promotional and one that is not. In this organizationally pluralistic, "multiple epistemic" or "multiparadigmatic" setting, every knowledge-producing group seems to have "an angle," "a bias" or "a perspective" from which they collect their own data and spin their interpretations. In such a "hyperreal" environment, in Jean Baudrillard's (1983) famous description, it becomes increasing difficult to distinguish between the "spin documents" and "talking points" of think tanks or the public relations spokespersons of pharmaceutical laboratories and the pronouncements of traditional, university based experts or researchers. Under the interestization of all things created by neoliberal knowledge conditions "not-for-profit" knowledge begins to look and sound the same as that produced under the profit motive. In this case, it is the organizational plurality of knowledge making and the corresponding end of the university and professional monopoly over knowledge that generates perspectivism and epistemic uncertainty. This reign of perspectivism or the "postmodernization of knowledge" is, consequently, not simply the result of some cultural evolution of knowledge as found in the exhaustion of Western metanarratives of truth or the rise of multicultural or postcolonial critiques of European logocentrism as cultural theorists have argued but the outcome of a new political and economic regime under which knowledge is increasingly produced and spread.

While changes in private knowledge production in think tanks and corporations over the last few decades have made this type of knowledge look and sound like university-produced knowledge, university-produced knowledge has itself also begun to look and sound much more promotional and entrepreneurial. Thanks in part to the withdrawal of public monies to support knowledge production in universities, its knowledge must now take on the very same promotional and marketing strategies found in product promotion in the marketplace, including sophisticated media relations, sponsorship, spin off products and "for pay" types of exhibits, such as found with the Ida exhibit in New York.[9] In the new entrepreneurial model, it is the particular style of knowledge that can enlist a paying audience and that can, consequently, generate a market that will survive. Here a new pop and promotional science becomes the model of what good, self-supporting, pseudo-event, market-based science looks like. Good, consumer friendly knowledge requires marketing and a public relations "buzz" like the proper promotion of any other product.

The neoliberal push for efficiencies has also helped change the very form knowledge now takes. As Georg Simmel (1990) pointed out in *The Philosophy of Money*, one of the features of a market society is the transformation of amorphous and ill-defined qualitative characteristics into precise, concrete and measurable quantitative ones. Much as the advent of the monied economy allowed goods to be rationalized and made more mobile and transportable, contemporary knowledge is also being rationalized and made more transportable through its transformation into formula and through its digitization (see Striphas, 2009). Knowledge that is slow, cumbersome, laborious and overly "complex" to create or "store" can't easily be "disaggregated," packaged and transported in order to enter the marketplace where, according to neoliberal principles, its value and usefulness can be determined. Consequently, just as market economies create precise and standardized measurements and calculations of time, amount, distance and weight in order to function more efficiently as exchange mechanisms, knowledge too is undergoing its own unique version of rationalization and standardization in order to be more effectively and efficiently exchanged in a marketplace. In order to be transportable and moveable within an increasing fast-paced marketplace, knowledge that can be reduced to a formulistic application is faster and, consequently, better by the prevailing standards of performativity than that which cannot be easily reduced in this manner—much like the formulaic development and application of pop music. In such a setting, it becomes possible to talk about the "velocity of knowledge" in the same way that economists talk about the "velocity of money." Knowledge, like inventory control management in an automobile plant, can be converted into "just-in-time" for particular knowledge consumers to fill what Lyotard (1984: 50) referred to as their "memory banks." As a result the new flexible and speedy knowledge, like movies on cable television or internet, can be presented "on demand" and "as needed." Formula increases the speed at which knowledge can be produced thus fulfilling both neoliberal expectations and the requirements of the various academic audits that measure performance by research productivity and the market's needs for quickly produced, "relevant" and disposable knowledge. As this occurs, "knowledge and its acquisition are increasingly valued in instrumental terms, and understood not as the discovery of truths so much as regulated practices and the exercise, at different levels of cognitive skills" (Henkel, 2007: 90). Users are now able to use technology in order to "stock more information, to improve their competence and optimize their performances" (Lyotard, 1993: 62).

Second, not only is the speed of knowledge production and dissemination greatly increased through knowledge's transformation into formula and technique, the actually form in which knowledge is displayed and distributed has been undergoing a significant transformation as well. In this Googleization of knowledge, as we might call it, knowledge is both disaggregated and digitized in order to turn it into easily transportable and quickly sellable bits of information. In essence, digitization is to the new knowledge economy what automation was to the industrial one. Digitization allows knowledge to be broken into segments and sold "by the piece," "on demand" and "as needed" rather than in its bulkier, older, slower and less transportable form. It creates what Lyotard (1991) referred to as the "streaming of culture." This streaming makes knowledge more readily available and, hence, more immediately marketable and generally more "consumer friendly." As this Googleization proceeds, knowledge is reduced to sellable "bundles" of easily transmittable information or "micro-excerpts" as G. Pascal Zachary (2009) refers to them. These bundles enable knowledge to be disaggregated by being broken into individual chapters, paragraphs and even sentences to be sold. This creates an epistemic sorting system that threatens the survival of those works "best suited for book treatment, sustained criticism and analysis; imaginative long-form writing; and the patient unraveling of the mystery of how things work (and why things fall apart)" (Zachary, 2009: B4). Critics charge that much like newspapers or TV news have been replaced by abbreviated websites, tabloid news or sounds bites, knowledge under these new conditions risks being reduced to easily digestible bits of information or "knowledge stones," as Nietzsche called them.

In the broader informational context, the ongoing Googleization of knowledge can be seen as analogous to what happened with the conversion of analog music into digital MP3 files. Beginning in the early 2000 with the advent of sites such as Napster and Apple's iTunes music could be purchased and downloaded online. iTunes subsequently required that musicians "disaggregate" their music by agreeing to allow their music to be purchased "by the song" instead of in an entire album or CD form. With regard to knowledge, this digitization enables a company such as Google, Amazon or individual publishers to engage in a hyper-marketization by selling individual chapters or journal articles or to identify individual pages with the needed information. This, in combination with simple word searching and "text mining" capabilities and technologies, such as portable digital readers such as Kindle or the iPad, enable the further disaggregation of a text into smaller, individually marketable components. This move enables knowledge workers to be faster and more productive since they only need to focus on the specific bits of information that are relevant for their particular "knowledge project" rather than engaging in a time-consuming consideration of the work as a whole. It also allows successful works to be more quickly imitated and copied. In the end the market benefits from this digitization because knowledge has become streamlined, rationalized and better managed and like the music on iTunes or the movies on Netflix, "available on demand."

5 Creating the "Clever Country"
Neoliberalism, Knowledge Society Policies and the Restructuring of Higher Education

> People are born with talent and everywhere it is in chains. Fail to develop the talents of any one person, we fail Britain. Talent is 21st century wealth. (Blair, 1999)

> Knowledge Society. n. What advanced capitalism looks like to intellectuals, once they have been assimilated into its mode of production. (Fuller, 2000: 83)

> The great scientific revolution is yet to come . . . it will ensue when men collectively and cooperatively organize their knowledge for application to achieve and make secure social values. (Dewey, 1998: 3)

> The generalisation of public education makes it possible to recruit this line of laborers from classes that had formerly no access to such education and that were accustomed to a lower scale of living. At the same time this generalisation of education increases the supply and thus competition. With a few exceptions, the labor-power of this line of laborers is therefore depreciated with the progress of capitalist development. The wages fall, while their ability increases. (Marx 1967: 354)

From corporate boardrooms to government office buildings to the laboratories of science parks and universities, "innovation" has become one of the most ubiquitous and lauded terms of the last few decades. In theses places, as well as a score of others, a relatively simple, neoliberal inspired formula has often been applied to highlight the importance of innovation to both the economy and society-at-large. In this formula, increases in knowledge, particularly techno- and bioscientific knowledge, is said to lead to more product innovation and entrepreneurialism which, in turn, will drive new forms of consumption and augment profits for companies and stockholders. This process will culminate in economic growth, lower unemployment rates, better paying jobs and a higher standard of living for all. In this economic formula knowledge becomes the newest form of capital and entrepreneurialism and innovation became the mechanisms through which economies and nations are led from the gritty and scarcity prone smokestack economies of the past into a rosy, cleaner and abundant post-industrial future. This future will be marked not by the control of raw materials or labor, as in the old industrial system, but by the creation, utilization and management of knowledge. This will generate a situation where individual freedom, innovation and creativity are finally and forever freed from the "dead hand" of the industrial or state bureaucracy.

Going by such epochal names as "the information society," "the knowledge society, " "knowledge capitalism" or "the learning society," this new social form became in many nations the *fine de siècle* utopian vision of the late twentieth and early twentieth-first centuries and signaled the dawn of what some referred to as the new "knowledge century." The father of modern management, and one of the early theoreticians and promoters of the formation of this new knowledge society, Peter Drucker (1993: 8), went so far as to describe this new social form as a "post-capitalist society" where "the basic economic resource—'the means of production,' to use the economist's term—is no longer capital, nor natural resources (the economist's land), nor labor. It is and will be knowledge."[1]

Making this knowledge society come to fruition has been the expressed mission of number of political actors and parties in national and local governments, various international organizations and transnational policy networks over the last few decades. These groups, ranging from the World Bank to the European Union to the OECD, have promoted the knowledge society as a bold new frontier where flexible and well-educated knowledge workers produce smartly and efficiently while continually creating innovative new products to fuel the marketplace and profit making. "The knowledge economy conjures a world of smart people, in smart jobs, doing smart things, in smart ways for smart money, increasingly open to all rather than a few" (Brown and Hesketh, 2004: 1). All these happy knowledge workers producing all these new cell phones and pharmaceuticals then become happy consumers who, thanks to all the wealth generated by the innovations of the new knowledge-based economy, flock to new "consumer super-hubs" to buy new gadgets and drugs of their own to make their lives happier, more efficient and more fulfilling. This cycle of "endogenous growth" (Romer, 1990) repeats itself, proliferates and magnifies until the whole world benefits as the raising tide of "wealth through innovation" causes everyone everywhere to experience dramatic increases in their standard of living and ability to consume. In this new growth system "the action of knowledge upon knowledge" is to become "the main source of productivity" (Castells, 1996). Nation states, regions, cities, institutions and individuals who fail to embrace and act upon this new roll knowledge is now called upon to play risk impoverishment, lack of competitiveness and obsolescence in the world economy. Bluntly put, those places that learn how to effectively create innovation systems that utilize knowledge effectively will become the wealth machines of the new global economy, while those who don't will provide their labor power and wait-staff.

Universities occupy a particularly special place in this new economic configuration and the creation of these new national, regional and city-based "innovation systems." Knowledge society proponents envision universities as the engines of economic growth. They are to become essentially what the "coal mines were to the industrial economy" (Castells and Hall, 1994: 231). They are to do this by providing the new epistemic materials for post-industrial production, by becoming the setting for entrepreneurial innovation, business incubation and technology transfer and by providing a well-trained and flexible labor force that can continuously be retrained with useful skills as economic conditions and the needs of corporations change. However, if knowledge is to become the centerpiece for such a radical new social order and economic form then universities must, like the smokestack industries that the knowledge economy is supposed to be replacing, be significantly retooled and reorganized themselves. They too must undergo a creative destruction of their own kind where older and unproductive strategies of a by-gone era are dismantled and reconfigured. In this retooling, universities must be streamlined, remolded and remade by the forces of the market in order to become more rationally organized, economically responsive, "accountable," and to produce economically useful products. Otherwise, they too risk becoming obsolete. This "last reformation" of the university, as Robert Nisbet (1971) described it in the early 1970s, requires that the state actively work to remake public universities to serve as what an OECD (2002: 13, 55) report described as "catalysts and organizers" of innovative "knowledge flows" between universities and the market. To make this happen universities must be redirected to serve the interests of the national, regional or local economy rather than following their own independent pathways.

This chapter examines the connection between neoliberal-inspired knowledge society policies and various university reform efforts that have occurred over the last few decades around the world. The first section of the chapter traces the early history of science policy that began to take shape during the 1930s, principally in the contexts of the U.S. and the U.K. This section explores how the tension between liberal and socialist learning politics found in the creation of early science policies set the stage for the knowledge society and economy policies that would first begin to emerge in Europe and the United States in the 1960s and would later become a catalyst for university reform. The second section of the chapter looks at how the conceptualization of the knowledge society that emerged during this time became linked through a network of "global policy flows" with the neoliberal politics of the 1980s and 1990s. It is here that the particular ideas of harnessing knowledge more directly for production become intertwined with neoliberal politics. The third subsection examines how these latter knowledge policies have shown up in a few specific national tertiary policies and reform efforts, such as those found in the Spellings Commission in the U.S., the development of the Research Assessment Exercise and the Dearing Report in United Kingdom, the Dawkins reforms in Australia and the European Union's "Lisbon Strategy" and "Bologna Process." I conclude the chapter with a discussion of how knowledge society policies are influencing the making of a market of and for higher education.

THE "REPUBLIC OF SCIENCE" OR "SCIENCE FOR THE PEOPLE"? EARLY SCIENCE POLICY IN THE U.S. AND THE U.K.

Under what social and political conditions does knowledge become a regulated activity in need of a "policy?" In the U.S. the idea of directly linking national aspirations of the state with the control of knowledge is quite old. Indeed, Alexis de Tocqueville (1847: 53) worried in the early part of the nineteenth century about how in the U.S. "a science is taken up as a matter of business and the only branch of it which is attended to is such as admits of an immediate practical application." In the U.S. some of the specific links are traceable to the nineteenth century with the founding of such groups as the National Institute for the Promotion of Science in 1840, housed in the U.S. Patent Office, and later the agricultural extension offices created in the Hatch Act of 1887 and also in the founding of MIT in 1861. However, the idea of creating and coordinating specific governmental policies to guide knowledge making in general was primarily a product of the second two-thirds of the twentieth century. As we saw in Chapter 3, prior to World War II the linkage between government, foundations, industry and knowledge-making institutions was clearly evident; however, it was generally topically limited, highly localized and relatively uncoordinated. During this period there was a strong division of epistemic labor in which governments performed applied, socially beneficial research in areas such as geological mapping, civil engineering and conservation; large industrial laboratories, such those that emerged at DuPont and General Electric in the early twentieth century, performed research that was most likely to yield industrial products and profits and universities conducted the bulk of what came to be called "basic science." In this model of dispersed knowledge making university-produced knowledge was relatively independent of both the state and market. University-produced knowledge was most often funded either by the university itself as part of its overall mission and purpose or through various private research and philanthropic foundations. When direct knowledge transfer happened, such as in the cases of the foundations at the University of Wisconsin or MIT, it was often on a relatively small scale. In addition, prior to this timeframe the structural and ideological conditions for knowledge to be directly transferred from universities to either state or market were simply not present. In this instance, knowledge partially because of its political insularity could not easily move about. Also, generally speaking, university produced knowledge was simply not seen as a vital economic commodity or administrative tool nor were specific organizational mechanism in place to transfer it out of the university in the first place.

Sustained efforts to change this arrangement began to appear in the both the U.S. and the U.K. in the 1930s. In the U.S. the progressive politics of the early part of the twentieth century was responsible for creating what came to be called a "technocracy movement" that sought to forge expert created governmental science policies that would guide and link both economic recovery and the development of scientific knowledge (see Turner, 2003: 117). In the U.K. the National Efficiency Movement and the writings of Karl Pearson, of Pearson's R statistics fame, promoted similar efforts to use the state to develop a science that would be more directly in service of the needs of society (see Searle, 1971). Also during this time in the U.K. J. D. Bernal, the renowned crystallographer and one of the early founders of the sociology of science, published his influential account of science, *The Social Function of Science* (Bernal, 1939). Bernal, using the socialist model of science being developed in the Soviet Union as a guide, called for a much stronger and more direct connection between the state and scientific research in order to better serve the needs of society. Other publications, such as J. G. Crowther's (1941) *The Social Relations of Science* and Lancelot Hogben's *Science for the Citizen* (1938), also amplified this call for a government-directed science that would be much more problem oriented and responsive to immediate and chronic social needs. In this reading, the privately produced or directed knowledge of foundations with their various "agendas" or industries with their concern for profit were not always capable of contributing to the greater good of society. In addition, even the publically accessible basic science generated by universities seemed too uncoordinated and insular to find its way into state led programs of societal betterment. Only government was capable of generating and managing a complex system intent on directing science for the public good.

In the U.S. the movement toward greater involvement of the state in science began to come to fruition in 1933 with the Roosevelt administration and the formation of Science Advisory Board (SAB) or the "scientific cabinet" as it came to be called. The SAB sought to emulate efforts that began toward the end of World War I when Woodrow Wilson initiated a limited type of coordination of scientific activities for the war effort with the formation of National Research Council (NRC), an offshoot of the National Academy of Science (NAS). After the war the Council continued its work but returned to an independent status under the NAS. The NRC advocated for an exclusively privately funded and controlled research strategy involving foundations, philanthropists and universities (Geiger, 1986: 256). The NRC was highly skeptical of any direct government involvement in the steering of scientific activity in universities fearing the corruption of science by governmental interests. While the SAB sought to forge a new path in the relationship between government and university-produced science by supporting a more active role for government, it too was divided between those who wanted a much more direct involvement of the government in university science and those who, following the direction set by the NRC and NAS, called for the continuation of an independent science free from government support or steering.[2]

Although the SAB was short-lived due to divisions within and outside of the Board and its goal of connecting science and government was rather limited it did signal the launch of a much more concentrated effort on the part of a number of scientific groups to forge a closer relationship between university science and government (see Cochrane, 1978: 358). Much of the SAB's efforts were taken up by the much broader National Planning Board whose name was later changed to the National Resource Committee (NRC). In 1938 the NRC published its influential report on science entitled, *Research—A National Resource*. The report, like those of the SAB, called for a closer connection between science and government. Specifically, it sought to more directly integrate federal support with existing private science funding, such as the Rockefeller Foundation (see Geiger, 1986: 263). However, the report also retained the NRC's deeply seated fear of the takeover of science by the state. The report maintained that government-sponsored research should be "organized and conducted as to avoid the possibilities of bias through subordination in any way to policy-making and policy-enforcing" (National Resources Committee, 1938: 4).

These early efforts to forge a closer relations between university knowledge production and the government in the U.S. during the 1930s were caught between liberals who feared state involvement and steering and who preferred the private support provided by foundations or the universities themselves and progressives who argued that that traditional system was broken and needed a new, more state-centered or socialist model of science funding. Those who called for more direct government support and steering believed that privately supported knowledge creation, with its random application and focus on the "pet projects" of wealthy philanthropists, was not capable of contributing to technological advancement or the larger social good. On the other hand, the liberal conceptualization of knowledge feared that the centralization and control of the state threatened to make university knowledge subservient to the political aspirations of the state.

In the U.K. similar positions on the proper role of science and state were exemplified in the Polanyi-Bernal debates that pitted Michael Polanyi's (1951; 1962)[3] liberal stance on science against the leading proponent of a more socialist conceptualization, J. D. Bernal (1939)—one such exchange appeared on the BBC in the early 1940s. Polanyi, a one time member of Hayek's Mount Pelerin Society and, for a time later on, a fellow member of the Committee on Social Thought at the University of Chicago with Friedrich Hayek, wanted to defend a science independent of state control. Echoing Ludwig von Mises's and Hayek's contention that society is and ought to be a spontaneous creation of freely acting and associating individuals, Polanyi maintained that science itself was a unique "dynamic order" that could not nor should not be planned. Such an order constituted what he called "the republic of science" (Polanyi, 1962: 54). In his republic members of knowledge making communities were connected to one another by the "mutual adjustment of individual interests" (Polanyi, 1962: 54). Such a situation, like social order in general, meant that it is both impossible and undesirable to "steer science" from either the inside or outside because its movements depend on the unique internal organization and pace of problem solving evident in particular fields (see Henkel, 2007: 89). In this sense the state could never plan science "nor could science be fully rationalized according to some sort of external authoritarian scheme" (Turner, 2003: 134). It was "irreducibly free and unadministrable" (Turner, 2003: 135). Attempts to steer it would ruin the internal ordering of scientific fields and make knowledge less innovative or capable of uncovering truths. In 1940 Polanyi, fearing the growing directing of science by government, particularly with the infatuation with Soviet science, and the influence of Bernal's socialist leaning *The Social Function of Science*, founded the Society for Freedom in Science to promote a liberal political conceptualization of knowledge (see McGucken, 1978; Shils, 1947).

Bernal, on the other hand, sought to forge a science that was much more directly guided and funded by the state and could be used more readily to improve social conditions. In his view, independent funding created a patchwork science that only produced sporadic advances in areas that were of immediate interests to philanthropists, industrialists and foundations. In areas where there was no interest to be manifest or profit to be made, there was no advancement. Such a science did not provide the broader funding necessary for scientific advancement and the growth of society in a technological age. In his view, the division between applied and pure science that was created under the liberal politics of university science funding was unnecessary. Indeed, that divisions itself was described by the communist theoretician N. I. Bukharian as an outgrowth of the inner conflict of capitalist societies (see Polanyi, 1946: 8). In this conceptualization knowledge and social utility were one and the same. For Bernal and others in Britain who wanted the government to take a much more active role in science funding "science was not being adequately utilized for the benefit of mankind, that the capitalist order in Great Britain was frustrating science by preventing its benefits from reaching society at large" (Shils, 1947: 80). The war had created a situation where "we had learned for the first time how to carry on scientific work rapidly and effectively" (Bernal in Polanyi, 1951: 86). It had shown that knowledge, particularly science, could be an effective state-directed public good since markets were simply unable to provide the scale of planning and investment necessary to sustain large scale scientific research (see Callon, 1994: 397). Likewise its search for profit could be detrimental to the interests of society or its advancement. To help institutionalize this view of a state-centered science the British Association for the Advancement of Science formed its Division for the Social and International Relations of Science in 1938 (Polanyi, 1946: 7).

In the U.S. the conflict between a more liberal, Polanyi-style "republic of science" and Bernal's more socialist "people's science" was waged on somewhat more moderate terms between Democratic Senator Harley Kilgore of West Virginia and Vanneavar Bush, director of the U.S. Office of Scientific Research and Development and author of the influential 1945 report *Science—The Endless Frontier*. Kilgore had become convince during World War II that the only way war production would succeed was through "an agency run by public spirited professionals—a technological high command" (Kevles, 1977: 8). He carried this idea over to the advancement of science in the postwar years. Kilgore believed that science could only advance through subsidization and direction by the state (see Price, 1968: 35). Although Bush's report leaned more toward the liberal defense of the autonomy and freedom of science, it also contained elements of the more socialist emphasis on the modern necessity of a publicly financed and guided science. It also contained ideas that would later become reconfigured and incorporated into various knowledge society policies in Europe and the United States. Evoking the strongly liberalist image of the independent pioneer, Bush argued,

> The pioneer spirit is still vigorous within this nation. Science offers a largely unexplored hinterland for the pioneer who has the tools for the task. The rewards of such exploration both for the Nation and the individual are great. Scientific progress is one essentially key to our security as a nation, our better health, to more jobs, to a higher standard of living, and to our cultural progress.

Bush (1945: 12) also took up the liberalist creed with the warning that "freedom of inquiry must be preserved under any government support of science." To accomplish this, Bush (1945: 34) called for the creation of a "National Research Foundation" to "develop and promote a national policy for scientific research and scientific education." As Bush (1945: 33) described it, the "basic principles" that must underlie all government support of science and ones that should serve as the guide for this new foundation should "promote research through contracts or grants to organizations outside the Federal Government." It should also "leave the internal control of policy, personnel and the method and scope of the research to the institutions themselves" (Bush, 1945: 33). Government support of science should also assure "complete independence and freedom for the nature, scope, and methodology of research carried on in institutions receiving public funds" (Bush, 1945: 33).

Bush's call was finally fulfilled after nearly five years of contentious political battles, particularly with Senator Kilgore who wanted a much stronger role for the government in science, and liberals such as Frank Jewett of the National Academy of Sciences who wanted to roll back government support of science to pre-war levels, with the creation of the National Science Foundation (NSF) in 1950 (see Kevles, 1977; Fuller, 2000: 121). Under the NSF model, a compromise of sorts was established between the two models of science funding. This position, where science would be as Polanyi (in Shils, 1947: 81) disparagingly referred to it, "half-free" would come to define much of the relationship between science and the state in the post–World War II era both in the U.S. and the U.K. Here government would take a much more active role in science but not through direct control, such as with expanding or establishing government laboratories, which the law establishing the NSF expressly forbad, or the Soviet model of science admired by Bernal and others in the Division for the Social and International Relations of Science (see Kevles, 1977). Instead, science funding would be built around a competitive "project and grant system" where scientists would be encouraged to apply for government support for particular projects. The foundation would be a government agency under the control of the president but its members would be selected from the scientific community who would use the established practices of peer review to determined awards. Such a system would preserve the liberal value of the autonomy of university science and the fear of government steering and the more socialist calls for more directly and actively harnessing science in service to society. It would also preserve the internal peer culture of academia where scientists themselves and not government bureaucrats or the marketplace would continue to make decisions about what constituted worthwhile and hence fundable science. These conflicts from the 1930s and 1940s would provide both the rhetorical and political framing for the knowledge society polices that would begin to emerge in the 1960s and eventually the impetus for reforming universities.

NEOLIBERALISM, THE TRIPLE HELIX AND THE EMERGENCE OF THE KNOWLEDGE SOCIETY

Until the 1960s much of the debate over science policy centered on the proper role of the state in the funding and directing of university science and science in general. As a result different nation states adopted different science-funding formulas which generated a wide variety of "public science systems" (see Whitley, 2007: 13). In some national contexts, universities remained autonomous, but different forms of knowledge were steered through grant funding. In some instances this grant funding was controlled through the peer review of other knowledge makers. In other situations it was directed by science policy experts and bureaucrats. In some systems, universities were more tightly controlled by the state and funding was often in the form of targeted grants that could be directed toward certain types of knowledge production or certain knowledge producers. A few scientists, such as *Scientific American* publisher Gerald Piel (1966: 12), worried that the growing reliance on the government projects and grants system that emerged after World War II had created a situation where "the independence of the university scientist would seem to be heavily compromised." In this situation an independent, pure science was often seen as loosing out to government directed applied science. Critics feared that the "pressure for immediate results, and unless deliberate polices are set up to guard against this applied research invariably drives out pure" (Dubridge, 1946: 14). In these debates over government control and steering of science, the Soviet model of science held particular sway, with critics pointing to the authoritarian debacle of Lysenkoism[4] as an indication of what could happen if science fell completely under government control. On the other hand, however, advocates of government control touted the successes of government supported science, particularly during the two world wars and in the U.S. with the government-directed space program.

Of secondary importance in these discussions was the role industry and business should play in the larger nexus of science, government and society. Even Vandaneer Bush's (1945: 21) more politically liberal work *Science—The Endless Frontier* maintained that the best way to "strengthen industrial research" was for the government "to support basic research and develop scientific talent." Industry was fully capable of meeting "the challenge of applying new knowledge to new products" (Bush, 1945: 22). It was, however, not able "to meet the additional demands of increased public need for research" (Bush, 1945: 22). Industrial research and development and university basic science were still generally viewed as separate domains where industrial research was a derivative of and only indirectly connected with the generally independent production of basic knowledge occurring in universities. Industries didn't produce pure knowledge, as such, but when possible and feasible took the basic science and discoveries of universities science or their own scientific activities and converted them into marketable products.

During the 1960s and 1970s two interrelated developments began to alter these framings of the proper role of governments, the universities and business and industry in knowledge production in the U.S. and elsewhere. As these developments became incorporated with the emerging neoliberal politics of the 1970s and 1980s, a new "triple helix" of government, university and business—one recognizable today in national and regional innovation systems and university reforms—was born. The first of these developments was the advent of a new discursive framing of the role knowledge was now called on to play in society that appeared in newly emerging conceptualizations of the so-called knowledge society or economy. The other was the emergence of specific knowledge policies advocated by group such as the Organization for Economic Cooperation and Development (OECD) and later the World Bank to promote and enhance the development of the new knowledge society. Over time these policies would become embedded in international policy networks and would be taken up by various neoliberal learning think tanks and, later, became a key part of various neoliberal government reform agendas.

The specific descriptions and theoretical conceptualization of the emerging knowledge society begins to appear it a few related but distinguishable forms in the 1960s and early 1970s (see Bullen et al., 2004: 12–13). One form grew out of the publication of Harvard University's Management Professor Peter Drucker's 1959 book *Landmarks of Tomorrow*. In the subsequent decades, Drucker would become both one of the leading theoreticians of the origins and dynamics of the new knowledge society and one of its central proponents. In *Landmarks of Tomorrow* he argued that "society must be an 'education society' today—to progress to grow, even to survive" (Drucker, 1959: 114). In this work Drucker becomes the first to use terms such as "knowledge work" and "knowledge worker" to describe a new occupations and forms of capital that relied less on raw materials and more on knowledge for production. Here, "educated people are the 'capital' of a developed society" (Drucker, 1959: 120). In his later 1969 work *The Age of Discontinuity* Drucker (1968: 264) described the emergence of a new economy where "knowledge has become the central 'factor of production'" (Drucker, 1968: 264). For Drucker (1993: 8) "the leading social groups of the knowledge society will be 'knowledge workers'—knowledge executives who know how to allocate knowledge to productive use, just as the capitalists knew how to allocate capital to productive use; knowledge professionals, knowledge employees."

Another source of the knowledge society can be found in Fritz Machlup's 1962 work *Distribution of Knowledge in the United States* and his discussion of the growth of "knowledge industries" in the U.S. Machlup calculated that with the growth of white collar workers 29 percent of the U.S. economy was a result of "knowledge industries" such as research and development, education and information service industries. Another source can be traced to discussion of post-industrialism associated most closely with Daniel Bell (1973) and Alain Touraine (1974). For Bell (1973) universities were fast becoming "the axial structures" and scientists the "pivotal occupation group" in an emerging post-industrial society where knowledge was driving the economy. When coupled with the emerging computer technologies, a new societal form that would forever change the way work was conducted and the way the economy operated was in the making.

These efforts to identify the features and parameters of something called the knowledge society also began to show up in policy documents during the 1960s, particularly those of the OECD. Since its formation knowledge and education have featured prominently in the efforts by the OECD to promote economic development in member states. However, the way this was to occur has changed rather dramatically over the ensuing decades as the ideas of economic liberalism became more politically dominant within the organization. The OECD's early knowledge policy documents featured a strong Keynesian understanding of the role of government in knowledge creation. Its 1963 report *Science, Economic Growth and Public Policy* (OECD, 1963: 9), for example, proclaimed that economic growth calls for "deliberate action and planning." The report maintained that the lessons of the "Keynesian revolution has produced a more realist theory for explaining short-term fluctuations in employment, incomes and prices" (OECD, 1963: 15). Government, therefore, should take a much more active role in promoting knowledge for economic growth and in overcoming the "inadequacies of the market mechanism" (OECD, 1963: 47). These sentiments were extended in the 1972 OECD report *Science Growth and Society: A New Perspective* that resulted from a "reassessment" of OECD science and knowledge policy. The Report concluded that "Science and technology are an integral part of social and economic development, and we believe that this implies a much closer relationship between policies for science and technology and all socio-economic concerns and governmental responsibilities than has exited in the past" (OECD, 1972: 96).

During the 1970s and 1980s these ideas of more directly harnessing education and knowledge for economic growth also became a central feature of various national reports issued by OECD investigators. In this system of evaluation, governments would often invite an OECD panel to visit the country and assess its economy in general or its education system at various levels. The OECD reports and its ideas, language and economic framing then would often serve as the basis for the founding of national panels or commissions and the subsequent releasing of "white papers" and reports advocating for education reform, such as those found in the prelude to the "Tomorrow's School" plan in New Zealand.

Efforts to forge new knowledge policies and national education reforms were also supported by a new theoretical emphasis in economics on knowledge and the formation of "human capital," as well as the new, more general role economists, many of whom were University of Chicago trained, were coming to play in all varieties of social policy formation in a number of countries. For instances, Gary Becker's (1964) human capital theory that first emerged in the 1960s often was cited as a way of rethinking the relationship between economic growth, education and the expansion of human capital. Instead of education being a good in itself because of its effects on personal enlightenment or national identity—or what Becker (1964: 249) refers to as the "residual effects" of "social gain"—it is recast as something that increases an individual's skills and marketability. In this human capital model, wage differences are not socially and politically forged allotments but a result of the fact that "some persons earn more than other simply because they invest more in themselves" (Becker, 1964: 245). In the 1970s groups such as the Business-Higher Education Forum, the Government-University-Industry Research Roundtable, The Committee for Economic Development in the United Kingdom and the Carnegie Foundation for the Advancement of Teaching in the United States became important promoters of efforts to draw upon such an economic framing in order to better marketize universities and bring them in direct service of the economy (Arshad-Ayaz, 2007: 82).

As a result of these rhetorical, theoretical and political changes by the 1980s, there is a clearly discernable redirection of OECD policies toward education. During this time OECD documents adopted a more neoliberal take on the relationship between knowledge, economy and state where governments were seen as less active but more supportive players. In this case the state is either to reduce its role in directly supporting education, as in "roll back" forms of neoliberalism or to become an instrument to remold education to better enable markets to function. In either case, social policies should support first and foremost market interests rather governmental ones. As part of these reformulations, the OECD advocated a new arrangement of government, university science and industry that would place business and economics as the center of knowledge making and dissemination. Early OECD documents, like the national science policies that preceded them, contained a strong Keynesian flavor with an emphasis on an activist state in order to bring about the knowledge society. In this role the state was seen as providing a necessary balance between markets and larger social interests.

Just as human capital theory helped reorient the policy treatment of education beginning in the 1960s, during the late 1980s and 1990s OECD recommendations began to reflect a new theoretical and policy movement in economics referred to as "new growth theory" or "endogenous growth theory." The principle proponent of the theory, Paul Romer (1990), a former economist at the University of Chicago and now at Stanford University, essentially argued that economic growth is not a matter of the increasing the quantities of existing goods but is directly tied to the ability of nations and economies to generate new ideas (see Peters and Besley, 2008). In this context "the stock of human knowledge determines the rate of growth" (Romer, 1990: S71). As such, "market incentives . . . play an essential role in the process whereby new knowledge is translated into goods with practical value" (Romer, 1990: S72). This economic principle applies both to wealthy nations who must work to continuously create a knowledge economy and institutions that can constantly generate new, novel ideas to sustain economic growth and to poor countries that can be lifted from poverty by drawing from and properly utilizing this knowledge stock. As Romer frames it, "if a poor nation invests in education and does not destroy the incentives for its citizens to acquire ideas from the rest of the world, it can rapidly take advantage of the publicly available part of the worldwide stock of knowledge" (Romer 2007).[5] Embedded in this theory is the idea that knowledge, like a natural resource, only needs to be properly tapped in order to fulfill its ultimate promise and potential.

In the early 1980s with the emergence of neoliberal political regimes the OECD identified what they considered to be "a changing relationship"

(OECD, 1982) between the university and the community and called for "the reappraisal of the special position of the university" in society (OECD, 1983: 55). In 1987 the OECD issued perhaps its most comprehensive report to date on higher education entitled *Universities under Scrutiny*. According to the report only "radical groups," some of whom were housed in universities, were delusional enough to "embrace the image of a society in which economic considerations take second place to quality of life." Such "nostalgic" considerations led these radicals to not pay attention to the "realities of economic competition" (OECD, 1987: 12). The report warned that universities would not be able to cope with the new demands being placed on them "without external intervention" (OECD, 1987: 23). The report issued a number of important "issues for policy," including an increased focus on applied areas, vocationalism, efficiency, productivity and accountability to various "external constituents." Also, it called for a closer link between theory and practice where the academic staff "must have some first-hand familiarity with professional practice" (OECD, 1987: 102). The report also maintained that the curriculum too must undergo a reform in order to more in alignment with "long-term economic trends and secular changes in employment patterns" without becoming overly narrow (OECD, 1987: 104). Likewise, the report identified an "increasing need for the exercise of leadership which takes appropriate initiatives and sets priorities and directions. . ." (OECD, 1987: 103). To accomplish this the report maintained that university administration would need to dismantle strong forms of collegial control that made universities less manageable and replace them with strong, corporate style administrators.

These reports of the 1980s and the growing influence and popularity of new growth theory served as guides for the OECD's highly influential 1996 report *The Knowledge-Based Economy* (see Warsh, 2006). This report continued the theme of the "crisis of performance" that was increasingly found in documents on tertiary education throughout the 1980s and early 1990s. This report also continued the call for the creation of more explicit and direct policies that linked university knowledge production to economic output (see Bullen et al., 2004a: 12). To accomplish a more complete harnessing of the economic impact of knowledge it might now be "necessary to modify or reject the idea that science is a public good" (OECD, 1996: 22). In the report the neoliberal-inspired ideas of managing knowledge and universities better in order to either create more products for the marketplace or reduce state spending become much more overt and urgent. Now the role of nation states was not to drive knowledge creation, as it had been in earlier reports, but, as a later report described it, to act as "catalysts and organizers" in the "dynamising of national innovation systems" (OECD, 2002: 55). The report was followed in the late 1990s with the report *Benchmarking Knowledge Based Economies* (OECD, 1999) that provided particular elements and empirical indicators of the knowledge economy and specific ways in which countries could measure their own implementation of knowledge society policies.

By the middle of the 1990s, the World Bank joined the OECD in its efforts to further marketize knowledge and reorganize universities. It soon became one of the central global advocates for the creation of knowledge societies by placing knowledge and innovation issues at the heart of its economic development initiatives. During this time the World Bank began to move away from a more limited "piece meal" approach that targeted particular nations or regions with specific projects toward a broader thematic vision of development drawn in part from endogenous growth theory. It also began moving from exclusively promoting policies of economic liberalizations to ones seeking to further embed neoliberalism globally (Griffin, 2006). At this point the Bank began to refer to itself as "the knowledge bank" and sought to promote what it called "knowledge for development." Particularly influential in this new emphasis on knowledge was their 1994 report *Higher Education: The Lessons of Experience* (World Bank, 1994), *Indigenous Knowledge for Development: A Framework for Action* (World Bank, 1998) and the 1999 report *Knowledge for Development* (World Bank, 1999). Like those of the OECD, the World Bank policies reflected the basic neoliberal ideal that knowledge should and could be harnessed as a development or growth strategy that would enable both developed and "underdeveloped" nations to compete in the global economy and, as a result, increase their standard of living (see Kenway et al., 2004).

In its 2002 report *Constructing Knowledge Societies: New Challenges for Tertiary Education*, the Bank extended its efforts to promote "knowledge for development" to the modification of university structure and increasing student access through user fees and loans. In the report inequality in educational opportunities are referred to as "imperfections and information asymmetries that constrain the ability of individuals to borrow adequately for education" (World Bank, 2002: 76). In order to promote knowledge and universities in both developed and "transition" societies, it was necessary for states to establish a "coherent policy framework," an "enabling regulatory environment" and "appropriate financial incentives" in order to promote "innovation," "human capital formation," and to further "national innovation systems" (World Bank, 2002: 83). The state's role in this process was to "put in place an enabling framework that encourages tertiary education institutions to be more innovative and responsive to the needs of a globally competitive knowledge economy and the changing labor market requirements for advanced human capital" (World Bank, 2002: 6). Part of this "enabling regulatory environment" and "enabling framework" involved encouraging rather than stifling "innovations in public institutions" and promoting "initiatives by the private sector to expand access to good-quality tertiary education" (World Bank, 2002: 87). This included removing "cumbersome administrative requirements that limit private tertiary education" (World Bank,

2002: 88). It also included the creation of national standards and "quality assurance" mechanisms and the promotion of "institutional autonomy" (World Bank, 2002: 89). When these reforms are in place, financial incentives could then "be applied creatively to steer tertiary education institutions more effectively toward compliance with quality, efficiency, and equity goals" (World Bank, 2002: 91).

Promoting a knowledge society and knowledge as development also became a key part of the efforts of other groups such as the U.S. Agency for International Development (USAID) through its "knowledge management program" and the United Nation's Educational, Scientific and Cultural Organization (UNESCO) over the last few decades. In 2005 UNESCO released its own knowledge society report entitled *Toward Knowledge Societies* (2005). The report rhetorically echoed those of the OECD and World Bank in arguing for the importance of knowledge for economic development and the needs of an emerging knowledge society. The UNESCO report departed from the other reports, however, in its worries about "the "dangers of an excessive commodification of knowledge" (UNESCO, 2005: 22).

What separated the OECD knowledge reports of the 1960s and early 1970s and their later documents or those of the World Bank and UNESCO is not only simply the historical context in which they were written but the specific ways they conceptualize knowledge, economy and society and their interrelationship. For these early reports knowledge is, first and foremost, to be harnessed in service of state or national interests. These state interests are translated as being the same as those of "society." Knowledge is conceived here as a public good that will propel the progress of the nation state and societies. By the time of the OECD and World Bank reports of the late 1980s and 1990s the rhetoric and public policy had shifted toward a much more neoliberal vision of the role of knowledge in directly providing innovation for the marketplace and the role of the state in creating conditions for that to happen. Now only through "desocializing" knowledge by rejecting the "idea that science is a public good" (OECD, 1996: 22) and turning it into a private commodity through the assistance of governments could national interests be served. As a knowledge society document from New Zealand described it "This is a market led approach to economic development, not one that is centrally planned. The intention is to unleash the productive potential of the private sector not to replace it" (New Zealand Ministry of Economic Development, 2002: 22). In this transition a neoliberal model of the triple helix relation of state, industry and science emerged and replaced the more state-centered model that dominated much post World War II science and early knowledge society policies. In the neoliberal model the state moved to being a supporting player rather than the central player in knowledge policy it had played from the 1930s until the 1970s.

THE BIRTH OF THE ENTERPRISE UNIVERSITY: NEOLIBERALISM AND TERTIARY EDUCATION REFORM

While the science policies of the post–World War II era that granted the state a much more active role in knowledge production greatly affected the size and status of universities, they did not, by and large, alter their internal structure or operation. These polices with their "indirect direction" of knowledge through the project and grants systems, their support of "basic research" and their hands off approach to the curriculum, research and teaching allowed the basic departmental and collegial structures that had emerged under the Humboldtian *Kulturstaat* and other similar university models in late nineteenth century to largely remain intact. The merger of neoliberal politics, theoretical visions of the knowledge society of the future and the specific knowledge society policies of groups like the OECD and World Bank would in the 1990s and 2000s, however, began to dramatically change this structure. Indeed, in this new model rather than working within the traditional organizational, collegial and epistemic parameters of the university, as occurred in previous state-guided science policies of the post–World War II era, the structure of universities was increasingly seen as significant part of the problem. Universities now increasingly were viewed, as an influential report on higher education in the U.S. referred to them, "both the problem and the solution" (NCSL, 2006: 2). While universities were seen as holding the potentials of the newly emerging knowledge society in their hands, they were much to removed and protected from the market to operate optimally or to provide the knowledge resources and products necessary to grow the new knowledge-based economy. In addition, their internally focused epistemology was increasingly seen less as a virtue that generated novelty and innovation and more as a form of self-indulgence that kept them too far removed from responding to the more immediate needs of the economy. Simply put, universities were much too independent and self-directed to serve the role they were now being called on to play in the new neoliberal order. They urgently needed redirection, reorganization and a new epistemic focus. As a result, neoliberal politicians and policies called for the transformation of the traditional university into the "enterprise university" (Marginson and Considine, 2000) or "entrepreneurial university" (Etzkowitz, 2008) with a heightened focus on innovation, vocationalism, knowledge transfer, marketability, workforce needs and adherence to the cost-saving and moralizing discipline imposed by the bottom line. They were again called on to serve the needs of society, however, now that "society" had become reconfigured to mean markets and the economy and not "humankind," "citizenship," "the public," "enlightenment," or even the nation state.

By the 1990s and early 2000s, the reform of higher education advocated by the OECD and others became a central feature of neoliberal reform efforts in many nations around the world. These reforms were often circulated through a network of consultants and policy advisors as they moved from place to place and by various professional groups and international foundations through their international conferences and meetings (see Rhoades and Sporn, 2002; Rhoades, 2005: 25; Beerkens, 2008: 23). These networks then fused with the efforts of think tanks and political parties into a global, transnational education policy network that both spread ideas of neoliberal reforms and helped to erode more locally or nationally generated policies (see Kenway et al., 2004: 136). As with primary and secondary education reform discussed in the next chapter these groups often employed various 'crisis narratives" that foretold the "downward spiral" or the "declining by degrees" of universities and decried their lack of transparency, accountability and out and out arrogance. As a response to this "crisis" a large number of "special commissions" or panels were convened by various neoliberal learning governments to investigate "the state of the university." These panels, in turn, released various reports and "white papers" advocating change, often with language directly borrowed from OECD, World Bank and think tank reports. As is common with panels and committees of these types, these particular university reform commissions and panels were usually stocked with individuals both within and outside of universities who were sympathetic to neoliberal political goals. In the U.K., university reform was guided by such reports as the Dearing Report (1997) and more recently the Browne Report. In New Zealand reform was guided by the *Tertiary Education Green Paper* of 1998 and the *Report of the Special Task Force* in 2001. In France reform was initiated with the *Plan for the University of the Third Millennium*, 2000. In Spain it was directed by the *Bricall Report* (2000). In South Africa reform was led by the *Report of the Council on Higher Education* (2000). In Australia revisions were led by *Higher Education: A Policy Discussion Paper, An Agenda for the Knowledge Economy* (2001) and more recently with the *Review of Australian Higher Education* (2008) or "Bradley Report." In India change was initiated with the report *India as Knowledge Superpower: Strategy for Transformation* (2001).

Of these various reforms launched over the last couple of decades some of the most sweeping ones have occurred in Australia. As with other neoliberal reform efforts in other national contexts, these reforms have been guided by a more general reorientation of public policy that began to emerge in the 1980s. In the late 1980s then Australian Prime Minister Bob Hawke at the opening of the Japanese funded National Science and Technology Center in Canberra declared that Australia must strive to become "the clever country" by investing much more in technology, science and science education. Generating this "clever country" then became a centerpiece of his 1990 election campaign. For Hawke and others creating this "clever country" required a fundamental change in the way the Australian education system at all levels operated.

Specific neoliberal style reforms of the university sector in Australia began in 1987 when universities where reorganized under Labour Minister for Employment, Education and Training and former Finance Minister John Dawkins (1987) and his influential white paper *Higher Education: A Policy Discussion Paper* that became part of the Higher Education Funding Act of 1988. These "Dawkins reforms," much like those that would soon occur in the U.K., eliminated the division between colleges of advanced education, institutes of technology and universities and developed a national funding formula in the name of creating a more efficient university system. The reforms employed an "autonomy for accountability" approach where universities were given more control over local decision-making and resource allocation in exchange for greater accountability to the government (see Dollery et al., 2006). The Dawkins reforms also reintroduced student fees for university attendance through the "Higher Education Contributions Scheme"—fees which had been abolished in the 1970s. Most critical for the future of higher education these reforms also sought to reorient Australian universities more directly toward the goal of economic growth. This was to be accomplished, in part, by remolding vice-chancellors into more corporate style CEOs, encouraging universities to pursue international students for revenue and, as with post-Bayh-Dole universities in the United States, to engage in more commercial ventures with business in order to increase revenues.

Such calls for education reform were reinforced by a litany of other, more general economic reports issued by various groups in the late 1980s and throughout the 1990s on the need to make the Australian economy more globally competitive. One such report, the "Garnaut Report" (1989), sought to initiate domestic reforms in response to increasing international competition. In the early and mid 1990s, this view was reinforced by the "Hilmer Report" (Hilmer, 1993) which called for dramatic new measures to improve Australia's international competitiveness. This was soon echoed by the Business Council of Australia's *Australia 2010* report that called for "establishing a competitive economic climate in which enterprises and individuals operate in an open environment with incentive to compete, to innovate and to manage the risks they face" (BCA, 1993: 7). In 1995 this call was followed by the Karpin Report (1995: 106) or *Enterprising Nation: Renewing Australia's Managers to Meet the Challenges of the Asia-Pacific Century* which sought to promote "a positive enterprise culture" in order to promote competitiveness throughout all levels of the Australian economy (see Beeson and Firth, 1998).

During this time the Australian government also began moves to evaluate universities through a performance-based funding initiative called the "Australian Composite Index." The Index, like the RAE in England, measured each university's research activity in order to determine the allocation of university funding. The Index later evolved into a more elaborate research assessment exercise called the "Research Quality Framework" (RQF). This assessment included much more detailed assessment measures and panels to rate the quality of research. In the RQF up to a quarter of university funding for teaching and research were directly tied to the outcomes of the evaluation system (Glaser and Laudel, 2007: 128). The measures were intended to be so precise that an individual researcher could know the exact amount that each of his or her publications added to the university's income. The RQF also began to focus more on research output and "influence" rather than simply on research activity. In 2007 the RQF was again changed with the introduction of the Excellence in Research for Australia Initiative (ERA). This approach sought to simplify the process and rectify some of the problems found in the RQF. After a limited discipline run in 2009, the ERA was applied to all disciplines in 2010 and again modified shortly afterward (see Rowbotham, 2011).

Some of the most important market-driven policy changes to higher education in Australia came during the 1990s. Indeed, "university organization changed more during the 1990s than in the previous 40 years" (Marginson and Considine, 2000: 39). Some of the most important of these changes came during the Coalition government of John Howard as a result of the West Committee's *Review of Higher Education Financing and Policy* (1997). Although a white paper failed to follow the report, its view of generating a student-driven market for higher education in Australia would serve as a template for future reforms both in Australia and elsewhere (see Pick, 2004). The report argued that "if our higher education system is to make the contribution to Australian society that we envisage in the next century and also operate at an internationally competitive level, we need to rethink fundamentally the way that we finance and regulate our universities" (West Committee, 1997). The report put forward thirty-eight specific recommendations for university reform including a move toward a "student-centered funding" formula where student would receive loans that would be paid back when they were employed. This funding approach, which would later become a global model (see Bollag, 2007), argued that by increasing fees to students and switching to loan support that a market for education would be created that would make higher education more demand driven. University fees would be capped, however, over time even those could possibly be removed as the quasi-market was transformed into a true market. As with previous reports, the West review also issued an urgent call to "increase the responsiveness of higher education research to the needs of the users of that research" (West Committee, 1997).

The West review was followed by a series of reform documents such as the 1999 paper entitled *Knowledge and Innovation: A Policy Statement on Research and Research Training* issued by D. A. Kemp the Minster of Education. The White Paper outlined a number of criticism of the Australian tertiary education system, such as, "1) government funding incentives do not sufficiently encourage diversity and excellence; 2) research in our universities is too often disconnected from the national innovation system; 3) there is too little concentration by institutions on areas of relative strength; 4) research degree graduates are often inadequately prepared

Creating the "Clever Country" 149

for employment; and there is unacceptable wastage of private and public resources associated with long completion times and low completion rates for research degree students" (Australian Department of Education, Training and Youth, 1999: 1). In 2001 this report was followed with *An Agenda for the Knowledge Nation* written by the "Knowledge Nation Task Force" and released by the Australian Labor Party as part of their 2001 campaign. Like the reports that preceded it, the report maintained that "Australia is facing a national crisis . . . the only way forward is become a courageous and effective Knowledge Nation in which everyone participates and shares the benefits" (Knowledge Nation Task Force, 2001). As would become common in Labour documents of the 2000s, the new "Knowledge Nation" was projected as a society that "will break down barriers. It will be inclusive, closing the disturbing gaps between the cities and the bush and between elitist and populist opinion with courage—arguing for a fresh vision of life, an updating of Ben Chifley's 'light on the hill' for the twenty-first century" (Knowledge Nation Task Force, 2001).[6] In this new situation universities were again called upon to reorganize and reorient their missions toward economic goals. This could happen, however, only if the university became more "flexible." For this flexibility to happen universities would need to compete in a market and be guided by consumer choice, incentives and funding formulas (Pick, 2004: 108).

More recent reforms have stemmed from the *Review of Australian Higher Education* (2008) or the "Bradley Report" and the Labour governments' of Rudd and Gillard response found in the government's white paper *Transforming Australia's Higher Education System* (2009). These reports have led to more spending on higher education but have connected that spending with more "quality assurance arrangements" overseen by the newly created Tertiary Education Quality Standards Agency (TEQSA), which replaces and consolidates activities previously performed by the Australian Universities Quality Agency and state governments. Unlike current changes in the U.K., those in Australian have moved back to the more "roll out" neoliberalism's emphasis on using markets to generate "a fairer Australia"—a social capitalism" in former prime minster Rudd's (in Coorey, 2009) terms. Despite the focus, however, most of the rhetoric and policy in these documents still focuses on expanding economic productivity, increasing student choice, treating knowledge as skill enhancement and on generating, what has become a new phrase in many recent global documents on higher education reform, an "economically sustainable university system."

In the U.S., with its large private system of higher education and decentralized control in the fifty states, similar neoliberal calls for university reform began to emerge in the early 1990s. The most significant reform efforts, however, were undertaken during the G. W. Bush administration with the formation in 2005 of the Commission of the Future of Higher Education, also known as the "Spellings Commission," directed by Margaret Spellings the Secretary of Education. The Commission's final report

150 *Neoliberalism and Restructuring of Knowledge and Education*

"A Test of Leadership: Charting the Direction of U.S. Higher Education" (U.S. Department of Education, 2006) called for important changes in the ways higher education in the U.S. operated. In the Commission view universities had become "increasingly risk-averse, frequently self-satisfied and unduly expensive" (U.S. Department of Education, 2006). They also had an "unwarranted complacency" and "a remarkable absence of accountability." Spelling called for a concerted effort to "make sure our higher education system continues to spur innovation and economic growth and gives more Americans the chance to succeed in the knowledge economy" (U.S. Department of Education, 2006).

The Report maintained that "the continued ability of American postsecondary institutions to produce informed and skilled citizens who are able to lead and compete in the 21st-century global marketplace may soon be in question" (U.S. Department of Higher Education, 2006: 13). The Commission further maintained that "higher education must change from a system primarily based on reputation to one based on performance" (U.S. Department of Education, 2006: 21). The report argued that

> with too few exceptions, higher education has yet to address the fundamental issues of how academic programs and institutions must be transformed to serve the changing needs of a knowledge economy. We recommend that America's colleges and universities embrace a culture of continuous innovation and quality improvement by developing new pedagogies, curricula, and technologies to improve learning, particularly in the area of science and mathematical literacy. (U.S. Department of Education, 2006: 25)

To do this it was imperative for universities to create "performance measures" to be recorded and published. Specifically, the report called for the establishment of what it termed a "consumer friendly" national database where colleges and universities would report such information as graduation rates and job placement results. Eventually the database could be expanded to include "student learning outcomes" in order to move accountability forward and enable more informed consumer choice among parents and students.

To makes these reforms, Spelling proposed changes to the accrediting system that would force the independent regional accrediting agencies to examine and report on student outcomes. Efforts at implementing some of the recommendations of the commission stalled, however, when groups such as the American Association of Universities began to questions both the costs and the loss of autonomy that the new system might impose. The resistance to such measures crystalized in 2008 when universities were able to insert language in the reauthorization of the Higher Education Act that prohibited the Education Department from using federal accreditation to create standards which universities were required to follow (Basken, 2008:

A19). In the decentralized American higher education system, liberalism had successfully countered neoliberalism, at least temporarily, and only at the national level.

With the failure of the Spellings Commission to effect change at the broad national level, neoliberal policy initiatives shifted to individual states. In the same year the Spellings Commission released its influential report the National Council of State Legislatures released its own report entitled, *Transforming Higher Education, National Imperative—State Responsibility* (2006). Echoing similar themes as were found in the Spellings Commission Report, the NCSL's report argued that, "there is a crisis in American higher education"...and "it up to the states—and specifically state legislators—to alter the course of higher education" (NCSL, 2006: 1). As such, "legislators should demand that institutions improve their productivity. Every other sector of the economy is guided by this principle, but higher education has, for some reason, been except from concepts of efficiency" (NCSL, 2006: 10). According to the report we now live in a new age where "globalization demands different priorities, different skills and different knowledge" (NCSL, 2006: 1). In this new world, "the nation is losing its competitiveness because it has failed to focus on how higher education reenergizes U.S. competitiveness and revitalizes the states" (NCSL, 2006: 2). Among the NCSL's central recommendations was to "hold institutions accountable for their performance" (NCSL, 2006: 7) through "performance-based funding." In such a system there would be direct "incentives and consequences of institutional performance" (NCLS, 2006: 7). State-supported universities should also be encouraged "to embrace innovation" and to "encourage partnerships" particularly with businesses who "can be excellent partners in helping to understand the weakness in the current system and designing innovative solutions" (NCLS, 2006: 9).

Rather than being slowed down by the economic downturn that began in 2008 neoliberal reforms of higher education have actually intensified in the U.S. but largely at the level of individual states. Indeed, the financial crisis seems to have spurred a neoliberal resurgence in the U.S. directed at decreasing state support of universities, curtailing the collective bargaining rights of public sectors workers in general, including professors, demanding increased efficiencies and accountability and increasing the university's economic focus. Some states, such as California and Nevada, have made drastic cuts to their higher education budgets, while states such as Texas and Florida have undertaken efforts to remold higher education entirely through the introduction of new methods of accountability. As mentioned earlier at Texas A&M University, for example, a new program was initiated in 2010 that calculated and displayed the "financial contributions and liabilities" of each faculty member at the university (see Simon and Banchero, 2010: C1–C2). In this formula individual professors were rated by "funds generated" from tuition and grants and then compared with the faculty member's salary. This was soon followed by a similar initiative in the University of Texas system. In both cases these initiatives were pushed along by the neoliberal think tank Texas Public Policy Foundation who have become a champion of a long series of neoliberal education changes in the state.

In the European Union education reforms have taken a similar route of extolling the virtues of the knowledge society but with a much stronger rhetorical emphasis on expanding opportunity and accessibility (although individual members such as Germany have followed a more vigorous program of university reform). Such an approach became an integral part the "Lisbon Strategy" first established in 2000. One of the central goals of the Strategy was to make the European Union "the most competitive and dynamic knowledge-based economy in the world capable of sustainable economic growth with more and better jobs and great social cohesion" (Commission of European Communities, 2000). As part of the strategy in 2000 the European Union pledged to become the most competitive knowledge based economy in the world with the goal of a 3 percent investment in Research and Development by 2010 (European Commission, 2000, see also Perry, 2006: 203). The EU also established the European Research and Innovation Area (ERIA) to order to create a "Europe of Knowledge."[7]

In 1999 EU education ministers announced the signing of the "Bologna Declaration of 19 June 1999." The declaration followed up on an earlier declaration at the Sorbonne that stressed the importance of universities for economic growth in the EU. The Bologna Declaration and the Bologna process that came with it were designed to rationalize national university systems in order to ease the movement and transfer of students between them. As part of this, the process established the "harmonization" of the structure of academic programs of various EU members by creating greater "compatibility and comparability of the systems of higher education" (The European Higher Education Area, 1999). This was to be accomplished in order to give "its citizens the necessary competences to face the challenges of the new millennium, together with an awareness of shared values and belonging to a common social and cultural space" (The European Higher Education Area, 1999; see also Musselin, 2005). Among the new procedures introduced were the "easily readable and comparable degrees," the establishment of standardized "cycles" of graduate and undergraduate degrees, the "promotion of mobility" of students and the establishment of "quality assurance" mechanisms with "comparable criteria and methodologies" (The European Higher Education Area, 1999). By the late 2000s the agreement had expanded to include over 45 countries and 5600 public and private universities with over 16 million students (Robertson and Keeling, 2008: 224).

In England neoliberal style reforms of higher education began to unfold with the election of Thatcher and the appointment of Keith Joseph as education secretary. The first important policy document to appear was *A Strategy for Higher Education into the 1990s* written for Keith Joseph by the University Grants Committee in 1984 (UGC, 1984). The report first laid out the idea of a "selective approach" to research funding in order to "ensure that resources for research are used to best advantage" (UGC, 1984, par. 1.9). Out of this report and others came a new type of performance based funding for universities called the Research Selectivity Exercise (RSE) which was eventually renamed the Research Assessment Exercise (RAE). This performance-based funding approach for research would soon become a model for evaluating and funding university research around the world. The first rudimentary RSE, conducted in 1986, included only a short description of achievements, a list of the five best publications in the department and data on research incomes (Martin and Whitley, 2010). Later the RAE was modified to include individual publications rather than simply those the department considered its best.[8] Other important higher education policy changes of the early Thatcher period come from the Jarratt report of 1985. This report advocated for the growth of a more efficient, corporate style university with calls for strategic planning, financial transparency, a line-management style of operations and fewer university committees (Leisyte et al., 2010: 272).

Another key set of policies was enacted in the 1992 Further and Higher Education Act. This Act developed a new funding system for universities in England and Wales and required the establishment of "Quality Assessment Committees" (QAC) to measure and report on quality within the university. In 1997 such efforts at quality control culminated in the establishment of an overall government agency, the Quality Assurance Agency for Higher Education (QAA) to monitor "how well they meet their responsibilities, identifying good practice and making recommendations for improvement" (QAA, n.d.). The Agency governing board contains members of higher education institutions, public officials and business leaders. In the past, universities themselves and the QACs were largely responsible for quality control, curriculum content and degree standards. The groups mission is to both safeguard "the public interest in the sound standards of higher education qualifications and "informing and encouraging continuous improvement in the management of the quality of higher education" (QAA. n.d.).

In 1996 the National Committee on the Inquiry into Higher Education (NCIHE) was formed to offer suggestions on further reforming higher education. The 2000-page Committee's report, *Higher Education in a Learning Society* (1997), or the "Dearing Report" as it became known, was the first major review of education in the UK since the 1960s. The report called for some ninety-three specific reforms of higher education, including the introduction of after graduation student fees, increased money for research and a refocusing of universities toward their communities. In many ways this Report can be seen as a transitional document that contained both traditional appeals to academic freedom and personal growth and more neoliberal notions of the economic and utilitarian purposes of higher education. The report declared that "in the next century, the economically successful nations will be those which become learning societies: where all are committed, through effective education and training, to lifelong learning" (NCIHE, 1997: 3). The Report warned that, "A lifelong career in one organization will become increasing the exception. People will need the knowledge and skills to control and manage their own working lives" (NCIHE, 1997: 3). As a result universities could no longer do "more of the same" but must "adapt to the needs of a rapidly changing world and to new challenges" (NCIHE, 1997: 7). Not only will universities be forced to change their ways because of their new role in the learning society, they also will be faced with students who are becoming "increasingly discriminating investors in higher education" who are "looking for quality, convenience, and relevance to their needs at a cost they consider affordable and justified by the probable return on their investment of time and money" (NCIHE, 1997: 7).

The Dearing Report was followed in 1998 with new Labour's white paper *Our Competitive Future: Building the Knowledge Driven Economy* (Department of Trade and Industry, 1998) and the *UK Competitiveness Indicators* and in 2002 with the so-called *Lambert Review* commissioned by the Treasury and the Department of Education and Skills. These reports largely deemphasized the Dearing Report's discussion of various purposes of higher education and instead focused almost exclusively on its economic role (Brooks, 2008). In 2003 Labour released the white paper *The Future of Higher Education* which became a foundation for the Higher Education Act of 2004 (The National Archives, 2004). The document extolled the virtues of higher education which allows graduates "to get better jobs and earn more than those without higher education." One of the most significant outcomes of the 2004 Act was to increase tuition fees from £1200 to £3000 per year and, similar to the Australian system, to "back load" these through loans that would be repaid after graduation and only when an adequate income was received. Students from lower incomes would also be able to have part of the fee waived.

Most of these post-Dearing reform efforts have been directed at further devolving state support for higher education by shifting more costs directly to students while simultaneously increasing enrollments to meet the needs of the knowledge society. Such devolution was said to benefit students and parents who would have more choice and to generate a market for education since students would be paying directly and, as good consumers, would demand more for their money. It would create in, Tony Blair's words, "the beginnings of choice and contestability" (Blair in Brooks, 2008: 235) which would create an "economically sustainable" higher education system. Generating more accountability and consumer choice was also instrumental in the establishment of the National Student Survey in 2005 as part of the broader Quality Assurance Framework for Higher Education. The Survey allows graduating students to assess and report on their experiences at particular universities. The results are then posted in league table form.

More recently with the return of a "roll back" style of neoliberalism in the "Big Society" policies of the Cameron Coalition government efforts have intensified to move further along to generate a market for higher education. In June 2011 the Cameron government released its anticipated "white paper" on higher education, *Higher Education: Students at the Heart of the System* (Department of Business, Innovation and Skills, 2011). The white paper's goal is to finally "put students in the driving seat" by generating a market for higher education. This is to accomplished primarily through four efforts, (1) further shifting of fees to students though loans, (2) generating new "best buy facts" and a consumer rights "student charter" that essentially generates a contract between the student and his or her university, (3) allowing universities to compete for higher scoring students and rewarding those universities who "combine good quality with value for money," and (4) expanding private universities in the English system including those operating on a for-profit basis. In 2010 the Browne report *Securing a Sustainable Future for Higher Education*, previously commission by the Labour government, had set the stage for this latest round of reforms with its recommendation to dramatically increase fees for students attending British universities and to move the financing if higher education to student loans (The National Archives, 2011). In 2010 the government announced that fees would be increased up to £9000 by 2012. Under the proposals outlined in the new white paper, the university sector would be "diversified" by opening it up to competition from groups such the American company Apollo which operates the University of Phoenix in the U.S. and BPP in Britain. This proposal would include allowing private universities to expand their operations and take over and run universities who face closure as a result of the financial pressures imposed by the newly created market for higher education (see Chronicle of Higher Education, 2011).

What is particularly striking about all these commissions, reports, white papers and actual university reforms in these various national contexts is their similarity. Indeed, taken together they seem to comprise a "neoliberal reform trope" exhibiting an often-tireless parade of similar framings, rhetorical phrasing and proposed solutions. Despite variations in national political systems and political parties all the ones examined here reflect in some manner neoliberalism's interconnected central tenants of devolving state financial support, expanding privatization either in funding and/or delivery, increasing "quality control" measurements and oversight agencies, commercializing university research and, the ultimate goal, enabling consumer choice in a higher education marketplace. At some points in time and under different variants of neoliberalism and with different political parties one of these tenants may be emphasized over another. Also, at some points the language of social inclusion and equality associated most closely with "roll out" neoliberalism may be present, while at others times the rhetoric of austerity and individual responsibility of "roll back" neoliberalism may be more pronounced. However regardless of these variations in method and rhetorical tone these neoliberal tenants serve as a compass to orient the direction in which the new entrepreneurial university must now go regardless of the particular politics of time and place.

MAKING A MARKET OF AND FOR HIGHER EDUCATION

On the surface it would appear that the neoliberal emphasis on harnessing higher education for economic development, the promotion of lifelong learning and increasing higher education participation rates found in various knowledge society policies would have hailed new halcyon days for universities. Since productive workers require constant access to information and knowledge in order to be able to quickly change or update their "skill set" or "knowledge stock" and to stay competitive in the changing global economy and universities are key parts of new "national innovation systems," universities would seem to be the great beneficiaries of neoliberal knowledge society policies. This has not necessarily been the case, however, in either the areas of university funding or autonomy. While some universities have seen an increase in state funding, such as recently in Australia, they have had to pay for that increase with much closer inspection, steering and monitoring. And, conversely in cases where autonomy has been increased, usually only at the budgetary level, they have to purchase that limited autonomy with cuts in direct state funding. This has essentially created a type of "pushing out" policy, intended or not, where the only means for public universities to have the type of autonomy that had in the past is to become private or private like enterprises.

However, just as the public regarding view of knowledge described in Chapter 3 contained internal contradictions between knowledge as a public good and limited monopolistic ownership, the more recent neoliberal university reforms efforts also contain their own set of seeming contradictions drawn from a tension within variants liberalism itself. On the one hand, the classic liberal emphasis on devolved authority and university independence are sometimes touted as a virtue. While on the other hand there have been increased pressures to make universities more formally accountable by both deliberately steering their production of knowledge toward more market-centered products and by making them account for expenditures and the quality of their activities. However, on closer inspection what seem to be contradictory policies are in fact quite compatible with neoliberal views of the need of governments to "make markets." In this role it is the state's job to manufacture a market where one didn't exist before through political guidance. This produces an ironic situation where only more government control and steering can generate the type of environment where liberal attitudes and practices of "less government" and "more responsibility" can take hold. In other words, it is only through government concentrated power, of a certain variety, where neoliberal governmentality can be put into operation.

The seeds and contradictions of this ironic neoliberal transformation of universities were planted as early as the 1930s with the advocacy for more government directed science. This advocacy called for a much more activist state to direct the advancement of knowledge toward societal welfare. However, as this welfare state began to lose power and its activism became redirected to support markets with the rise of "roll back" neoliberalism in the late 1970s and 1980s, its role in determining the fate of public knowledge production in universities would too change. Both the political liberals who advocated for independent universities and untethered knowledge and the socialists who wished for more "science for the people" were displaced by a new, neoliberal arrangement. In this particular arrangement universities would increasingly come to both provide for the needs of markets and be made into a market themselves. Universities would not have the kind of autonomy "old school" political liberals such as Michael Polanyi had sought nor were they to serve the needs of the public in the way J.D. Bernal and other socialists had wanted but would now be made to serve a new master—the neoliberal state and economy nexus.

6 "An Island of Socialism in a Free Market Sea"
Building the Market-Oriented School[1]

These are the disadvantages of the commercial spirit. The minds of men are contracted, and rendered incapable of elevation. Education is despised, or at least neglected, and the heroic spirit is almost utterly extinguished. (Smith, 1997 [1766]: 20)

The establishment of the school system in the United States as an island of socialism in a free market sea reflected only to a very minor extent the early emergence among intellectuals of a distrust of the market and of voluntary exchange. (Friedman and Friedman, 1980)

[T]he necessary preparation, such as the learning of commercial details, languages, etc., is more and more rapidly, easily, generally, cheaply reproduced with the progress of science and popular education, to the extent that the capitalist mode of production organizes the methods of teaching, etc., in a practical manner. (Marx, 1967: 354)

It is only in the context of the grand narratives of legitimation—the life of the spirit and/or the emancipation of humanity—that the partial replacement of teachers by machines may seem inadequate or even intolerable. (Lyotard, 1984)

We've given away equality of opportunity in schooling for the shyster democracy of the marketplace. (Former New Zealand Prime Minister David Lange, 1999: 16)

With neoliberal theory as a foundation, new public management as an institutional mechanism and knowledge society policies as international guideposts, during the 1980s and 1990s neoliberal politician and policy makers set about the task of reforming a number of primary and secondary education systems in various places around the world. If government and other parts of the public sector could be made less costly, more efficient and more market-centered through the application of neoliberal tactics and policies so too could education institutions. Although liberal ideas about the decentralization of schooling have a long history involving sporadic applications, the specific neoliberal reform efforts at, "denationalizing schooling" as Milton Friedman (2005) referred to it, became more pronounced in the mid and late 1980s with the establishment of educational policies such as New Zealand's Tomorrow's School Plan in 1987 and the England and Wales Education Reform Act of 1988 (see Thrupp, 1998). From those locales, neoliberal education policies spread via various "policy borrowing networks" to places as diverse as Chile, Spain, Mexico, Hong Kong, Singapore, Sweden and the U.S. These reforms, like those in higher education explored in the last chapter, were usually preceded by a series of commissioned reports and "white papers" which sought to generate a moral panic surrounding the impeding education crisis created by inept teachers, poor performing students and the inability of schools to respond to the new challenges posed by global competitiveness and to reframe education in economic and human capital terms.

While each country's implementation of neoliberal primary and secondary education reforms was unique and dependent on the "national politics of place," much like the implementation of general neoliberal policies themselves, they were, nevertheless, drawn directly from broad neoliberal conceptualizations of the need to realign the relationship between state, society and the individual. As such, these reforms were integral parts of a concentrated global effort to use an assortment of market mechanisms and incentives to transform educational institutions in the name of efficiency, managerial oversight, devolution, parental choice, responsiblization, accountability and the "demands of the new global economy." Perhaps mostly importantly overall, these reforms were also directed at morally transforming schools from institutions supporting and operating on social interests, public welfare and equality of opportunity to ones centered on the neoliberal values of individualism, competition, contractual relations and "freedom of choice."

Although nationally variable, the neoliberalist educational models that began to emerge in the late 1980s and 1990s generally contained four basic elements. These elements often combined the "roll back" neoliberal emphases on privatization, devolution and reduction of state expenditures with the more "roll out" neoliberal focus on using a market friendly, activist state to create more favorable market conditions and hone skilled and flexible workers or "lifelong learners." In some cases these two versions were used together as part of general neoliberal reforms. In other instances, they existed alongside, usurped or became hybridized with other education models already in place. First, and perhaps most fundamental, of these elements was the argument that the market and its built-in efficiencies needed to be brought into the organization and management of public education. Here, as in other public organizations, privatization or quasi-privatization measures should be used to reorganize the way schools conduct themselves. This strategy often included decentralization, sometimes based on the American federalist education model and its locally controlled board of directors or trustees, and the subsequent devolution of authority and budgets, as well as the ability of parents and students to "choose" their school. Second, reflecting the new orientation of roll out neoliberalism's managerial-style state, was the promotion and extension of an "accountability movement" that argued that schools should be held more accountable for reaching certain enhanced, centrally established and monitored academic standards or goals. These standards, outlined by state education agencies, ministries or newly established quasi-agencies, such as England's Office of Standards in Education (Ofsted) and New Zealand's Education Review Office (ERO) were to be more directly reflective of the needs of companies operating in the global economy or the larger economic goals outlined in national and increasingly international knowledge society policies. They were also to be developed and controlled by these government agencies rather than being left to teachers or local authorities to determine. Third, and following directly from the second, "performance indicators," such as standardized tests scores, "league tables," audit reports, school inspection rankings or "school report cards," should be used to assess how well the established standards were being implemented and adhered to and if the state's educational goals were being met. These assessments exercises were often overseen by newly established or reorganized offices that were outside of the direct control of traditional state education departments or ministries. These new assessments were designed to provide indicators as to which schools were more effective and hence more "accountable" to the taxpayers and "stakeholders" that supported them. These scores could then be used to compare the performance of schools and teachers and to establish market-type competition and reward systems for those that were performing well and to punish those who were not, such as the linking of teacher retention and pay with test score performance, such as in New York state, or in the case of Washington, D.C., firing teachers who were deemed by student test scores to be deficient (Lewin, 2010). Finally, information from these indicators should then be made available to enable some form of school choice among parents, such as the voucher system or charter schools often favored in U.S. neoliberalist reform efforts, or the newly created "free schools" found in England or the "out of districting" of the early English and New Zealand models of reform. These parents and students, who were now recast as "education consumers" under these reforms, could use the information found in various performance indicators provided by the state to make informed, consumptive decisions about which school they wanted to send their children to or attend themselves as part of their own "life long learning strategy." Supporters of these neoliberal reforms contended that the competitive pressure spawned by the availability of this information would transform education from a bureaucratically imposed state obligation or mandate to a free market consumer choice, much like purchasing a car or television. In the newly created educational marketplace consumers could compare and decide for themselves which educational institution bests fit their desires, needs and budget. Somewhat like a shopping mall, people could choose from a range a products, from the upscale, custom boutique to the massified discount box store, compare their relative value, consult their budget (and increasingly their credit report) and make their own choice. With this, governments would, as J. S. Mill had hoped in the nineteenth century, be slowly removed from the education business.

Such neoliberal reforms not only sought to make knowledge and education commodities to be bought and sold in a marketplace or at least to act as if they were in marketplace, they also sought to place the fate of schools and teachers more directly under the dictates of market mechanisms and pressures. If schools failed to live up to established standards they ran the risk of losing their "business" and "customers" to other schools as students transferred out, much like a retailer who will go out of business if he or she fails to provide for their customers' needs. In other scenarios schools would face some type of state funding or auditing sanction or, as was the case with the U.S.'s "No Child Left Behind," have the school's administrators be removed or potentially be shut down altogether. In some cases the compensation of school personnel would also become more market centered through the expansion of merit or performance-based pay formulas, which is some places, such as Florida in 2010, entailed ending the tenure system for teachers all together. Or, in other cases, with the establishment of well-compensated administrators, such as the "superheads" in Britain who become CEOs and take on the reins of poor performing schools. Such an approach even appeared at the university level, as in the case of Kent State University in Ohio, with the introduction of what was termed a "success bonus pool" that awarded professors bonuses when the university exceeded its goals in the areas of "status improvement," student retention and fund raising (Masterson, 2008: A1).[2]

In this chapter I want to examine a few examples of how neoliberal education reforms efforts have played out over the last few decades in the contexts of New Zealand, England and Wales and the U.S. These case studies are not intended to be thorough histories of these reform efforts but a summary of a few of the key changes in each country and their connection with neoliberal ideals and politics. I begin, however, with a more general discussion of some of the precursors that converged in the 1970s to provide the general framework that neoliberal education reforms would follow, such as Milton Friedman's call for school vouchers in the 1950s, the move toward a "human capital" conceptualization of education in the 1960s and the "accountability in education movement" associated initially with Leon Lessinger that arose in the early 1970s. Afterward, I move to a discussion of the three different cases of neoliberal education reform. Finally, I conclude with a discussion of what these reforms have wrought and what is arguably their larger purpose with neoliberalism's moral and social revolution.

VOUCHERS, HUMAN CAPITAL AND ACCOUNTABILITY: THE PRECURSORS TO NEOLIBERAL EDUCATION REFORM

Education has been a central concern of various strains of liberal thought since the late eighteenth century. Although Adam Smith remarked that education was "no doubt, beneficial to the whole of society" and worried in his *Lectures on Justice, Police, Revenue and Arms* about the tendency of market economies to extinguish "the heroic spirit," (Smith, 1964), he also argued that the expense of education "might perhaps with equal propriety, and even with some advantage, be defrayed altogether by those who receive the immediate benefit of such education and instruction, or by the voluntary contribution of those who think they have occasion for either the one or the other." In the U.S., Thomas Paine (1942) advocated for an early form of a voucher system to address inequality in education in his 1791 work "The Rights of Man." A century later J. S Mill (1951: 88) issued one of the strongest liberal critiques of education when he decried state-directed education as "establish[ing] a despotism over the mind." "State education," in his description, is but a "mere contrivance for molding people to be exactly like one another" (Mill, 1951: 88). In this sense private, independent education was preferable because it created a variability of thought that countered the establishment of state-led dogma and indoctrination.

Despite liberal insistence of the need to make education privately purchased in order to either defray the costs, as in Smith's case, or avoid the concentration of government power and ideology, as for Mill, the late nineteenth and twentieth centuries became the heyday of publicly supported education in most Western countries. With the growth of state power and a more socialist or nationalist notion of the public good, education was generally seen as something that should be subsidized and controlled to varying degrees by governments acting to promote the larger public interest. Progressives, following educators such as Horace Mann (in Alexander and Alexander, 2005: 29), also often saw education as "the great equalizer of the conditions of men, the balance-wheel of the social machinery" that could be used to correct for some of the social problems of increasingly urbanized and heterogeneous modern societies and the social equalities of income and wealth generated by capitalist markets. Governments also came to recognize the value of state-controlled or -directed education as a means of civic or state socialization and as a way to cultivate and maintain national solidarity, loyalty and political participation.

While the seeds of some neoliberal-style education reform are clearly evident in classic liberalism, the specific theoretical justification and model for most contemporary neoliberal school reforms can be traced to a post–World

War II resurgence of liberalism and public interest theory, particularly as found in Milton Friedman's (1955) influential essay "The Role of Government in Education." Friedman, who built on both Paine's advocacy of school vouchers and Mill's fear of state indoctrination, argued that schools needed a radical "denationalizing." For Friedman (1955: 125), the "neighborhood effect" that was often used to legitimate state-controlled education appeared at first glance to make education a governmental concern because of the general welfare it provides to both the individual and the community as a whole. However, Freidman argued that the neighborhood effect does not automatically mean that it is the government's role to fund and direct education. Social benefits can and should be derived from the "voluntary associations" of individuals and the choices they make and not through the coercions of the state. For Friedman (1955: 129) "competitive private enterprise is likely to be far more efficient in meeting consumer demands than either nationalized enterprises or enterprises run to serve other purposes." Freidman argued that the role of government in education "has led not only to enormous waste of taxpayers' money but also to a far poorer educational system than would have developed had voluntary cooperation continued to play a larger role" (Friedman and Friedman, 1980: 187). Like government's bureaucratic "dead hand" in other areas, in education, it had squashed variability and innovation in the name of concentrating power and ameliorating inequality. For Friedman, the government's role should be strictly limited to maintaining "minimum standards" of education. In other words, it should work to improve "the operation of the invisible hand without substituting the dead hand of bureaucracy" (Friedman, 1955: 144). Among Friedman's recommendations was the financing of higher education through a type of "share investment strategy" where financial institutions would be guaranteed a certain share in the loan recipient's future income (Friedman, 1955; Friedman and Friedman, 1980: 184)—a plan that would come to fruition in a different form in the transfer of state support to student loans later on. Most importantly perhaps for the direction future neoliberal reforms of primary and secondary education would take, he also reintroduced the idea of education vouchers that had long lay dormant. The vouchers would be given to parents to allow them to select the school, private or public, to send their child. This would essentially end the state's monopoly over education and provide a market based on freedom of choice (Friedman, 1955: 127; Friedman and Friedman, 1980: 158–170). In the end Friedman believed that these vouchers would generate competition among schools, spur pedagogical innovation, discipline teachers and, overall, produce a much better, more efficient educational system.

In the 1960s fellow Mont Pelerin Society member Gary S. Becker also began advancing a new conceptualization of education that would also have an important effect on future education policy. In his theory of "human capital," Becker (1964) began to link educational attainment with both individual earnings and national economic growth. In this framing, education was seen as individual skill development, which would then connect with greater productivity and earnings. Investments made in human capital by the state or industry would, in the end, pay off for both the individual "investor" and the larger national economy. In Becker's fusion of education and economics the content of what students' received in education settings is conceptualized less as "enlightenment" or the molding of "citizenship" but rather as the acquisition of specific marketable skills or "human capital" that served direct economic purposes and which can then be "cashed in" by the individual for higher wages in the marketplace. In this reading poverty and inequality are not outcomes of the systemic failures of the market economy but an individual problem resulting from a lack of skills or skills being out of alignment with economic need.

In the early 1970s another movement with important future implications for education policy was put forward by Leon Lessinger (1970) in his book *Every Kid a Winner: Accountability in Education*. Subsequently the book became one of the central works in the development of what came to be called the "accountability movement" in education. Lessinger advocated a new strategy for school reform drawn from neoclassical economics that create a new form of "educational engineering" through the establishment of "performance contracts." These contracts would establish specific goals and expectations that schools needed to adhere to in order to keep or increase their funding. Such a move, Lessinger argued, would encourage schools to become more efficient and accountable and shift control from teachers and local officials to centralized departments of education. As Lessinger (1970: 30–31) described it, under this new system "school officials will have to adopt certain managerial procedures that both stimulate the demand for performance and help provide it." Under this new contractual system students will "acquire certain skills" as measured by independent auditors (Lessinger, 1970: 18). Those schools that lived up to their contractual obligations and succeed are deemed accountability and worthy of rewarding with future funding. Those that don't, deserve to fail.

During the 1970s, the ideas of Friedman, Becker and Lessinger became integral parts of the efforts of think tanks to formulate neoliberal policy recommendations and to recommend specific reforms in education and the public sector as a whole. Friedman's ideas were also given some credence in the U.S. when they became part of the Nixon administration's failed attempt to introduced vouchers in large New Hampshire schools in the early 1970s (see Friedman, 2005) and, a bit later, were an inspiration for Thatcher's "Assisted Places Scheme" that sought to provide vouchers for "able children from our poorest homes" (Boyson, 1979). Indeed, vouchers have remained a key ingredient of various neoliberal reform efforts throughout the 1980s and 1990s and live on today in a different form in the charter schools of the U.S. and the free schools of Sweden and England.

The contours and seeming contradictions found in the "loose-tight" (Nitta, 2008) configuration that is a feature of most late twentieth and early twenty-first century neoliberal education policy reforms efforts can be situated by linking the writings of Friedman, Becker and Lessinger. In this configuration, education is to be freed from state control in order to avoid state indoctrination and to save tax money while, simultaneously, it is also to become more tightly controlled through auditing and monitoring by the state to ensure accountability, improve quality and enable choice. From Friedman comes the general critique of government directed and funded education. Such a critique shows up in various privatization and "school choice" measures advanced at various times and in various contexts. From Becker comes the idea that the true purpose of education in a market-oriented society is really economic rather than social or political. It is, in this way of thinking, the obtainment of individual skills and capital that fuel individual earnings, the generation of wealth and societal economic growth and well-being. From Lessinger comes the idea that a contractual arrangement should be put into place to engineer educational performance and generate institutional accountability. Only such a contractual system can create the type of incentives necessary to motivate schools, administrators and teachers, spur reforms and promote "excellence." When merged these stances represent the oscillating dimensions of neoliberal reforms efforts in various national contexts. In this situation, education is to be viewed as a private resource rather than a public good or more precisely as a public good that can only be arrived out through its use as a private resource. Education should be less about society collectively paying for something that benefits society as a whole and more about individuals paying for the opportunity to enhance their own human capital and thus contribute more effectively to societal well-being. This being the case, education at all levels should be much more closely connected with the evolving economic needs of companies and firms. It should not be an institution controlled by education professionals promoting their or some particular group's ideals or part of the state efforts to increase loyalty but should follow the needs and dictates of employers operating in the marketplace and education consumers reacting to those perceived needs. These needs, in turn, can then be best assessed through the use of outside auditing and accountability measures, such as standardized testing, that are linked with reward and punishment mechanisms. Indeed, directing all this auditing to enable choice and establishing a market for education are the only functions government should have in public education.

NEW ZEALAND'S TOMORROW SCHOOLS[3]

New Zealand represents one of the most extensive neoliberal efforts to reform the state sector to be found any nation over the last few decades (see Boston, 1995). As such, it was also among the first nations to experiment with wholesale neoliberal inspired education reforms beginning in the late

1980s. It did this with a rapid and dramatic alteration to its school structure referred to as the Tomorrow's Schools Plan—a plan that one observer dubbed "the earthquake method" of educational change (Holdaway, 1989). As with educational reform in other countries, New Zealand's sweeping reforms of the late 1980s were brought about by a fundamental reconsideration of the role of the state in all social welfare and public domain matters that was led by neoliberal think tanks, policy makers, politicians and theoreticians. New Zealand's reforms were also influenced by a particularly strong and influential Treasury Ministry that during the 1980s had become an advocate for many neoliberal ideas and policies within the government, including reforming government through the application of Buchanan and Tullock's Public Choice Theory (see Openshaw, 2009: 175; Barrington, 1991: 296). In New Zealand these reforms were often referred to as "Rogernomics," as opposed to Reaganomics in the U.S., in reference to Roger Douglas who became Finance Minister in 1984. New Zealand's education reforms were also inspired by an influential 1983 OECD report that linked the country's increasing unemployment and declining economic productivity and standard of living of the 1970s and 80s with its overly centralized and bureaucratic education system. The report called on the government to establish much closer links "between education and economic planning" (OECD, 1983: 27)

Many of these neoliberal ideas crystallized in Treasury's report *Government Management* that was prepared for the incoming Labour government and prime minister David Lange in 1987 (The Treasury, 1987).[4] The Treasury report referred to the education system as one that "tends to run on its own track motivated by its own educational objectives which may be at variance with other objectives, including macro objectives, of the Government" (The Treasury, 1987: 18). The report also criticized the state-run education system as being "highly centralized" and unable to "adjust rapidly to the fast changing demands that are being put upon it" (The Treasury, 1987: 18–19). Under such circumstances, there appeared to be no reason for government to continue its "direct provision of education services" (The Treasury, 1987: 9). Reform was urgently needed.

These documents served as a precursor and motivation for Lange to form a taskforce to make recommendations for education reform.[5] The Taskforce to Review Educational Administration (TREA), chaired by Brian Picot, a grocery chain owner and former president of the Auckland Chamber of Commerce, set out in July of 1987 to fundamentally rethink the education system of New Zealand in the wake of the OECD report and criticisms offered up by the Treasury Ministry and others seeking education reform (see Openshaw, 2009; McQueen, 1991). As much as the report *A Nation at Risk* provided the policy foundation and much of the vocabulary for neoliberal education reforms in the U.S., the TREA's report *Administrating for Excellence* (TREA, 1988), or "The Picot Report" as it became known, served as a catalyst for primary and secondary education reform in New Zealand. The report decried the existing education system as "a creaky cumbersome affair" that is "not suited to the rapidly changing late twentieth century" (TREA, 1988: 22). One of the central criticisms levied in "The Picot Report" was the urgent need to decentralize New Zealand Schools. The report maintained that the primary problem with New Zealand's national education system was that is was "overcentralised and made overly complex by having too many decision points" (TREA, 1988: xi). As such, parents had little power or choice within a system that had historically been exclusively controlled by bureaucrats and teaching professionals. What was needed was a more consumer friendly system they gave parents in local schools the power to make choices; similar to what was also unfolding in England and Wales.

"The Picot Report" recommended that control of schools be decentralized by moving them out of the control of the Ministry of Education and into locally constituted and controlled Board of Trustees, much like as is found in school boards in the U.S. or the "independent board of governors" of the short lived grant maintained schools in England. This decentralization would be complemented by a strengthening of new national standards that would now be overseen by a new Education Ministry and a grouping of new offices such as the Education Review Office (ERO), which would be responsible for reviewing the progress of schools, the Teacher Registration Board (TRB), that would oversee teacher standards, and the New Zealand Qualifications Authority (NZQA) who would access all school qualifications (and later a division of Special Education Services). In October of 1989 the task force's recommendations were largely accepted and were passed as the "Tomorrow's Schools Plan." In 1991 the plan was amended and further liberalized under a new Nationalist government that did away with zoning requirements thus enabling parents to choose which school to send their children to.

The Tomorrow's Schools plan received mostly negative reviews from teachers in New Zealand's two major teachers' union, the New Zealand Educational Institute (NZEI) which represents primary and intermediate teachers, and the New Zealand Post Primary Teachers Association (PPTA) which represented teachers in secondary schools (see Grant, 2003). In essence many teachers believed that the general neoliberal reforms, with their public interest theory rhetoric of "producer interest" and the "capture" of education, portrayed teachers as untrustworthy and self-interested actors and disregarded their commitment and professionalism. The plan was also criticized in union circles as being a disguised attempt to destroy the autonomy, pay scale and professional control of teachers and their unions and to replace them with a purely consumer driven and profit-based educational model with lower autonomy and wages (see Gordon and Wilson, 1992).

While the teacher's unions were criticizing the Tomorrow's Schools plan for going too far in its introduction of a neoliberal decentralized, consumer model into education, others criticized the plan for not going far enough. Many of these criticisms were to be found in the book *Upgrading New Zealand's Competitive Advantage* (Crocombe et al., 1991). The book and the "Porter Project," named for the contributions of and the policy movement spawned by Harvard Business School professor Michael Porter, condemned the New Zealand education system for placing "a higher priority on the transmission of social values and academic training rather than on providing economically usefully skills" (Crocombe et al., 1991: 153). For Porter, New Zealand's economy had "fallen out of alignment with the mandates of modern international competition" (Porter in Crocombe et al., 1991: 8) because it had essentially become an overextended social welfare system that emphasized "wealth distribution" over "innovation and skills development" (Openshaw, 2009: 153). This system had also created "a glaring mismatch between the skills needed to upgrade the New Zealand economy and those provided by our education system" (Crocombe et al., 1991: 161). The solutions, according to the authors, were to upgrade New Zealand's human resources and human capital by establishing a much closer connections between educational institutions and businesses and by increasing the focus on educational innovation.

The "Porter Project's" work served as one of the central document for the 1992 curricular reforms found in the *New Zealand Curriculum Framework* (Ministry of Education, 1993). Specifically it helped push the neoliberal reform efforts away from the national structure and organizations of schools to the curriculum itself. The framework established the first significant curriculum guidelines in the wake of the Tomorrow Schools Plan. Tomorrow's Schools reforms had been about the reorganization of education and the lessening of state and professional control rather than specifically about pedagogical or curricular content. The *Curriculum Framework* called for creating "a workforce which is increasingly highly skilled and adaptable" (Ministry of Education, 1993: 1). It, like the 1988 education reforms in England and Wales, also identified "seven essential learning areas" that would serve as the focus of primary and secondary education and on which students would be tested.

In 2007 the New Zealand national curriculum underwent another, even more profoundly neoliberal-style overhaul. In keeping with the neoliberal emphasis on individual initiative and ending welfare state dependency, one of the central purposes of the new curriculum was to forge a student who is "enterprising and entrepreneurial." In the report launching the new curriculum, future students were described as being able to "seize the opportunities offered by new knowledge and technologies to secure a sustainable social, cultural, economic, and environmental future for our country" (Ministry of Education, 2007: 8). These students were also called upon to become "life learners" who continually "learn to learn." Implicit in the 2007 revised curriculum, and a "key competency," was an approach that sought to help students, in the words of the report, in "managing self."

Students who are capable of managing self were described as being "enterprising, resourceful, reliable, and resilient. They establish personal goals, make plans, manage projects, and set high standards. They have strategies for meeting challenges. They know when to lead, when to follow, and when and how to act independently" (Ministry of Education, 2007: 12). Interestingly in comparing the curriculum documents from 1993 to 2007 some key "educational values" of 1993 such as "honesty," "reliability" and "respect for the law" were replaced in the 2007 curriculum with "excellence," "innovation, inquiry and curiosity" and "community and participation."

From the late 1980s onward as National and Labour governments "came and went" neither party did little to alter the basic structure found in Tomorrow's Schools or the neoliberal curricular reforms first introduced in 1992. Generally speaking National governments wanted to expand budgetary devolution and school choice, while Labour governments emphasized assessment, equality of opportunity and increasing educational standards. Both, however, largely kept the market-centered neoliberal approach to education in tact (see Openshaw, 2009: 161–162). Despite the endurance of these neoliberal policies critics continued to argue that despite all these reforms and the condemnation of the older public welfare system of education there was "scant evidence of any tangible improvements to teaching and learning as a result of site based management" (Education Policy Response Group, 1999: 39). In the end it seemed, despite all the emphasis on a radical new model for education—one that made New Zealand the global poster child of neoliberal-style reforms—there appeared to be little educational improvement to show for it.

FROM THE NATIONAL CURRICULUM TO FREE SCHOOLS: EDUCATION REFORM IN ENGLAND AND WALES

Like New Zealand, neoliberal education reforms in England and Wales also followed an ironic decentralized/centralization or "loose-tight" arrangement. In this system the range of government shrunk, however, "where you were inside the range, there was no doubt who directed" (interviewee in Kogan and Hanney, 2000: 167). Under Margaret Thatcher and her second education secretary and fellow founder of the Centre for Policy Studies, Keith Joseph, she began limiting and refocusing state involvement in education beginning shortly after her election in 1979. The ideas she drew upon for specific education reforms had been around for some time, dating back to her own term as Secretary of State for Education and Science during the Heath government in the early 1970s and the so-called "Black Papers" of the 1960s and 1970s that advocated for market solutions to education reform, as well as in the writings of neoliberal think tanks such as the Institute of Economic Analysis, the Adam Smith Institute and Thatcher's own Centre for Policy Studies. Following the framework outlined in these documents, the main focus of early reform efforts were directed at laying the groundwork for creating a market for education by first revising how schools were organized within the national system of education. This system had largely been in place since the 1940s and was envisioned as a comprehensive "national system, locally administered." In this system money for school operations came from the central government but was administered and controlled by a Local Education Authority (LEA) (Whitty, Power and Helpin, 1998). However, for a neoliberal-style reorganization of the type Thatcher envisioned to occur the power held by LEAs would need to be considerably curtailed since they were in a position to effectively block any reform efforts led by the central government. The LEAs were also seen by the Thatcher government and others promoting neoliberal reforms as being overly bureaucratic, exceedingly focused on transmitting progressive social values rather than knowledge content and, perhaps most importantly, too much under the sway of teachers' unions and the Labour party, particularly in urban areas.

The neoliberal-style reform efforts of the early and mid-1980s were somewhat limited in scope, at least by later standards, and, somewhat like those in New Zealand, largely focused on expanding the power of parents, creating parental choice, limiting the role of the LEAs and promoting cultural conservative values, such as religious training. The 1980 Education Act gave parents the ability to express preferences for a school which the LEAs were obligated to consider. It also established the controversial "Assisted Places Scheme" that gave "academically able" poor students vouchers to attend school in other areas. Likewise, the 1984 Education Act created grants for various government-backed initiatives that further reduced the LEAs control over local education (see Miller and Ginsburg, 1991).

In 1987 school reform became a centerpiece of Thatcher's reelection campaign. After her reelection the initial devolutionary efforts to limit the power of LEAs and to create a market for education from the early 1980s culminated and intensified in 1988 with the Education Reform Act for England and Wales or "The Baker Act," named after secretary of state Kenneth Baker. The Act was one of the most sweeping reforms in British history and would serve as a template for global neoliberal-style reforms enacted elsewhere in the subsequent decades.[6] The Act contained four features that built on previous devolutionary efforts and also moved reform into new areas. These reforms included (1) the furthering of budgetary and control devolution through the "Local Management of Schools" initiative, (2) the establishment of a national curriculum in various "core" and "foundation" areas and the advancement of standards and periodic testing of students, (3) the publication of "league tables" reporting on how schools were meeting those new national standards and (4) the ultimate goal, the expansion of school choice provisions in order to further the generation of a market or quasi-market for education.

Under the Act authority over schools was further devolved with LEAs now only able to retain a small bit of government funding to allocate themselves. Under the Local School Management initiative almost all aspects of budgets and decision-making were essentially taken from LEAs and handed directly over to the schools. Also under this new system, funding was for the first time directly linked to the number of students attending a school. Parents were also now also able to select through "open enrollment" which school to send their children. In turn schools themselves could not decline students until they had reached their capacity. At that point the school could develop standards of admission to limit enrollment much like private schools. In addition, the Act introduced a new entity, the "grant maintained school," that allowed schools to bypass the LEAs altogether with funding grants coming directly from the government. These schools could be created through a ballot of parents and operated with their own independent board of governors. These would exist until they were eliminated during the Blair government and would serve as an inspiration for the establishment of free schools in 2010.

While the Act decentralized some control, or at least initiated a devolutionary strategy for bypassing the LEAs, it also created new forms of governmental centralization in the area of the curriculum and the introduction of a national examination system. The Act created a National Curriculum in the core areas of English, math and science and six foundation areas for all children in England's and Wales' schools. In addition, the Act provided for the first "attainment targets" where every child would be tested for achievement in core areas at the age of 7, 11 and 14 (see Le Grand, 2003: 108–109). The results of these tests would then be published by the Chief Inspector of Schools (which was later transformed into the Office of Standards in Education in the 1992 Education Reform Act) to provide information to parents to further enable them to select the best school where to send their children.

The next significant education act was the Education Act of 1992 under the Major government. This Act again sought to further decrease the power of LEAs and increase market-style competition. This was to be done primarily by increasing the amount of information being collected by schools through a reordering of the school inspection process. Previous school inspections had been performed by the independent Her Majesty's Inspectors (HMI) and the LEAs. The Act established a new non-ministerial Office of Standards in Education (Ofsted) to carry out inspections of schools by independently contracted inspectors who are selected and trained by Ofsted. These new inspectors would use a newly created *Ofsted Inspection Handbook* to guide their inspections (see Whitty et al., 1998: 20). Under the model HMIs still performed school inspections but under the direction of Ofsted. Ofsted, whose motto is "raising standards, improving lives," consists of private education experts and one so called lay expert who evaluate each school and issue a report card in areas such as "teaching and learning," "care, guidance and support" and "leadership and management." The scores form inspection reports are summarized in league tables that are then published to increase school choice among parents. Now parents could analyze both school test scores on the National Curriculum and Ofsted inspections reports to help determine which school to select or put pressure on their schools to improve.

With the ascendency of Labour in1997 after eighteen years on the sidelines, the education reforms launched by Conservatives were to the surprise of many educators and critics general strengthened rather than abandoned (see Glennerster, 2002). Such a consistent orientation is also found in Australia, the U.S. and New Zealand where changes from Conservative to Labour or Republican to Democrat has shown few changes in the general neoliberal direction of education policy. Dropped under the Labour government, however, were the controversial "Assisted Places Scheme" and its voucher program and the "grant maintained school." Under the Blair policies school inequality and social justice again returned as a central issue for education policy makers, particularly in schemes such as the Education Action Zones (EAZs) for underperforming schools; however, these reforms were to be accomplished through market-style methods rather than welfare state intervention.

The general orientation toward education and the key piece of policy introduced during Blair's term were summarized early on in his term in the white paper *Excellence in Schools*. The paper maintained that education was to be "the top priority" of the government (DfEE, 1997). The new focus of education reform would, however, be on "standards" rather than with the Conservatives emphasis on "structural reform," since, as the report framed it, "standards matter more than structures" (DfEE, 1997). Under this new orientation, schools that failed would be identified, intervention would take place and funding and the intensity of future reviews by Ofsted would be tied to improvement in test scores, similar to the reform which would occur later in the U.S. in its "No Child Left Behind" policy.

More recently neoliberal education reforms have intensified under the Cameroon Coalition government and its attempts to create a new "education revolution." Michael Gove, the Education Secretary, has stated, "What I'd like to do is to ensure some of the radicalism that we used to have education policy returns" (Harrison, 2010). These new reforms have again revolved around expanding consumer choice this time through the establishment of so-called "free schools" based on those in Sweden and American charter schools and the extension and modification of Blair's urban "academy schools" concept to all schools. Free schools, like charter schools, are schools that a group of people can establish and still receive funding directly from the central government. These free schools will be able to establish their own admission policies and salaries and make approved variations to the National Curriculum, although they will still face Ofstead inspection. Over time this would allow parents to select from a variety of schools with variations of styles and curricula. The new free schools are forms of the broader academy schools where now all public schools in England will have the option be become "grant maintained" and be able to by-pass the LSAs completely. These academy schools will also have the option of being managed and operated by outside companies. These academy schools, like free schools, will also have the ability to choose their own curriculum.

As with education reforms in New Zealand and those happening in higher education in the U.K., those in England and Wales have shifted with the varieties of neoliberalism in place. Labour governments tend to emphasize markets as a means to generate more equality, while Conservatives focus on the ability of markets and privatization to devolve state responsibility. However, what has been consistent in both cases is the central role the market and consumer choice are now called on to play in education.

FROM "A NATION AT RISK" TO "NO CHILD LEFT BEHIND" AND BEYOND: EDUCATION REFORM IN THE U.S.

Initiatives to bring market-style reforms to the American education system are actually quite old. Indeed, with its federated political system, strong economic liberalist streak and array of private schools the American system has sometimes been an exemplar for various neoliberal reforms around the world, although at home it has often been attacked by neoliberals for not being marketed oriented and liberal enough.[7] Although in the U.S. the specific neoliberal attempts to reform education were theoretically established by Milton Friedman in the 1950s and flirted with during the Nixon administration in the early 1970s, it was not until the 1980s with the rise of the "roll back" neoliberalism of Ronald Reagan that these ideas began to be put forward as specific reform efforts and education policy, and then only slowly. As with the rhetoric appearing in other national contexts, neoliberal reformers in the U.S. cited the decline of the U.S. economy in the late 1970s and early 1980s as evidence that the "command economy" policies and the welfare state had failed and, by implication, so too had their inefficient and misdirected education system.

Much of the neoliberal outrage of the early 1980s was directed at the elevation of the office of education in the Department of Health, Education and Welfare (HEW) to a cabinet-level position under the administration of Jimmy Carter in 1979. Prior to this, most federal education policy was overseen by a relatively small office within the HEW with limited responsibilities. Education issues were left almost entirely to the individual states with the federal government providing some funding through various "Title Programs" directed primarily toward poor students and for the pre-school program "Project Head Start" but the generally federal government provided very little steering of education policy. Critics contended that the new federal department marked a significant foray of the federal government into the educational domains of the individual states and was, consequently, a violation of the constitutional rights of states to control their schools.

Efforts to abolish the Department of Education never materialized despite support from the Reagan administration. However, neoliberal reforms did make important inroads following Reagan's establishment of the National Commission on Excellence in Education. In 1983 the commission released its report entitled *A Nation at Risk*. This report, which helped make popular the soon to become trite terms of "educational excellence" and "the learning society," linked together education as a nationalist goal and its importance in global economic competition. Prior to this education reform was largely a local matter built around the general rationalistic goals of the individual states or broad national concerns, such as the science education reform efforts that began after the launch of Sputnik in the late 1950s. Using the alarmist rhetoric that would became a hallmark of these types of reports, *A Nation at Risk: The Imperative for Education Reform* warned that "history is not kind to idlers." To shake people from their complacency the report called for the creation of a "Learning Society," in which public, private, and parochial schools; colleges and universities; vocational and technical schools and institutes; libraries; science centers, museums, and other cultural institutions; and corporate training and retraining programs offer opportunities and choices for all to learn throughout life" (National Commission on Excellence in Education, 1983). The report further argued that

> The time is long past when American's destiny was assured simply by an abundance of natural resources and inexhaustible human enthusiasm, and by our relative isolation from the malignant problems of older civilizations. The world is indeed one global village. We live among determined, well-educated, and strongly motivated competitors. We compete with them for international standing and markets, not only with products but also with the ideas of our laboratories and neighborhood. (National Commission on Excellence in Education, 1983)

Although the report received considerable attention at the time it was released, it provided only five very general policy recommendations beyond a renewed commitment by government, communities and schools to put more focus on education.

A Nation at Risk was soon followed by a series of similar reports such as the *Carnegie Corporation of New York's Education and Economic Progress: Toward a National Educational Policy* (1983), *The Committee for Economic Development's Investment in Our Children* (1985), *The Business and Higher Education Forum's America's Competitive Challenge: The Need for National Response* (1983), *The Committee for Economic*

Development's Strategy for United States Industrial Competitiveness (1984) and the *Twentieth Century Fund Task Force's Making the Grade* (1983) (see Martin, 1991: 342). All of these report in some manner echoed *A Nation at Risk* by advocating for the remolding of education in response to declining standards and inevitable changes occurring in the U.S. and global economy.

Altogether A Nation at Risk did little to directly change public education policy in the U.S., it did begin to shift the rhetoric and national education agenda toward the obtainment of new, more economically centered educational goals (see Nitta, 2008: 27). It also served as a seminal document and set the stage for a number of specific reforms attempted first under the administrations of George H. W. Bush and finally obtained under the administration of Bill Clinton in the 1990s. Echoing Leon Lessinger from the 1970s, Clinton called for "accountability in education" through testing and increasing standards as part of a more general push for accountability and "outcomes assessment" in government guided by the principles of New Public Management (see Nitta, 2008: 54). In terms of education, the Clinton administration introduced two key pieces of legislation during the 1990s, the *Goals 2000: Educate America Act and the Improving America's Schools Act of 1994*. *Goals 2000* was the first law to establish national goals for education and to mandate state devised testing to measure adherence to those standards (see U.S. Department of Education, 1994). Among the goals outlined in the Act were to increase parent participation levels and to make the U.S. first in mathematics and science achievement. The Improving America's Schools Act further solidified these goals by directly linking federal support to states that could show movement toward meeting the goals outlined in Goals 2000. Also, included in this legislation was a "school choice" provision that mandated that schools create systems that allowed parents to select schools within their area. It also provided incentives for states to create more "magnet schools" which were to serve as "models of school reform efforts."

While the policy documents of the 1980s established economic priorities for education in the U.S., it was the acts passed under the Clinton administration that began to make these priorities actionable. The policies enacted under his term dropped some of the more conservative cultural elements that has been prevalent in 1980s reform efforts, such as a return to school prayer, but retained and magnified the emphasis on economic priorities in education. Most importantly, however, it added specific enforcement, auditing and steering mechanisms to achieve these economic priorities. Education was now to be primarily about economic priorities, and these priorities would be assessed and federal funding linked to how goals were being met. Clinton era reforms were generally accepted on both side of the political spectrum, although those on the left worried about the assault on teachers and their unions that was a part of the rhetoric spurred by these measures and those on the right lamented the absence of a return to morality in the schools.

Neoliberal think tanks have played an active role in U.S. school reform efforts going back to the 1970s; however, it was during the 1990s and early 2000s that their role in shaping education policy became much more pronounced. During this time several neoliberal-leaning think tanks, including the American Enterprise Institute, the Gates Foundation, the Hoover Institute and the Heritage Foundation released policy documents pushing for more market-centered education reforms in order to meet the demands of globalization. One of the most exemplary in this regard was the Heritage Foundation's "No Excuses Campaign" (see Carter, 2000). The Campaign advocated for many of the central features of neoliberal models of education reform including expanding the managerial power of principals, establishing measurable education goals and using "rigorous and regular testing" directed by individual states and not the federal government (Carter, 2000: 8–10). The report maintained that these features were very much compatible with vouchers and school choice. This document and others produced during the late 1990s and early 2000s provided much of the verbiage for the creation of what came to be called "No Child Left Behind." In the later part of the decade, another leading proponent of education reform, The Gates Foundation, ramped up its efforts to influence education reform in the U.S. In 2009 the Foundation spent $373 million to support various groups, such as The Alliance for Excellent Education, seeking to promote neoliberal-style changes in public education, including a $3.5 million grant to Harvard University to place "strategic data fellows" into schools to act as "entrepreneurial change agents" and funds to Teach Plus and Educators for Excellence to help counter the message of teacher unions in various states (Dillon, 2011: 3).

The most sweeping neoliberal-style reform came with the enactment of the "No Child Left Behind Act of 2001" (U.S. Department of Education, 2001). The Act essentially expanded and strengthened the reforms enacted during the Clinton administration. The Act, with its stated goals of "closing the achievement gap" between rich and poor students and school districts and ending what G. W. Bush called "the soft bigotry of low expectations" effectively combined elements of the previous neoliberal educational agenda with progressive's long standing emphasis on equality of opportunity and "improving the academic achievement of the disadvantaged." Only this time, as under Blair in England, "equality of opportunity' was framed not in terms of direct government action or increased educational spending but through the neoliberal mantras of flexibility, marketization, accountability and choice. The law established a series of increasingly severe penalties for schools that failed to make what was called "adequate yearly progress" (AYP) on state-designed and -mandated tests, including allowing parents to transfer their students out of a failing school, changing administrators and even eventually closing the schools that were deemed as failing to achieve AYP.

The early part of the twenty-first century also saw new emphasis placed on "charter" and "magnet" schools as part of the larger effort to expand school choice and as a result of the resistance to wide-scale use of school vouchers. As with free schools in Sweden and England, charter schools were essentially publicly funded schools where an individual state would grant a "charter" for a group of individuals, either for or not for profit, to launch a school in a particular community. On the other hand, "magnet" schools were still publicly funded but were "themed" to meet particular consumer niches, such as schools of art or science and technology. In the case of charter schools individual schools would receive funding from and be monitored by the state. In turn the school would be freed from some state regulation, as well as the collective bargaining rules of teacher unions. In New York City, charter schools were promoted by Joe Klein, the former chancellor of the New York City schools, as "a core part of our portfolio strategy" (Klein in Fisher, 2010: 74). As an assistant attorney general under the Clinton administration, Klein (in Fisher, 2010: 74) claims that he had learned two things about successful education, "competition and accountability." In New Haven, Connecticut, all the city's high schools were turned into "magnet" schools and when one school "failed" in 2011 a private, for-profit company, Renaissance School Services, was brought it to reorganize and run the school (see Smith, 2011).[8]

More recent neoliberal-style reforms efforts in the U.S. have occurred in individual states such as Florida which abolished tenure for teachers and at the federal level with the introduction of the "A Blueprint for Reform" (U.S. Department of Education, 2010) to reform "No Child Left Behind" and the "Race to the Top" initiative. "A Blueprint for Reform" has made the "promotion of innovation," "education entrepreneurship," "raising the bar" and "rewarding excellence" as some of its key provisions. In order to promote innovation, the "Race to the Top" initiative set up a competitive grant system where states were given "incentive funding" to experiment with new ways of organizing and conducting education in their schools. Under the grant system, those states "leading the way with ambitious yet achievable plans for implementing coherent, compelling, and comprehensive education reform" received Race to the Top funds while the less "innovative" did not (U.S. Department of Education, 2011).

Neoliberal reform efforts in the U.S. have also generally displayed the loose-tight configuration seen elsewhere. However, as a decentralized system these changes have been guided by federal policy and dollars but have been implemented at the state level. In one direction various privatization or quasi-privatization measures have been introduced to move education away from governmental control, such as the voucher system advocated by Friedman and others that has been experimented with in a few school districts or the more recent move to less regulated charter schools emphasizing variety and parental choice. Here there has been a fear of state power in the running of schools and a push to "denationalize schooling." In the other direction schools have been brought under much tighter regulations and auditing through the implementation of "accountability systems" and the "outcomes based assessment" contained in various high stakes testing, as in "No Child Left Behind" and its proposed revision in "A Blueprint for Reform." Also, as in England and Wales and New Zealand, it has not mattered much which political party launched the reforms since most strongly believe in the power of markets and choice rather than the welfare state to provide for quality schooling for all.

THE IMPORTANCE OF EDUCATION REFORM FOR NEOLIBERAL GOVERNANCE

Since their founding in the nineteenth century, Western public education systems have frequently been the targets of various reform-minded groups and organizations seeking to remold society by remaking education. Indeed, the massified public education systems that began to develop in the late nineteenth and early twentieth centuries themselves grew out of larger social reforms efforts launched in various nations in the latter half of the nineteenth century in the name of progress, equality of opportunity, modernization and societal advancement. Throughout its history, public education has, perhaps more than any other social institution, been the site of considerable moral panic about declining standards and the ceaseless introduction of trendy new curricula, assessments, procedures and "best practices" meant to improve the education of children. However, the neoliberal reforms of the last few decades have not been merely another attempt to "tweak" public education systems or to reshuffle the curriculum yet again but a much more fundamental attempt to completely and thoroughly reorganize the way education at all levels operates. As such, it represents a major shift in what should comprise the "public domain" and how this domain should be organized and controlled.

Under the Enlightenment and democratic models, at least in their unrealized ideal forms, education was seen as an aspect of personal and national developmental that called for action by the state acting in the public interest. As this vision unfolded in the twentieth century, the belief came to be that everyone should have access to knowledge through some degree of formal, state-directed public education through a certain level in order to become both "enlightened" themselves and a competent citizen in society. This, "neighborhood effect," to use Friedman's own term, made acquiring knowledge a public matter that should be directly supported and encouraged by governments operating to promote the public good. A broad, liberal form of learning was also of central importance in this model. While people may be specialized and access to knowledge stratified in various ways, there remained a basic "social literacy" and level of political awareness or citizenship that should ideally be shared by all within a particular nation state.

Likewise, everyone should also have access to this personal development and social literacy through the availability of free libraries, free schools and free or subsidized higher education. Such public institutions would be funded collectively through progressive forms of taxation. However, the neoliberal model of knowledge and education that emerged over the last few decades, with its emphasis on privatization, choice, meeting economic needs and providing accountability, seeks to create an entirely new condition for education where, as Ball (2003) describes it, "value replaces values" Indeed, in this model being "enlightened, "socially literate" or "politically aware" are no longer in themselves central foci of education. If they have importance at all, it is only in the context of direct marketable skills, the development of human capital, personal earnings or to assist in the gaining of a national competitive advantage. For instance, knowledge of the classics or medieval history is only meaningful if can be parlayed into something marketable such as advertising campaigns, computer gaming or "Renaissance Fairs." In the neoliberal model of education there is no one set of state directed knowledge that people need to acquire in order to become enlightened or socially or politically literate just as there can be, as Hayek (1948) described it, no one set of knowledge available to correctly direct a command economy. Advocating one knowledge form over another is, from this reading, unnecessary, authoritarian and even elitist. Instead of these social or government-directed goals, there are individual skills and perspectives that one must choose to acquire and frequently modify as needed in order to fit with evolving needs of the marketplace. Education exists to help the individual acquire those skills he or she needs in order to succeed in a particular economic place and climate—which too is ever modulating. People are certainly free to choose any course of action they want, such as becoming well versed in philosophy, anthropology or medieval history or selecting a "low rated school," however, there will always be a "market cost" levied on that particular decision that will eventually redirect behavior. Here equality of opportunity where all schools should provide a similar quality of education, at least theoretically, is replaced with a market stratified system.

Given all these neoliberal attempts to fundamentally rework education, what have actually been the specific outcomes of these now several-decades-long efforts? Also, how successful have these efforts been and, more fundamentally, have they made education better? At first glance the more grandiose visions of complete privatization or a full "denationalization of schooling" and "vouchers for all" seem to have been tempered somewhat over the ensuring decades by the "politics of policy implementation" generated by various forces of resistance, such as teachers' unions and welfare state politicians. The direct privatization attempts of public education or the indirect privatization through vouchers approach advocated by Freidman, the Institute of Economic Research and others seems to largely have had their day in most countries, at least for the time being, although in some contexts they continue to oscillate between rejection and a miraculous resurrection. As evident in New Zealand's most recent curricular reforms or the U.S.'s "Blue Print for Reform" and "Race to the Top" initiatives, most education policies today still contain elements of both the more socialized vision of education with its emphasis on social inclusion, equality and critical thinking historically promoted by teachers and educational theorists alongside the more neoliberal emphasis on cost reductions, economic goals, accountability, assessment and entrepreneurialism associated with neoliberal politicians, think tanks and reformers. Much like the hybrid political landscape of today discussed in Chapter 1, today's education policy environment is, like those of the past, continuously morphing around new coalitions (see Kliebard, 1995). As Openshaw (2009: 183) describes this situation, in today school environment we are surround by "a bewildering muddle of neoliberal, bicultural, constructivist and equity concepts, with little or no acknowledgment of any contradictions between them."

However, while the contemporary education policy scene is undoubtedly multivariate if we look deeper and more transnationally neoliberal reforms are still very much in vogue and more globally pronounced than perhaps ever before. Despite the economic downturn that began in 2008 that would have seemingly called neoliberal policies that created the crisis into question and despite the hybridization and the retention of older educational approaches and philosophies, the more general framing of education today has clearly undergone a seismic shift under neoliberal policies. In this sense, even the older approaches, whether they are labeled, "enlightenment," "nationalistic" or "progressive," have become reinterpreted and repositioned within the more general neoliberal instrumentalist and economistic framing of education. Indeed, what made neoliberal ideals palatable to many progressives was its adoption of the language of using education to generate mobility and end inequality, such as Bush's "No Child Left Behind."

Yet, the central question remains, have these reforms actually produced better schools? Choice and rudimentary markets or quasi-markets have emerged and state auditing and monitoring has substantially increased but does that means students are better educated? Providing answers to these questions is difficult if not impossible since the answer depends on the political manner in which "better" is defined. Also the very contemporary "measures" that are used to assess "betterment" are themselves reflections of particular ideas about what should properly constitute the purpose of education, what is measurable and the specific assessments and measures that result from this. In this sense, measurement is a deeply political and pragmatic endeavor rather than simply an epistemic process where, as Ian Hacking (1983: 137) reminds us, "we represent into order to intervene, and we intervene in light of representation." For example, the league tables, high stakes testing results and international comparison surveys that are often cited as evidence of the progress or decline of schools or national education systems are themselves outcomes of particular neoliberal policy framings of knowledge and education. Not only is this a matter of content in terms of what "core areas" or domains are included and which are not, i.e., math and reading above social studies and art but also at a more fundamental level what values or norms are appropriate in schools and which are not, such as in New Zealand's promotion of "entrepreneurial values" in its curriculum. In this case as particular assessment measures are used over and over, they become self-sustaining features of the neoliberal framing of education and often legitimate the need for even more assessment and for more neoliberalization of education. In other words, if choice fails to deliver it is because there was not enough choice.

However, even if we set the "politics of measurement" aside for a moment, there remains scant empirical, "measurable" evidence that neoliberal reforms have actually improved education in any context, and that which does exist is often produced by neoliberal-leaning think tanks or government organizations themselves. Indeed, this paucity of evidence is similar to that first used to argue for the need for neoliberal reforms to compensate for school's spiraling decline in the first place. Interestingly some of the biggest proponents of early neoliberal reforms have come to doubt their effectiveness. David Lange, the former Prime Minster who helped direct the Tomorrow's School plan in New Zealand, later expressed displeasure with the direction these reforms had taken. In a speech "Another Day for Tomorrow's Schools" he declared that "we've given away equality of opportunity in schooling for the shyster democracy of the marketplace" (Lange, 1999: 16). Likewise, Diane Ravitch who spend much of her early career advocating for neoliberal-style reforms in the U.S. now believes these reforms, particularly as found in all the attention and effort placed in the charter school movement, to have been greatly overblown (see Ravitch, 2010). Indeed, much of the evidence for reform seems to suggest that little has changed and that any rise in test scores may have been actually a self-fulfilling prophecy resulting from more attention being paid to testing itself, i.e., from teaching to the test (see Whitty 2002). Or, in the case of the supposed success of former grant-maintained, charter or free schools, increases in scores were actually the result of a "creaming" that occured as better students abandoned their home schools and congregated in particular schools through new systems of choice (see Hayden, 2004).

Also much education research now cast doubt on the often-grandiose claims of neoliberal reformers that choice will end inequality in education, "close the achievement gap" or, in G. W. Bush's terms, stop the "soft bigotry of low expectations." Indeed, much research seems to show the opposite. Primarily this results from a lack of attention to the variety of things that markets actually do. Fundamentally, there is an inherent and necessary stratification built into the neoliberal conceptualization of education and their use of markets or quasi-markets to correct the problems in education. Despite the rhetorical focus on "closing the achievement gap," neoliberal reforms actually rely on and produce a highly stratified market for education. Indeed, market stratification is what makes some markets and "products" more appealing, marketable, expensive and, ultimately, "better" than others. Such a process is seen as some students flock to so-called "better schools" with better reputations, real or imagined, and other remain in their local "crappy" schools. They are, consequently, also what makes some forms of knowledge and education more "valuable" and expensive than others in an educational marketplace. Without differentiation and stratification, whether real or imagined—p.r. or market driven—there can be no markets only the reciprocal exchange of a gift economy. Yet, as research in different contexts shows, the power to choose is itself unequally distributed (see Tomlinson, 2001). For instance, evidence from neoliberal education reforms in New Zealand and Belgium report an increased stratification occurring under neoliberal systems of school choice (see Lauder and Hughes, 1999; Vandenberghe, 1998). In the rush to propose markets as panaceas for education problems neoliberals seem to have forgotten that markets, while certainly generating competition and variability, also generate stratification and inequalities. In fact it was similar past inequalities that led to the establishment of the massified public schools systems of the last century.

If the outcomes of neoliberal reform have been dubious at best, why has education reform figured so prominently in the efforts of neoliberal reformers across the globe? Why have millions of dollars and countless hours of effort been expended writing reports, assessing schools and redesigning curriculum when the results are so meager or even by some accounts counterproductive? Also, if learning has not really improved much, charter or free schools have not proven that remarkable and the "achievement gap" has widened rather than narrowed, why do neoliberal education policies still seem to be so popular and "the only option?" The answers to these questions seem to be that these reforms were not about the "improvement" of education as such but a key component of a larger political and moral project of remolding the public sphere and realigning the relationship between government, economy and individual. Although neoliberal education reforms have been cast in the modernization narrative as "improvements" to the curriculum, pedagogy, school governance, teacher training or school administration, they are fundamentally about restructuring and reculturing society not just education. In the case of education, as in the case of other contexts, neoliberalism is a moral movement of broad societal reform posing as a pragmatic, realist and "economically sustainable" means of improving schools.

Some of the most compelling evidence that this is a far-reaching moral revolution and not just a revision in the organization of education comes from those who have been the point of all these education reforms in the first place—students themselves. Indeed, the true outcome of neoliberal policies can perhaps be best understood by looking at the "enterprise culture" created by "the new system of morality 'taught' by schools" (Ball, 1994:

146). In one interview study from New Zealand, for instance, neoliberal education reforms there were found to have produced a student who "had a strong sense that 'it's all down to me'" and that they were the exclusive "bearers of their own risk" (Higgins and Nairn, 2006: 219). Survey-based studies in Australia have also tracked the movement of students toward a more "economic/utilitarian perspective" as the result of the implementation of neoliberal policies in that country (Pick and Taylor, 2009: 73). In the U.S. an annual survey of first year university students at the University of California at Los Angeles found in 1971 that 37 percent though that it was important to be well off financially, while 73 percent said that "developing a meaningful philosophy of life" was important. By 2009 that percent had virtually reversed with 78 percent indicating the importance of being well off financially and 48 percent declaring the importance of having a meaningful life philosophy (Zernike, 2010: 16).

What these studies arguably point to is the depth of the neoliberal moral revolution and its decollectivization efforts. Education it is but one part, important as it may be, of generating a particular new type of political and societal arrangement. Indeed, promoting such a revolution is what brought liberalism back from the dead in the first place during the height of Keynesian orthodoxy. The traditional values of nation, community and cooperation that were key parts of the past education system are to be replaced with those of individualism and competition (see Whitty et al., 1998: 91). The school, consequently, is the place were those values are taught both explicitly in the design and content of the curriculum and implicitly in the very context and organization of the schools. In the next chapter, I will be concerned with outlining some of the outcomes that the more general moral shift that all these reforms efforts to knowledge making and education have sought to introduce.

7 Aligning Markets and Minds
The Responsibilized Self in the New Entrepreneurial Culture

> In acquiring new productive forces men change their mode of production; and in changing their mode of production, in changing the way of earning their living, they change all their social relations. (Marx, *The Poverty of Philosophy*)

> Utilitarians ... reduced the world to a dead mechanism, destroyed every element of cohesion, made society a struggle of selfish interest, and struck at the very roots of all order, patriotism, poetry, and religion. (Stephen, 1902: 192)

> The money economy ... is in fact one of the most potent institutions in our whole culture. In sober truth it stamps its pattern upon wayward human nature, makes us all react in standard ways to the standard stimuli it offers, and affects our very ideals of what is good, beautiful and true. (Mitchell, 1937: 371)

> Man is no longer man enclosed, but man in debt. (Deleuze, 1992)

> Whenever a single definite object is made the supreme end of the State, be it the advantage of a class, the safety or the power of the country, the greatest happiness of the greatest number or the support of any speculative idea, the State becomes for the time inevitably absolute. (Acton, 1907 [1862]: 288)

If one of the ultimate goals of neoliberalism was to "change the soul," as Margaret Thatcher famously put it, there is considerable evidence that within the last ten years the goal was well on its way of becoming realized. A 2007 poll conducted in Britain by the HeadlightVision Project at the Henley Centre found that more than half of the two thousand respondents felt that "looking after oneself" was a more effective strategy for handling the future than "looking after the community's interests." Ten years earlier the same poll found that 70 percent of those surveyed placed looking after the community's interest ahead of looking after one's own was preferable (Sears, 2007: 37). Even more striking the poll also found that those in lower socio-economic groups were more likely to report the importance of "looking after oneself" rather than the community's interest as more important when compared with those in upper income brackets. Another revealing survey, this time a cross-national opinion poll, found that between 1983 and 2001 the levels of mistrust of individuals and institutions increased substantially in the U.S., Ireland and the U.K., sites of some of them most dramatic neoliberal and new public management reforms of the past few decades (Judt, 2010: 19).

Such findings lend support to the argument that after over three decades of neoliberal politics and policies, as contested and incomplete as they may have been and continue to be, the changing of soul that Thatcher and other neoliberal politicians have worked so deliberately to achieve has made remarkable inroads not only politically and economically but also in the reshaping of everyday beliefs, lifestyles and opinions. The traditional welfare state, with its particular notions of citizen rights, collectivized wellbeing, progressive taxation and socialized risk, has, in many places been either reduced to an outdated and disdained institution in need of elimination or a second rate, backup alternative to a fully functioning market society. In this "post welfarist regime of the social" (Dean, 1999: 173) a new "conservative modernization" (Dale, 1989–1990: 4) has emerged that has generated a new, more individualist moral project of self-care and with it a new system of performance government to oversee and guide the making of a new moral self.

While it is often tempting to treat the rise of neoliberalism as simply a spotty and incomplete "minimalist state" ideology advocated by financial firms or the "rentier class" or as the flexing of the political muscle of global corporations, it is important to keep in mind that it is, like classic liberalism itself, a profoundly moral project as well. Since its inception it has sought nothing short of the creation of a new "morality of enterprise" (Power, 2007: 195) or "habitat of subjectification" (Rose, 1999: 178) built on the principles of individual responsibility, autonomy, individual choice and a rejection of all collectivist framings and solutions. This new system is buoyed by the belief that "individuals can shape autonomous identity for themselves through choices in taste, music, goods, styles and habits" (Rose 1999: 178). In this sense, despite neoliberals' insistence that they are rolling back the state and limiting the size of government, their active promotion of "autonomy and freedom of choice, require for their functioning a complex array of technologies if they are to operate" (Miller and Rose, 1993: 86). In other words, neoliberalism's anti-government stance has required a new form of what Foucault referred to as "governmentality" or technologies of power emphasizing and promoting an ongoing "self-care" and "ethical work" (Foucault, 1997: 265) in order to convert its anti-collectivist ideals into practice.[1] In this neoliberal system, a new being, a consumer citizen, is required, perhaps we could even say forced, to engage in constant acts of personal responsibility, choice and risk analysis in order to be an acceptable moral being and a proper citizen.

Through its proclamations of the return and triumph of the self-interested economic agent, neoliberalism's "responsibility talk" is also its "morality talk" (Ruhl, 2005: 72). Neoliberalism, like its older variant described by John Dewey (1935: 38) in the 1930s, places an "unceasing glorification of the virtues of initiative, independence, choice and responsibility." As such, it is a deeply moral project that often deceptively poses as an amoral or naturalistic claiming only to reflect human nature, a love of freedom and the "realities of the world." Neoliberalism is, in essence, an attempt to remake society as a collection of individuals—to, as Guy Debord (1995: 137) describes it, "restructure society without community." In this sense, the social is no longer a place that makes freedom possible through its enabling rules, boundaries and culture but "a site of constraint" (Rose, 2004: 180). Society, as sociologically conceived, holds people back by prohibiting them from entrepreneurializing, choosing and self-actualizing.

In this final chapter, I want to explore some of the manifestations and outcomes of the neoliberal moral project of the last few decades. It is my contention that all of neoliberalism's epistemic and pedagogical projects taking place in various forms and in various places must be seen in the context of its larger moral project and the "ethical work" it wishes to accomplish. In other words, neoliberal changes to knowledge and education are not just "policy shifts" or an inevitable economic reframing of epistemic activities as a response to globalization but part of a more fundamental, politically guided attempt to restructure society through a radically new "production of behaviors" (Ozga, 1998: 147) and the generation of very different "ethical subjects" (see Foucault, 1997: 265). In this chapter, I specifically want to focus on what type of social order and people get made or are at least attempted to be made under neoliberal forms of governmentality. This "aligning of market and minds" involves both the ways in which particular forms of subjectivity are constructed, internalized and reinforced and the creation of a larger moral ordering or an "intersubjective network," if you will, that creates, sustains and supports that particular form of subjectivity. It also, as we have seen in previous chapters, presupposes the recasting, reconstituting and dismantling altogether of an array of social institutions, regimes of truths and social discourses that have supported other notions of the social, politics and governmentality. In this sense we can conclude that "socio-economic systems do not simply create new products and perceptions. *They also create and recreate individuals*" (Hodgson, 1999: 76).

To investigate this neoliberal "making up of people," as Ian Hacking (1986) once described it, I want to look at three interconnected processes that are part of the creation of a new moral order and new forms of neoliberal ethical subjectivity: the consumerization of choice, the individualization of risk and the entrepreneurialization of work. Before exploring these specific new modes of subjectivity, however, I briefly discuss some of the dimensions of the moral projects of liberalism and neoliberalism. I conclude the chapter with a discussion of the distinction between a market society and social markets and the limits of liberalism.

THE MORAL PROJECTS OF NEOLIBERAL GOVERNMENTALITY

While the classic liberalism that emerged in the eighteenth and nineteenth centuries had enormous political and economic consequences, it should be understood first and foremost as a moral project of reform. Over time this moral project presented itself as a new mode of governmentality that sought to reimagine and reconfigure various existing relationships between the individual, society and government. David Hume was among the first to describe the link between the moral missions of early liberalism and the unique form of govenmentality it sought to introduce. In his words,

> In contriving any system of government, and fixing the several checks and controls of the constitutions, every man ought to be supposed a knave and to have no other end, in all his actions, than private interest. By this interest, we must govern him and, by means of it, notwithstanding his insatiable avarice and ambition, co-operate to the public good.

Recognizing actors as "selfish knaves" rather than "gallant knights" created not only a new understanding of human nature and social order but with them a new relation between governance and the governed (see Le Grand, 2003).

Adam Smith (1966), the great moral philosopher of Glasgow, also cast early liberalism as a doctrine centrally concerned with the relationship between the "passion of self-love" and social order. For Smith this basic motive, along with those of sympathy, the desire for freedom, propriety and the propensity to exchange goods and to work, when unhindered and spontaneous, worked in concert with the motives of others to generate individual happiness and the greater social good. Most famously it was in *The Theory of Moral Sentiments* and his discussion of wealth and the wealthy where Smith first laid out the relationship between "the selfish passions," economic exchange and the greater "public interest." As Smith described it, under a liberal order the wealthy are "led by an invisible hand to make nearly the same distribution of the necessaries of life which would have been made had the earth been divided into equal portions among all its inhabitants" (Smith, 1966 [1759]: 264–265). Some fifteen years later in the *Wealth of Nations*, Smith (1904 [1776]: 184) elaborates on the moral, social and economic workings of this invisible hand:

> Every individual necessarily labours to render the annual revenue of the society as great as he can. He generally neither intends to promote the public interest, nor knows how much he is promoting it ... He intends

only his own gain, and he is in this, as in many other cases, led by an invisible hand to promote an end which was no part of his intention. Nor is it always the worse for society that it was no part of his intention. By pursuing his own interest he frequently promotes that of the society more effectually than when he really intends to promote it. I have never known much good done by those who affected to trade for the public good.

In this moral and political system nature worked through the basic human sentiments to increase wealth and generate a harmonious social order (Pribram, 1983: 132). It was best able to do this without any guidance from the outside. Indeed, altering these natural sentiments would destroy this natural balance and the social equilibrium it created.

The moral projects of liberalist reform lay buried in the early twentieth century by both its own tendencies to promote economic "freedom of contract" over political "freedom of choice" and the growth of a more communalistic notion of the relationship between the individual and state. In the latter instance, the "knights" once again returned but now in the form of enlightened bureaucrats and experts who would help direct and manage society for the greater good. In the mid twentieth century, the moral projects of neoliberalism was given a rebirth in Hayek's works, particularly his essay "*Individualism*: *True and False*" based on a lecture delivered at University College Dublin in 1945 (Hayek, 1948). In the essay Hayek (1948: 6–7) defended the moral project of classic liberalism from socialistic and Keynesian challenges by distinguishing between two forms of individualism—one found in the "rationalist pseudo-individualism" of Cartesianism and the other in the spontaneous, collaborative individualism of Scottish liberalism. In the first the individual is engaged in "designing and directing" society for rational purposes. In the latter society is but the outcome of spontaneous interactions of individuals. The individual here is not the rational "comprehender" or designer but the actionable, self-interested person. In describing the tendency of critics to reduce Adam Smith's and "his group" writings to "the bogey of the 'economic man,'" Hayek (1948: 11) writes, "it would be nearer the truth to say that in their view man was by nature lazy and indolent, improvident and wasteful, and that it was only by the force of circumstances that he could be made to behave economically or carefully to adjust his means to his ends." Hayek (1948: 11) further argues that "we can still learn more about the behavior of men from the *Wealth of Nations* than from most of the more pretentious modern treatises on "social psychology." In this new liberal system "we must face the fact that the preservation of individual freedom is incompatible with a full satisfaction of our views of distributive justice" (Hayek, 1948: 22). Such a view produces a form of governance where the "need of conscious control" is eliminated and inducements are put into place to enable "individuals do the desirable things without anyone having to tell them what to do" (Hayek, 1945: 527).

Aligning Markets and Minds 189

As neoliberalism emerged in the 1970s it sought to recapture the moral projects first launched in the age of classic liberalism and which, according to neoliberal proponents, had been silenced by the more collectivist ethos, morality and politics of the twentieth century. Perhaps nowhere is this political morality more evident than in British politics of the last few decades. In the late 1980s Margaret Thatcher (1987), famously summed up the anti-collectivist moral thrust of the "roll back" phase of early neoliberalism. In her words,

> I think we have gone through a period when too many children and people have been given to understand" I have a problem, it is the Government's job to cope with it!" or "I have a problem, I will go and get a grant to cope with it!" "I am homeless, the Government must house me!" and so they are casting their problems on society and who is society? There is no such thing! There are individual men and women and there are families and no government can do anything except through people and people look to themselves first.

For Thatcher and other neoliberals the state was necessary to "preserve both liberty and order," however, it should no longer be the "good fairy at every christening, a loquacious and tedious companion at every stage of life's journey, the unknown mourner at every funeral" (Thatcher in Rose, 1999: 139). Such a view required a new morality of choice where "a moral being is one who exercises his own judgment in choice on matters great and small" (Thatcher in Russel, 1978: 104–105). These sentiments were echoed by Keith Joseph (1975: 57) who argued that it was necessary for government to "re-create the conditions under which the values we cherish can form the cement of our society. Our job is to recreate the conditions which will again begin to permit the forward march of embourgeoisment which went so far in Victorian times." In the U.S. similar pronouncements were made by Ronald Reagan's Director of the Office of Management and Budget, David Stockman (1986: 11), who called for the urgent need to "cut the umbilical cord of dependency that ran from Washington to every nook and cranny of the nation."

Almost a decade after Thatcher infamous remarks about the end of society and as neoliberalism began moving from its roll back to roll out phase, the soon to be British Primer Minister and Leader, Tony Blair, declared a similar but more nuanced, neoliberal moral mission during a 1996 speech entitled "Faith in the City—Ten Years On." He declared,

> we must create a society based on a notion of mutual rights and responsibilities, on what is actually a modern notion of social justice—'something for something.' We accept our duty as a society to give each person a stake in its future. And in return each person accepts responsibility to respond, to work to improve themselves. (in Blair, 1996: 298)

His statement echoed comments made a few weeks earlier at a speech in Singapore where he declared that what people really want is "independence, dignity, self-improvement, a chance to earn and get on" (in Blair, 1996: 293).

The economic downturn of the late 2000s surprising did little to dampen the enthusiasm for this new neoliberal moral order, at least in many corridors of power. In early 2011 the Coalition government of David Cameron declared as part of his "Big Society" initiative that enterprise is the "only strategy" for growth. To "boost enterprise" required government to "be on the side of everyone in the country who wants to create jobs, and wealth and opportunity" (Wheeler, 2011). In his view, "enterprise is not just about markets—it's about morals, too. We understand that enterprise is not just an economic good, it's a social good" (in Wheeler, 2011).

Although these statements obviously came at different historical moments, from different political parties with different agendas, they illustrate key dimensions of neoliberal governmentality and its particular themes of voluntary action and moral responsibility that are at the heart of it attempts to reformulated the relationship between state and individual. With Blair the concept of society is resurrected from its Thatcherian imposed death but is reconceptualized in a neoliberalized form of shared, moral obligation among free choosing individuals, who, much like a corporate shareholder, works to see that the company, or in this case the nation state, that he or she "owns" performs optimally in order to protect both their own interests and those of the state. The key differences between classic liberalism and neoliberalism also lie in these statements and the modes of governmentality they represent. In classic liberalism the "government cannot override the rational free conduct of governed individuals without destroying the basis of the effects it is seek to produce" (Burchell, 1993: 271). In other words, government must always be in accord with the "natural liberty" and "self-passions" (Smith, 1904) residing in the individual actor. If not, it risks both illegitimacy as a governmental form and disequilibrium and catastrophe as an economic system. In contrast, in neoliberalism such an ordering of state and economy is an "artifact" (Hayek, 1979) that needs ongoing governmental and institutional assistance in order to achieve its goals of individual liberty, freedom and economic efficiency. In other words, people's rationality, freedom and self-interested action need ongoing institutional support in order to be made and sustained. It is, consequently, the role of government to create the conditions where markets, freedom and self-interest can be realized. In both systems individualism, rationality and choice provide the basis of the moral order; however, in the former case it simply flows from an underlying human nature that should not be disturbed, and can only be thrown a kilter by government action, while in the latter it needs to be "consciously contrived" (Burchell, 1993: 271) by being activated and continuously protected through governmental action and policies.

This new neoliberal moral ordering generated a radical new form of what Foucault famously referred to as "governmentality." This new form of governance "does not abandon the 'will to govern'" (Miller and Rose, 2008: 211) but merely reconfigures it. Indeed, within the particular theoretical framing the voluntary action and self-care of neoliberalism is not to be considered innate or natural attributes but as a new form of governmentality that is enacted on and through individual action. In this sense neoliberalism introduces an anti-government governmentality. Essentially neoliberal governmentality puts into place what we might call a guided freedom, or in the language of contemporary economics a "behavioral economics," where autonomous individuals are to be continuously disciplined by governing policies that shape and utilize their freedom (Miller and Rose, 2008: 212). This should not be mistaken with truly autonomous forms of self-regulation, which neoliberalism is highly suspicious of (see Peters, 2005: 131) but as a managed freedom. In administering this guided freedom there is also a switch from the "positive knowledges" of human conduct where society was to be steered by the knowledge generated by social engineers and experts to a new breed of "calculative regimes of accounting and financial management" (Miller and Rose, 2008: 212). In this new neoliberal mode people are disciplined not through the tactics associated with either an administered or democratically planned society but through an "ethical citizenship" or "a governing by community" (Rose, 1999: 475). Here the rules associated with the "spontaneous orderings" and "associations" often generated by the "objective realities" of markets, economics and financial accountability serve as a new means of governmentality and control. People are guided by these "micro-moral domains" of these associations and "do not depend upon political calculations and strategies for their rationales" (Miller and Rose, 2008: 212). In this rational order an individual "must be accountable for each of his or her actions and submit them to the approval of the community, under the threat of exclusion" (Amable, 2011: 14). In these neoliberal systems, government should not directly determine the nature of these orderings but create and monitor the conditions for a disciplined and self-committed self-ordering to occur. The amoral moralism created by such a guided or perhaps forced freedom creates, in turn, a "degovernmentalization of the state" and a "de-statization of government" (Miller and Rose, 2008: 212). States do not govern in the traditional sense of representing the interest of society and the "greater good" but rather through becoming the great auditor or assessor charged with seeing to it that all individuals everywhere and in all contexts engage in self-care, including social organizations and government themselves. Simply put, in this system social control is not about telling people what to do directly through social policy, bureaucratic mandates or even the peer pressure of democratic decision making but through adherence to the principle of choosing. In the end the results may be the same, in the sense that

THE CONSUMERIZATION OF CHOICE

"Freedom of choice," "voluntary action," and their assumed corollary "freedom of contract" lie at the heart of both the liberal and neoliberal moral projects. As we saw in the first chapter, liberals and neoliberals argue that when political and decision-making systems try to impose a choice either from the outside in the name of the people, the proletariat, god, progress or the state they become authoritarian as they try to insinuate or force a particular decision, moral visions and course of action rather than relying on the spontaneous organization generated by the manifestation of individual self-interested action. This authoritarianism can take the form of a monarch who seek to exercise his or her will, such as in the critiques leveled by classic liberals; the expert driven social systems envisioned in the nineteenth century by Saint-Simon and Comte and found later in Keynesian economic management; or twentieth century socialist governments that sought to act on behalf or in the name of "the people" or society. In this reading, and in keeping with public interest and principle-agent theories all human actions are "interested," even those performed by the allegedly enlightened, selfless planners and technocrats who want to run society in the name of the people and the "greater good." This being the case, decision-making should always be located in the dispersed and "spontaneously guided" market of individuals selecting and choosing what course of action to follow and what to consume in order to fulfill their own interests and to manifest control over those domains that interest them. It is only under such a decentralized market arrangement where a truly spontaneous, free and non-authoritarian social order can emerge.

Such a view of the way decision-making happens or should happen stands in contrast to the more collectivist or sociological understanding of freedom and choice—a framing that is at the heart of the workings of the welfare state. Here choice and freedom are much less instrumentally rational and consumer driven and much more deeply embedded in a variety of cultural assemblages. Here choice is not determined by the assessments and actions of atomistic individuals in the context of acting alone but by the influences of preexisting social conditions or states and intersubjective acts, such as religion, tradition, gender, ethnicity or class that make certain choices possible and correct. In other words, individual freedom first requires a society. This society is not limiting and repressive but contextual and enabling. In this framing the absolute free choice of liberalism is either impossible, since individuals are always embedded in social forms that shape knowledge, thought or action, or a political ideology, since in can only serve as an illusionary myth to support a particular truth regime and hierarchical ordering. Choice, then, is always and necessarily contextual. In the collectivist model of what T. H. Marshall (1950: 34) called "social citizenship" if an individual action brings about unintended consequences or unforeseen risks, these can be mediated by the collective and the protection provided by the clan, tribe or state. In this sense, as Karl Polanyi (1957: 163–164) famously framed it, no one person starves in a collective system unless everyone starves; however, once they are pried from the protection of the collective via the individualizing effects of the market economy, individual starvation becomes a real possibility. Indeed, it is that very threat of starvation that sustains relations in a market economy.

The role of knowledge in such a consumer-centered liberal order is considerably different from that found in a more collectivist and expert-based one. In a collectivist system, tacit forms of knowledge are often either dispersed throughout the group or, as in the Enlightenment model, controlled by experts. However, even in instances where knowledge is concentrated in particular places, such as universities and agencies, and is controlled by particular people, such as scientists and experts, it still remains oriented toward the goal of collective dispersion and social improvement. In keeping with the Enlightenment metanarrative described in Chapter 3, knowledge is at its best and most accurate when it is produced and screened by a professionalized group of people who follow their own professionally constituted methodological procedures and public regarding ethics of responsibility. Afterward, that knowledge is to be made available to those who wish to use it in the public domain or through public education. Also it can and should also be used by governments to create the greater public good.

What collectivists see as a virtue of public availability liberals see as a vice of state control. In the neoliberal system knowledge is conceived of as a personal tool or private resource that individuals make in order to manifest their self-interests and that they consume and utilize in varying forms in order to make choices affecting their lives. Knowledge, in this sense, provides the informational platform on which individual choice and action can happen. Knowledge is never nor should it ever be located in one particular individual or group (see Hayek, 1949). Here, a person's "knowledge needs" are strictly pragmatic and idiosyncratic. They include only those items individuals believe they need to make consumptive decisions in the marketplace of life. In this system tacit knowledge is either unworthy of commodification because it can't be adequately priced by a market or in some instance by limiting its flow over times it too can be commodified and converted into a fictitious commodity in order to be bought and sold to others. Also, knowledge in this system does not necessarily need to be made or screened exclusively by experts but can be gathered by the individual from an array of sources or, in the language of the OECD, "knowledge markets." Once gathered, this knowledge becomes part of the "intellectual assets" from which information consumers may use to select a course of action. Indeed, from this vantage point knowledge is simply another form of information to be included in the larger calculus of choice. In this calculus some knowledge forms may be more valuable than others and, therefore, demand a higher price. The course of action selected is, then, intermingled with other consumers gathering their own information with their own methods and making decisions in a stratified market for knowledge, such as status differences of universities. The end result of all this cost-benefit decision-making and spontaneity is an optimal knowledge market, good government and social consensus. The ultimate standing, truthfulness or judiciousness of that consensus is ultimately irrelevant or unknowable since the larger course of action followed by "society" becomes an assemblage of the consumptive choices of individuals. In this system, some people inevitably make choices that are "bad." However, these choices are bad not because of some absolute moral or epistemic pronouncement or a decision's correspondence with some ultimate underlying reality but because they are out of alignment with the decisions of the majority as manifest in their particular choices and "what the market will bear."

Putting this particular conceptualization of the intersection of knowledge and consumer choice into action has been one of the defining goals of neoliberalism over the past few decades and one of its rationales reformulating knowledge making and distributing institutions. From hospitals to schools to universities to government agencies, the ability of individuals to assess information and make informed (or even misinformed) consumer choices lie at the heart of neoliberalism's transformative social agenda. This agenda can be clearly seen in the new configuration of medical knowledge, insurance and health care that has emerged in several countries over the last few decades (see Shaw, 2007). Under the collective and expert driven system, the locus of control was with the medical community and individual doctors. In this model, the collective knowledge generated by the medical community was used by doctors to diagnosis and treat patients (see Greener, 2009). The pronouncements of doctors were considered to be their "best take" based on their professionally accrued understanding or expertise and the knowledge available. Under a more neoliberal influence model, however, the locus of control has shifted from the medical community and the doctors who are embedded in it to the individual patient-consumer who must now take the information provided by doctors, along with other information they deem pertinent, such as costs, alternative interpretations and treatments found in a variety of sources and then make a decision on their particular treatment. The viewpoints of doctors and the medical community are not viewed as the primary determinate or sole consideration of individual action but simply another factor to be considered by the "medical consumer" when making a decision about his or her health care. In all situations people must weigh and choose a number of "interested opinions" and interpretations of varying weight, which they too must determine, and then select their own unique, individual course of action.

In this model consumer choice comes to constitute the highest form of sovereignty—a "consumer sovereignty," in the description of Ludwig von Mises (1983). This sovereignty contends that "consumer interest counts above all other interests" (Peet, 2007: 73). In this "consumerization of citizenship" (Needham, 2003), consumer choice is not just a matter of the rational economic sorting and optimization of goods and services but a democratic means through which social order, governance and harmony is achievable in a free society. A free society is, hence, an entity that can only be generated by the spontaneous actions of free and self-interested individuals making consumptive choices. Social order is achievable in this model through the interactive balancing or "mutual checking" of the actions and opinions of self-interested consumer citizens acting independently but for an unknown greater good. As this new citizen-consumer hybrid makes decisions based on her or his assessment of a situation and purchase goods and services, they are essentially casting a vote based on their own individual preferences (see Johnston, 2008). In this "voting" process, self-interest is pitted against and, in the end balanced by, the self-interest of other citizen-consumers. The end result is a largely unnoticeable harmonization of social relations that resembles the equilibrium of the "invisible hand" of market. This harmonization produces "large-scale, non-intimate collectivities unified by the ritualized fantasies of collective expenditure" (Appadurai in Foster, 1995: 153).

In a genuinely free society, consequently, consumer choice is the only proper arbitrator of what is good or bad or right and wrong. There is no moral teleology or compass present here that should determine in which direction a society should go or what precise moral order should be followed. Indeed, any group that seeks to "move" society one way or the other based on a political or moral vision risks upsetting both freedom and social equilibrium. This produces, as Debord (1995: 15) has described it, a society of the spectacle where "everything that appears is good; whatever is good will appear" (Debord, 1995: 15). In the "enormous positivity" (Debord, 1995: 15) generated under these conditions, if something "sells" or is the object of consumer choice, whether it is a product or idea, and can generate a market, it is good, true and just. If it can't, it deserves to fail and fall by the wayside regardless of some alleged overall rationality, value, morality or importance to one group.

Not only is this type of consumerism envisioned as new means of governmentality where individuals must discipline and govern themselves through their own individual efforts, but it is also seen as serving as the basis of new mode of social obligation, moral ordering or sociality. In this sense, consumption is not simply the manifestation of the pleasure principle in action but is now, as Baudrillard (1988: 48) reminds us, "the citizen's duty." As he describes it,

One is obliged to be an enterprise of pleasure and satisfaction; one is obliged to be happy, to be in love, to be adulating/adulated, seducing/seduced, participating, euphoric, and dynamic. This is the principle of the maximization of existence by the multiplication of contacts and relations, by the intensive use of signs and objects, and by the systematic exploitation of all the possibilities of pleasure . . . He is therefore not passive: he is engaged, in continuous activity. Otherwise he runs the risk of being satisfied with what he has and of becoming asocial. (Baudrillard, 1988: 48)

Here the patriotic duty of the citizen and individual self-interest are merged into one. As Rose (1999: 145) describes it, in this situation freedom "is redefined: it is no longer freedom from want . . . it is the capacity for self-realization which can be obtained only through individual activity." As new self-actualizing, consumer citizens, individuals must essentially adopt a "fun morality" (Baudrillard, 1988: 49) drawn from utilitarian pain/pleasure principles in order to continually selected from the options offered by the market for achieving happiness. If they do not choose or choose not to choose, they risk a socially imposed death since they have violated the new ethic of choice that lies at the heart of the neoliberal consumer society.

In the end these newly instituted neoliberal systems of choice create citizen consumers who, to quote Giddens (1991), "have no choice but to choose." In this unending and spiraling "reflexive project of self . . . individuals are forced to negotiate lifestyle choices among a diversity of options" (Giddens, 1991: 81). In doing so, they increasingly face the "paradox of choice" (Schwartz, 2005) where the proliferation of options to choose from both overwhelms human capacity and leaves all decisions in doubt. Here each choice creates a number of new choices until individuals are frozen by the exponential potentiality of each choice that confronts them. They may also face the realization that many of these so-called choices are, in the end, not necessarily genuine ones but more "the illusion of liberty by sanctioning strictly controlled choices" (Duncan, 2003: 470).

This championing of "freedom of choice" also entails and goes hand in hand with the promotion of a "freedom of contract." When a consumer makes a selection they are essentially entering into a contract with others. Such an agreement assumes contractual responsibilities and obligations on the part of both parties. Such a contractual arrangement between parties extends beyond consumers in the marketplace to the way neoliberal governance should operate. Instead of rights afforded to all, as in the welfare state model, the "new contractualism" of neoliberalism posits "contractual governance" with a *quid pro quo* arrangement between governments and its citizens (see Jayasuriya, 2002). In this arrangement of "carefully controlled external incentives" (Duncan, 2003: 472), citizens may receive governmental or social assistance, such as welfare, subsidized education loans, health care insurance or unemployment compensation, but only with the explicit understanding that it comes with certain obligations on their part. This return represents not only a contractual obligation to the state but also to the "taxpaying members of society" who support the state and its social programs. In turn, those who are supporting these social programs deserve certain "guarantees" for their investment in human capital. Those who continually drain the public coffers are, consequently, morally reprehensible because they drain other's privately accumulated wealth and have been unable to live up to their part of the neoliberal social contract.

By creating situations where individuals must select from a preselected menu of options in schools, retirement accounts, medical insurance, etc., neoliberalism acknowledges, legitimates and even celebrates the existence of unequal variations in "purchasing power." These variations are seen as inevitable, non-correctible and even desirable features of an imperfect and obtainment-oriented world where knowledge and good choices combine to become the roadmap and moral template for determining individual success or failure. The market always distributes goods rationally, if unfairly (unless of course it has been altered). Or, in other, more Social Darwinist terms that would have resonated with Herbert Spencer, inequality is an outcome of improper planning, unless the political and legal systems have somehow failed to provide the proper conditions for competition. As Spencer put it, "the poverty of the incapable, the distresses the come upon the imprudent, the starvation of the idle, and those shouldering aside of the weak by the strong" are merely outcomes of a "far seeing benevolence" (Spencer, 1850: 323). Inequality is the result of failure, and failure here is the result of bad or unfortunate individual choices. In this system people are either "flotsam" who are capable of adjusting to the continual currents of change or "jetsam" who are dispelled from the system for their lack of trying or bad luck (Pick, 2004: 104). Inequality is, thus, always an individual problem and never a reflection on the rational economic system which distributes things or the political system that allows and sets the conditions for such an economic system to operate.

THE INDIVIDUALIZATION OF RISK

In the neoliberal framing, choosing is to be stripped of its broader cultural and moral context, "desocialized," "unleashed" and, subsequently, transformed into consumer-driven action. However, the proliferation of this disembedded and free-floating consumer choice generates a host of new organizational and individual risks. Indeed, risk becomes so prevalent in this new system of spiraling choice that even a market itself can be made from it in the forms of various insurances, such as those for "bundled investments," that can safeguard individuals and firms from "risky situations." At its core and paralleling the rise of neoliberalism, governance in the last half of the twentieth century increasingly came to be about the analysis and management of risk (see Beck, 1992), leading to a type of "risk management of everything" (Power, 2004: 42). In the new neoliberal model of risk management individuals are called on to engage in a "new prudentialism" (O'Malley, 1992) in order to continuously evaluate their own risks in everyday life that may put his or her education or future livelihood at risk. These risks are not "social problems" to be shared or tempered by the state or government in general but "ethical" or personal ones that must be shouldered exclusively by the individual. Such a prudentialism demands the creation of a new asocial moral being—an "actuarial self" that employs an probabilistic rationality to continuously gage conditions and make appropriate adjustments (Peters, 2005).

In contrast to the increased individualization of risk found in neoliberalism, socialist and more Keynesian forms of governance treated risk essentially as a social problem that required collective and/or state intervention to measure, monitor and correct. These forms of governance sought to manage risk through a series of state planning and intervention initiatives, the assessments of officially trained experts and the proper application of bureaucratic organization and authority. In this more "social insurance" model one of the central roles of government is to reestablish a modern form of "tribal protection" (see Polanyi, 1944) in order to insulate individuals from the risk imposed from such everyday life events as bad health and unemployment. Governments are to do this by spreading costs across the entire population and, in some instances, by progressively distributing the costs to those with the ability to pay (see N. Rose, 1993: 293), such as in the case of state pensions or unemployment benefits. The welfare state model of risk employed a particular "calculative rationality" (Power, 2007: 22) where bureaucracies collected data for processing and initiated social policy through state bureaucratic mechanisms. In this model risk is not simply a personal matter to be shouldered by individuals alone but a collective, social or national concern that requires an equitable distribution across all members. Here all members are protected, and in turn all members are called on to share the cost burdens of that protection. In this approach risk is a socially manageable problem if it is properly analyzed by an objective "political science" and properly steered and distributed by a welfare state.

The neoliberal take on risk is much more individualized in both its assessment and the burden it may impose. In this case risk is largely, if not exclusively, an individual or family matter to be assumed by the responsiblized consumer citizen rather than a matter for the collective or the state. In this instance risk should be managed by the self-aware and self-reflexive individual who utilizes the information and knowledge available to maneuver himself or herself and perhaps his or her family through the series of risky situations that are a natural or inevitable part of the uncertainties of modern life, including the economic crises of market economies themselves. In this understanding, economic upheavals and uncertainties are viewed as natural and inevitable rather than things created by a particular political economy, historical configurations and political power. In the neoliberal reading it is "uncertainty that makes us free" (Bernstein, 1998: 229). Consequently, the ability to properly weather an economic downturn or any other uncertainty is an outcome of those who have been the most adept at monitoring and reacting to risky situations, which is, in turn, a further reflection of the larger entrepreneurial cunningness of the individual. Under this model, individual health, well-being and financial security are directly attributable to the free choices an individual makes within the possible options offered up by the market. Here, "collective responsibility is replaced by one in which individuals are ultimately apportioned responsibility, even for things (crime, health and job training) that are social in their scope" (Ruhl, 2005: 102). Likewise, in this privatized model of risk, as with choice, failings are attributable to the bad decision-making, irrationality or simply the bad luck of the individual and are, consequently, his or her responsibility and not that of the state.

In adopting this individualized view of risk, neoliberalism has sometimes ironically set up governing systems whose central activities are not to manage large scale social risk but are, as part of both neoliberalism's moral project and devolving budgets, to "push risk off"—to actively relocate risk from the state to the individual (see Cheshire and Lawrence, 2005: 438). Here people are forced to be free through a new form of "insitutionalised individualism" where they are "invited to constitute themselves as individuals: they plan, understand, design themselves and acts as individuals—or, should they fail, to lie as individuals on the bed they have made for themselves" (Beck and Beck-Gernsheim, 1996: 438 and 26). In this "all necessity and certainty is being replaced by artistry ... we are becoming—helplessly—high-wire dancers in the circus tent" (Beck and Beck-Gernsheim, 1996: 24).

Such a relocation of risk can be found in a variety of policies and procedures introduced by neoliberal governments over the past few decades, ranging from housing policies that push the risk and costs of low and moderate income housing to individuals, the sick individual who must "shop around" for the best treatment or the future retiree who must now manage their future retirement. For example, with the advent of both national and private pension funds in the early and middle part of the twentieth century, the government either guaranteed a pension upon retirement or, in the case of private plans, professionally trained money managers took employee and employer contributions, pooled them and invested them in often relatively safe or so-called conservative investments, such as long-term government bonds. Upon retirement the retiree received a monthly pension often with an annual cost of living adjustment. In the U.S. this arrangement began to change with the Employee Retirement Security Act of 1974 (see Clowes, 2000: 6). With this Act employee contributions began to move from the relatively safe areas of government bonds into various individual and packaged equities. In the case of private pension funds, they also began to move from the hands of more local or company-based money managers to the hands of large investment firms. This had the immediate effect of flooding the commodities and mutual fund markets with pension money and raising the price of individual equities. Later, particularly with the advent of the Internet and "online investing management," and 'individualized retirement plans" or "defined contribution plans," individuals were pushed to become more actively involved in both the management and the particular allocation of their own retirement funds. The new technology allows individuals to check their retirement fund as much as they want and to readjust their allocations as they see fit, regardless of their knowledge or expertise about investing. As Clowes (2000: 4) describes this situation,

> Many are now able to match their investment with their own financial status, future financial needs, and risk tolerance. They themselves decide how much they will invest in growth stocks or value stocks, large-cap or small cap stocks, bonds, or guaranteed investment contracts through their decisions about how much to put into which mutual fund options offered by their employers. These employees have become investors, and some are becoming long-term-oriented as their investment pools increase.

Neoliberal reformers promoted this new approach as a way of "empowering" individuals to look after their own future finances and of pushing the risks and burdens of financing one's retirement from corporations and the state to the individual. As in other aspects of life, it was now up to the individual to research various funds, compare products, make prudent investments and vigilantly watch the stock market—a place where their future well-being is now tied. The "successful retiree" is one who is smart enough to have saved and invested wisely, much like the successful firm, entrepreneur or organization that is capable of surviving the "natural" ups and downs of business cycles.

In this way of thinking, pensions, with their socialized responsibility and costs, were much too collectivistic and expensive for companies and the state to maintain. In the pension system everyone with the same years of service received the same payout with adjustments based on salary. There was little room for individual choice, control and investment levels. By shifting the retirement from a pension system to an individual retirement account, companies could quickly increase shareholder profit and the value of their stock by unloading the burden and risk of their employees' pension. Likewise, the state itself could either curtail or end all together their support for people's retirement. This would enable markets to be further supported either through the lowering of taxes, as required by "roll back" neoliberals, or shifted to policies to created added value to markets, as required in "roll out" neoliberalism.

A similar relocation of risk can be seen in U.S. housing policy since the 1980s and is one of the causes of the "housing bubble" of the early 2000s.

Aligning Markets and Minds   201

Prior to this time, most U.S. housing policies recognized some direct role for government in providing housing. This might occur through direct or indirect loans for those in the working class to federal housing projects for the poor (or even the building of the experimental mixed income town of Greenbelt, Maryland, in the 1930s). However, beginning with the Housing Act of 1974 under the Nixon administration, a new more market-centered approach was slowly introduced into American housing policy. This approach was carried forward in the policies adopted by subsequent administrations. The first phase of "roll back" policies, as found in the Reagan administration, slashed the budget of the Department of Housing and Urban Development (HUD) from $30 billion to $9 billion. In the late 1980s, Newt Gingrich even called for the complete elimination of HUD.

In the early 1990s, housing policy begins to take another turn, this time from the "roll back" form of neoliberalism that simply wanted to reduce or eliminate public spending to a more "roll out" form that wanted to use state policies to establish markets as a mechanism for social change and for disciplining behavior. This approach begins to become apparent in the National Affordable Housing Act of 1990. The act sought to privatize most public housing by selling off units, creating housing vouchers to generate a market for low-income housing and allowing for a greater role of tenants in decision-making in the public housing that remained. These polices were amplified during the Clinton and G. W. Bush administrations, particularly with the "Quality Housing and Work Responsibility Act" of 1998, as the federal support for housing continued to diminish and markets were put in its place for almost everyone seeking housing. In these policies, the housing needs of the working poor or the lower middle would be taken care of by the market, where quasi-government groups like Freddie Mac and Fannie Mae were encouraged to lower their eligibility requirements for purchasing loans in order to expand home ownership through the market. This would help spur competition among private banks to expand loans to those traditionally outside of the private housing market, using in many cases "sub-prime rates."[2]

Since the 1980s both the moral and practical message of U.S. housing policy has been that lower- and middle-income people should not be dependent on the government to directly provide or subsidize their housing needs. Instead, and in keeping with neoliberal models of governance, government support would be directed toward enabling the market to provide the housing support people needed and could afford. In order to make this system operate, those needing housing would be required by prevailing economic circumstances to become more responsible, rational and concerned with their self-interest. They were not to be dependent "wards of the state" that were "on the dole," as they had been under the welfare housing system, but were now individuals who needed to be taught moral lessons through the market. If things are unequal it is essentially your responsibility to figure out how to correct it through your own innovation.

The relocation of risk from the state to the individual is also evident in the way higher education is now funded in many national contexts. Indeed, university degrees themselves are increasing viewed by students as less general preparation for life and work and more as a type of insurance for "minimizing risk and uncertainty" (Pick and Taylor, 2009: 76). In this way of thinking, although a university degree may not provide a guarantee of well- paying and stable employment in the flexible new economy, without it students see their employment futures and incomes as much less predictable. This change in thinking has been driven by a change in the way public higher education is paid for. As we saw in Chapter 5, prior to the adoption of neoliberal policies, higher education in many Western societies was viewed as the collective responsibility of the state. In this welfare state model, the state provided either some or all of direct funding for the operation of universities, as in Germany, the U.K. and New Zealand or the "block funding" of individual American states. Over the last few decades, however, neoliberal policies have begun to push for a type of "user pay" system similar to that advocated in other parts of the public sector. In the user pay system, the cost of higher education is decollectivized and shifted away from the corporations (though taxes) and the state to the individual. In the case of the U.S., which generally already had a more liberal and individualized system to begin with, the emphasis shifted from governmental grants to private loans even for the poor. In other cases, such as England today, this has meant a dramatic increase in the amount students pay for tuition and a switch from government subsidizes toward individual student loans. These loans and user fees, in turn, make both students and knowledge institutions more dependent on financial markets themselves as predicted in the rating agency Standard and Poor's (2003) report *Higher Education: Changing by Degrees.*

In all these situations, the consumer citizen come face to face with the risk-aware subject as people are "forced to 'do' consumer" (McDonald et al., 2007: 432). In these situations retirees, homeowners and students have no choice but to choose, but those choices, whatever they may be, have risks that the individual himself or herself must be willing or made to shoulder. Ultimately, it is up to them to oversee their retirement portfolios by screening investments, sorting out prospectuses and making prudent investment decisions or to finance their own housing or to make an informed investment in their own education and retraining. In the end, a person's failure to compete or wrong decisions in the competition is ultimately the individual's fault and not that of the government, or society for that matter. Bad or unfortunate decisions are risks the individual must now assume and are due to the individual's own greed, incompetence, laziness, lack of foresight or maybe just simply bad luck and has nothing to do with the workings of the self-regulating economy or the governing responsibilities of the liberalist state. The economy is merely playing itself out based on its own internal equilibrium and laws. Indeed, "being ahead of the curve" by interpreting and benefiting from the up-and-down movement of such business cycles is now one of the central jobs of the risk-aware consumer citizen. Likewise, governments are not responsible for a particular individual's well-being but only for providing the legal provisions that allow individual decisions making and choice to take place. If the individual fails to properly anticipate or is imprudent, he or she alone must pay the price—the collective can no longer be held responsible to protect people from a risky world.

THE ENTREPRENEURIALIZATION OF WORK

Two of the great ideals and icons of neoliberalism are the risk-aware consumer and the risk-taking entrepreneur. The risk-aware consumer is projected as a sovereign citizen who makes consumptive choices and, as a consequence, creates economic and social equilibrium alongside the independent action of his or her fellow choosers. A parallel and equally powerful neoliberal ideal and icon to this risk aware, consumer citizen is the risk-taking entrepreneur. The "cult of the entrepreneur" (O'Malley, 2000: 480) projects him or her as the idealized, rugged individualist who scans the horizon looking for opportunities, accesses the risk of those opportunities and makes a selection that will benefit him- or herself and ultimately, but not deliberately, society as a whole through the creation of nifty new products, services, jobs and economic growth. This entrepreneur is often conceptualized as a "lone wolf" who "goes it alone" or the "creative genius" who "sees ahead of the curve" and is unhampered by the actions of the collectivist herd or the rules of state or organizational bureaucratic intrusions. He or she will stand or fall solely based on individual foresight, hard work and luck. Under neoliberal governments, these icons are, however, not simply unobtainable idealized conceptualizations of the "ought." They also serve as guideposts to a host of specific state policies designed to remold social circumstances and the workplace and to transform "employees into entrepreneurs" (Rose, 1999: 156). In this transformation, the worker is no longer thought of as a "social creature seeking satisfaction of his or her need for security, solidarity and welfare, but as an individual actively seeking to shape and manage his or her own life in order to maximize its returns it terms of success and achievement" (Miller and Rose, 1993: 100). Indeed, a truly rational and efficient market cannot be manifest until the worker himself or herself is no longer the "victim" of capitalist exploitation but "is the active and voluntary promoter of capitalism" (Amable, 2011: 13).

With the promotion of this new entrepreneurial icon neoliberalism has sought "the generalization of an 'enterprise form' to all forms of conduct" (Burchell, 1993). In this scheme all organizations and individuals would be better off if they could only manage to throw off the chains of bureaucratic organization and the collective protection associated with organized capitalism and the welfare state and were to adopt the "free spiritedness" and opportunism of the entrepreneur. Under both socialist and the more stable bureaucratic or organized capitalism spawned by Keynesian economic policy, the great iconic heroes and behavioral model of the economy was, in contrast, the omnipresent and rational industrial manager and his or her parallel, the life-time unionized employee. The industrial manager used his or her particular managerial skills to institute new cost-cutting procedures throughout an organization and to streamline production in the name of efficiency. The manager was beholden to, and his fate often rested with, the long-term interest of the company and its shareholders. He or she was, however, also rule-bound by the very rationalizing systems of organization and procedures that he or she helped introduce and by the ones imposed on him or her by the welfare state or from negotiated labor contracts. Workers, in this context, were often, at least in certain core economic sectors in industrialized nations, shielded from change or insecurity by the protection afforded by collective bargaining that came with belonging to a union or profession. They were, as described by Hayek (1979: 111), "strangers to those rules of the market which have made the great society possible. To them, the market economy is largely incomprehensible; they have never practiced the rules on which it rests and its results seem to them irrational and immoral." Such membership protection and power enabled collective rights and benefits to be negotiated with management who recognized, perhaps begrudgingly, that the overall fate of the company rested with the abatement of labor conflict and the development of agreed upon rules of work provided through collective bargaining. Here, "the labour of individual subject was linked into economic flows, conduct was regularized, access was provided to all kinds of social benefits as a *quid pro quo* for regularity of employment" (Rose, 1999: 157). When economic conditions declined, displaced workers would be taken care of by a generalization of the costs and pain directed by the state, through such programs as unemployment compensation or government-sponsored employment programs.

The neoliberal promotion of entrepreneurialism is a deliberate attempt to destroy the bureaucratic, organized capitalism model (Lash and Urry, 1987) described above and remold the nature of work both at the level of organizations and firms and the day-to-day experience of individual workers. At the broader level of organizations this is to be accomplished by making work become more flexible or "post-Fordist" by making it more responsive to the rapid ebbs and flows of capital and the "needs of the global economy." In this new work situation "instability is meant to be normal" (Sennett, 1998: 31) or even valorized as permitting new opportunities for individual renewal and growth. Work is to become a "vulnerable zone" where "employment must ceaselessly be earned . . . under the constant threat of 'down-sizing'" (Rose, 1999: 158). According to the neoliberal logic as global markets and consumer demand change, workers need to be able to freely flow to the places, industries and occupations where jobs are being created. As these markets ebb and recede, new labor flows will emerge. Wages must also be allowed to "free float" with the going rate of the national and international labor market. Workers must also be capable of changing or updating their skill to meet constantly evolving demands. In order to accomplish this, workers in this situation are to become much less protected by the collective, such as in the protections afforded by unions, professions and the collective bargaining and labor regulations created by the state, and much more individually competitive in the market for labor.

This adaptation also applies to the situation of "lifelong learning" which has become a key part of more recent neoliberal education policies (see Brine, 2006). Here, not only is the student to be held responsible for paying for his or her own education or "skill enhancement" but they must also pay for ongoing job retraining and "skill enhancement" at different stages throughout their lives. In this situation changes in the global economy and the rapid flow of capital call for the quick retooling of workers. This is to be paid for not by tax monies but by the individual who must continuously (re)invest in him- or herself by maximizing their own human capital in order to remain employable (see Olssen, 2006). In this situation "the mandate and authority for education shall no longer be exclusively bound to institutions and their agents, but partly shift to the learning individual" (Tuschling and Engeman, 2006: 458). If an industry, technology or job becomes obsolete, the workers must take it upon themselves to restock their knowledge and skill inventory. They must learn new technologies that will make them more competitive in the labor market. They should not simply sit back and allow economic changes to overwhelm them but should anticipate and become self-actualized, risk-aware and self-promotional. This requires a worker who, like the vigilant consumer who wishes to push down prices but must work in concert with the entrepreneur who wishes to promote his or her self-interest and wealth, must continuously gage economic circumstances and who is able and willing to adjust to the market's unceasing creative destruction. Governments may assist in this retraining unless a phase of "rollback" is called for by economic circumstances, however, it is primarily the responsibility of the lifelong learner to read the economic "tea leaves," make informed choices and make an investment in their own human capital.

In this new work situation, individuals are demanded, as Foucault describes it, to make "entrepreneurs of themselves" (Foucault in Olssen, 2006: 219). They must become as cunning and self-serving as the iconic entrepreneur. In this context the goal is for both workers and managers to become entrepreneurs who are each capable of spotting an opportunity and optimizing it for personal gain. This rugged and rational individualist is capable of making him- or herself more marketable and wealthier only through his or her own innovation and ingenuity not through the false protection of the state, union or society. Individuals, therefore, do not need the protection of the collective and its socialization of gain, which only obstructs creativity and siphons off the workers' own initiative and innovation. They are, in contrast, much better served by "going it alone," "going against the crowd" and "forging their own path" just like the advice offered up in CEO advice books. By acting in such a manner, and in keeping with the liberal credo, the individual is not just advancing him or herself but is an active part of the building of a spontaneous and forever evolving social order—as a selfish self-interest breeds a self-sustaining society.

With the end of bureaucratic or "organized capitalism" brought about by neoliberal ideas and policies all forms of work and all workers, from the McDonalds fry cook to the elementary school teacher to the hospital physician, are to become "entrepreneurialized." Transforming workers into entrepreneurs requires an array of new state-directed social and economic policies. In this sense, the children of the "creeping collectivism" of the twentieth century do not understand what is morally required of them and must be remade (see Marquand, 1992: 68). Government policy must be directed toward helping the individual entrepreneurialize by either removing collective protections that "hold people back," such as rolling back collective bargaining rights or by creating situations where individuals can be retrained and recredentialed quickly. Work is now to become not only more flexible and piece- or project-based but also void of protections by systematically removing or discouraging collective protection, as described by Polanyi (1944). Work is to be "freed" or untethered to float with the vicissitudes of the market. However, this "right to work" is not presented as a new form of exploitation of labor by capital but actually a freeing of labor from the collective conditions of its own enslavement and servitude; thereby, releasing each person's potential, marketability and ultimate fulfillment. Indeed, economic insecurity is not a social problem to be solved by a welfare state but is relabeled as an opportunity for the individual to reinvent him or herself. Workers are now, like the entrepreneur, free to have the pride and sense of accomplishment gained by living by their own wits and manifesting their "inherent freedom" even if that freedom is politically manufactured.

THE LIMITS OF LIBERALISM

In some contexts, particularly the U.S. and the U.K., neoliberalism has become so pervasive that it has "become incorporated into the commonsense way many of us interpret, live in and understand the world" (Harvey 2005: 3). This naturalization makes neoliberal ideas and practices seem simply as the right, smart or only prudent thing to do, or in the famous words of Thatcher, "there is no other option." After all, shouldn't people ultimately be responsible for their own well-being? Do they not pay taxes to support the government and social programs and, as consequence, should be able to demand options, transparency and accountability? Do we not exist in world where consumer demand should dictate price and product availability? The seeming normalness with which many people would answer yes to these questions signals the ways in which neoliberal ideas, discourse and practices have become naturalized and self-evident over the course of the last few decades. Yet while these ideas and practices have become normalized, we also have "paid a big price for the uncritical acceptance of neoclassical theory" (North, 1990: 131).

While all the social changes introduced by neoliberalism over the last few decades may seem new and inevitable, it is important to keep in mind that similar issues and concerns are at least a couple of centuries old. Indeed, one of the central concerns of nineteenth- and early twentieth-century social theory was with the relationship between the emerging modern market economy and the new forms of social relations it was generating. Social theory with its collectivist vocabulary and group framing arose, at least in part, as a counter movement and narrative to the economic individualism, contractualism and psychologism present in much of eighteenth- and nineteenth-century liberalist thought. As such, it may also provide some of the vocabulary and framework necessary for containing and rethinking neoliberalism today. For classical social theorist such as Karl Marx, Georg Simmel, Ferdinand Tonnies, Max Weber, Emile Durkheim and, a bit later, Karl Polanyi the thing we have come to label in the West as modernity is expressly defined, at least to a significant degree, by the new forms of social relations and societal form produced in an age increasingly dominated by markets, individualized economic exchange and contractual relations between strangers.

In *On the Jewish Question* (1972 [1843]), Marx described some of the contours of the newly emerging forms of subjectivity evident in the ideas and practices of eighteenth- and nineteenth-century liberalism and the market society. In his description for this new liberal subject, "the only bond between men is natural necessity, need and private interest, the preservation of their property and their egoistic persons" (Marx, 1972: 43). For this individual, "the world is no more than a Stock Exchange, and he is convinced that he has no other destiny here below than to become richer than his neighbour. "Trade has seized upon all his thoughts, and he has no other recreation than to exchange goods" (Marx, 1972: 49). Under these circumstances society was not seen as an enabling and stabilizing presence in life but as "a system which is external to the individual and [as] a limitation of his original independence" (Marx, 1972: 43).

Emile Durkheim's target was less the particular conditions of capitalist production than the more general liberal attempts to conceptualize a society and "the social" based exclusively on contractual relations, particularly as found in the writings of Herbert Spencer. For Durkheim (1964 [1893], "the concept of social contract is today therefore very difficult to define ... not only are there no societies that have had such an origin but there are none whose present structure bears the slightest trace of contractual organization." For Durkheim "contracts are the result of society, not its cause"

(Sulkunen, 2007: 326). Contracts must rely on already existing social bonds and relations and therefore can't be sustained without a background of socially constituted mutual trust. The economy, that entity that Adam Smith and other liberals sought to distinguish from society and explain through the natural sentiments of individuals, Durkheim sought to explain through preexisting social bonds among societal members. Consequently, dissolving the distinction between society and economy or "economizing morality" (Shamir, 2008: 3) by grounding it in an individualistic and contractual system which ignores the presence of the social is either an illusion or, if actively pursued, a cause of pathological social disintegration and perhaps even in the end the birth of a new "tribalism."[3]

Nineteenth- and twentieth-century social theorists essentially took what liberal theorist considered to be universal features of humankind, such a self-interest, instrumental reasoning and economic exchange, and historicized and relativized them. In doing so they sought to sketch out the theoretical and practical limits of liberalism in order to make possible their political reconsideration and reorientation. The neoliberalism of the last few decades didn't necessarily change these modern social relations as much as it redirected, enhanced and valorized them. The very features that social theorist saw as tearing society apart and generating massive inequalities, alienation and anomie, liberals and neoliberals took as making happiness, dignity, harmony and social order possible.

Marx's and Durkheim's critique of the emerging market society and its variations was greatly tempered in the twentieth century by many factors, including movements launched in Marx's own name. The forces they and other social theorists described did not go away, however. They were, to use the language of Karl Polanyi (1944), merely balanced or tempered by various "recollectivization" efforts of the twentieth century. Indeed, capitalism, in all its varied historical and national forms, such as "Atlantic," "Rhineland," bureaucratic, liberalist or neoliberalist must in their own way reduce things to commodities and market relations. However, the way they do this and the counterbalances put in place to limit or corral the market and commodification are highly variable across time and space. Under neoliberalism these efforts to reduce things to commodities and market relations have not been just confined to the boundaries of traditional market domains or commodities but have expanded to include all human endeavors and objects. In this, the market economy has effectively become, or is moving toward becoming, the market society. The institutions and the cultural practices that once limited the domain and tempered markets and held the marketization of social and moral life in check, at least under certain circumstances, are themselves being reduced to either markets or commodities. For example, in the twentieth century the welfare state, although it was never really anti-market, played an increasingly active role in containing the market and limiting its impact on particular domains and dimensions of life. As described earlier, in this system risk was socialized and the cost was progressively distributed. However, with the return of a particular virulent style of liberalism in neoliberalism that containment has now been lifted and with it, in the language of Karl Polanyi, the "tribe" was once again being disaggregated.

The framing of the individual and his or her relationship to society is obviously much different in neoliberalism than in social theory or the welfare state model. As I argued in the introduction to this book, in the neoliberal framing of governance or society, citizenship or cultural membership does not automatically convey societal rights. Instead neoliberalism posits a market-determined, "opportunity society" with a form of "contingent citizenship" (Lunt, 2009: 10) where individual actions and responsibility earn one a position and standing in the social order. There is consequently, "no rights without responsibilities" (Giddens, 1998). Such a configuration fits well with and sustains a more entrepreneurial, risk-aware and consumer-minded social ordering and subjective form. Instead of citizen rights that are afforded to all as members of society or a shared opportunity structure where some limits are place on inequality, neoliberalism introduces "achieved" or "purchased" rights and opportunities that must be earned through the display of proper individual behavior. Once earned through responsible action, these rights can be essentially "cashed in" to acquire what one needs and show his or her overall value to the market and state through his or her economic activity. In introducing this particular consumer citizenship, neoliberals, like some of their liberal predecessors, reposition the individual as the starting point for all forms of action by making it appear as a natural independent entity that is in concert with "the way things are" or perhaps should be. With this, society is rethought as a collection of individuals who produce an always changing social order as they make their choices. As John Dewey (1935: 39) described this form of liberalism, "The underlying philosophy and psychology of liberalism led to the conception of individuality as something ready-made, already possessed, and needing only the removal of certain legal restrictions to come into full play. It was not conceived as a moving thing, something that is attained only by continuous growth. Because of this failure, the dependence in fact of individuals on social conditions was made little of."

However, even economists in the neoclassical camp have seen that a complete individuation, interestization, contractualism and subsuming of everything to the market can have disastrous social consequences, even to the functioning of the market itself (see Shipman, 1999). Indeed, there is an ironic tendency for a market "to devour its supporting social structures" (Baert and Shipman, 2005: 157). It is in this sense that some argue that inherent contradictions of capitalism require that it must sometimes be "saved from itself" (see Bootle, 2009). This means that "the legitimacy of markets may depend on keeping them in their proper place" (Plant, 1992:

99). Echoing ideas found in classical social theory, Francois Perroux (in Albert, 1993: 104) argued,

> For any capitalist society to function smoothly, there must be certain social factors which are free of the profit motive, or at least of the quest for maximum profits. When monetary gain becomes uppermost in the minds of civil servants, soldiers, judges, priests, artists or scientists, the result is social dislocation and a real threat to any form of economic organisation. The highest values, the noblest human assets—honour, joy, affection, mutual respect—must not be given a price tag; to do so is to undermine the foundations of the social grouping. There is always a more or less durable framework of pre-existing moral values within which a capitalist economy operates, values which may be quite alien to capitalism itself.

Joseph Schumpeter (1976: 423) who is repeatedly and somewhat ironically invoked as a proto-neoliberal theoretician echoed these views when he remarked that "no social system can work which is based exclusively upon a network of free contracts between (legally) equal contracting parties and in which everyone is supposed to be guided by nothing except his own (short-run) utilitarian ends." In this sense "the stock exchange is a poor substitute for the Holy Grail" (Schumpter quoted in Bell, 1973: 66).

However, what happens when such ideas of a fully developed market society do indeed become the "Holy Grail" and are used as the guidepost for an array of politics and policies well beyond the traditional domain of the market? What happens when liberalism is pushed to its extremes in new, neoliberal forms and governance and social institutions are made to solely serve the interests of markets rather than their own historically constituted forms of action? Dewey, Perroux and Schumpter in different ways recognized that "liberalism driven to extremes may become its opposite" (Hodgson, 1999: 83). In this case an uncontained liberalism generates an illiberalism that leads to a "colossal liberal absolutism" (Hart, 1955: 285). This absolutism drives "all social forms and ideologies . . . to the margins" (Hodgson, 1999: 38). Such a situation creates a scenario where only market mechanisms are deemed as solution to all human problems in every context and at all times. When this happens, as Fukuyama (1992) has framed it, those who were once "kept out of politics and the military" because of their concern with making money are now free to bring their principles to bear on all social institutions and practices. The result is that "their restlessness would lead them to propose innovations at home or adventures abroad with potentially disastrous consequences for the polity" (Fukuyama, 1992: 316).

As Hodgson (1999: 83) and others have pointed out, the desire of neoliberals to extend market principles to all domains of life essentially derives from a confusion of "personal freedom" with "freedom of the market." This conflict was a result of the inherent friction between the two variants of liberalism discussed in Chapter 1. In the first, all of society must be transformed into a market—a market society. In the other, more Durkheimian and Deweyian influenced model, it is society that makes markets possible—a social market. By turning all aspects of society into an individualistic and contractual market, neoliberals destroy the very basis of markets. In other words, destroy the social and moral bonds that make up the social through the introduction of markets and market individualism into all aspects of life and you ironically destroy not only the very possibility of social order but the possibility of markets themselves effectively operating. In other words, a "market society of strangers" as conceived in neoliberalism is ultimately impossible. Its unceasing individualization, atomization and hypercompetitiveness in all domains of life generate a social and cultural cynicism or "enlightened false consciousness" (Sloterdijk, 1988) and erosion of trust that eventually fragments or dissolves all moral orders. In this sense, there can be no society composed exclusively of hyper-individualists, hermits or contract lawyers. Moral order can't be generated or sustain on the basis of isolated, non-interactants or contracts and legal-market relations. In other words, as Dewey framed it, "the actual 'laws' of human nature are laws of individuals in association, not of beings in a mythical conditions apart from association." In relaying on and trying to generate a "mythical condition" of lone, forever self-interested players, neoliberalism has perhaps unknowingly sown the seeds of its own demise; although such demise may take decades to play itself out politically. [4]

Over the course of the last few decades there has clearly been a seachange in the way we think about and experience the relationship between individual, state and economy. With it the way we think about and practice knowledge and education have also changed rather dramatically. In many respects, the changes of the last few decades have happened so slowly and particularlistically that we have generally failed to understand what is happening and why. They have appeared to be merely inevitable and irreversible outcomes of the functioning of something we simply call "the economy." Lest we forget, however, neoliberalism's project of self and society never unfolded in the way it was promoted nor has its practices become complete or hegemonic. It is, after all, a political project and social movement existing alongside and in opposition to other projects and movements. Neoliberalism and its utopian capitalism forget that the economic theories on which they are based are in themselves abstractions rooted in particular politically forged historical circumstances and practices. As Marx and Engels (1982: 100) put it in their critique of the utopian socialist Proudhon, "He fails to see that *economic categories* are but *abstractions* of those real relations, that they are truths only in so far as those relations continue to exist." Neoliberalism's reality, hence, resides not in its theories that capture economic reality or the way things are but in the politically forged practices that constitute and sustain it. Even the individualism, consumerism and contractualism so key to neoliberal ideals and governance are predicated upon the maintenance of what are, in the end, historically fragile forms of social relations.

Notes

NOTES TO CHAPTER 1

1. This view can also be found in the Singapore Sessions sponsored by the Singapore Economic Development Board. They describe their approach as a means to determine "how we can make it profitable for companies to innovate for the developing world" and to move from "marginal missions to profit margins" (see www.singaporesessions.com).
2. As Keynes (1926: 9) pointed out, this approach was also brought about by the successes of "socialized production" during World War I and the desire to "repeat it in peace conditions."
3. During World War II, Keynes and Hayek became friends while sharing air warden shifts in Cambridge (see Fox, 2009: 90).
4. They also founded the journal *Ordo* to which Hayek contributed articles. There was a close relation between the Ordoliberal school and Chicago School economics after World War II (Burchell, 1993: 270).
5. These ideas of a Social Market Economy became ensconced it West German social and economic policy after 1948.
6. This time period also marked what Charles Jencks (1984) described as the death of modern architecture and its particular dream of molding and directing social reform through rational design. In March of 1972 the modernist Pruitt-Igoe public housing project in St. Louis was destroyed just over twenty years after its construction.
7. Early efforts to politically revitalize liberalism took a number of different forms. One such form involved the installation of a particular Chicago style of neoliberal economics in corridors of power around the world. In this case, economists trained in neoliberal economic theory began to move around the globe with the more general expansion and growing influence of the profession of economics in the 1970s and the "economization" of social policy (see Fourcade, 2006; Caliskan and Callon, 1998). A second form, and perhaps most important for domestic policy, involved specific political efforts to create or expand policy centers, think tanks and political networks to promote neoliberal policies and to elect public officials that would promote neoliberal ideas. Indeed, Hayek believed that to effectively change things it was first necessary to change the minds of intellectuals. Only they were capable of redirecting "the climate of opinion" (Hayek, 1967).
8. In terms of neoliberalism's influence on knowledge policy and education, it important to note that Powell had served as a member of the Richmond City School Board and was also a members of the Virginia State Board of Education before the memo was written.

9. Neoliberalism was further popularized in the 1980 PBS documentary *The Power to Choose* that featured Friedman discussing and defending the neoliberal stance on government and economy.
10. As R. H. Tawney (1924: 35) described it in the early part of the twentieth century, an entire science of society (i.e., economics) was founded "upon the assumption that the appetite for economic gain is a constant measurable force, to be accepted, like other natural forces. . ." As Gary Becker (1976: 14) put it, "the economic approach provides a valuable unified framework for understanding all human behavior." For Adam Smith this new science flowed from the six basic motives of human nature: "self-love, sympathy, the desire to be free, a sense of propriety, the habit of labor, and the propensity to truck, barter and exchange"(Dowd, 2000: 29).
11. Margaret Thatcher (1987; also see Chapter 7 in this work) famously put it in an interview: "I think we have gone through a period when too many children and people have been given to understand "I have a problem, it is the Government's job to cope with it!" or "I have a problem, I will go and get a grant to cope with it!" "I am homeless, the Government must house me!" and so they are casting their problems on society and who is society? There is no such thing! There are individual men and women and there are families and no government can do anything except through people and people look to themselves first."
12. For example, Adam Smith's views on the Navigation Acts and usury laws adopted a more nuanced position than simply advocating for *laissez-faire*.
13. As both Marx and Polanyi remind us, the functioning of market economies are predicated on the ability of the state to put into place laws that create and support private property and assist capital accumulation. The state, is nevertheless, depicted by liberalists as an obstacle to freedom and individualism. This problematic generally works on two levels. On one level it is government spending itself that is the problem. Governmental spending is a burden that essentially robs the private sector of opportunity. On another level, the state monopolizes all it touches and eliminates the ability of an enterprise to produce a profit.
14. However, as Polanyi (1944), Dumont (1986) and others have argued, prior to the rise of liberal economics markets were seen as extensions of and as embedded within the normative systems of religions or cultures. They were not seen as independent, unique or natural entities but things that were directly connected to the larger norms and social processes present throughout society at a particular moment in time.
15. This is perhaps most evident in the austerity measures that were forced on governments in Greece, Portugal and Ireland in 2010. They were also leverage in the debate over deficit spending during this time in the U.S.
16. For example, as Richard Sennett (1998: 22–23) has pointed out, the length of time stocks have been held on British and American exchanges dropped by 60 percent from the mid early 1980s through the late 1990s. More recently this trend has created what is referred to as "high frequency trading" where high-speed computers are used to place very short-term bets. In the case of Tradebot, in Kansas City, the average time a stock was held was 11 seconds. By some estimation high-frequency trading now makes up 40–70 percent of all trading in the United States (Creswell, 2010)
17. See the article at www.clipsyndicate.com/publish/video/749747/bridgeport_looks_abroad_for_teachers.
18. An interesting example of the stakeholder society in action can be found in an advertising campaign put forward by a group calling themselves "The People of the Oil and Natural Gas Industry" (PONGI) that began running

on U.S. television stations in the spring of 2008. During this time PONGI (the API) began running a television ad entitled "Do You Own an Oil Company." The ad stated: "If you're wondering who owns 'Big Oil,' chances are good the answer is 'you do'" (see www.energytomorrow.org/economy/Do_You_Own_an_Oil_Company_.aspx). The argument put forward was that since most people's retirement portfolios and mutual fund holdings likely contained some oil stocks the entity denigrated as "big oil" was actually the millions of ordinary shareholders who held stock in oil companies.
19. In the view of neo-Marxists and Karl Polanyi, liberalism and neoliberalism are not now, nor have they ever been, anti-state. Liberalist rhetoric aside, both theorists argued markets needs the state in order to exist. As Antonio Gramsci (1971: 160) framed it, "*laissez-faire* too is a form of State 'regulation,' introduced and maintained by legislative and coercive mean . . . not [an] expression of economic facts." Echoing this view Karl Polanyi (1957 [1944]) likewise argued, "There was nothing natural about laissez faire; free markets could never have come into being merely by allowing things to take their course . . . Laissez faire itself was enforced by the state." In other words, markets are not natural entities that grow out of a self-centered human nature or natural harmony rather they are artificial formations that must suppress other forms of economic exchange and which must use a particular type of political authority to create their conditions for existence. For Marx and subsequent Marxists, of course, the spontaneous, natural market is one of the great ideologies of capitalism.

NOTES TO CHAPTER 2

1. These systems have also spawned and fueled a vast "performance indicator industry" (Hood, 1991: 9) whose job it is to create new, more detailed measures that gage and report on performance that can be purchased from various private companies.
2. This perhaps helps explain why Rosenthal's (2002) study of doctors in Sweden, the U.K. and the U.S. found a growing belief that they were being deliberately and systematically removed from most important policy and managerial decisions under NPM. Also, the Changing Academic Profession survey of faculty found a considerable decline in the perception of faculty power and influence in many countries (Cummings and Finkelstein, 2009).

NOTES TO CHAPTER 3

1. Such a view may be returning today with the "cut and paste" and choreography found in the postmodernization of knowledge.
2. Such a view can be found in Adam Smith's (1904 [1776]: 418) *The Wealth of Nations* where he sees patents and copyrights as justifiable because they compensate companies "for hazarding a dangerous and expensive experiment, of which the publick is afterward to reap the benefit."
3. As Habermas (1989) has noted this early public sphere was only truly public to a few. In this somewhat ironic framing, "private property is the entrance ticket to the public sphere . . . [o]nly as a property-owning, educated individual can private man engage in the public sphere" (Wirtèn, 2008: 35). The further expansion, socialization and democratization of this sphere would be one of the most important cultural and political accomplishments of the twentieth century.

4. In the early part of the twentieth century, university departments increasingly came less under the control of university presidents or powerful chairs and become more autonomous and in control of their own personnel and curriculum (see Geiger, 1986: 37).
5. A famous case in this regard involved James Watt's refusal to license the steam engine after he patented it in 1769. In this instance, patent protection allowed Watt to essentially sit on the invention without others being able to add to it (see Sell and May, 2001: 472–473).
6. One of the most important patent law cases in this regard was the U.S. Supreme Court's 1917 overturning of the 1912 decision involving the A. B. Dick Company. The original 1912 Dick decision had allowed the company to require purchasers of is mimeograph machine to also buy its ink, although the ink itself was not patented (Sell and May, 2001: 486). In overturning the 1912 decision, the court maintained that such patent maneuvers constituted a monopoly and was a violation of the 1914 Clayton Act that forbade monopolistic control. As such knowledge, even if in technological form, belonged in the public domain where other knowledge makers could, under the political concepts of innovation and the public domain and the legal guidelines of "fair use" and "patent life," advance an argument or improve upon an existing patent.
7. While it could be argued that these remarks are more rhetorical than a real description of universities in the nineteenth century, it would be virtually impossible to find a university president who would make such remarks today.
8. In the Humboldtian university, as Fuller (2000: 83) has described it, "in one fell swoop free floating gadflies were flattened into civil servants."
9. A similar emphasis on the importance of epistemic independence was later exemplified in the joint *Statement of Principles on Academic Freedom and Tenure* issued and adopted in 1940 by the American Association of University Professors (AAUP) and Association of American Colleges (now the Association of American Colleges and Universities). The statement maintained that "the common good depends upon the free search for truth and its free expression" (AAUP, 1940: 3). It provided professors "full freedom in research and in the publication of the results" as well as freedom in the classroom (AAUP, 1940: 3).
10. The University also began to publish a cost/benefit analysis of each professor that calculated their monetary cost to the university versus the amount of money they produced through grants and student tuition.
11. The fear of monopolization found in the Statute of Anne and the U.S. Constitution reflected some of the thinking about knowledge during this time. Likewise, the liberal fear of the stifling effects of monopolization was not necessarily driven by a disproval of the larger inequalities in wealth that were created by the centralization of resources as they were for socialists. These were, after all, viewed as inevitable private outcomes of individual achievements. Here, "citizens are equal, but only in their capacities as citizens, not as private individuals" (Boyle, 1996: 26). Instead, political liberals feared that monopolies denied individuals their livelihood and autonomy and limited the ability of the public to use information to make informed decisions and to become innovative.

NOTES TO CHAPTER 4

1. In one sense this resembles the way corporations have replaced the traditional workforce with contingent workers who work on "projects" and within "fields of work" (see Sennett, 1998: 22).

2. In some instances the exercises have helped established universities fend off challenges from upstart universities or the polytechnics by using the evaluations to keep their research funding.
3. Interestingly and predictably the assessment movement has also spawned private companies that provide support services. For example, a company called Scopus provides various types of rankings to assist managers in decision-making (see www.scopus.com). Scopus describes itself as "the optimal data source for research performance measurement." In an ad appearing *The Chronicle of Higher Education* in 2008, Peter Brimblecome of the University of East Anglia describes the value of Scopus in the following way, "As financial resources become more scarce, it is more critical to identify research and researchers who are the most productive and on the right track." The ad claims that it is now easy to "evaluate and prioritize resource allocation by departments or fields," to allow the "managerial revolution and its expansion into the professions about tenure and promotion" and to "promote your institution for funding and recruitment" (*The Chronicle of Higher Education*, January 11, 2008: A15).
4. Such an approach can be found in the move to a clinical model of training teachers in the U.S. In this model teachers ironically know less content but more ways to disseminate the content they know less about (see AACTE, 2010; NCATE, 2010).
5. For instance, the now over $1.5 billion K-12 standardized testing industry (McLaren 2003: 43) has becomes one of the mechanisms through which the vague, amorphous and qualitative dimensions of knowledge are transformed into knowable and measurable quantitative epistemic units.
6. This is evident in the 2010 move in the U.S. by National Council for Accreditation of Teacher Education to make teaching a "skills based profession." Rather than being versed in teaching philosophies, histories and modes of learning, students in teacher preparation programs are now to be taught skills directly related to classroom management. In this case, teachers are not expected to be creative professionals who develop their own strategies but are to delivery technicians who convey the "best practices" as deemed by departments of education, administrators and curriculum experts.
7. Such a process can also be found in a recent effort sponsored by the Carnegie Foundation to encourage academic publishers to disaggregate their publications. In the university-based and public-regarding system of knowledge production where costs are socialized, trade publications were sometimes viewed skeptically as being only useful in a few situations where the knowledge needed to be popularized to a large audience.
8. Several memorable cases in this regard have involved trade secrets and public relations efforts of pharmaceutical research companies. In one instance, a medical researcher at the University of North Carolina, John Buse, presented a paper revealing heart complications with GlaxoSmithKline's diabetes drug, Avandia. In 2006 the drug had $2.2 billion in U.S. sales. Buse was, subsequently, threatened with legal action by the company. He eventually signed a document agreeing not to discuss his concerns with the drug in public (Harris, 2010: A3). A similar incident involving the same drug also took place at the University of Pennsylvania.
9. While such a Barnum-like scientific spectacle is not necessarily new in the world of science, as in the case of the Piltdown Hoax, for example, it does reveal the extent to which knowledge must promote itself in order to be deemed worthy of large-scale support. An interesting example of this new promotional science in action can be found in 2009 with the discovery of a skeleton named Ida in Germany. While the discovery of a skeleton is

somewhat common in paleontology, Ida was quickly dubbed as "the missing link" and promoted as one of the great discoveries of science. The "news conference" unveiling the "missing link" at the Museum of Natural History in New York included a light show and the launching of a website named. www.revealingthelink.com. As a prelude to a book and a documentary entitled "The Link" on Ida's discovery shown on The History Channel, narrated by Sir David Attenborough, the news conference featured a curtain to unveil the skeleton by the mayor of New York, Michael Bloomberg.

NOTES TO CHAPTER 5

1. In addition, new positions, such as chief knowledge officer (CKO), have arisen in corporations to help better manage the organization's use and dissemination of knowledge (see Foote et al., 2001).
2. Although not directly financed by the government but partly supported by the Rockefeller Foundation, the nine-member SAB's first task was to inquire "into the objectives, personnel, duplication and coordination of scientific work" (Dupree, 1957: 351; see Gray, 1934). Its central goal was to gain government support for a variety of nongovernmental research (see Geiger, 1986: 257). The SAB's first major report entitled "Recovery Program of Science Progress" linked economic recovery with science funding in universities by calling for a "New Deal" for science. This new initiative called for a significant use of public funds to support various scientific projects that would in turn contribute to the recovery efforts being undertaken by the Roosevelt administration (Dupree, 1957: 353). The Board's Chair and President of MIT, Karl Compton, subsequently launched a media campaign to convince Americans of the need for a broad based, government sponsored science policy. Compton (1934: 7) argued that the time had come for "the development of scientific discovery into an operating industry, to create employment, business wealth, health and satisfaction." Foreshadowing some of the arguments that would be made in the economic downturn of the first decade of the twenty-first century, he (in Gray, 1934) tried to convince Congress and the public "that if one-tenth the money which has been lost in this depression had been put into a wise program of research, the other nine-tenths would never have been lost."
3. Michael was also brother of Karl Polanyi author of *The Great Transformation*.
4. Lysenkoism refers to a case in Soviet agricultural science where the ideas of Lamarckian biology were promoted by and became the official orthodoxy of the Communist Party.
5. This particular article appeared in the Liberty Fund's *Concise Encyclopedia of Economics*. The Liberty Fund is an American group organized over fifty years ago "to encourage the ideal of a society of free and responsible individuals" (see www.libertyfund.org).
6. The same year the Australian government released *Backing Australia's Ability*. The report called for the urgent need to create a flexible workforce to spur future innovation. This was followed in 2003 with the government's *The Innovation Report of Backing Australia's Ability 2003–04—Real Results, Real Jobs* that sought to illustrate Australian progress in meeting the goal of becoming a knowledge society as laid out by the OECD's benchmarking report of 1999.
7. Also among these reforms an emphasis was placed on "lifelong learning" in member states. Here lifelong learning is envisioned as "an essential policy strategy for the development of citizenship, social cohesion, employment and

for individual fulfillment" (European Commission, 2002: 2). Such a vision connects with the idea of a flexible workforce that can quickly adjust to changing conditions. It also involves a system whereby the worker must take it up on him- or herself to continuously possess skills that are in demand. This essentially shifts the burden of education from state and business to the individual (see Olssen, 2006; Tuschling and Engeman, 2006).
8. By 2008 the RAE had expanded to involve over 700 assessors combing through some 180 thousand publications and issuing ratings (see Hicks, 2008: 6). Discussions are also underway to change the RAE to a new Research Excellence Framework.

NOTES TO CHAPTER 6

1. The phrase "an island of socialism in a free market sea" is taken from Milton and Rose Friedman's essay on education (Friedman and Friedman, 1980).
2. The pool made its first payout in December of 2009 when 819 continuing faculty members received $2855.00 each (Kent State University, n.d.).
3. Portions of this section draw on interviews with educators and policy makers conducted in New Zealand in the spring of 2009.
4. In the National Party, Ruth Richardson, the Party Spokesperson on Education and one of the central advocates of education reform in New Zealand borrowed her ideas directly from Friedman's plan for education vouchers (Grant, 2003: 225). These became part of the National Party's general educational agenda, although they were never enacted.
5. Lange later expressed displeasure with the competition that the national government later introduced into the Tomorrow's Schools plan.
6. The Act was influenced and given legitimacy by Brian Caldwell and Jim Spinks' (1988: vii) book *The Self-Managing School* that set forth an agenda for moving schools away from centralized control while maintaining accountability "to a centralized authority for the manner in which resources are allocated."
7. For example, in the early twentieth century the National Association of Manufacturers (1905) called for more training "in the arts of production and distribution" in order to respond to the economic threat posed by "international competition," particularly from Germany.
8. As with reform elsewhere key to many of these forms efforts was an emphasis on a "data driven form of decision making" or "what works" strategies where teaching is based directly on the outcomes of standardized testing. In this approach companies such as Wireless Generation or Blue Ribbon Testing began providing online testing of students and feedback to teachers. As Larry Berger (in Fisher, 2010: 76), the president of Wireless Generation described it, "education is in a revolution of sophisticated analysis of data set." One such data driven experiment in New York City has students receive their lessons plans on "airport-style overhead monitors in the morning according to how they performed on a quiz the afternoon before" (Fisher, 2010: 76).

NOTES TO CHAPTER 7

1. Foucault saw such power less as a "historically specific vehicle for an eternal will to power" and more as the deployment of particular "political and intellectual technologies" (see Hunter, 1993: 181). In this sense, power is not, as it had been for Weber and others, a coercive force pressing down on the individual from above but a field of both self and social organization.

2. In the 1990s and early 2000s this becomes coupled with the broader financialization of the economy discussed in Chapter 1 that sought to increase the speed and expand the domains of finance. As part of this expansion, new financial instruments were created that enabled banks to bundle subprime loans and market them as investments. In this system, the normal risk factors of equity and the possibility of default would be covered by a continuously expanding market and the rising price of houses.
3. A few decades later in his classic essay "The Great Salesroom," C. Wright Mills (1956) described an updated, mid twentieth century version of the liberal subject at work in one of the most liberalist of societies, the United States. In this instance the rise of corporations had transformed the atomistic and egoistic nineteenth-century liberal into a mid twentieth century "organization man" (Whyte, 1956) who sold not only products but themselves as well. The person's entire being was now enveloped in sales and the new retail form, including his or her emotions and emotional labor (see Hochschild, 1983).
4. Part of the issue here involves the neoliberal assumption, as in the "sentiments" of Smith, that humans are naturally insatiable. As Lea et al. (1987: 111) argued, "the axiom of greed must be rejected because real people, unlike Home economicus, are not insatiable." Likewise Marshall Sahlins (1972) contented that unlike market economies tribal economies do not create insatiable want." Such materialism, "springs from the notion, sedulously cultivated by the class in power, that the creative capacities of individuals can be evoked and developed only in a struggle for material possessions and material gain" (Dewey, 1935: 89).

References

AACTE (American Association of Colleges of Teacher Education). 2010. *The Clinical Preparation of Teachers: A Policy Brief.* Washington, DC: AACTE.
AAUP (American Association of University Professors). 1940. Statement of Principles on Academic Freedom and Tenure. Retrieved from www.aaup.org/AAUP/pubsres/policydocs/contents/1940statement.htm.
Abbott, Malcolm. 2006. "Competition and Reform of the New Zealand Tertiary Education Sector." *Journal of Education Policy* 21 (3): 357–387.
Ackerman, Bruce and Anne Alstott. 1999. *The Stakeholder Society.* New Haven, CT: Yale University Press.
Acton, Lord. 1907 [1866]. *A History of Freedom and Other Essays.* London: Macmillan.
Adorno, Theodore, and Max Horkheimer. 1991 [1944]. *The Dialectic of Enlightenment.* New York: Continuum.
Agger, Ben. 1988. *Fast Capitalism.* Urbana: University of Illinois Press.
Albert, Michel. 1993. *Capitalism Against Capitalism*, trans. by P. Haviland. London: Whurr Publishers.
Alexander, Kern, and M. David Alexander. 2005. *American Public School Law* (6th edition). Belmont, CA: Wadsworth.
Amable, Bruno. 2011. "Morals and Politics in the Ideology of Neo-Liberalism." *Socio-Economic Review* 9 (1): 3–30.
Anyanwu, Chika. 2004. "Innovation and Creativity in the Humanities: Accepting the Challenges." Pp. 71–81 in J. Kenway, E. Bullen and S. Robb (eds.), *Innovation and Tradition: The Arts, Humanities and the Knowledge Economy.* New York: Peter Lang.
Apple, Michael. 1998. "Under the New Hegemonic Alliance: Conservatism and Education Policy in the United States. Pp. 79–99 in K. Sullivan (ed.), *Education and Change in the Pacific Rim: Meeting the Challenges.* Wallingford, UK: Triangle Books.
Arshad-Ayaz, Adeela. 2007. "Globalisation and Marginalisation in Higher Education." *Education and Society* 25 (1): 77–93.
Association of University Technology Managers. 2007. "US Licensing Activity Survey." Retrieved from www.autm.net/AM/Template.cfm?Section=FY_2007_Licensing_Activity_Survey&Template=/CM/ContentDisplay.cfm&ContentID=2805.
Australian Department of Education, Training and Youth. 1999. *Knowledge and Innovation: A Policy Statement on Research and Research Training.* Retrieved from http://www.dest.gov.au/archive/highered/whitepaper/heading.htm.
Baert, Patrick, and Alan Shipman. 2005. "University under Siege? Trust and Accountability in the Contemporary Academy." *European Societies* 7 (1): 157–185.

Bacon, Francis. 1960. "Aphorisms on the Composition of Primary History." Pp. 273–284 in F. H. Anderson (ed.), *The New Organon and Related Writings.* Indianapolis: Bobbs-Merrill Educational Publishing.
Bailey, R. 1994. "British Public Sector Industrial Relations." *British Journal of Industrial Relations* 32: 113–136.
Ball, S. J. 1994. *Education Reform: A Critical and Post-structural Approach.* Buckingham: Open University Press.
———. 2003. "The Teacher's Soul and the Terrors of Performativity", *Journal of Education Policy* 18 (2): 215–228.
Barnes, Barry and David Edge (eds.). 1982. *Science in Context: Readings in the Sociology of Science.* Milton Keynes: Open University Press.
Barrington, J.M.. 1991. *Report to the Ministry of Education: OECD : Educational Evaluation and Reform Strategies.* Wellington, NZ: Victoria University.
Basken, Paul. 2008. "Colleges Emerge the Clear Winner in the Battle Over Accreditation." *The Chronicle of Higher Education*, February 1: A19.
Baudrillard, Jean. 1983. *In the Shadow of the Silent Majorities, or the End of the Social.* New York: Semiotext(e).
———. 1988. *Selected Writings* (ed. by M. Poster). Stanford, CA: Stanford University Press.
Baxandall, Rosalyn, and Elizabeth Ewen. 2001. *Picture Windows: How the Suburbs Happened.* New York: Basic Books.
BCA (Business Council of Australia). 1993. *Australia 2010: Creating the Future in Australia.* Melbourne: BCA.
Beck, John, and Michael F.D. Young. 2005. "The Assault on the Professions and the Restructuring of Academic and Professional Identities: A Bernsteinian Analysis." *British Journal of Sociology of Education* 25 (2): 183–197.
Beck, Ulrich. 1992: *Risk Society: Towards a New Modernity.* London: Sage.
———. 2000. *What Is Globalization?* Cambridge: Polity Press.
Beck, Ulrich, and E. Beck-Gernsheim. 1996. "Individualization and the 'Precarious Freedoms': Perspectives and Controversies of a Subject-Orientated Sociology." Pp. 23–48 in P. Heelas, S. Lash and P. Morris (eds.), *Detraditionalization: Critical Reflections on Authority and Identity.* Cambridge, MA: Blackwell.
Becker, Gary. 1964. *Human Capital: A Theoretical and Empirical Analysis, with Special Reference to Education.* New York: Columbia University Press.
———. 1976. *The Economic Approach to Human Behavior.* Chicago: University of Chicago Press.
Beerkens, Eric. 2008. "University Polices for Knowledge Societies: Global Standardization, Local Reinvention." *Perspectives in Global Development and Technology* 7: 15–36.
Beeson, Mark, and Ann Firth. 1998. "Neoliberalism as Political Rationality: Australian Public Policy Since the 1980s." *Journal of Sociology* 34 (2): 215–231.
Bekelman, J. E., Li, Y., and C. P. Gross. 2003. "Scope and Impact of Financial Conflicts of Interest in Biomedical Research: A Systematic Review." *Journal of the American Medical Association* 289: 454–465.
Bell, Daniel. 1973. *The Coming of Post-Industrial Society: A Venture in Social Forecasting.* New York: Basic Books.
Bergeron, Suzanne. 2008. "Shape-shifting Neoliberalism and World Bank Education Policy: A Response to Steven Klees." *Globalisation, Societies and Education* 6 (4): 349–353.
Berle, Adolf, and Gardiner Means. 1991 [1933]. *The Modern Corporation and Private Property.* New Brunswick, NJ: Transaction.
Bernal, J. D. 1939. *The Social Function of Science.* London: George Routledge & Sons.

———. 1953. *Science and Industry in the Nineteenth Century*. Bloomington: Indiana University Press.
Bernstein, Basil. 2000. *Pedagogy, Symbolic Control and Identity: Theory, Research, Critique* (revised edition). Lanham, MD: Rowman & Littlefield.
Bernstein, Peter. 1998. *Against the Gods: The Remarkable Story of Risk*. New York: Wiley.
Biddle, Justin. 2007. "Lessons from the Vioxx Debacle: What the Privatization of Science Can Teach Us About Social Epistemology." *Social Epistemology* 21 (1): 21–39.
Blair, Tony. 1996. *New Britain: My Vision of a Young Country*. London: Basic Books.
———. 1999. "Blair Promises Britain and Era of Equality and Opportunity." Retrieved from http://www.guardian.co.uk/politics/ 1999/sep/29/labourconference. labour6.
Blume, Stuart. 1974. *Toward a Political Sociology of Science*. New York: The Free Press.
Blumenthal, D. Gluck, M., Louis, K.S., Soto, A. and D. Wise. 1986. "University-Industry Research Relations in Biotechnology: Implications for the University." *Science* 232: 1361–1366.
Bollag, Burton. 2007. "Financing for Higher Education Shifts to Private Sector Worldwide." *Chronicle of Higher Education* 53 (50): A36.
Boltanski, Luc, and Eve Chiapello. 2005. *The New Spirit of Capitalism* (trans. by G. Elliott). London: Verso.
Books Rights Registry. 2011. "Google Book Settlement." Retrieved from www.googlebooksettlement.com/ agreement.html.
Bootle, Roger. 2009. *The Trouble with Markets: Saving Capitalism from Itself*. London: Nicholas Brealy Publishing.
Boston, Jonathan (ed.). 1995. *The State Under Contract*. Wellington, NZ: Bridgett Wilson Books.
Bousquet, Marc. 2008. *How the University Works: Higher Education and the Low-Wage Nation*. New York: New York University Press.
Bourdieu, Pierre. 1998. "The Essence of Neoliberalism." Retrieved from http://mondediplo.com/1998/12/ 08bourdieu.
———, 2003. *Firing Back: Against the Tyranny of the Market 2* (trans. by L. Waquant). New York: New Press.
Boyle, James. 1996. *Shamans, Software, & Spleens: Law and the Construction of the Information Society*. Cambridge, MA: Harvard University Press.
———. 2003. "The Second Enclosure Movement and the Construction of the Public Domain." *Law & Contemporary Problems* 66: 33–75.
———. 2009. *The Public Domain: Enclosing the Commons of the Mind*. New Haven, CT: Yale University Press.
Boyson, Rhodes. 1979. "Education Concern." *Daily Mail* June 25.
Braverman, Harry. 1974. *Labor and Monopoly Capital: The Degradation of Work in the Twentieth Century*. New York: Monthly Review Press.
Brine, Jacky. 2006. "Lifelong Learning and the Knowledge Economy: Those That Know and Those That Do Not—The Discourse of the European Union." *British Educational Research Journal* 32 (5): 649–665.
Brooks, Peter. 2011. "Our Universities: How Bad? How Good?" *New York Review of Books* March 24: 10–13.
Brooks, Rachel. 2008. "Government Rhetoric and Student Understandings: Discursive Framings of Higher Education 'Choice.'" Pp. 232–247 in D. Epstein, R. Boden, R. Deem, F. Rizvi and S. Wright (eds.), *World Yearbook of Education 2008, Geographies of Knowledge, Geometries of Power: Framing the Future of Education*. London: Routledge.

Brown, Michael F. 2003. *Who Owns Native Culture?* Cambridge, MA: Harvard University Press.
Brown, Phillip, and Anthony Hesketh. 2004. *The Mismanagement of Talent: Employability and Jobs in the Knowledge Economy.* Oxford: Oxford University Press.
Buchanan, James. 1972. "Toward Analysis of Closed Behavioral Systems." Pp. 11–23 in J. Buchanan and R. Tollison (eds.), *Theory of Public Choice: Political Applications of Economics.* Ann Arbor: University of Michigan Press.
———. 1984. "Politics without Romance: A Sketch of Positive Public Choice Theory and Its Normative Implications." Pp. 11–22 in J. Buchanan and R. Tollison (eds.), *The Theory of Public Choice—II.* Ann Arbor: University of Michigan Press.
Buchanan, James, and Tullock, Gordon. 1962. *The Calculus of Consent.* Ann Arbor: The University of Michigan.
Bullen, Elizabeth, Jane Kenway and Simon Robb. 2004. "Can the Arts and Humanities Survive the Knowledge Economy? A Beginner's Guide to the Issues." Pp. 10–22 in S. Robb, E. Bullern and J. Kenway (eds.), *Innovation & Tradition: The Arts, Humanities and the Knowledge Economy.* New York: Peter Lang.
Burchell, Graham. 1993. "Liberal Government and Techniques of the Self." *Economy and Society* 22 (3): 267–282.
Burton, Robin. 1997. "Popular Health, Advanced Liberalism and *Good Housekeeping* Magazine." Pp. 223–248 in A. Peterson and R. Bunton (eds.). *Foucault, Health and Medicine.* London: Routledge.
Burtscher, Christian, Pasqualoni, Pier-Paolo and Alan Scott. 2006. "Universities and the Regulatory Framework: The Austrian University System in Transition." *Social Epistemology* 20 (3–4): 241–258.
Bush, Vannevar. 1945. *Science: The Endless Frontier, A Report to the President.* Washington, DC: U.S. Government Printing Office. Retrieved from www.nsf.gov/od/lpa/nsf50/vbush1945.htm.
Business and Higher Education Forum, American Council on Education. 1983. *America's Competitive Challenge: The Need for National Response.* Washington, D.C.: American Council on Education.
Caldwell, Brian, and Jim Spinks. 1988. *The Self-Managing School.* East Sussex: Falmer Press.
Caliskan, Koray, and Michel Callon. 2009. "Economization, part I: Shifting Attention From the Economy towards Processes of Economization." *Economy and Society* 38 (3): 369–398.
Callon, Michel. 1994. "Is Science a Public Good? Fifth Mullins Lecture, Virginia Polytechnic Institute, 23 March 1993." *Science, Technology and Human Values* 19 (4): 395–424.
———. 1998. "Introduction: The Embeddedness of Economic Markets in Economics." Pp. 1–57 in M. Callon (ed.), *The Laws of the Markets.* Oxford: Blackwell Publishers.
Carnegie Corporation of New York. 1983. *Education and Economic Progress: Toward a National Educational Policy.* New York: Carnegie Corporation.
Carter, Samuel Casey. 2000. *No Excuses: Lessons from 21 High Performing, High- Poverty Schools.* Washington, DC: Heritage Foundation.
Cassidy, John. 2010. "Right and Wrong New Labour." *New York Review of Books* LVII (11), June 24: 57–60.
Castells, Manuel. 1996. *The Rise of the Network Society.* Cambridge, MA: Blackwell.
———. 2000. *The Information Age: Economy, Society and Culture, Vol. 1* In *The Rise of the Network Society* (2nd edition). Malden, MA: Blackwell.

Castells, Manuel, and P. Hall. 1994. *Technopoles of the World*. London: Routledge.
Chandler, Alfred. 1977. *The Visible Hand: The Managerial Revolution in American Business*. Cambridge, MA: Harvard University Press.
Cheshire, Lynda, and Geoffrey Lawrence. 2005. "Neoliberalism, Individualisation and Community: Regional Restructuring in Australia." *Social Identities* 11 (5): 435–445.
Ciancanelli, Penny. 2008. "(Re)producing Universities: Knowledge Dissemination, Market Power and the Global Knowledge Commons." Pp. 67–84 in D. Epstein, R. Boden, R. Deem, F. Rizvi and S. Wright (eds.), *Geographies of Knowledge, Geometries of Power: Framing the Future of Higher Education*. London: Routledge.
Clark, Gordon L., and Dariusz Wojcik. 2007. *The Geography of Finance: Corporate Governance in the Global Marketplace*. New York: Oxford University Press.
Clarke, John. 2004. "Dissolving the Public Realm? The Logics and Limits of Neo-Liberalism." *Journal of Social Policy* 33: 27–48.
Clarke, John, and Janet Newman. 1993. "The Right to Manage: A Second Managerial Revolution?" *Cultural Studies* 7 (3): 427–441.
———. 1997. *The Managerial State: Power, Politics and Ideology in the Remaking of Social Welfare*. Thousand Oaks, CA: Sage Publications.
Clawson, Dan. 1997. "Editor's Note: Market Censorship—Books Under Attach." *Contemporary Sociology* 26 (5): vii–viii.
Cloke, Ken, and Joan Goldsmith. 2002. *The End of Management and the Rise of Organization Democracy*. San Francisco: Jossey-Bass.
Clowes, Michael J. 2000. *The Money Flood: How Pension Funds Revolutionized Investing*. New York: John Wiley & Sons, Inc.
Cochrane, Rexmond. 1978. *The National Academy of Sciences: The First Hundred Years, 1863–1963*. Washington, DC: National Academy of Sciences.
Cohen, Joseph, and Miguel Centeno. 2006. "Neoliberalism and Patterns of Economic Performance, 1980–2000." Pp. 32–67 in D. Massey, M. Sanchez and J. Behrman (eds.), *Chronicle of a Myth Foretold: The Washington Consensus in Latin America*. Thousand Oaks, CA: Sage Publications.
Collins, Randall. 1998. *The Sociology of Philosophies: A Global Theory of Intellectual Change*. Cambridge, MA: Harvard University Press.
Collins, T., and S. Tillman. 1988. "Global Technology Diffusion and the American Research University." In J. T. Kenny (ed.), *Research Administration and Technology Transfer*. San Francisco: Jossey Bass.
Committee for Economic Development. 1984. *Strategy for United States Industrial Competitiveness*. New York: Committee for Economic Development.
Compton, Karl. 1934. "Science Still Holds a Great Promise: An Answer to Those Who Contend That Ills of Today Can Be Blamed on Technology." *New York Times* December 16.
Cooper, Andrew. 2000. "The State of Mind We're In." *Soundings* 15: 118–138.
Cooper, Simon. 2002. "Post-Intellectuality? Universities and the Knowledge Industry." Pp. 207–232 in S. Cooper, J. Hinkson and G. Sharp (eds.), *Scholars and Entrepreneurs*. North Carlton, Australia: Arena Publications.
Coorey, Phillip. 2009. "Time for New World Order: PM." *The Canberra Times* January 31. Retrieved from http://www.canberratimes.com.au/news/national/national/general/time-for-a-new-world-order-pm/1421121.aspx#.
Cope, Bill, and Mary Kalantzis. 2008. "The Social Web: Changing Knowledge Systems In Higher Education." Pp. 371–384 in D. Epstein, R. Boden, R. Deem, F. Rizvi and S. Wright (eds.), *Geographies of Knowledge, Geometries of Power: Framing the Future of Higher Education*. London: Routledge.

Cozzens, Susan. 2007. "Death by Peer Review? The Impact of Results–Oriented Management in U.S. Research." Pp. 225–242 in R. Whitley and J. Glaser (eds.), *The Changing Governances of the Sciences: The Advent of Research Evaluation Systems*. Dordrecht: Springer.

Creswell, Julie. 2010. "Speedy New Traders Make Waves Far from Wall St." *New York Times*. May 16.

Crockett, Richard. 1995. *Thinking the Unthinkable: Think-Tanks and the Economic Counter-Revolution, 1931–1983*. London: Fontana Press.

Crocombe, Graham, Enright, Michael and Michael Porter. 1991. *Upgrading New Zealand's Competitive Advantage*. Auckland: Oxford University Press.

Crowther, J. G. 1941. *The Social Relations of Science*. New York: MacMillan.

Cummings, William, and Martin Finkelstein. 2009. "Global Trends in Academic Governance." *Academe*, November–December: 31–34.

Dale, Roger. 1989/1990. "The Thatcherite Project in Education: The Case of the City Technology Colleges." *Critical Social Policy* 9 (3): 4–19.

Darnton, Robert. 2009. "Google and the Future of Books." *New York Review of Books* 56 (2), February 12.

———. 2011. "Google's Loss: The Public's Gain." *New York Review of Books* 58 (7), April 29.

Davies, Bronwyn. 2003. "Death to Critique and Dissent? The Politics and Practices of New Managerialism and of 'Evidence-based Practice.'" *Gender and Education* 15 (1): 91–103.

Davies, Bronwyn, Jenny Browne, Susanne Gannon, Eileen Honan and Margaret Somerville. 2005. "Embodied Women at Work in Neoliberal Times and Places." *Gender, Work and Organization* 12 (4): 343–362.

Dawkins, John. 1987. *Higher Education: A Policy Discussion Paper*. Canberra: AGPS.

De Tocqueville. Alexis. 1899. *Democracy in America*. New York: Colonial Press.

Dean, Mitchell. 1999. *Governmentality: Power and Rule in Modern Society*. Thousand Oaks, CA: Sage Publications.

———. 2008. "Governing Society: The Story of Two Monsters." *Journal of Cultural Economy* 1 (1): 25–38.

Debord, Guy. 1995. *The Society of the Spectacle*. New York: Zone Books.

Deleuze, Gilles. 1992. "Postscript on Societies of Control." Retrieved from http://www.n5m.org/n5m2/media/texts/deleuze.htm.

Denham, Andrew, and Mark Garnett. 1998. *British Think-Tanks and the Climate of Opinion*. London: UCL Press.

Dent, Mike. 2002. "Introduction: Configuring the 'New' Professional." Pp. 1–16 in M. Dent and S. Whitehead (eds.), *Managing Professional Identities: Knowledge, Performativity and the 'New' Professional*. London: Routledge.

———. 2006. "Disciplining the Medical Profession? Implications of Patient Choice for Medical Dominance." *Health Sociology Review* 15: 458–468.

Dent, Mike and Stephen Whitehead. 2002. *Managing Professional Identities: Knowledge, Performativity and the 'New' Professonal*. London: Routledge.

Department of Business, Innovation and Skills. 2011. "*Higher Education: Students at the Heart of the System*. London: The Stationary Office Limited.

Department of Trade and Industry. 1998. *Our Competitive Future: Building the Knowledge Driven Economy*. London: HMSO. http://www.dti.gov.uk/comp/competitive/wh_int1.htm

Derby, Charles, William Schwartz and Yale Magrass. 1990. *Power in the Highest Degree*. New York: Oxford University Press.

Dewey, John. 1935. *Liberalism and Social Action*. New York: G. T. Putnam's Sons.

———. 1998. *The Essential Dewey, Volume I* (ed. by L. Hickman and T. Alexander). Bloomington: Indiana University Press.

DfEE. 1997. *Excellence in Schools, White Paper*. London: DfEE.

Dillon, Sam. 2011. "Behind Grass-Roots School Advocacy, Bill Gates." *The New York Times*, May 22: 1 and 4.

Dollery, B., Murray, D. and Crase, L. 2006."Knaves or knights, pawns or queens? An evaluation of Australian higher education reform policy."*Journal of Educational Administration*44(1): 86–97.

Douglas, Mary. 1982. *In the Active Voice*. London: Routledge and Kegan Paul.

Dowd, Douglas. 2000. *Capitalism and Its Economics: A Critical History*. London: Pluto Press.

Downs, Anthony. 1957. *An Economic Theory of Democracy*. New York: Harper and Row.

Drucker, Peter. 1954. *The Practice of Management*. New York: Harper.

———. 1959. *Landmarks of Tomorrow*. New York: Harper.

———. 1968. *The Age of Discontinuity: Guidelines of Our Changing Society*. New York: Harper & Row.

———. 1993. *Post-Capitalist Society*. New York: Basic Books.

Dubridge, Lee. 1946. "Science and National Policy." *Bulletin of the Atomic Scientists* 1 (11):12–14.

Du Gay, Paul. 2006. "Machinery of Government and Standards in Public Service: Teaching New Dogs Old Tricks." *Economy and Society* 35 (1): 148–167.

Dunne, Stephen, Stefano Harney and Martin Parker. 2008. "The Responsibilities of Management Intellectuals: A Survey." *Organization* 15 (2): 271–282.

Dumenil, Gerard, and Dominique Levy. 2004. *Capital Resurgent: Roots of the Neoliberal Revolution* (trans. by D. Jeffers). Cambridge, MA: Harvard University Press.

Dumont, Louis. 1986. *Essays on Individualism: Modern Ideology in Anthropological Perspective*, Chicago: University of Chicago Press.

Duncan, Grant. 2003. "Worker Compensation and the Governance of Pain." *Economy and Society* 32 (3): 449–477.

Dupree, A. Hunter. 1957. *Science in the Federal Government: A History of Policies and Activities to 1940*. Cambridge, MA: Harvard University Press.

Durkheim, Emile. 1964. *The Division of Labor in Society* (trans. by G. Simpson). New York: The Free Press.

Education Policy Response Group. 1999. *Against the Tide: A Critique of the Coalition Government's Education Policy Proposals, 1997–1998*. Palmerston North, N.Z: Kanuka Grove Press.

Eisenberg, Rebecca and Richard R Nelson.2002. "Public vs. Proprietary Science: A Fruitful Tension?" *Daedalus* 131 (2): 89–101.

Elias, Norbert. 1978. *The Civilizing Process* (trans. by E. Jephcott). New York: Urizen Books.

Epstein, Gerald A. 2005. "Introduction: Financialization and the World Economy." Pp. 3–16 in G. Epstein (ed.), *Financialization and the World Economy*. Northampton, MA: Edward Elgar Publishing.

Esty, Daniel, and Andrew Winston. 2009. *From Green to Gold: How Smart Companies Use Environmental Strategy to Innovate, Create Value, and Build Competitive Advantage*. New York: Wiley.

Etzkowitz, Henry. 2002. *MIT and the Rise of Entrepreneurial Science*. London: Routledge.

———. 2008.*The Triple Helix: University-Industry-Government Innovation in Action*. New York: Routledge.

European Commission. 2002. *European Report on Quality Indicators of Lifelong Learning*. Brussels: European Commission.

European Council. 2000. *Conclusions of the European Council, March 23–24*, SN100/00. Retrieved from http: www.europarl.europa.eu/summits/lis1_en.htm.

European Higher Education Area. 1999. "The Bologna Declaration of 19 June 1999." Retrieved from www.ond.vlaanderen.be/hogeronderwijs/bologna/documents/MDC/BOLOGNA_DECLARATION1.pdf.
Ezrahi, Yahron. 1971. "The Political Resources of American Science." *Social Studies of Science* 1 (2): 117–133.
Felix, David. 2005. "Why International Capital Mobility Should be Curbed and How It Could be Done." Pp. 384–408 in G. Epstein (ed.), *Financialization and the World Economy*. Northampton, MA: Edward Elgar.
Fisher, Daniel. 2010. "What Educators Are Learning from Money Managers." *Forbes* June 7: 72–78.
Florida, Richard. 2002. *The Rise of the Creative Class*. New York: Basic Books.
Foote, Nathaniel, Eric Matson and Nicholas Rudd. 2001. "Managing the Knowledge Manager." *McKinsey Quarterly* 3: 120–130.
Foucault, Michel. 1977. "What Is an Author?" Pp. 124–127 in D. Bouchard and S. Simon (eds.), *Language, Counter Memory, Practice*. Ithaca, NY: Cornell University Press.
———. 1991 [1978]. "Governmentality" (lecture at the College de France, February 1, 1978). Pp. 87–104 in G. Burchell, C. Gorden, and P. Miller (eds.), *The Foucault Effect: Studies in Governmentality*. Hemel Hempstead: Harvester Wheatsheaf.
———. 1991. *Remarks on Marx: Conversations with Duccio Trombadori*. New York: Semiotext(e).
———. 1997. *Ethics*. London: Penguin Books.
Fourcade, Marion. 2006. "The Construction of a Global Profession: The Transnationalization of Economics." *American Journal of Sociology* 112 (1): 145–194.
Fox, Justin. 2009. *The Myth of the Rational Market: A History of Risk, Reward and Delusion on Wall Street*. New York: Harper Collins.
Foster, Robert. 1995. "Print Advertisements and Nation Making in Metropolitan Papua New Guinea." Pp. 151–181 in R. Foster (ed.), *Nation Making: Emergent Identities in Postcolonial Melanesia*. Ann Arbor: University of Michigan Press.
Friedman, Milton. 1955. "The Role of Government in Education." Pp. 123–144 in R. Solo (ed.), *Economics and the Public Interest*." New Brunswick, NJ: Rutgers University Press.
———. 1962. *Capitalism and Freedom*. Chicago: University of Chicago Press.
———. 2005. "Free to Choose: After 50 Years, Education Vouchers are Beginning to Catch On." *Wall Street Journal* June 9.
Friedman, Milton, and Rose Friedman. 1980. *Free to Choose: A Personal Statement*. New York: Harcourt Brace Jovanovich.
Freire, Paulo. 1970. *Pedagogy of the Oppressed* (trans. by M. Bergman Ramos). New York: Herder and Herder.
Freidson, Eliot. 1994. *Professionalism Reborn: Theory, Prophecy and Policy*. Chicago: University of Chicago Press.
Frye, Northrope. 1957. *Anatomy of Criticism: Four Essays*. Princeton, NJ: Princeton University Press.
Fuchs, Stephan. 1992. *The Professional Quest for Truth: A Social Theory of Science and Knowledge*. Albany, NY: SUNY Press.
Fuchs, Stephan, and Steven Ward. 1994. "What is Deconstruction, and Where and When Does It Take Place? Making Facts in Science; Building Cases in Law." *American Sociological Review* 59: 481–500.
Fuller, Steven. 2000. *The Governance of Science: Ideology and the Future of the Open Society*. Buckingham: Open University Press.
Fukuyama, Francis. 1992. *The End of History and the Last Man*. New York: Free Press.
Funtowicz, S. O., and J. R. Ravetz. 1993. "The Emergence of Post-Normal Science." Pp. 85–123 in R. von Schomberg (ed.). *Science, Politics and Morality: Scientific Uncertainty and Decision Making*. Dordrecht: Kluwer.

Gains, Jane. 1995. "Reincarnation as the Ring on Liz Taylor's Finger: Andy Warhol and the Right of Publicity." Pp. 131–148 in A. Sarat and T. Kearns (eds.), *Identities, Politics and Rights*. Ann Arbor: University of Michigan Press.

Galison, Peter, and Bruce Hevly (eds.). 1992. *Big Science: The Growth of Large-Scale Research*. Stanford, CA: Stanford University Press.

Galison, Peter, Bruce Hevly and Rebecca Lowen. 1992. "Controlling the Monster: Stanford and the Growth of Physics Research, 1935–1962." Pp. 46–77 in P. Galison and B. Hevly (eds.), *Big Science: The Growth of Large-Scale Research*. Stanford, CA: Stanford University Press.

Gamble, Andrew. 1988. *The Free Economy and the Strong State: The Politics of Thatcherism*. Durham, NC: Duke University Press.

Garnaut, R. 1989. *Australia and the Northeast Asian Ascendancy*. Canberra: AGPS.

Geare, Alan, Fiona Edgar and Ian McAndrew. 2006. "Employment Relationships: Ideology and HRM Practice." *International Journal of Human Resource Management* 17 (7): 1190–1208.

Geiger, Roger. 1986. *To Advance Knowledge: The Growth of American Research Universities, 1900–1940*. New York: Oxford University Press.

———. 2004. *Knowledge & Money: Research Universities and the Paradox of the Marketplace*. Stanford, CA: Stanford University Press.

Gewirtz, Sharon, and Stephen Ball. 2000. "From 'Welfarism' to 'New Managerialism': Shifting Discourses of School Headship in the Education Marketplace." *Discourse: Studies in the Cultural Politics of Education* 21: 253–270.

Gibbons, Michael, Camille Limoges, Helga Nowotny, Simon Schwartzman, Peter Scott and Martin Trow. 1994. *The New Production of Knowledge: The Dynamics of Science and Research in Contemporary Societies*. London: Sage Publications.

Giddens, Anthony. 1991. *Modernity and Self-Identity: Self and Society in the Late Modern Age*. Cambridge: Polity Press.

Glaser, Jochen, and Grit Laudel. 2007. "Evaluation without Evaluators: The Impact of Funding Formulae on Australian University Research." Pp. 127–151 in R. Whitley and J. Glaser (eds.), *The Changing Governance of the Sciences*. Dordrecht: Springer.

Gleeson, Denis, and Farzana Shain. 1999. "Managing Ambiguity: Between Markets and Managerialism—A Case Study of 'Middle' Managers in Further Education." *The Sociological Review* 47 (3): 461–490.

Glennerster, Howard. 2002. "United Kingdom Education 1997–2001." *Oxford Review of Economic Policy* 18: 120–136.

Gordon, Colin. 1991. "Governmental Rationality: An Introduction." Pp. 1–52 in G. Burchell, C. Gordon and P. Miller (eds.), *The Foucault Effect: Studies in Governmentality*. Chicago: University of Chicago Press.

Gordon, Liz, and Geoff Whitty. 1997. "Giving the 'Hidden Hand' a Helping Hand? The Rhetoric and Reality of Neo-Liberal Educational Reform in England and New Zealand." *Comparative Education* 33: 453–457.

Gordon, Liz, and K. Wilson. 1992. "Teacher Unions in New Zealand." Pp. XX–XX in B. Cooper (ed.), *Labor Relations in Education: An International Perspective*. Westport, CT: Greenwood Press.

Grafton, Anthony. 2010. "Britain: The Disgrace of the Universities." *New York Review of Books* April 8: 32.

Gramsci, Antonio. 1971. *Selections from the Prison Notebooks*. London: International Publishers

———. 1988. *The Gramsci Reader*. London: Lawrence and Wishart.

Grant, David. 2003. *Those Who Can Teach: A History of Secondary Education in New Zealand for the Union Perspective*. Wellington, NZ: Steele Roberts Ltd.

Gray, George. 1934. SCIENCE SHARES IN NATIONAL PLANNING: The Work of the New Advisory Board May Set the Pace of American Progress for Another Century or More. *New York Times*, January 21.
Gray, John. 1989. "Hayek on the Market Economy and the Limits of State Action." Pp. 127–139 in D. Helm (ed.), *The Economic Borders of the State*. Oxford: Oxford University Press.
Greenberg, Daniel S. 2007. *Science for Sale: The Perils, Rewards, and Delusions of Campus Capitalism*. Chicago: The University of Chicago Press.
Greener, Ian. 2009. "Toward a History of Choice in UK Health Policy." *Sociology of Health and Illness* 31 (3): 309–324.
Grey, Christopher. 1999. "'We Are All Managers Now'; 'We Always Were': On The Development and Demise of Management." *Journal of Management Studies* 36: 561–585.
Griffin, P. 2006. "The World Bank." *New Political Economy* 11 (4): 872–581.
Griswold, Daniel. 2009. *Mad About Trade: Why Main Street American Should Embrace Globalization*. Washington, DC: Cato Institute.
Gumport, Patricia, and Stuart Snydman. 2002. "The Formal Organization of Knowledge: An Analysis of Academic Structure." *The Journal of Higher Education* 73 (3): 375–408.
Gunn, J. A. W. 1969. *Politics and the Public Interest in the Seventeenth Century*. London: Routledge and Kegan Paul.
Habermas, Jurgen. 1989. *The Structural Transformation of the Public Sphere*. Cambridge, MA: MIT Press.
Hacking, Ian. 1983. *Representing and Intervening: Introductory Topics in the Philosophy of Natural Science*. Cambridge: Cambridge University Press.
———. 1986. "Making Up People." Pp. 222–236 in T. Heller, M. Sosna and D. E. Wellbury (eds.), *Reconstructed Individualism: Autonomy, Individuality, and the Self in Western Thought*. Stanford, CA: Stanford University Press.
Hagstrom, W. O. 1974. "Competition in Science." *American Sociological Review* 39: 1–18.
Hainge, Greg. 2004. "The Death of Education, a Sad Tale (DEST): Of Anti-Pragmatic Pragmatics and the Loss of the Absolute in Australian Tertiary Education." Pp. 35–57 in J. Kenway, E. Bullen and S. Robb (eds.), *Innovation & Tradition: The Arts, Humanities and the Knowledge Economy*. New York: Peter Lang.
Halévy, Elie. 1966. *The Era of Tyrannies: Essay on Socialism and War*. New York: University Press.
Hammer, Michael, and James Champy. 1993. *Re-engineering the Corporation*. New York: Harper Business.
Hann, Chris. 2007. "A New Double Movement? Anthropological Perspectives on Property in the Age of Neoliberalism." *Socio-Economic Review* 5 (2): 287–318.
Hardin, Garrett. 1968. "The Tragedy of the Commons." *Science* 162: 1243–1248.
Harris, Abram L. 1939. "Pure Capitalism and the Disappearance of the Middle Class." *Journal of Political Economy* June: 276–301.
Harris, Gardiner. 2010. "Research Ties Diabetes Drug to Heart Woes." *The New York Times* February 20: A1, A3.
Harrison, Angela. 2010. "Schools are Promised an Academies 'Revolution.'" *BBC News* May 26.
Harrison, Bennett. 1994. "The Dark Side of Flexible Production." *Technology Review* 97(4): 38–45.
Hartwell, R. M. 1995. *A History of the Mont Pelerin Society*. Indianapolis: Liberty Fund.

Hartz, Louis. 1955. *The Liberal Tradition in American: An Interpretation of American Thought Since the Revolution.* New York: Harcourt, Brace, World.
Harvey, David. 2005. *A Brief History of Neoliberalism.* New York: Oxford University Press.
Hayden, T. 2004. "The Strange Death of the Comprehensive School in England and Wales, 1965–2002." *Research Papers in Education* 19 (4): 415–432.
Hayek, Fredrich A. 1944. *The Road to Serfdom.* Chicago: University of Chicago Press.
———. 1960. *The Constitution of Liberty.* Chicago: University of Chicago Press.
———. 1945. "The Use of Knowledge in Society." *The American Economic Review* 35 (4): 519–531.
———. 1948. *Individualism and Economic Order.* Chicago: University of Chicago Press.
———. 1949. "The Intellectuals and Socialism." Retrieved from http://mises.org/daily/2984.
———. 1967. *Studies in Philosophy, Politics and Economics.* London: Routledge & Kegan Paul.
———. 1978. *The Denationalization of Money: The Argument Refined: An Analysis of the Theory and Practice of Concurrent Currencies.* London: Institute of Economic Affairs.
———. 1979. *Law, Legislation and Liberty, Vol. III: The Political Order of a Free People.* London: Routledge and Kegan Paul.
———. 1984. *The Essence of Hayek* (ed. by C. Nishiyama and K. Leube). Stanford, CA: Stanford University Press.
Head, Simon. 2011. "The Grim Threat to British Universities." *New York Review of Books* January 13: 58–64.
Heckscher, Charles. 1995. *White Collar Blues: Management Loyalties in an Age of Restructuring.* New York: Basic Books.
Heckscher, Charles, and Anne Donnellon (eds.). 1994. *The Post-Bureaucratic Organization: New Perspectives on Organizational Change.* Thousand Oaks, CA: Sage Publications.
Heilbrunn, Jacob. 2008. "Whose Conservatism Is It?" *New York Times*, September 28: 6.
Henkel, Mary. 2007. "Can Academic Autonomy Survive in the Knowledge Society? A Perspective from Britain." *Higher Education Research & Development* 26 (1): 87–99.
Hicks, Diana. 2008. "Evolving Regimes of Multi-University Research Evaluation." Working Paper #27, Ivan Allen College School of Public Policy, Georgia Tech.
Hilmer, F. 1993. *National Competition Policy.* Canberra: AGPS.
Higgins, Jane, and Karen Nairn. 2006. "'In Transition:' Choice and the Children of New Zealand's Economic Reforms." *British Journal of Sociology of Education* 27 (2): 207–220.
Hochschild, Arlie. 1983. *The Managed Heart: Commerialization of Human Feeling.* Berkeley: University of California Press.
Hodgson, Geoffrey. 1999. *Economics and Utopia: Why the Learning Economy Is Not the End of History.* London: Routledge.
Hogben, Lancelot T. 1938. *Science for the Citizen.* New York: A. A. Knopf.
Holbrook, Karen, and Eric Dahl. 2004. "Conflicting Goals and Values: When Commercialization Enters into Tenure and Promotion Decisions." Pp. 89–102 in D. Stein (ed.), *Buying in or Selling Out? The Commercialization of the American Research University.* New Brunswick, NJ: Rutgers University Press.
Holdaway, T. 1989. "An Outsider's View of Tomorrow's Schools." *New Zealand Journal of Educational Administration* 4: 35–40.

Hood, Christopher. 1991. "A Public Management for All Seasons?" *Public Administration* 69 (Spring): 3–19.
Hounshell, David. 1992. "Du Pont and the Management of Large-Scale Research and Development. Pp. 236–261 in P. Galison and B. Hevly (eds.), *Big Science: The Growth of Large-Scale Research*. Stanford, CA: Stanford University Press.
House of Representatives. 2008. "The Bayh-Dole Act (P.L. 96–5190), Amendments to the Patent and Trademark Act of 1980—the Next 25 Years. Washington, DC: Government Printing Office.
Hunter, Ian. 1993. "Personality as a Vocation: The Political Rationality of the Humanities." Pp. 153–192 in M. Gane and T. Johnson (eds.), *Foucault's New Domains*. London: Routledge.
Hyde, Lewis. 1983. *The Gift: Imagination and the Erotic Life of Property*. New York: Vintage Books.
International Centre for Trade and Sustainable Development. n.d. Retrieved from http://ictsd.org/.
International Monetary Fund. n.d. "Articles of Agreement of the International Monetary Fund." Retrieved from www.imf.org/external/pubs/ft/aa/aa04.htm.
James, Paul, and Douglas McQueen-Thomson. 2002. "Abstracting Knowledge Formation: A Report on Academia and Publishing." Pp. 183–206 in S. Cooper, J. Hinkson and G. Sharp (eds.), *Scholars and Entrepreneurs*. North Carlton, Australia: Arena Publications.
Jameson, Frederic. 1991. *Postmodernism or, the Cultural Logic of Late Capitalism*. Durham, NC: Duke University Press.
Jayasuriya, Kanishka. 2002. "The New Contractualism: Neo-Liberal or Democratic?" *The Political Quarterly* 73 (3): 309–320.
Jencks, Charles. 1984. *The Language of Post-Modern Architecture*. New York: Rizzoli.
Jessop, Bob. 1994. "The Transition to Post-Fordism and the Schumpeterian Workfare State." Pp. 13–37 in B. Burrows and B. Loader (eds.). *Towards a Post-Fordist Welfare State?* London: Routledge.
Johnston, Josee. 2008. "The Citizen-Consumer Hybrid." Ideological Tensions and the Case of Whole Food Markets." *Theory and Society* 37 (3): 229–270.
Joseph, Keith. 1975. *Reversing the Trend—A Critical Reappraisal of Conservative Economic and Social Policies*. London: Barry Rose.
Judt, Tony. 2010. "Ill Fares the Land." *New York Review of Books* LVII (7), April 29: 17–19.
Kant, Immanuel. 1979 [1798]. *The Conflict of the Faculties* (trans. M. Gregor). New York: Abaris Books.
Kant, Rosabeth. 1989. "Careers and the Wealth of Nations: A Macro-Perspective on the Structure and Implications of Career Forms." Pp. 506–521 in M. B. Arthur, D. T. Hall and B. S. Lawrence (eds.), *Handbook of Career Theory*. Cambridge: Cambridge University Press.
Karpin Report (Report of the Industry Task Force on Leadership and Management Skills). 1995. *Enterprising Nation: Renewing Australia's Managers to Meet the Challenges of the Asia-Pacific Century*. Canberra: AGPS.
Kelty, Christopher. 2008. *Two Bits: The Cultural Significance of Free Software*. Durham, NC: Duke University Press.
Kent State University. n.d. Retrieved from www.einside.kent.edu/?type=art&id=92319.
Kenway, Jane, Elizabeth Bullen and Simon Robb. 2004. "Global Knowledge Politics and 'Exploitable' Knowledge." Pp. 135–149 in J. Kenway, E. Bullen and S. Robb (eds.), *Innovation & Tradition: The Arts, Humanities and the Knowledge Economy*. New York: Peter Lang.

Kerr, Clark. 1964. *The Uses of the University.* Cambridge, MA: Harvard University Press.
Kettl, Donald. F. 2000. *The Global Public Management Revolution.* Washington, DC: Brookings Institution Press.
Kettl, Donald, and John DiLulio, Jr. (eds). 1995. *Inside the Reinvention Machine: Appraising Governmental Reform.* Washington, DC: The Brookings Institution.
Kevles, Daniel. 1977. "The National Science Foundation and the Debate over Postwar Research Policy, 1942–1945: A Political Interpretation of Science—The Endless Frontier." *Isis* 68 (1): 4–26.
———. 1992. "K1S2: Korea, Science, and the State." Pp. 312–333 in P. Galison and B. Hevly (eds.), *Big Science: The Growth of Large-Scale Research.* Stanford, CA: Stanford University Press.
Keynes, John Maynard. 1926. "The End of Laissez-Faire." London: Hogarth Press. Retrieved from www.panarchy.org/keynes/laissezfaire.1926.html.
———. 1964. *The General Theory of Employment, Interest and Money.* New York: Harcourt Brace and World.
Klees, Steven. 2008. "A Quarter Century of Neoliberal Thinking in Education: Misleading Analyses and Failed Policies." *Globalisation, Societies and Education* 6 (4): 311–348.
Kleinman, Daniel Lee, and Steven P. Vallas. 2001. "Science, Capitalism, and the Rise of the 'Knowledge Worker'? The Changing Structure of Knowledge Production in the United States." *Theory and Society* 30: 451–492.
Kliebard, Herbert. 1995. *The Struggle for the American Curriculum: 1893–1958.* New York: Routledge.
Knowledge Nation Task Force. 2001. *Agenda for the Knowledge Nation: Report of the Knowledge Nation Taskforce.* Retrieved from http://www.katelundy.com.au/2001/10/30/an-agenda-for-the-knowledge-nation-1-.
Kogan, Maurice, and Stephen Hanney. 2000. *Reforming Higher Education.* London: Jessica Kingsley.
Kohler, Robert. 1991. *Partners in Science: Foundations and Natural Scientists, 1900–1945.* Chicago: University of Chicago Press.
Krause, Elliott. 1996. *Death of the Guilds: Professions, States, and the Advance of Capitalism, 1930 to the Present.* New Haven, CT: Yale University Press.
Krimsky, S. 2003. *Science in the Private Interest: Has the Lure of Profits Corrupted Biomedical Research?* Lanham, MD: Rowman & Littlefield.
Krippner, Greta. 207. "The Making of U.S. Monetary Policy: Central Bank Transparency and the Neoliberal Dilemma." *Theory & Society* 36: 477–513.
Krucken, Georg. 2003. "Learning the 'New, New Thing': On the Role of Path Dependency in University Structures." *Higher Education* 46: 315–339.
Lamont, Michele. 2009. *How Professors Think: Inside the Curious World of Academic Judgment.* Cambridge, MA: Harvard University Press.
Lange, David. 1999. "Another Day for Tomorrow's Schools." *DELTA: Policy and Practice in Education* 51 (1): 11–22.
Larson, Magali. 1977. *The Rise of Professionalism: A Sociological Analysis.* Berkeley: University of California Press.
Lash, Scott, and John Urry. 1987. *The End of Organized Capitalism.* Madison: University of Wisconsin Press.
Latour, Bruno. 1993. *We Have Never Been Modern.* Cambridge, MA: Harvard University Press.
Lauder, Hugh, and David Hughes. 1999. *Trading in Futures: Why Markets in Education Don't Work.* Buckingham: Open University Press.
Lea, Stephen, E. G. Tarpy, M. Roger and Paul Webley. 1987. *The Individual in the Economy: A Survey of Economic Psychology.* Cambridge: Cambridge University Press.

Le Grand, Julian. 2003. *Motivation, Agency and Public Policy: of Knights and Knaves, Pawns and Queens.* Oxford: Oxford University Press.

Leisyte, Liudvika, Jurgen Enders and Harry de Boer. 2010. "Mediating Problem Choice: Academic Researchers' Responses to Changes in their Institutional Environment." Pp. 266–290 in R. Whitley, J. Glaser and L. Engwall (ed.), *Reconfiguring Knowledge Production Changing Authority Relationships in the Sciences and their Consequences for Intellectual Innovation.* Oxford: Oxford University Press.

Lemke, Thomas. 2001. "'The Birth of Bio-Politics': Michel Foucualt's Lecture at the College de France on Neoliberal Governmentality." *Economy and Society* 30 (2): 190–207.

Leslie, Stuart W. 1993. *The Cold War and American Science: The Military-Industrial-Academic complex at MIT and Stanford.* New York: Columbia University Press.

Lessig, Lawrence. 2001. "Copyright's First Amendment." *University of California Los Angeles Law Review* 48 (5): 1057–1073.

———. 2004. *Free Culture: How Big Media Uses Technology and the Law To Lock Down Culture and Control Creativity.* New York: The Penguin Press.

———. 2008. *Remix: Making Art and Commerce Thrive in the Hybrid Economy.* New York: Penguin.

Lessinger, Leon. 1970. *Every Kid a Winner: Accountability in Education.* New York: Simon and Schuster.

Lewin, Tamar. 2010. "School Chief Dismisses 241 Teaches in Washington." *New York Times* July 24: A8.

Lipman, Pauline. 2007. "'No Child Left Behind': Globalization, Privatization and the Politics of Inequality." Pp. 35–58 in E. W. Ross and R. Gibson (eds.), *Neoliberalism and Education Reform.* Cresskill, NJ: Hampton Press.

Locke, John. 1980 [1690]. *Second Treatise of Government.* Indianapolis: Hackett Publishing Company.

Lowen, Rebecca. 1997. *Creating the Cold War University: The Transformation of Stanford.* Berkeley: University of California Press.

Lunt, Neil. 2009. "The Rise of a 'Social Development' Agenda in New Zealand." *International Journal of Social Welfare* 18: 3–12.

Lyotard, Jean-Francois. 1984. *The Postmodern Condition: A Report on Knowledge* (trans. by G. Bennington and B. Massumi). Minneapolis: University of Minnesota Press.

———. 1991. *The Inhuman: Reflections on Time.* Cambridge: Polity.

———. 1993. *Libidinal Economy.* London: Athlone.

Machlup, Fritz. 1962. *Production and Distribution of Knowledge in the United States.* Princeton, NJ: Princeton University Press.

Macintyre, Clement. 1999. "The Stakeholder Society and the Welfare State: Forward to The Past!" *Contemporary Politics* 5 (2): 121–135.

Macintyre, Stuart. 2002. "Funny You Should Ask for That: Higher Education as a Market." In S. Cooper, J. Hinkson and G. Sharp (eds.), *Scholars and Entrepreneurs.* North Carlton, Australia: Arena Publications.

MacKenzie, Donald, Fabian Muniesa and Lucia Siu (eds.). 2007. Do Economists Make Markets? : On the Performativity of Economics. Princeton, NJ: Princeton University Press.

Mandeville, Banard. 1957. *The Fable of the Bees: or Private Vices, Public Benefit.* Oxford: Clarendon Press.

Mannheim, Karl. 1991. *Ideology and Utopia: An Introduction to the Sociology of Knowledge* (trans. by L. Wirth and E. Shils). London: Routledge.

Marcuse, Herbert. 1964. *One Dimensional Man: Studies in the Ideology of Advanced Industrial Society.* Boston: Beacon Press.

Marginson, Simon. 1994. *Education and Public Policy in Australia*. Melbourne: Cambridge University Press.

Marginson, S., and M. Considine. 2000. *The Enterprise University: Power, Governance and Reinvention in Australia*. Cambridge: Cambridge University Press.

Marquand, David. 1992. "The Enterprise Culture: Old Wine in New Bottles?" Pp. 61–72 in P. Heelas and P. Morris (eds.), *The Values of the Enterprise Culture: The Moral Debate*. London: Routledge.

Marshall, T. H. 1950. *Citizenship and Social Class*. Cambridge: Cambridge University Press.

Martin, Ben, and Richard Whtley. 2010. "The UK Research Assessment Exercise: A Case of Regulatory Capture? Pp. 51–80 in R. Whitley, J. Glaeser and L. Engwall, *Reconfiguring Knowledge Production*. Oxford: Oxford University Press.

Martin, Don. 1991. "The Political Economy of School Reform in the United States." Pp. 341–368 in M. Ginsburg (ed.), *Understanding Educational Reform in Global Context: Economy, Ideology, and the State*. New York: Garland.

Marvizon, Juan Carlos. 2008. "How to Succeed in an Academic Career." *Academe* 94 (6): 25.

Marx, Karl. 1972 [1843]. "On the Jewish Question." In R. C. Tucker (ed.). *The Marx-Engels Reader*. New York: Norton.

———. 1967. *Capital: A Critique of Political Economy, vol. III* (ed. by F. Engels). New York: International Publishers.

———. 1996. *Capital: A Critique of Political Economy, vol. I* (trans. by B. Forkes). New York: Penguin/New Left Review.

Marx, Karl, and Friedrich Engels. 1982. *Collected Works, Vol. 38*. London: Lawrence and Wishart.

Masterson, Kathryn. 2008. "If Kent State Beats Goals, Professors Will Profit." *Chronicle of Higher Education* September 12, LV (3): A 1, A 20.

———. 2009. "Research and Inventions Earn Big Bucks for American Universities." Chronicle of Higher Education. January 27th: A16.

Matasar, Richard. 1996. "A Commercialist Manifesto: Entrepreneurs, Academics, and Purity of the Heart and Soul." *Florida Law Review* 48 (5): 781–811.

May, Christopher, and Susan Sell. 2006. *Intellectual Property Rights: A Critical History*. Boulder, CO: Lynne Rienners Publishers.

McCauley, Michael. 2005. *NPR: The Trials and Triumphs of National Public Radio*. New York: Columbia University Press.

McDonald, Ruth, Nicola Mean, Sudeh Cheraghi-Sohi, Peter Bower, Diane Whalley and Martin Roland. 2007. "Governing the Ethical Consumer: Identity, Choice and the Primary Care Medical Encounter." *Sociology of Health & Illness* 29 (3): 430–456.

McGucken, William. 1978. "On Freedom and Planning in Science: The Society for Freedom in Science, 1940–46." *Minerva* 16 (1): 42–72.

McLaren, P. 2003. *Life in Schools: An Introduction to Critical Pedagogy in the Foundations of Education* (4th edition). Boston: Allen and Brown.

McQueen, Harvey. 1991. *The Ninth Floor: Inside the Prime Minister's Office—A Political Experience*. Auckland: Penguin.

McSherry, Corynne. 2001. *Who Owns Academic Work? Battling for Control of Intellectual Property*. Cambridge, MA: Harvard University Press.

Medema, Steven. 2009. *The Hesitant Hand: Taming Self-Interest in the History of Economic Ideas*. Princeton, NJ: Princeton University Press.

Merton, Robert. 1968. *Social Theory and Social Structure*. New York: The Free Press.

———. 1968b. "The Matthew Effect in Science." *Science* 159 (January 5): 56–63.

Mill, J. S. 1951. *Utilitarianism, Liberty and Representative Government*. New York: Dutton.

Miller, D. R. Henry, and Mark Ginsburg. 1991. "Restructuring Education and the State in England." Pp. 49–84 in M. Ginsburg (ed.), *Understanding Educational Reform in Global Context: Economy, Ideology, and the State*. London: Garland Publishing.

Miller, Peter, and Nikolas Rose. 1993. "Governing Economic Life." Pp. 75–105 in M. Gane and T. Johnson (eds.), *Foucault's New Domains*. London: Routledge.

———. 2008. *Governing the Present: Administering Economic, Social and Personal Life*. Cambridge: Polity.

Mills, C. Wright. 1959. *The Sociological Imagination*. New York: Oxford University Press.

Ministry of Education. 1993. *The New Zealand Curriculum Framework*. Wellington: Learning Media.

———. 2007. *New Zealand Curriculum*. Wellington: Learning Media.

Mirowski, P., and E. Sent (eds.). 2002. *Science Bought and Sold: Essays in the Economics of Science*. Chicago: University of Chicago Press.

Mises, Ludwig von. 1932. *Socialism: An Economic and Sociological Analysis* (trans. by J. Kahane). New Haven, CT: Yale University Press.

———. 1935. "Economic Calculation in the Socialist Commonwealth." Pp. 87–130 in F. Hayek (ed.), *Collectivist Economic Planning*. London: George Routledge.

———. 1949. *Human Action: A Treatise on Economics*. London: William Hodge.

———. 1983. *Nation, State and Economy: Contributions to the Politics and History of Our Time* (trans. by L. B. Yeager). New York: New York University Press.

Mitchell, Wesley. 1937. *The Backward Art of Spending Money and Other Essays*. Cambridge, MA: Harvard University Press.

Mittelstrass, Jürgen. 2003. "Knowledge as a Good: Science, Education, and the Commodification of Knowledge." *TRAMES: A Journal of the Humanities & Social Sciences* 7 (4): 227–236.

Montesquieu. 1989 [1748]. *The Spirit of the Laws* (ed. by A. Cohler, B. Miller and H. Stone). Cambridge: Cambridge University Press.

Moore, Barrington, Jr. 1984. *Privacy: Studies in Social and Cultural History*. Armonk, NY: Sharpe.

Morey, Ann. 2003. "Major Trends Impacting Faculty Roles and Rewards: An International Perspective." Pp. 68–84 in H. Eggins (ed.), *Globalization and Reform in Higher Education*. Berkshire: Open University Press.

Morley, Louise, and Naz Rassool. 2000. "School Effectiveness: New Managerialism, Quality and the Japanization of Education." *Journal of Education Policy* 15 (2): 169–183.

Mowery, David, Richard Nelson, Bhaven Sampat and Arvids Ziedonis. 2004. *Ivory Tower and Industrial Innovation: University-Industry Technology Transfer Before and After the Bayh-Dole Act in the United States*. Stanford, CA: Stanford University Press.

Muller, Jerry. 2002. *The Mind and the Market: Capitalism in Modern European Thought*. New York: Anchor Books.

Murray, Laura. 2003. "Just Another World for Nothing Left to Lose?: Public Domains and Intellectual Property Law." *American Quarterly* 55 (4): 739–748.

Musselin, Christine. 2005. "Change or Continuity in Higher Education Governance: Lessons Drawn from Twenty Years of National Reforms in European Countries." Pp. 65–79 in I. Bleiklie and M. Henkel (eds.), *Governing Knowledge: A Study of Continuity and Change in Higher Education*. Dordrecht: Springer.

National Archives. 2004. "Higher Education Act 2004," Retrieved from http://www.legislation.gov.uk/ukpga/2004/8/contents.

———. 2011. "Securing a Sustainable Future for Higher Education in England." Retrieved from http://webarchive.nationalarchives.gov.uk/+/hereview.independent.gov.uk/hereview/ report/.

National Association of Manufactures. 1905. "Report of the Commission of Industrial Education, 1905." In *American Education: A Documentary History, 1870–1970*. New York: Teachers College Press.

National Commission on Excellence in Education. 1983. *A Nation at Risk: The Imperative for Education Reform*. Washington, DC: Government Printing Office.

National Performance Review. 1995. *Putting Customers First '95: Standards for Serving the American People*. Washington, DC: Executive Office of the President.

National Resources Committee. 1938. *Research—A National Resource*. Washington, DC: Government Printing Office.

NCATE (National Council for Accreditation of Teacher Education). 2010. *Transforming Teacher Education Through Clinical Practice: A National Strategy to Prepare Effective Teachers*. Washington, DC: NCATE.

NCIHE (National Committee on the Inquiry into Higher Education). 1997. *Higher Education in a Learning Society*. Retrieved from bei.leeds.ac.uk/Partners/NCIHE/.

NCSL (National Conference of State Legislatures). 2006. "Transforming Higher Education, National Imperative—State Responsibility." Washington, DC: National Conference of State Legislatures.

Neave, G. 1988. "On the Cultivation of Quality, Efficiency and Enterprise: An Overview of Recent Trends in Higher Education in Western Europe, 1986–1988." *European Journal of Education* 23: 7–23.

Needham, Catherine. 2003. *Citizen-Consumers: New Labour's Marketplace Democracy*. London: Catalyst.

New Zealand Ministry of Economic Development. 2002. *Growing an Innovative New Zealand*. Retrieved from http://unpan1.un.org/intradoc/groups/public/documents/apcity/unpan005946.pdf.

Newfield, Christopher. 2003. *Ivy and Industry: Business and the Making of the American University: 1880–1980*. Durham, NC: Duke University Press.

———. 2008. *Unmaking the Public University: The Forty-Year Assault on the Middle Class*. Cambridge, MA: Harvard University Press.

Newman, Janet. 1998. "Managerialism and Social Welfare." Pp. 333–374 in G. Hughes and G. Lewis (eds.), *Unsettling Welfare: The Reconstruction of Social Policy*. London: Routledge.

Newman, John Henry. 1996. *The Idea of a University*. New Haven, CT: Yale University Press.

Nisbet, Robert. 1971. *The Degradation of the Academic Dogma: The University in America, 1945–1970*. New York: Basic Books.

Niskanen, William. 1971. *Bureaucracy and Representative Government*. Chicago: Aldine Press.

Nitta, Keith. 2008. *The Politics of Structural Education Reform*. New York: Routledge.

North, Douglass. 1990. *Institutions, Institutional Change and Economic Performance*. Cambridge: Cambridge University Press.

Nowotny, Helga, Scott, Peter and Michael Gibbons. 2001. *Re-Thinking Science: Knowledge and the Public in the Age of Uncertainty*. Cambridge: Polity.

OECD (Organization for Economic Co-Operation and Development). 1963. *Science, Economic Growth and Public Policy*. Paris: OECD.

———. 1972. *Science, Growth and Society*. Paris: OECD.

———. 1982. *The University and the Community*. Paris. OECD.

———. 1983. *Review of National Policies for Education: New Zealand*. Paris: OECD.

———. 1987. *Universities Under Scrutiny*. Paris: OECD.

———. 1996. *The Knowledge-Based Economy*. Paris: OECD.
———. 1999. *Benchmarking Knowledge Based Economies*. Paris: OECD.
———. 2002. *Dynamising National Innovation Systems*. Paris: OECD.
———. 2004. *Innovation in the Knowledge Economy: Implications for Education and Learning*. Paris: OECD.
Olssen, Mark. 2006. "Understanding the Mechanisms of Neoliberal Control: Lifelong Learning, flexibility and Knowledge Capitalism." *International Journal of Lifelong Education* 25 (3): 213–230.
Olssen, Mark, and Michael Peters. 2005. "Neoliberalism, Higher Education and the Knowledge Economy: From the Free Market to Knowledge Capitalism." *Journal of Education Policy* 20 (3): 313–345.
O'Malley, Pat. 1992. "Risk, Power and Crime Prevention." *Economy and Society* 21, 252–275.
———. 2000. "Uncertain Subjects: Risks, Liberalism and Contract." *Economy and Society* 29 (4): 460–484.
Orwell, George. 1989. *Nineteen Eight-Four*. London: Penguin.
Osborne, David, and Ted Gaebler. 1992. *Reinventing Government: How the Entrepreneurial Spirit Is Transforming the Public Sector*. Reading, MA: Addison-Wesley Publishing.
Outhwaite, William. 2006. *The Future of Society*. Malden, MA: Blackwell.
Ozga, Jenny. 1998. "The Entrepreneurial Researcher: Re-Formation of Identity in the Research Marketplace." *International Studies in the Sociology of Education* 8 (2): 143–153.
Paine, Thomas. 1942 [1791]. *Basic Writings of Thomas Paine*. New York: Wiley.
Palumbo, Antonino. 2001. "Administration, Civil Service, and Bureaucracy." Pp. 127–138 in K. Nash and A. Scott (eds.), *The Blackwell Companion to Political Sociology*. Oxford: Blackwell Publishers.
Parker, Martin. 2002. *Against Management: Organization in the Age of Managerialism*. Malden, MA: Polity Press.
Peck, J., and A. Tickell. 2002. "Neoliberalizing Space." *Antipode* 34 (3): 380–404.
Peet, Richard. 2007: *Geography of Power: Making Global Economic Policy*. London: Zed Books.
Pels, Dick. 2003. *Unhastening Science*. Liverpool: Liverpool University Press.
Perkin, Harold. 1992. "The Enterprise Culture in Historical Perspective: Birth, Life, Death—and Resurrection?" Pp. 36–60 in P. Heelas and P. Morris (eds.), *The Values of the Enterprise Culture*. London: Routledge.
Perry, Beth. 2006. "Science, Society and the University: A Paradox of Values." *Social Epistemology* 20: 201–219.
Peters, Michael, and Tina Besley. 2008. "Academic Entrepreneurship and the Creative Economy." *Thesis Eleven* 94: 88–105.
Peters, Michael. 2005. "The New Prudentialism in Education: Actuarial Rationality and the Entrepreneurial Self." *Educational Theory* 55 (2): 123–137.
Pick, David. 2004. "The Reflexive Modernization of Australian Universities." *Globalisation, Societies and Education* 2 (1): 99–116.
Pick, David and Jeannette Taylor. 2009. "'Economic Rewards are the Driving Factor': Neo-liberalism, Globalisation and Work Attitudes of Young Graduates in Australia." *Globalisation, Societies and Education* 7 (1): 69–82.
Piel, Gerald. 1966. "Federal Funds and Science Education." *Bulletin of the Atomic Scientists* (May) 22 (5): 10–15.
Plant, Raymond. 1992. " Enterprise in Its Place: The Moral Limits of Markets." Pp. 85–99 in *The Values of the Enterprise Culture* (ed. by P. Heelas and P. Morris). London: Routledge.
Polanyi, Karl. 1957 [1944]. *The Great Transformation: The Political and Economic Origins of Our Time*. Boston: Beacon Press.

Polanyi, Michael. 1946. *Science, Faith and Society.* London: Oxford University Press.
———. 1951. *The Logic of Liberty.* Chicago: University of Chicago Press.
———. 1962. "The Republic of Science: Its Political and Economic Theory." *Minerva* 1 (1): 54–73.
Pollard, A., and P. Triggs (with P. Broadfood, E. McNess and M. Osborn). 2000. *What Pupils Say: Changing Policy and Practice in Primary Education.* London: Continuum.
Pope, Alexander. 1824. *The Poetical Works of Alexander Pope, Esq..* London: Jones and Co.
Powell, Lewis. 1971. "The Powell Memo." Available at www.democrarcy.org/corporate_accountability/powell_memo_lewis.html.
Power, Michael. 1997. *The Audit Society: Rituals of Verification.* New York: Oxford University Press.
———. 2004. *The Risk Management of Everything: Rethinking the Politics of Uncertainty.* London: Demos.
———. 2007. *Organized Uncertainty: Designing a World of Risk Management.* Oxford: Oxford University Press.
Prasad, Monica. 2006. *The Politics of Free Markets: The Rise of Neoliberal Economic Policies in Britain, France, German and the United States.* Chicago: University of Chicago Press.
Pribram, Karl. 1983. *A History of Economic Reasoning.* Baltimore: Johns Hopkins University Press.
Price, Derek J. de Solla. 1963. *Little Science, Big Science.* New York: Columbia University Press.
Price, Don. 1968. "Federal Money and University Research." Pp. 23–51 in H. Orlans (ed.), *Science Policy and the University.* Washington, DC: Brookings Institution.
QAA (Quality Assurance Agency for Higher Education). n.d. "About Us." Retrieved from www.qaa.ac.uk/aboutus/ WhatWeDo.asp.
Ravitch, Diane. 2010. "The Myth of Charter Schools." *New York Review of Books* November 11: 22–24.
Readings, Bill. 1996. *The University in Ruins.* Cambridge: Harvard University Press.
Rhoades, Gary. 1998. *Managed Professionals: Unionized Faculty and Restructuring Academic Labor.* Albany, NY: SUNY Press.
———. 2005. "Distinctive Local Continuities Amidst Similar Neo-Liberal Changes: The Comparative Importance of the Particular." Pp. 11–28 in I. Bleiklie and M. Henkel (eds.), *Governing Knowledge: A Study of Continuity and Change in Higher Education.* Dordrecht: Springer.
Rhoades, Gary, and Barbara Sporn. 2002. "Quality Assurance in Europe and the U.S.: Professional and Political Framing of Higher Education Policy." *Higher Education* 43 (3): 355–390.
Ricardo, David. 1973. *Principles of Political Economy and Taxation.* New York: Dutton.
Rich, Andrew. 2004. *Think Tanks, Public Policy, and the Politics of Expertise.* New York: Cambridge University Press.
Robertson, Susan, and Ruth Keeling. 2008. "Stirring the Lions: Strategy and Tactics in Global Higher Education." *Globalization, Societies and Education* 6 (3): 221–240.
Robertson, William. 1972 [1769]. *View of the Progress of Society.* Chicago: University of Chicago Press.
Romer, Paul, 1990. "Endogenous Technological Change." *Journal of Political Economy* 98 (5): S71–S102.
———. 2007. "Economic Growth." In D. Henderson (ed.), *The Concise Encyclopedia of Economics.* Indianapolis: The Liberty Fund.

Rose, M. 1993. *Authors and Owners: The Invention of Copyright*. Cambridge, MA: Harvard University Press.
Rose, Nikolas. 1990. *Governing the Soul*. New York: Routledge.
———. 1993: "Government, Authority and Expertise in Advanced Liberalism." *Economy and Society* 22 (3): 283–300.
———. 1999. *Powers of Freedom: Reframing Political Thought*. Cambridge: Cambridge University Press.
———. 2004. "Governing the Social." Pp. 167–185 in N. Gane (ed.), *The Future of Social Theory*. London: Continuum.
Rosenthal, Marilynn. 2002. "Medical Professional Autonomy in an Era of Accountability and Regulation." Pp. 61–80 in M. Dent and S. Whitehead (eds.), *Managing Professional Identities: Knowledge, Performativity and the 'New' Professional*. London: Routledge.
Rousseau, Jean Jacques. 1992 [1755]. *Discourse on the Origin of Inequality*. Indianapolis: Hackett Publications.
Rowbotham, Jill. 2011. "End of an ERA: Journal Rankings Dropped." *The Australian* May 30. Retrieved from www.theaustralian.com.au/higher-education/end-of-an-era-journal-rankings-dropped/story-e6frgcjx-1226065864847.
Ruhl, Lealle. 2005. "Liberal Governance and Prenatal Care: Risk and Regulation in Pregnancy." Pp. 71–93 in P. O'Malley (ed.), *Governing Risks*. Burlington, VT: Ashgate.
Russel, T. 1978. *The Tory Party: Its Policies, Divisions and Future*. Harmondsworth: Penguin.
Ryan, Michael P. 1998. *Knowledge Diplomacy: Global Competition and the Politics of Intellectual Property*. Washington, DC: Brookings Institution Press.
Sachs, Jeffrey. 2005. *The End of Poverty: Economic Possibilities for Our Time*. New York: Penguin Press.
Sahlins, Marshall. 1972. *Stone Age Economics*. London: Tavistock.
Saltman, Kenneth. 2006. "The Right-Wing Attack on Critical and Public Education in the United States." *Cultural Politics* 2 (3): 339–358.
Say, Jean-Bapiste. 1964. *A Treatise on Political Economy; or, The Production, Distribution and Consumption of Wealth*. New York: A. M. Kelly.
Scaff, Lawrence. 1991. *Fleeing the Iron Cage: Culture, Politics and Modernity in the Thought of Max Weber*. Berkeley: University of California Press.
Schimank, Uwe. 2005. "'New Public Management' and the Academic Profession: Reflections on the German Situation." *Minerva* 43: 361–376.
Schumpeter, Joseph. 1942. *Capitalism, Socialism and Democracy*. New York: Harper & Brothers.
———. 1976. *Capitalism, Socialism and Democracy* (5th edition). London: Routledge.
Schwartz, Barry. 2005. *The Paradox of Choice: Why More is Less*. New York: Harper Collins.
Schweber, S. S. 1992. "Big Science in Context: Cornell and MIT." Pp. 149–183 in P. Galison and B. Hevly (eds.), *Big Science: The Growth of Large-Scale Research*. Stanford, CA: Stanford University Press.
Searle, G. R. 1971. *The Quest for National Efficiency: A Study in British Politics and Political Thought, 1899–1914*. Oxford: Blackwell.
Sears, Neil. 2007. "Ten Years of Labour Has Left Us More Selfish Than Before." *Daily Mail* February 5: 37.
Sell, Susan, and Christopher May. 2001. "Moments in Law: Contestation and Settlement in the History of Intellectual Property." *Review of International Political Economy* 8 (3): 467–500.

Sen, Amartya. 2009. "Capitalism Beyond the Crisis." *New York Review of Books* LVI (March 20): 27–30.
Sennett, Richard. 1998. *The Corrosion of Character: The Personal Consequences of Work in the New Capitalism.* New York: W. W. Norton.
Shamir, Ronen. 2008. "The Age of Responsiblization: On Market-Embedded Morality." *Economy and Society* 17 (1): 1–19.
Shapin, Steven, and Simon Schaffer. 1985. *Leviathan and the Air-Pump: Hobbes, Boyle and the Experimental Life.* Princeton, NJ: Princeton University Press.
Shapin, Steven. 2008. *The Scientific Life: A Moral History of a Late Modern Vocation.* Chicago: University of Chicago Press.
Shaw, Sara. 2007. "Driving out Alternative Ways of Seeing: The Significance of NeoLiberal Policy Mechanisms for UK Primary Care Research." *Social Theory & Health*, 5 (4): 316–337.
Shenhav, Yehouda. 1986. "Dependence and Compliance in Academic Research Infrastructures." *Sociological Perspectives* 21 (1): 29–51.
Shils, Edward. 1947. "A Critique of Planning—The Society for Freedom in Science." *Bulletin of the Atomic Scientists* 3 (3): 80–82.
Shipman, Alan. 1999. *The Market Revolution and Its Limits: A Price for Everything.* London: Routledge.
Shonfield, Andrew. 1965. *Modern Capitalism: The Changing Balance of Public and Private Power.* New York: Oxford University Press.
Simmel, Georg. 1990. *The Philosophy of Money* (2nd edition). New York: Routledge.
Simon, Stephanie, and Stephanie Banchero. 2010. "Putting a Price on Professors." *Wall Street Journal*, October 23–24: C1–C2.
Simon, William. 1978. *A Time for Truth.* New York: Reader's Digest Press.
Slater, Don, and Fran Tonkiss. 2001. *Market Society: Markets and Modern Social Theory.* Cambridge: Polity.
Slaughter, S., and L. L. Leslie. 1997. *Academic Capitalism: Politics, Policies and the Entrepreneurial University.* Baltimore: Johns Hopkins University Press.
Sloterdijk, Peter. 1987. *The Critique of Cynical Reason* (trans. by M. Eldred). Minneapolis: University of Minnesota Press.
Smith, Abbe. 2011. "New Haven Schools Hire Renaissance School Services to Take Over Clemente." *New Haven Register* May 23.
Smith, Adam. 1904 [1776]. *An Inquiry into the Nature and Causes of the Wealth of Nations.* London: Methuen.
———. 1964 [1896]. *Lectures on Justice, Police, Revenue and Arms.* New York: A. M. Kelley.
———. 1966 [1759]. *The Theory of Moral Sentiments.* New York: A. M. Kelley.
———. 1997 [1766]. "Lecture on the Influence of Commerce on Manners." Pp. 17–20 in D. Klein (ed.), *Reputation: Studies in the Voluntary Elicitation of Good Conduct.* Ann Arbor: University of Michigan Press.
Soros, George. 2010. "The Real Danger to the Economy." *New York Review of Books* November 11: 16.
Spencer, Herbert. 1850. *Social Statistics.* London: Appleton.
Sprigman, Chris. 2002. "The Mouse that Ate the Public Domain." Retrieved from writ.news.findlaw.com/commentary/20020305_sprigman.htm.
Spring, Joel. 1998. *Education and the Rise of the Global Economy.* Mahwah, NJ: L. Erlbaum and Associates.
Standard and Poor. 2003. *Higher Education Changing by Degrees: University Credit Rating.* London: Standard and Poor.

Stefancic, Jean, and Richard Delgado. 1996. *No Mercy: How Conservative Think Tanks and Foundations Changed America's Social Agenda.* Philadelphia: Temple University Press.
Stein, Donald. 2004. "A Personal Perspective on the Selling of Academia." Pp. 1–16 in D. Stein (ed.), *Buying in or Selling Out? The Commercialization of the American Research University.* New Brunswick, NJ: Rutgers University Press.
Stephen, Leslie. 1902. *History of English Thought in the Eighteenth Century, Vol. II.* London: Smith, Elder, & Company.
Stockman, David. 1986. *The Triumph of Politics: How the Reagan Revolution Failed.* New York: Harper & Row, Publishers.
Strathdee, Rob. 2005. "Globalization, Innovation, and the Declining Significance of Qualifications Led Social and Economic Change." *Journal of Education Policy* 20 (4): 437–456.
Strathern, Marilyn (ed.). 2000. *Audit Cultures: Anthropological Studies in Accountability, Ethics and the Academy.* New York: Routledge.
Striphas, Ted. 2009. *The Late Age of Print: Everyday Book Culture from Consumerism to Control.* New York: Columbia University Press.
Sulkunen, Pekka. 2007. "Re-inventing the Social Contract." *Acta Sociologica* 50 (3): 325–333.
Swidler, A., and J. Arditi. 1994. "The New Sociology of Knowledge." *Annual Review of Sociology* 20: 305–329.
Symes, Colin. 1996. "Selling Futures: A New Image for Australian Universities? *Studies in Higher Education* 21 (2): 133–147.
———. 2000. "Real World Education: The Vocationalization of the University." Pp. 30–46 in C. Symes and J. McIntyre (eds.), *Working Knowledge: The New Vocationalism and Higher Education.* Buckingham: Open University Press.
Talib, Ameen Ali. 2001. "The Continuing Behavioural Modification of Academics Since The 1992 Research Assessment Exercise." *Higher Education Review* 33 (3): 30–46.
Taskforce to Review Administrative Education. 1988. *Administering for Excellence: Effective Administration in Education.* Wellington, NZ: Government Printer.
Tawney, R. H. 1926. *Religion and the Rise of Capitalism.* New York: Harcourt, Brace.
Thatcher, Margaret. 1987. "Interview for *Women's Own* Magazine." Retrieved from http://www.margaretthatcher.org/speeches/displaydocument.asp?docid=106689.
The Chronicle of Higher Education. 2008. Scopus Ad. January 11: A15.
The Treasury. 1987. *Government Management: Brief to the Incoming Government 1987 Volume II.* Retrieved from http://www.treasury.govt.nz/publications/briefings/1987ii.
Thompson, John B. 2005. *Books in the Digital Age: The Transformation of Academic and Higher Education Publishing in Britain and the United States.* Cambridge: Polity.
Thrupp, Martin. 1998. "Exploring the Politics of Blame: School Inspection and Its Contestation in New Zealand and England." *Comparative Education* 34 (2): 195–208.
An Instructive Comparison." *Journal of Education Policy* 16 (4): 297–314.
Thursby, Jerry, and Marie Thursby. 2004. "Buyer and Seller Views of University-Industry Licensing." Pp. 103–116 in D. Stein (ed.), *Buying in or Selling Out? The Commercialization of the American Research University.* New Brunswick, NJ: Rutgers University Press.

Tocqueville, Alexis de. 1847. *Democracy in America* (7th edition). New York: Edward Walker.
Tomlinson, S. 2001. *Education in a Post-Welfare Society.* Buckingham: Open University Press.
Touraine, Alain. 1974. *The Post-Industrial Society: Tomorrow's Social History.* New York: Wildwood House.
Turner, Stephen P. 2003. *Liberal Democracy 3.0: Civil Society in an Age of Experts.* London: Sage Publications.
Tuschling, Anna, and Christoph Engemanm. 2006. "From Education to Lifelong Learning: The Emerging Regime of Learning in the European Union." *Educational Philosophy and Theory* 38 (4): 451–469.
Twentieth Century Fund Task Force. 1983. *Making the Grade: Report of the Twentieth Century Fund Taskforce on Federal Elementary and Secondary Education Policy.* New York: Twentieth Century Fund.
UGC (University Grants Committee). 1984. *A Strategy for Higher Education into the 1990s: The UGC's Advice.* London: HMSO.
UNESCO. 1993. "Wilhelm Von Humboldt, 1767–1835." *Prospects: The Quarterly Review of Comparative Education* 23 (3/4): 613–623.
———. 2005. *Towards Knowledge Societies.* Paris: UNESCO Publishing.
United Nations Development Program. 2004. *Unleashing Entrepreneurship: Making Business Work for the Poor.* New York: United Nations Development Program.
University of California Office of Technology Transfer. n.d. "The Bayh-Dole Act: A Guide to the Law and Implementing Regulations." Retrieved from www.ucop.edu/ott/faculty/bayh.html.
University of Pennsylvania. n.d. "Executive Doctorate in Higher Education Management." Retrieved from www.gse.upenn.edu/hem.
U.S. Code Collection. n.d. Retrieved from www4.law.cornell.edu/uscode/35/200.html.
U.S. Department of Education. 1994. "Goals 2000: Educate America Act." Retrieved from http://www2.ed.gov/legislation/GOALS2000/TheAct/index.html.
———. 2001. "PUBLIC LAW 107–110—JAN. 8, 2002." Retrieved from www2.ed.gov/policy/elsec/leg/esea02/107–110.pdf.
———. 2006. *A Test of Leadership: Charting the Direction of U.S. Higher Education, A Report of the Commission Appointed by Secretary of Education Margaret Spellings.* Washington, DC: U.S. Department of Education.
———. 2010. ESEA Blueprint for Reform. Washington, DC: Government Printing Office.
———. 2011. "Race to the Top Fund." Retrieved from http://www2.ed.gov/programs/racetothetop/index.html.
U.S. Government. 1998. "Copyright Term Extension." Retrieved from www.copyright.gov/legislation/s505.pdf.
Useem, Michael. 1976. "Government Influence on the Social Science Paradigm." *The Sociological Quarterly* 17 (2): 146–161.
Usher, Robin. 2000. "Imposing Structure, Enabling Play: New Knowledge Production and the 'Real World' University." Pp. 98–110 in C. Symes and J. McIntyre (eds.), *Working Knowledge: The New Vocationalism and Higher Education.* Buckingham: Open University Press.
Vandenberghe, Vincent. 1998. "Educational Quasi-Markets: The Belgian Experience." In W. Bartlett, J. Roberts and J. Le Grand (eds.), *A Revolution in Social Policy.* Bristol: Policy Press.
Veblen, Thorstein. 1918. *The Higher Learning in America: A Memorandum on the Conduct of Universities by Business Men.* New York: B. W. Huebsch.

Volcker, Paul. 2010. "The Time We Have Is Growing Short." *New York Review of Books* LVII (11), June 24: 12–14.
Walras, Leon. 1984. *Elements of Pure Economics, or, the Theory of Social Wealth.* Philadelphia: Orion Editions.
Warsh, David. 2006. *Knowledge and the Wealth of Nations: A Story of Economic Discovery.* New York: W. W. Norton & Company.
Webb, Diana. 2007. *Privacy and Solitude in the Middle Ages.* London: Hambledon Continuum.
Weber, Max. 1947. *The Theory of Social and Economic Organization* (trans. by A. M. Henderson and T. Parsons). New York: Oxford University Press.
———. 1958. "Science as a Vocation." Pp. 129–156 H. H. Gerth and C. W. Mills, *From Max Weber: Essays in Sociology.* New York: Oxford University Press.
———. 1968. *Economy and Society* (trans. by E. Fischhoff). New York: Bedmister.
Weinberg, Alvin. 1961. "Impact of Large-Scale Science." *Science* 134: 161–164.
West Committee. 1997. *Review of Higher Education Financing and Policy.* Retrieved from http://www.dest.gov.au/archive/highered/hereview/.
Wheeler, Brian. 2011. "David Cameron Says Enterprise is Only Hope for Growth." *BBC News*, March 6. Retrieved from bbc.co.uk/news/uk-poliitcs-12657524.
Whitley, Richard. 2007. "Changing Governance of the Public Sciences." Pp. 3–27 in R. Whitley and J. Gläser (eds.), *The Channing Governance of the Sciences: The Advent of Research Evaluation Systems.* Dordrecht: Springer.
Whitty, Geoff. 2002. *Making Sense of Education Policy.* London: Paul Chapman Publishing.
Whitty, Geoff, Power, Sally and David Halpin. 1998. *Devolution and Choice in Education: The School, the State and the Market.* Buckingham: Open University Press.
Whyte, William. 1956. *Organization Man.* New York: Simon and Schuster.
Willmott, Hugh. 2003. "Commercialising Higher Education in the UK: The State, Industry and Peer Review." *Studies in Higher Education* 28 (2): 129–141.
Wirtén, Eva Hemmungs. 2008. *Terms of Use: Negotiating the Jungle of the Intellectual Commons.* Toronto: University of Toronto Press.
Wren, D. 1994. *The Evolution of Management Thought.* New York: John Wiley.
Woodmansee, Martha. 1984. "The Genius and the Copyright: Legal and Economic Conditions of the Emergence of 'the author.'" *Eighteenth-Century Studies* 17 (4): 425–448.
Woodward, W., and R. Smithers. 2003. "Clarke Dismisses Medieval Historians." *The Guardian* May 9: 7.
World Bank. 1994. *Higher Education: The Lessons of Experience.* Washington, DC: The World Bank.
———. 1997. *The State in a Changing Society: The Lessons of Experience.* Washington, DC: The World Bank.
———. 1998. *Indigenous Knowledge for Development: A Framework for Action.* Washington, DC: The World Bank.
———. 1999. *Knowledge for Development.* Washington, DC: The World Bank.
———. 2002. *Constructing Knowledge Societies: New Challenges for Tertiary Education.* Washington, DC: World Bank.
World Trade Organization. 1994. "Agreement on Trade-Related Aspects of Intellectual Property." Retrieved from www.wto.org/english/tratop_e/trips_e/t_agm0_e.htm.
Yunus, Muhammad. 2009. *Creating a World Without Poverty: Social Business and the Future of Capitalism* (with Karl Weber). New York: PublicAffairs.

Zachary, G. Pascal. 2009. "Will Bits of Books Be All That Remain?" *The Chronicle Review* October 2: B4–B5.

Zemsky, Robert, Gregory Wegner and William Massy. 2005. *Remaking the American University: Market-Smart and Mission-Centered*. New Brunswick, NJ: Rutgers University Press.

Zernike, Kate. 2010. "Career U: Making College 'Relevant.'" *New York Times Education Life* January 3: 16–17, 25.

Ziman, John. 2000. *Real Science: What It Is and What It Means*. Cambridge: Cambridge University Press.

Index

A
A Nation at Risk report, 166, 173–175
Academic Ranking of World Universities, 54
Accountability, 3, 6, 7, 8, 9, 26, 29, 30, 50, 53, 54, 57, 60, 63, 66, 67, 69, 70, 102, 112, 114, 115, 117, 119, 142, 146, 147, 150, 151, 154, 159, 161, 162, 175, 176, 177, 179, 180, 191, 206, 219; in education movement, 160, 164–165
Achievement gap, 176, 181, 182
Adam Smith Institute, 169
Adequate Yearly Progress (AYP), 176
Advanced liberalism, 1
Agreement on Trade-Related Aspects of Intellectual Property Rights (TRIPS), 194
American Association of Universities (AAU), 150
American Association of University Professors (AAUP), 65, 84, 216
American Education Corporation, 113
American Enterprise Institute, 27, 176
American Federation of Teachers (AFT), 65
Angel investors, 110
Anglo-American capitalism, 16, 39
Apollo Group, 155
Aristotle, 74
Assisted Places Scheme, 164, 170, 172
Association of University Teachers, 84
Atomic Energy Commission (AEC), 90
Audit society, 9
Auditing, 6, 7, 8, 18, 30, 32, 36, 43, 54, 55, 57, 58, 61, 62, 63, 64, 67, 69, 70, 102, 161, 165, 175, 177, 180
Autonomy for accountability, 54, 57, 147

B
Bacon, Francis, 79, 80, 100, 108
Baker Act, 170
Balanced Scorecard, 69
Basic science, 4, 91, 92, 107, 108, 109, 132, 133, 138
Baudrillard, Jean, 125, 195–196
Bayh-Dole Act, 11, 77, 92–94, 97, 106, 123, 147
Beck, Ulrich, 40, 67, 198, 199
Becker, Gary, 21, 25, 33, 140, 163–164, 165, 214
Bell, Daniel, 71, 139
Bernal, J.D., 87, 133, 134–137, 157
Bernstein, Basil, 66
Best practices, 64, 66, 178, 217
Big Society policies, 29, 155, 190
Bildung, 75, 116
Black papers, 27, 169
Blackboard Inc., 113
Blair, Tony, 18, 29, 30, 31, 129, 154, 171, 172, 176, 189, 190
Blue Ribbon Testing, 219
Blueprint for Reform, 177, 178
Bologna Declaration (or Process), 132, 152
Books Rights Registry, 96–97
Bourdieu, Pierre, 17, 34, 37, 64, 72, 74, 124
Bradley Report, 146, 149
Branding, 54, 57
Bretton Wood Accord, 20, 24, 38, 39
Bricall Report, 146
British Association for the Advancement of Science, 135–136
Browne Report, 146, 155

Buchanan, James, 25, 42, 50–51, 166
Bukharian, N. I., 135
Bureaucratic professionalism, 59, 61, 65, 119
Bush, G.W., 11, 149, 175, 176, 180, 181, 201
Bush, Vanneavar, 89–90, 136, 138
Business cycles, 19, 23, 200, 203
Business Process Reengineering, 69

C

Callon, Michael, 36, 135, 213
Cameron, David, 29, 155, 190
Carnegie Foundation, 140, 174, 217
Carter, Jimmy, 24, 173
Cato Institute, 27, 28
Center for the Study of Public Choice, 50
Central Banks, 20, 37
Centre for Policy Studies, 27–28, 169
Charter schools, 160, 164, 172, 177
Clarke, Charles, 121
Classic liberalism, 18, 19, 23, 31, 34, 35, 42, 162, 185, 187, 188, 189, 190
Clayton Act, 216
Clinton, Bill, 18, 29, 53, 175, 176, 177, 201
Committee for Economic Development, 140, 174
Communitarian (ism), 51, 60, 83
Comparative advantage, 35, 38, 40, 95
Compton, Karl, 218
Comte, Auguste, 192
Consumer citizen, 185, 195, 196, 198, 202, 203, 209
Consumer sovereignty, 31, 195
Copyright Term Extension Act (CTEA), 96
Corporate laboratories, 88, 109
Creative destruction, 6, 38, 43, 106, 120, 131, 205
Cultural commons project, 75
Curriculum Framework, 168
Customer relations, 54

D

Darnton, Robert, 79, 81, 96–97
Data driven decision making, 69, 219
Dawkins, John (see Dawkins reforms)
Dawkins reforms, 132, 147
Dearing Report, 132, 146, 153, 154
Debord, Guy, 46, 186, 194
Deleuze, Gilles, 184

Deming, E. Edwards, 64
Dewey, John, 33, 44, 69, 75, 101, 129, 186, 209, 210–211, 220
Disaggregate (tion), 56, 126, 127, 128, 209, 217
Disney Corporation, 96, 97
Douglas, Mary, 67
Douglas, Roger, 166
Drucker, Peter, 47, 130, 139
Durkheim, Emile, 77, 207–208, 211

E

Economization, 32, 36, 105, 213
EdInvest, 95
Education Act of 1992, 171
Education Action Zones (EAZs), 172
Education Policy Response Group, 169
Education Review Office (ERO), 160, 167
Education vouchers, 161, 162, 163, 164, 170, 176, 177, 179, 201, 219
Embedded liberalism, 20
Employee Retirement Income Security Act of 1974, 199
Endogenous growth theory, 104, 130, 141, 143
Enlightenment, 75, 98, 99, 103, 107, 140, 145, 164; concept of knowledge, 66, 79–81, 83–84, 90, 91, 102, 103, 105, 178, 180, 193
Entrepreneurial: values, 4, 36, 181; university, 123, 145, 156
Entrepreneurialism, 129, 180, 204
European Union, 9, 11, 14, 41, 130, 132, 152
Excellence in Research for Australia Initiative (ERA), 110, 148
Excellence in Schools Report, 172

F

Fair use, 75, 83, 96, 98, 107, 216
Fast capitalism, 3
Federal Reserve, 20, 37
Fictitious commodities, 71, 95
Foucault, Michel, 7, 12, 36, 37, 57, 81, 185, 186, 191, 205, 219
Free schools, 160, 164, 169, 171, 172–173, 177, 181, 182
Free trade, 17, 32, 38, 39, 40, 94
Free use, 98, 106
Freiburg School of Economics, 23
Freire, Paulo, 75

French Academy of Science, 80
Friedman, Milton, 15, 17, 21–22, 25, 28, 33, 34, 35, 36, 51, 105, 158, 159,161, 163, 164, 165, 173, 177, 178, 214, 219
Frye, Northrop, 101
Fuller, Steve, 129, 137, 216

G

Game theory, 33
Garnaut Report, 147
Gates Foundation, 176
General Agreement on Tariffs and Trade (GATT), 94, 104
General Agreement on Trade in Services (GATS), 94, 95
Generalization of costs, 55
Gift economy, 182
Gillard, Julia, 149
Glass-Steagall Act, 20, 38
Globalization, 10, 11, 39, 40, 70, 72, 73, 151, 176, 186
Goals 2000, 175
Golden age of capitalism, 1, 24
Google, 11, 12, 77, 96–97, 127, 128
Gove, Michael, 172
Government Performance and Results Act (GPRA), 53, 110
Governmentality, 7, 107, 121, 157, 185, 186, 187, 190, 191, 191, 195
Great Depression, 1, 16, 18, 20, 38, 89
Grid/group theory, 67

H

Habermas, Jürgen, 215
Hacking, Ian, 180, 186
Halevy, Eli, 15
Hardin, Garrett, 2, 106
Hastening of Science, 124
Hatch Act, 88, 132
Hawke, Bob, 9, 28, 146
Hayek, Friedrich, 15, 17, 20–23, 24, 27, 28, 38, 41, 43, 51, 103, 104, 134, 179, 188, 190, 193, 204, 213
Helvetius, 15
Henley Centre, 184
Heritage Foundation, 27, 28, 176
High commitment management, 63
High stakes testing, 8, 9, 178, 180
Higher Education Act, 150
Higher Education Act of 2004, 154
Higher Education Contribution Scheme, 147

Hilmer Report, 147
Homo economicus, 2
Hoover Institute, 176
Housing bubble, 200
Housing Policy (see United States housing policy)
Howard, John, 148
Human capital, 5, 25, 140, 141, 143, 159, 161, 162, 163, 164, 165, 168, 179, 197, 205
Human resource management, 8, 57, 62
Humanistic intellectuals, 68–69
Humboldt, Wilhelm, 86, 122,
Humboldtian university, 4, 115, 122, 145, 216
Hume, David, 187
Hurried empiricism, 124
Hyde, Lewis, 74, 75
Hyperreality, 125

I

Ida Exhibit, 126
Improving America's Schools Act, 175
Incentivization, 52, 110, 118
Institute of Economic Affairs (IEA), 27, 28, 169, 179
Intellectual property (law), 10, 11, 13, 18, 75, 76, 77, 85, 86, 87, 94–95, 98
International Finance Corporation, 95
International Monetary Fund (IMF), 20, 28, 39, 40, 41
Inventory control, 55, 127

J

Jefferson, Thomas, 74, 75
Jessop, Bob, 5, 43
Jewett, Frank, 136

K

Kant, Immanuel, 82, 107, 115, 122
Karpin Report, 147
Keith, Joseph, 27, 28, 152, 169, 189
Kerr, Clark, 90
Keynes, John Maynard, 15, 18, 19, 34, 213
Keynesianism, 3, 4, 18, 21, 22, 27, 30, 42
Kilgore, Harley, 136
Klein, Joe, 177
Knowledge for knowledge's sake, 4, 100
Knowledge Nation Task Force, 149
Knowledge society, 9, 10, 11, 12, 13, 14, 18, 89, 102, 106, 121, 129,

250 *Index*

130–132, 136, 137–141, 143–145, 152, 154, 156, 158, 160, 218
Knowledge transfer (*see* technology transfer)
Kulturstaat, 86, 145

L

Labor unions, 25, 32, 34, 35, 41, 59, 65, 167, 170, 175, 176, 177, 179, 205
Laissez-faire, 7, 20, 23, 30, 34, 35, 43, 44, 78, 214, 215
Lambert Review, 154
Lange, David, 158, 166, 181, 219
Latour, Bruno, 77
League tables, 54, 113, 160, 170, 172, 180
Lessig, Lawrence, 75, 96
Lessinger, Leon, 161, 164–165, 175
Lifelong learning, 160, 205
Lisbon Strategy, 14, 132, 152
Local Education Authority (LEA), 170–171
Local Management of Schools Initiative, 170
Locke, John, 17, 19, 28, 78
Lord Acton, 184
Louisiana Board of Regents, 121
Lyotard, Jean-Francois, 12, 13, 86, 102, 107, 108, 112, 117, 120, 121, 124, 127, 158
Lysenkoism, 138, 218

M

Machlup, Fritz, 139
Magnet schools, 175, 177
Managed economies, 21, 22, 24, 25
Managed professionals, 65
Management by stress, 64
Management through (by) objectives, 55, 57, 69
Managerial state, 7, 18, 36, 43
Managerialism, 13, 46, 47, 48, 49, 50, 60, 65, 66, 68, 84
Mandeville, Bernard, 33, 79
Manhattan Institute, 27
Manhattan Project, 89
Mann, Horace, 162
Mannheim, Karl, 99
Market economy, 7, 17, 24, 28, 35, 71–72, 108, 164, 193, 204, 207, 208
Market society, 22, 105, 126, 185, 187, 207, 208, 210, 211

Marshall, T.H., 193
Marx, Karl, 15, 39, 48, 71, 74, 78, 124, 129, 158, 184, 207, 208, 211, 214, 215
Massachusetts Institute of Technology (MIT), 88, 89, 90, 91, 132
Massification of education, 5, 63, 116, 178, 182
Matthew effect, 111
MBAization, 68
Merit pay, 119
Merton, Robert K., 107, 111
Metrics, 68; enterprise 113
Mickey Mouse Protection Act (see Copyright Term Extension Act)
Mill, J.S., 19, 78, 104, 161, 162, 162, 163
Mills, C. Wright, 220
Mises, Ludwig von, 17, 20, 21, 22, 31, 33, 134, 195
Mode I knowledge production, 107–109, 110, 112, 114, 115, 116, 117
Mode II knowledge production, 108–109, 110, 112
Monetary policy, 20, 37, 38
Mont Pelerin Society (MPS), 20–21
Montesquieu, Baron de, 1
Montessorianism, 75
Morrill Act, 86, 88
Mortgage backed securities, 38

M

National Academy of Sciences, 80, 133, 137
National Affordable Housing Act of 1992, 201
National Association of Manufactures, 219
National Commission on Excellence in Education, 174
National Committee on the Inquiry into Higher Education (NCIHE), 153
National Council for Accreditation of Teacher Education (NCATE), 217
National Council of State Legislatures (NCSL), 145, 151
National Curriculum, 9, 11, 28, 169, 170–172
National Curriculum (England and Wales), 9, 11, 28, 169–173
National Education Association (NEA), 65

Index

National Efficiency Movement, 133
National Institute for the Promotion of Science, 132
National Institutes of Health (NIH), 89
National Public Radio (NPR), 105
National Resource Committee, 134
National Science Foundation (NSF), 89, 137
National Student Survey, 154
Nazi science, 89, 100
Nazism, 20
New Democrats, 18, 29, 30, 43
New Labour, 18, 29, 30, 43, 154
New prudentialism, 198
New public management, 5, 8, 9, 10, 13, 18, 39, 46–73, 115, 158, 175, 185
New York University, 93
New Zealand Educational Institute (NZEI), 167
New Zealand Qualifications Authority (NZQA), 167
New Zealand Treasury, 166
Newman, John Henry, 85
Nisbet, Robert, 99, 110, 131
Nixon administration, 27, 164, 173, 201
No Child Left Behind, 6, 9, 11, 161, 172, 173, 176–178, 180

O

Off shoring of labor, 32
Office of Management and Budget, 189
Office of Naval Research (ONR), 89
Office for Standards in Education (Ofsted), 160, 171–172
Ordoliberals, 23, 29, 30, 43, 213
Organization for Economic Cooperation and Development (OECD), 6, 9, 14, 28, 40, 104, 130, 131, 138, 139, 140, 141, 142, 143, 144, 145, 146, 166, 193, 218
Out of districting, 160

P

Paine, Thomas, 1, 162, 163
Patronage system, 74, 79, 82
Pearson, Karl, 133
Performance contracts, 164
Picot Report, 166–167
Polanyi, Karl, 28, 35, 71, 95, 193, 198, 206, 207, 208, 209, 214, 215, 218
Polanyi, Michael, 23, 103, 134–136, 137, 157, 218

Pope, Alexander, 1
Porter Project, 168
Post Primary Teachers Association, 167
Post-bureaucratic organizations, 5, 49, 50, 64
Post-explanatory knowledge, 122
Post-Fordist production, 5, 10, 56, 58, 109, 117, 204
Post-intellectuality, 122
Post-normal science, 108
Powell memo, 27, 213
Private equity firms, 40, 93
Privatization, 6, 12, 13, 17, 18, 26, 32, 52, 74, 77, 78, 81, 85, 87, 91, 92, 95, 96, 98, 101, 106, 108, 155, 159, 165, 173, 177, 179
Productive labor, 47, 70–71, 73
Program Assessment and Rating Tool, 53, 110
Project Head Start, 173
Property rights theory, 28
Proudhon, Pierre-Joseph, 211
Public Broadcast System (PBS), 105, 214
Public choice theory, 8, 25, 50–51, 69, 166
Public domain, 3, 4, 12, 13, 42–43, 66, 72, 76–77, 79, 81–82, 84, 85, 87–88, 90, 92, 96–100, 104, 106, 123, 166, 178, 193, 216
Public professions (professionals), 47, 50, 57, 59, 60, 65, 69, 70, 72, 73, 106
Public/private hybrids, 52, 77, 98, 99, 115
Putting Customers First Movement, 53
Pythagoreanism, 74

Q

Qualifications and Curriculum Authority (QCA), 9
Quality Assessment Committees (QAC), 153
Quality Assurance Agency for Higher Education (QAA), 153
Quality Assurance Framework for Higher Education, 154
Quasi-markets, 6, 7, 32, 53, 113, 148, 170, 180, 181

R

Race to the Top, 177, 180
Ravitch, Diane, 181
Reagan, Ronald, 7, 18, 28, 166, 173, 174, 189, 201

Renaissance School Services, 177
Rentier class, 32, 40, 185
Rent-seeking behavior, 60
Research Assessment Exercise (RAE), 94, 111–112, 122, 147, 153, 219
Research productivity, 66, 127
Research Quality Framework (RQF), 111, 147
Responsibility center management, 55
Responsiblization (ized), 2, 5, 12, 13, 61, 62, 159, 198
Rhineland capitalism, 24, 43, 208
Rhoades, Gary, 11, 64, 146
Ricardo, David, 19, 35, 38, 40, 78
Risk: analysis of, 2, 16, 33, 61, 92, 150, 185; individualization of, 14, 147, 183, 186, 197–203; socialized, 185, 198
Rockefeller Foundation, 134, 218
Rogernomics, 166
Roll back neoliberalism, 7, 16, 18, 29, 30, 31, 42, 43, 44, 102, 105, 141, 155, 157, 159, 173, 189, 200, 210
Roll out neoliberalism, 18, 30, 41, 42, 44, 149, 155, 159, 160, 189, 200
Romer, Paul, 130, 141
Roosevelt administration, 133, 218
Rose, Nicholas, 1, 7, 16, 29, 44, 185, 186, 191, 196, 198, 203, 204
Rousseau, Jean-Jacques, 78, 101
Royal Society, 80
Rudd, Kevin, 149

S

Sahlins, Marshall, 220
Saint-Simon, Henri de, 192
Scholastic Corporation, 113
Schumpeter, Joseph, 6, 38, 43, 210
Science policy, 9, 89, 131, 132–137, 218
Scopus, Inc., 217
Self-interest, 2, 3, 28, 31, 32, 33, 34, 42, 50, 51, 60, 61, 62, 78, 80, 167, 186, 188, 190, 192, 193, 195, 196, 201, 205, 206, 208, 211
Self-managing schools, 219
Sennett, Richard, 204, 214, 216
Sey, Jean-Baptiste, 19
Shapin, Steve, 80, 91, 93, 110, 116
Simmel, Georg, 124, 126, 207

Simon, William, 27
Singapore Sessions, 213
Smith, Adam, 19, 21, 33, 34, 35, 78, 79, 103, 104, 158, 162, 187, 188, 190, 208, 214, 215, 220
Social Darwinism, 197
Social theory, 207, 209, 210
Society for Freedom in Science, 135
Sociology, 122, 133
Sonny Bono Act (see Copyright Term Extension Act)
Soros, George, 46
Soviet science, 100, 133, 135, 137, 138, 218
Soviet Union, 90, 133
Spellings Commission, 12, 131, 149–151
Spencer, Herbert, 19, 197, 207
Stakeholder society, 44, 214
Stakeholders, 7, 26, 30, 31, 32, 41, 42, 50, 66, 69, 110, 160
Standard and Poor's, 202
Statute of Anne, 81, 83, 216
STEM, 121, 122
Stockman, David, 189
Strategic plans, 49, 55, 57, 58, 153
Substantive rationality, 66–69
Superheads, 52, 161

T

Taskforce to Review Educational Administration (see Picot Report)
Tawney, R.H., 214
Tea Party Movement, 29
Technical intelligentsia, 68, 70
Technical rationality, 65–69
Technocracy movement, 133
Technology transfer, 12, 63, 87, 91, 93, 94, 118, 121, 131, 132, 145
Tertiary Education Quality Standards Agency, 149
Texas A&M University, 93, 105, 151
Texas Public Policy Foundation, 152
Thatcher, Margaret, 2, 5, 7, 16, 18, 27, 28, 94, 152, 153, 164, 169, 170, 184, 185, 189, 206, 214
Think tanks, 27–28, 44, 109, 115, 125, 126, 139, 146, 164, 166, 169, 176, 180, 181, 213
Third Way, 18, 29, 41, 42, 43
Tocqueville, Alexis de, 74, 87, 132
Tomorrow's Schools, 11, 140, 159, 165–169, 181, 219

Tonnies, Ferdinand, 207
Total Quality Management, 8, 64, 69
Touriane, Alain, 139
Tragedy of the commons, 2, 106
Triple helix, 108, 137, 138, 144
Trust, 9, 58–61, 65, 70, 73, 78, 119, 124, 185, 208, 211
Tullock, Gordon, 25, 42, 50–51, 166

U
Unbundling, 55
UNESCO, 9, 144
United Nations, 9, 17, 29
United States Constitution, 81, 83, 85, 174, 216
United States Housing Policy, 20, 200–201
University of California, 87, 90, 91, 93, 183
University of Chicago, 21, 141; economics department, 20, 21, 25, 140, 141, 213
University of Phoenix (see Apollo Group)
University of Texas system, 105, 132
User pays systems, 5, 52, 55, 114
Utilitarians, 44, 184
Utopian capitalism, 3, 17, 130, 211
Utopian socialism, 78, 211

V
Veblen, Thornstein, 46, 65, 87, 100
Velocity of knowledge, 127
Venture capital (capitalist), 10, 40, 67, 92–93, 100, 110, 118
Vocationalism, 142, 145

W
Walras, Leon, 19
Washington Consensus, 29, 41
Watt, James, 216
Wealth of Nations (see Adam Smith)
Weber, Max, 25, 33, 47, 48, 66, 67, 68, 72, 123, 207, 219
Welfare state, 1, 3, 7, 16, 19, 20, 23, 25, 26, 29, 43, 59, 65, 157, 168, 172, 173, 178, 179, 185, 192, 196, 198, 202, 203, 204, 206, 208, 209
West Committee, 148
White, Andrew, 85
Wisconsin Alumni Foundation, 87, 132
World Bank, 9, 14, 20, 28, 39, 40, 41, 43, 95, 104, 130, 138, 143–144, 146
World Intellectual Property Organization (WIPO), 95
World Trade Organization (WTO), 40–41, 77, 94–95